CIVIC WARS

CIVIC WARS

Democracy and Public Life in the American City during the Nineteenth Century

MARY P. RYAN

University of California Press

Berkeley   Los Angeles   London

University of California Press
Berkeley and Los Angeles, California

University of California Press, Ltd.
London, England

First Paperback Printing 1998

Library of Congress Cataloging-in-Publication Data

Ryan, Mary P.
    Civic wars : democracy and public life in the American city during
the nineteenth century / Mary P. Ryan.
        p.   cm.
    Includes bibliographical references (p.   ) and index.
    ISBN 0-520-21660-1 (alk. paper : pbk.)
        1. Political participation—United States—History—19th century.
    2. Political culture—United States—History—19th century.
    3. Democracy—United States—History—19th century.   4. City and
    town life—United States—History—19th century.   5. United States—
    Politics and government—19th century.   6. New York (N.Y.)—
    Politics and government—To 1898.   7. New Orleans (La.)—Politics
    and government.   8. San Francisco (Calif.)—Politics and government.
    I. Title.
    JK1764.R9   1997
    320.973—dc20   96-25530
                                                                CIP

Printed in the United States of America
9 8 7 6 5 4 3 2 1

The paper used in this publication meets the minimum requirements of
American National Standard for Information Sciences—Permanence of
Paper for Printed Library Materials, ANSI Z39.48-1984. ⊚

For Anne

CONTENTS

ILLUSTRATIONS

ACKNOWLEDGMENTS

I have practiced the historian's craft too long to pretend that I am the solitary author of the following pages. In creating this book I have transcribed, transmitted, and lifted out of context the work of countless chroniclers and historians, most of whom I will never meet. Because this investigation took me far from the fields of my training or expertise, I was dependent on a vast and rich secondary literature that deserves far more recognition than the simple citations in the bibliography. It would not diminish my debt to all these strangers by naming my personal and specific benefactors. My special thanks go to those very generous and tolerant colleagues who read messy early drafts of this book and tendered invaluable advice and criticism. In thanking them I also assure them that I have left abundant grounds for continuing debate and disagreement among us. I am most indebted to Thomas Bender, Robin Einhorn, Philip Ethington, Eric Foner, Michael Kazin, Suzanne Lebsock, Joseph Logsdon, Timothy Gilfoyle, Terence Mac-Donald, Christine Stansell, and Dell Upton.

Several institutions have generously supported this project with their funds, their facilities, and their staffs. My research commenced long ago at the Center for Advanced Studies in the Behavioral Sciences at Stanford University; it was sustained while I was a member of the faculty at the University of California at Berkeley; and it was rejuvenated for one ecstatic year when the French American Foundation sent me to the Center for North American Studies, École des Hautes Études en Science Sociales in Paris. I send special thanks to Jean Heffer, François Weil, and

Carolyn Kaufman at CENA. This project would never have been finished without the skillful efforts of graduate research assistants at Berkeley: Jennifer Gold, Valerie Mendoza, Jessica Weiss, and the heroic Gabrielle Tenaglia. I am deeply indebted to the librarians and staff of the Bancroft Library, Historic New Orleans Collection, Louisiana Division of the New Orleans Public Library, the Louisiana State Museum, and the Municipal Archives of New York. The editorial staff at the University of California Press—Sheila Levine, Nola Burger, and Scott Norton—has my gratitude and affection, as does my copy editor, David Severtson.

Finally, I would like to acknowledge those who diverted me from working on this book, yet kept me right on course to creating it, as together we walked city streets and reveled in public places. My heartfelt appreciation goes to old New York friends David Gurin, Bert Hansen, Carroll Seron, Joanne Vanek, and Judy Walkowitz. I am indebted to Joe and Mary Logsdon for introducing me to New Orleans, her restaurants, her fetes, her people. I thank Ted and Joby Margadant for the pleasures of their company on the boulevards of Paris as well as the streets of San Francisco. Thanks and a purple heart go to Judy Stacey and Carol Stack for rescuing me with walks through the neighborhood. Richard Busacca has done double duty as usual, by tending the homes fires when I escaped to distant cities and by joining me at city playgrounds near and far. I thank Anne Busacca-Ryan for constantly reminding me to cherish the cities of our world for their fun and for our future.

From Public Realm
to Civic Warfare

Those awaiting the turn of the millennium can easily find evidence for the gloomy forecasts often associated with such an ominous date. The approach of the year 2000 finds many observers of American civic life, including historians, in a curmudgeonly frame of mind, their pessimism fed by more than the usual references to rising crime, debased morals, and irresponsible youth. Complaints first heard in the mid-1980s about how the American citizenry was fragmenting into narrow circles of interest and identity had given way by 1995 to far more alarming and widespread signs of the disintegration of the national consensus. Those earlier squabbles about what was alternately labeled multiculturalism and political correctness paled next to the clashing cultures of the 1990s—urban riots, rural militia companies, and bombed-out federal buildings—while the new political identities that emerged in the 1960s might seem paper tigers compared to the insurgents of the 1994 congressional election who not only asserted themselves but also set out to dismantle the basic social programs that had, at least since the New Deal, linked Americans together in the recognition of basic public needs. Historians' alarm about the rumored demise of a unified national narrative might seem inconsequential in a popular culture that shunned the printed word as it sated itself on talk shows, MTV, and cyberspace. The end of the twentieth century threatened to bring not just the contest and rivalry to be expected in a democracy but a whole other order of change, a withdrawal from the civic project as we had known it.

1

Or so it might seem to an American Jeremiah at the fin de siècle. But the revelers who will gather in Times Square on New Year's Eve 2000 will doubtless encounter some less dyspeptic citizens. The omens of crisis in American public life can also be read as signs of civic rejuvenation. The revolt against Washington at the ballot box could also open a broader, more fundamental debate on the nature of the public trust. The babel in cyberspace might give voice to the otherwise isolated and inarticulate. Those who gather at a place such as Times Square on New Year's Eve, furthermore, obstinately refuse to cede public space to urban anomie or disorder. Indeed, the compulsion to gather in city space seems more vigorous than ever. Witness the proliferation of cafes, street fairs, and festivals in communities across the land. Since the mid-1970s Americans have invented whole new occasions for citywide parties: Halloween processions in Manhattan, annual jazz festivals in New Orleans, foot races across San Francisco that bring as many as 100,000 giddy runners into the streets. I would bet that many Americans will greet the next century as the occasion to come joyously together, right in the heart of the city. Not all Americans have lost the will to fashion some facsimile of a civic whole.

As always, the markers of change can be read in many ways. And much depends on where we stop to read the signs of the times, be it, for example, on city streets or in front of TV screens. What strikes this observer at the end of the twentieth century is not the expected prophecies of national disorder and moral and political damnation but the fear that Americans are withdrawing from civic space as we have known it, be it in electoral campaigns, public festivals, or everyday encounters with one another. In the past Americans managed to contain their rowdy civic behavior within the bounds of acceptable differences and were linked together by both regular associations of town and city life and a common print culture, the very institutions that fostered the American experiment in pluralistic democratic politics beginning in the eighteenth century. The differences among Americans in the late twentieth century, by contrast, rarely come together in the same public square or on the same page of newsprint. Civic life seems socially adrift.

This book faces this troubling contemporary prospect in the perverse manner of a historian: To better read the signs of change before me, I have intentionally turned backward. By examining civic life a century ago I hope to acquire some sharpened perception, even some ideas, about how to exercise citizenship in these shifting times. In so doing I have adopted a spatial strategy just as curious as my temporal move backward. At a time when the connecting tissue of civic life seems as insubstantial as the airwaves of mass media, I have set up my historical laboratory in concrete places, in three nineteenth-century cities. In New York, New Orleans, and San Francisco I have found some solid ground on which to confront these civic fears and hopes. In the last century these cities were arguably as full of cultural differences and as fractured by social and economic changes as any metropolis today, and they provided equally challenging conditions under which to create civic communication and identity. My years of foraging through these corners of the American past have not yielded reassuring portraits of virtuous and harmonious communities that can serve as models or admonitions for the present. What I found instead is a trail of contestation that goes back well beyond a century. What I learned, slowly and reluctantly, still incompletely, is the necessity of facing these recurrent cultural and political collisions, of embracing these civic wars as an essential feature of modern democracy. But before I report on this exercise of retrospective citizenship, a brief comment on some of the personal concerns and more abstract cogitation that informed and preceded it is in order.

Undertaken as both a historian's project and a citizen's mission, my exploration began in the early 1980s amid growing unease with the fragmentation of the historical record that had accompanied the success of the new social history. The elaboration and diversification of our history that occurred in the 1970s and 1980s left a larger, infinitely improved, but more splintered picture of the past. The disarray among historians, the cracks in old syntheses, and the refuse of an untenable consensus were more than by-products of a quantitative expansion of the population included in the official historical record. A skilled and patient historian could fashion a social history from the studies of different races, classes, ethnic groups, gender cultures, sexual orientations, ages, and so forth. (My colleagues do it every day in survey courses and textbooks.) But to be a usable and living history rather than a sociological portrait, we are told that the parts of this enlarged picture need to be stitched together into a moving narrative. It needed a focal point, some major characters, a plot. In the past the focal point had been politics on the national level. The central characters had been political leaders, and the plot ended in the uniformity of a common culture or at the apex of intellectual hegemony or political power.[1]

These ways of giving narrative coherence to history certainly remained available to painstaking historians willing to draw the links between the social and the political, the local and the national, the social and the cultural, the everyday and the election day. Yet a rush to synthesis often traveled the same well-worn paths, sacrificing the rich record compiled by social historians, finding the easiest point of unity among the powerful and prominent, and in the end giving starring roles to the white, male, educated, and affluent. Still searching for some way of bringing America's diverse peoples together on one plane of analysis, but without subjecting them to the brute authority of a central government or the cultural tyranny of national character, I came upon the idea of the public, a symbol of the possibility of unification without homogenization, of integration without assimilation. In my first musings it evoked a broad and visible political space where a society's members might come together without forfeiting their multiple social identities, where they mounted debates rather than established consensus. In the first instance the public was no more than an invitation to imagine a historical plane of commonalty and connection that did not pulverize differences, where power was recognized without erasing the less powerful.[2]

From the first the word *public* had a second and especially seductive reference point as well. This attraction was as much personal and aesthetic as scholarly and political, and it was rooted in my own niche in American history. For someone growing up female after World War II, in a small town where my lower-class Roman Catholic parentage was still a mark of marginalization, the public gleamed as an object to covet, a kind of brass ring. As a female child of a small town in the 1950s I also saw the public as a liberation from stultifying privacy. It was a way out of the house. It summoned images of a gregarious, open, cosmopolitan, new, heterogeneous, anonymous world free of the constrictions of family and the straitjacket of gender identity. To my parents' generation the coveted public signaled the aspirations of the "little guy" for a public voice that was heard only as recently as the New Deal. In my adolescence the public prize was the election of the first president who shared my family's religious affiliation. My own political consciousness would take form within those social movements of the 1960s that made the dreams and protests of millions of once-silenced Americans a public matter. To this very day, when my gender remains drastically underrepresented in positions of state power and legislative deliberation, the public still glows with the aura of a brass ring. For a feminist the public remains an object of not fully requited desire. The turns in my own life and the jolts of American politics since the 1970s have not dimmed the utopian imaginings of the word; they have only made them seem more precious as they receded from the political horizon. In sum the word that set the course of this book is bloated with social, personal, as well as political promises. In its first incarnation the subject of this book was impossibly broad, simply a study of American public life in the nineteenth century.

Although my search for the "public" was singular, personal, and a mite eccentric, it was hardly solitary. The word *public* has one of the longest and most distinguished lineages in the Western dictionary of keywords. From the perspective of the history of ideas my musings about the public are a dilute and base remnant of the classic vocabulary of *polis, politeia,* and *res publica.* The word *public* was present at the reputed origins of Western political culture, in its Renaissance, and at the moments of greatest trial. The public was a conceptual life raft for political thinkers, most notably Hannah Arendt, trying to set a humanistic political course in the wake of twentieth-century totalitarianism. Yet I have kin much closer than these in my association with the public. The public is very much in the American grain. The word had a particularly prominent place in the vocabulary of the Progressives and appeared in the titles of books by Walter Lippman, Robert Park, and John Dewey in the 1920s. And in the 1990s the chorus of concern for the public is full of historians, social scientists, literary critics, and veterans of the social movements of my generation, including most especially feminists.

My original fealty to the word *public* inspired a conversation with political theorists that became a long, rambling section of this book's penultimate draft. The empirical historical study that followed, however, broke the bounds of this theory and became a meandering story of how Americans came together, for better and for worse, to share and shape a conjoined life. That account, which will begin with chapter 1, is not a paean to the public but a story I will call "civic wars." Before that story begins, however, I offer the reader the briefest report on my foray into the body of political philosophy to which I remain indebted.

The classic formulation of the public, especially as interpreted by Hannah Arendt, offers the loftiest inspiration for the study and practice of public life. Brought down from the Acropolis, this tradition heralds the public realm, as Arendt names it, as the place where citizens surrender their private concerns and come together as equals to deliberate about the common good. It is in the public realm, set aside from petty material interests and devoted to mutual respect and rational discourse, that humans express their highest natures and achieve a semblance of immortality. Yet as many critics, most notably Hannah Pitkin, have pointed out, whether it be ancient Greece or the Italian Renaissance re-

publics, the public realm was as narrow in its membership as it was lofty
in its idealism. It was a gathering place of elite males, many of them
slavemasters.[3]

For a more democratic social base, contemporary political philosophers turn more often to the work of Jürgen Habermas. By locating his
"public sphere" in the eighteenth-century West, Habermas opened up
civic life to a much broader citizenry and wider realm of rights and freedoms. His public sphere was a "realm of our social life in which something approaching public opinion can be formed. Access is guaranteed
to all citizens. A portion of the public sphere comes into being in every
conversation in which private individuals assemble to form a public
body." Habermas brought the public sphere not only into modern times
but into a broad historical plane of analysis. By locating public life outside the state, finding it in the press and the cafes and clubs of eighteenth-
century European capitals, wherever public opinion could be formed,
Habermas placed the humanistic political ideals on the grounds of social
practice and in the reach of many. His public sphere has been adapted by
many historians and literary scholars and is an indispensable guide
through the research for this book.[4]

Yet Habermas himself was circumspect in his own historical mapping
of the public sphere. Clinging to high standards of "rational-critical discourse," Habermas was wary of finding a genuine public sphere outside
the bourgeoisie and after the eighteenth century. To open a flank of the
public sphere in the nineteenth century, I next turned to the American
tradition of political philosophy and to John Dewey's *The Public and Its
Problems.* Conceived as a pragmatic human creation, not as an a priori rational norm, Dewey's public was an act of human discovery and organization that could, or could not, be found in any historical circumstance.
His formula for creating a public specified only this: "We take as our
point of departure from the objective fact that human acts have consequences upon others, that some of these consequences are perceived,
and that their perception leads to subsequent effort to control action so
as to secure some consequences and avoid others." Dewey then con-
strues a public that, theoretically, could exist anywhere, even in the most
unseemly civic spaces of America in the 1990s.[5]

Writing in 1927, Dewey rarely gave specific social or political content
to the public. His major historical reference was to the New England
community of face-to-face public assembly. Reconvening a town meeting is not a strategy likely to revive the public in the late twentieth century. An update to Dewey's public can be found, however, in a number

of contemporary writers, including postmodernists and neopragmatists, many of them veterans of the social movements of the 1960s. They argue for a public created through the piecemeal identification of new political constituencies. Social movements not only make new public claims for isolated groups but expand the rights of all. The feminist movement is a prime example of this pluralistic expansion of the public; it not only enrolled the second sex in the public realm but formulated whole new sets of human rights, naming them such things as privacy, reproductive freedom, family entitlement. These contemporary theorists dispute the singularity of the classic notion of the public but reclaim the term in the plural or prefix it with adjectives such as heterogeneous or democratic.[6]

At this point in the search for a civic lodestar I came to wonder if the public should be the exclusive focus of my attention. A qualifying term used by everyone from Dewey on began to assume a central place in my thinking. That term was *democratic*. Turning directly to recent democratic theorists, most notably Claude Lefort and Chantal Mouffe, I found classic and Renaissance notions of the public demoted to secondary importance, behind the political practices of representative government dating from the nineteenth century. Lefort focuses not on a preconceived public realm but on the process of representation, the ways in which the "people" become sovereign. To democratic theorists such as Lefort the participation of the people is the measure of civic well-being, and yet who the people are is never established in any finite, stable, or absolute way. Democratic politics and decisions about the conjoined life of a polity are worked out in an unremitting practice whereby citizens name, assert, and give meaning to themselves and one another. "The identity of the people remains latent. . . . Representation is dependent upon a political discourse and upon a sociological and historical elaboration always bound up with ideological debate." Convinced that the democratic public I valued requires this unremitting representative practice, I retitled my project *The Public and the People* and vowed to place the two concepts in constant, fluid relationship to one another.[7]

Once the search for civic ideals shifts from the Olympian plane of the polis to the pragmatic practices of democracy, the public sphere or realm splinters, inevitably and unregrettably, into more mundane and multiple political spaces. Democratic theorists are particularly intent on locating politics in actual physical spaces, historical sites that are public in the more pedestrian, colloquial, but critical way—in their openness and accessibility to the people. The writings of Lefort and Dewey no less than those of Habermas refer at critical points to mundane public places called, variously, civil society, New England communities, face-to-face ties—that is, multiple, finite, often small and decentered publics where people formulate their democratic aspirations and mobilize for political action. Conversely, one cannot imagine Dewey's pragmatic method of locating the public or Lefort's model of popular democracy operating in private space—the intimacy of the home, the recesses of the individual soul, and what Habermas calls the "rooms and anterooms of bureaucracies." By decentering politics and underplaying the role of the state, democratic theorists invest the social space between the government and the private home with more significance, by default if not intention. Even Hannah Arendt was enticed into this earthbound social dimension of the public as a "space" where "men act together in concert."[8]

Theories of democracy seem especially to gravitate toward this social and spatial public. The germination of democratic institutions may even require open, accessible, shared space, sites where the people can actually see each other in all their diversity and can mobilize, debate, form identities, and forge coalitions. Contemporary theory also adumbrates an aesthetic dimension to public democracy that is nurtured by the diverse and unpredictable encounters possible in open social space. Lefort repeatedly and approvingly quotes Tocqueville's observation that the "ceaseless agitation which democratic government has introduced into the political world influences all social intercourse. I am not sure that on the whole, this is not the greatest advantage of democracy."[9]

As the course of this search for the public shifted from the classic public to modern democracy it was inevitable that it should come back to Alexis de Tocqueville. First, Tocqueville's own search for a political system and culture to succeed the *ancien regime* led not just to democracy but to a social rendering of the public: It was founded not in the superior virtue of Americans but in their inveterate habit of forming groups to obtain common social goals. "Wherever, at the head of some new undertaking you see the government in France, or a man of rank in England, in the United States you will be sure to find an association. ...Thus, the most democratic country on the face of the earth is that in which men have, in our time, carried to the highest perfection the art of pursuing in common the object of their common desires, and have applied this new science to the greatest number of purposes." Tocqueville's democracy was composed of associated peoples, of voluntary organizations, or of local governments; his is a politics of public sociality. It is Tocqueville who located civic life in a place that is most congenial to this investigator. Its coordinates are not the goodness and virtue of the classic public sphere, nor the austerity of pure pragmatic practice, but the democratic associations of people.

Tocqueville guides the story that follows in a second, fundamental way: He identified the empirical center of the history of democracy peculiar to the United States. He discovered democracy not just in association but in a critical place and time. Touring America in 1831 and 1832, he was struck by sights such as these: "The people of one quarter of a town are met to decide the building of a church; there, the election of a representative is going on; a little further, the delegates of a district are posting to the town in order to consult some local improvements; the laborers of the village quit their ploughs to deliberate upon the project of a road or a public school." Tocqueville located democracy, in other words, in relatively dense human settlements, towns, villages, or cities. Tocqueville's America is distinguished not just from the classic or Enlightenment public sphere but also from another great theory of American democracy, Turner's frontier thesis, which traced the distinctive politics of the United States not to public associations but to the individual freedoms practiced in the supposedly open territories of the American West.

The human settlements that so sparked Tocqueville's political imagination point to an ideal time and place in which to examine the democratic public practices of an associated people. Tocqueville's visit, occurring in the second quarter of the nineteenth century, intersected with the moment when the term *democracy* became the best designation of the new nation's political ideology and institutions. By 1825, despite some contrary and curmudgeonly opinions, American politicians operated on the assumption that the people had to be consulted in public matters. A stance of superiority to the mass of men and deference to the opinions of the better sort, once proudly espoused by the likes of John Adams and James Madison, was now taboo. In the second quarter of the nineteenth century the term *democracy* was rarely qualified by allusions to those aspects of republican theory that constrained the voice of the people within the confines of a mixed constitution, with its aristocratic and monarchical elements. The frank exhaltation of democracy had become the presumption of national politics with Jackson's bank message in 1832. Ever since, politicians have courted the common man and bowed to the people in their homeliest aspects and humbler statuses. After acknowledging the accomplishments of a generation of historians who traced survivals of a republican ethic in nineteenth-century America, it is time to give this explicitly democratic strand of American political history a central place as of the 1830s. Thereafter neither politicians nor historians could sanction restrictions on popular participation in government, no matter how rational and critical were the discussions that transpired within the public sphere.[10]

The triumph of democratic rhetoric was no mere chimera but the product of a slow yet revolutionary change in the methods of representative government. The chief element in this transformation was the expansion of the elected sector of the government, which under republican theory and early American practice was kept in balance by constitutional restraints and restrictions on suffrage. By the date that begins this study, and exemplified by the New York State Constitution of 1821, legislative bodies were elected more directly, and property restriction on both voting and office holding had been abolished for white males. Democratic life was breathed into these representative procedures by political parties, mobilizations in civil society that the "founding fathers" had once bitterly excoriated. Still suspect as late as 1820, partisan loyalty was the focal point of politics by the raucous presidential election of 1840. With it came the assumption of permanent opposition, contest, and debate in public affairs and the removal of inhibitions about partisan loyalty. It was in the process of partisan elections that a public constituted itself in a participatory and expressive way. Only after several decades of practicing democratic politics in heated electoral contests for relatively low political stakes did Americans begin to invest public institutions with the extensive administrative power and responsibilities associated with the modern state—things (such as income taxes and standing armies) that were established during the Civil War.[11]

Although this democratic public life was acted out on the national stage and orchestrated with particular virtuosity during presidential elections, its origins and constitution can be discerned best at the local level by eavesdropping, like Tocqueville, on the political practices of associated Americans. Those ubiquitous meetings that dotted his itinerary, while less remote and more down to earth than those in the Acropolis, seem far too bucolic to offer models for democratic practice in late twentieth-century America. Tocqueville painted Americans as a relatively settled, homogeneous people who traced a cultural and political ancestry to Anglo-Saxon England. While he pointed out, perhaps correctly, that democracy flourished under such homogeneous social conditions, the village setting did not subject the democratic public to a severe test, certainly not by contemporary standards of diversity and disorder. My strategy in selecting exact sites for this study was to place the representative institutions established by 1825 in direct confrontation with a particularly heterogeneous and fractious people. Therefore, I mounted my historians' canvas squarely in the middle of rapidly growing, soon industrialized, garishly diversified cities.

To maximize the pressures on public life, I chose three sites that also reflected regional differences and antagonisms; one north and one south of the great rent in the nineteenth-century national order and a third located in the contested territory of the West. These three particular cities, New York, New Orleans, and San Francisco, meet my criteria for being ungainly, urban mongrels. Each is the antithesis of the other putative cradles of democracy, the New England town or the sparsely settled frontier where a sense of the common good or the unanimous public interest could be read off the surface of social relations within a relatively homogeneous community. The diversity of the citizenries of New York, New Orleans, and San Francisco precluded any assumption of an organic, automatic public consensus. Each was a port city tied to a transoceanic hinterland and open to waves of immigration. Already by the Revolution, New York boasted a cosmopolitan history. Having passed from Dutch to English colonial control, it hosted a mix of Western European immigrants along with significant numbers of African-born slaves and tolerated a range of religious sects as well as the usual number of urban infidels. The roots of city people were even more tangled in New Orleans. French, Spanish, English, African, Afro-Caribbean, and American Indian accents mingled in one of the most polyphonic cultures on this planet. The transient population that hastily staked a claim beside the Bay of San Francisco in 1849 was fed by especially strong demographic currents from the South. Migrants from Australia, Chile, Mexico, and elsewhere in Latin America pitched their tents beside refugees from back East. Soon the ocean traffic came from Asia, bringing thousands of Chinese. In none of these cities is there much evidence that the simmering social diversity ever boiled away. During the Civil War and after each city experienced vicious interracial conflict at the time that it admitted enough immigrants to make one third to one half the population foreign born.

The heterogeneity of the city was not as easily corralled into a single political jurisdiction as historians often assume. Even the national affiliation of each of these cities was a recent, fragile, and reversible creation. New York was invaded by the British as late as 1812. The teleology that affixes a basic stable national identity on the ports of North America is especially inappropriate to the other cities in this triad. In just one month, November 1804, New Orleans officially passed from Spanish to

French to U.S. authority. Well into the 1840s, city business was still conducted in French. The national identity of the settlement beside San Francisco Bay was also unstable. In just a few decades the hunting and fishing grounds of native Ohlone Indians passed through the hegemony of the Spanish crown, to the Republic of Mexico, and on to some fortune hunters calling themselves the Bear Flag Republic before it became a U.S. territory and finally a sovereign state in the Union. Then, in 1861, the Union itself was violently torn in two, causing particularly bitter internal political divisions in these three cities.

The instability of nationality during the nineteenth century is just one indication that democratic civic life is not a simple transcription from a singular national culture, nor is it centered in a singular political institution such as the state. Accordingly, this search for the public will focus not on centers of government but on the far more dispersed and elusive habitats of the people. The people of course do not present themselves to historians directly, transparently, as pure essences. A major objective of this investigation is to discover how people actually defined themselves as political actors and recognized one another. At best, some citizens left fleeting, partial, and ambiguous traces of themselves on selective sets of documents, few of which bear those exquisite signs of authenticity characteristic of the elite citizens who transcribed their lives and thoughts for posterity. Of necessity the search for the democratic public will be conducted in that second-class stock of historical documents called the published sources. It is there, in published proceedings of municipal governments, printed guides to city life, public commentaries of literate citizens, and above all the daily newspapers that the public discloses itself to citizens and historians.

The impurities of these raw materials do not require an apology, for in this instance they have their virtues as well as their limitations. Michael Warner, among others, has demonstrated how the emergence of the democratic public in the modern West was inextricably bound up with publication. Until the mid-eighteenth century the idea of calling upon officials to publish, much less explain or justify, their actions was considered libelous. Soon thereafter, the first halting attempts to question colonial authority took the form of demands for the publication of colonial procedures and mushroomed into a printing industry premised on the radical assumption of open debate, public discussion, and governmental accountability to citizens. The political literature of the early national period was more than a printed transcript of public debate. The process of publishing government actions created an imaginary but consequential republic of letters. Print linked author to reader and readers to one another in an ongoing, widespread, deeply thought if unspoken conversation. A political culture of print made government a public rather than a private matter; it was critical to the democratization of civic life.[12]

By 1825 the republic of letters was on its way to becoming a democracy of print. With steady growth of the penny press the majority of adult males became parties to the public discussions on a whole range of political issues. Early in the century the expensive newspapers not only were few, of narrow distribution, and small in size but scarcely mentioned local or national events. It was through the fiercely partisan campaigns of the press in the 1830s and 1840s that readers were introduced to a daily diet of public discussion of local and national politics. By 1850, when the press began to assume a nonpartisan but nonetheless politically engaged stance, the whole electorate was mobilized by newsprint. Circulation figures in individual cities reached to six digits, newspaper offices became gathering spots for obtaining political information, and even the illiterate congregated on street corners and in grogshops for a public reading of the dailies. After midcentury the press became more aggressive in courting and organizing public opinion by sending reporters onto the streets to survey and report on grassroots political discussions. Through it all newspaper editors were major public actors, candidates for public office, sponsors of major public projects, targets of violent crowd action and even assassination. By the late nineteenth century the big city newspapers had come to dominate civic space itself: the office towers of the *New York Herald, San Francisco Chronicle,* and *New Orleans Picayune* provided a spatial as well as an ideological focal point of public life. By scanning pages of newsprint, the chief informant for this account of the people and the public, the historian becomes witness to the oral, the imagined, the distorted, the living public.[13]

As the printed nexus of an extended, multivoiced conversation the newspaper may be as close as historians can get to the voice of the public. This is not to say that these published records speak of the people any more accurately and authentically than does any other species of historical document. At the same time newspapers and published records supply an admirably complete empirical record of local events and public actions. Nearly every political body, from Sunday school societies to the city council, reported to the local newspapers while very few deposited their private papers in historical archives. Repeatedly, the fullest, most intricate and extended accounts of public events are to be found in neither the minutes of the city council nor the private papers of mayors but in the newspapers. Once again it was Tocqueville who spied the practical as well as the theoretical significance of the press for democracy. He noted that an independent press was not only the "chief, and so to speak, the constitutive element of liberty" but the most efficient channel of communication and most audible call to the association so necessary to democracy. In Tocqueville's pithy but overly modest image the city presses "drop the same thought into a thousand minds at the same moment." This newspaper democracy has the final advantage that it extends across time as well as across the space of the city, making the historian just another citizen reader.[14]

The following chapters report one citizen's reading of this public record. My selective itinerary through this boundless universe has been plotted around a few signposts, or what Dewey called markers, of the public. My route will begin among the people and circle slowly in on the more formal institutions of the public. The first marker of the public is within the domain of everyday sociability, of face-to-face or shoulder-to-shoulder encounters between city residents, most of whom were strangers to one another if not representatives of alien cultures. This public life transpired in streets, squares, and parks, places of informal, casual, largely unplanned social interaction. The search for the public begins here, because such actual social interactions may nurture, undermine, or otherwise fundamentally condition the discovery of a more formal and organized public. Dewey, among others, maintained that sustained face-to-face associations (like those of the New England town of his birth) were the necessary precondition for discovering a public. Portraits of urban sociability such as those drawn by Lyn Lofland or Richard Sennett point to city streets as schools of public spirit more appropriate to complex modern cultures. City sidewalks were spaces where citizens could learn the cosmopolitan skills of discerning and accepting differences. The most exquisite evocation of such urban civility came from the pen of Jane Jacobs, who described the makings of the public on the sidewalks of New York some thirty years ago. "The sum of such casual, public contact at a local level—most of it fortuitous, most of it associated with errands, all of it metered by the person concerned and not thrust upon him by any one—is a feeling for the public identity of people, a web of public respect and trust and a resource in time of personal or neighborhood need."[15]

I have been alert to any evidence that city people found the first dim recognition of a public identity in encounters like these. The civilities of the streets may be the most basic training exercises of democratic citizenship. The possibility of nurturing such public civility, as Jacobs clearly demonstrated, depends on the sidewalks themselves, on the actual physical organization of city space. Accordingly, charting the roots of the public in everyday sociability has required attention to the changing organization of urban space—such things as the layout of streets, creation of parks, maintenance of squares, and construction of public buildings.

These spaces are also the sites of a second flank of my research in which I examine how public culture was organized through civic ceremonies. The performances and festivities that were enacted in public spaces on civic holidays served as both staging grounds and exercises of public life. Fourth of July parades, to give the obvious example, brought city residents together in a short-term commitment to some larger civic identity. In the process the celebrants might acquire a cultural cohesion that would gird them to undertake more costly and difficult public projects. At the very least public ceremonies allowed vast numbers of citizens to learn, invent, and practice a common language that could be converted to other civic or political uses. This public record is subject, like any other, to different readings. It can, in the manner of some symbolic anthropologists, be seen as the reservoir of a complex but seamless community identity, a pool reflecting an unproblematic common culture. But in the three bustling towns under study here, public ceremony is just as likely to present fractured images, outlines of the distinctive publics that formed in each city: ethnic contingents who skirmished on the sidelines of parades, racial minorities who were banished to the back of the line of marches, women who could be found only back stage or on the balconies, whole classes who strategically retreated from public festival. This second part of the investigation is an especially sensitive measure of the degree of public consciousness among the people. It may speak either of unity or diversity, harmony or conflict, exclusion or openness, but it always puts a large and vivid representation of the people on or near a public stage. The luxurious ceremonial life of the last century will at least reveal some of the many possibilities of the urban civic imagination.[16]

The ceremonial civic lessons were carried onto the next plane of my analysis, to a space of more formal and directly political public action. Perhaps the most intense focus of public attention in a nineteenth-century city was not a promenade or parade, neither casual socializing nor festive solidarity, but a knock-down-drag-out political contest called an election campaign. The operating principles of urban politics in 1825 and after was not an allegiance to some Olympian public good but a radically democratic procedure, an agreement to disagree. Conventional wisdom downplays the level of permissible disagreement and tells us that American electoral procedures compressed the diversity of the people into two parties with narrow ideological differences. In these three cities between 1825 and 1880, however, the voting public was far more distended than dualistic. Even the most rigid schemes of classifying partisan politics recognize three party systems in less than fifty years—Federalists and Democratic Republicans, Jacksonians and Whigs, Democrats and Republicans. At the local level the major parties regularly splintered into contending factions that were joined by an array of serious and sometimes successful contenders for local power, chief among them working men, abolitionists, nativists, and municipal reformers. An investigation of these partisan formations of the public, their ceremonies and symbols, as well as their platforms and speeches will be a critical test of the democratic public.

Because neither elections nor city council meetings ever enrolled all the people or expressed all public needs, it is also necessary to be attentive to the many occasions when politics spilled into the streets, in less than civil ways. Vociferous, often violent crowds took regularly to the streets of New York, New Orleans, and San Francisco to articulate interests, opinions, and demands that had not been heard in the more formal arenas of political discourse and decision making. Although the rioting public included relatively large cross sections of the urban population, it was more likely than a civic ceremony or a political party to enroll the more disorganized populations—the poor, unenfranchised, women, racial minorities, underrepresented peoples. In addition to functioning as an active part of the public, these urban crowds broke the silence of the formal public about certain issues and certain citizens: They are essential reminders that the democratic procedures of the nineteenth century consulted and enacted the will of only some people.

Much of the heterogeneity of the democratic public was washed out when established governments took action in the name of the whole polity. In the end only a few of the infinite matters of public relevance (or, in Dewey's terms, indirect consequences) reached city hall. Groups such as racial minorities and women seldom were able to place issues of greatest concern to them on the public agenda, much less translate them into public policy. Accordingly, any attempt to retrace the steps whereby people discovered the public must move beyond the space of discourse, demonstration, and contention to consider public decisions and public policies. At this final plane of analysis the discrepancy between the public and the people will appear once again and in boldest relief, inscribed in the limited number of issues, interests, and public goods that culminated in government actions.

In fact the range of municipal actions in the nineteenth century was relatively small, and extremely hesitant: from partial responsibility for street improvements, to private contracting of major services such as the water supply, and occasionally a major investment in civic improvement such as a municipal hall or grand park. Although a number of historians have shown how antebellum cities were busy staging grounds of different public interests, they had a very small set of public programs and services to show for themselves. There is still little reason to expect that these three cities managed to disprove Sam Bass Warner's interpretation of nineteenth-century urban history as the domain of the private city. Too often the machinations of the capitalist market, rather than democratic deliberations, were left to determine the public good. During and after the Civil War, furthermore, military force, governmental bureaucracy, and corporate franchises became larger forces in municipal life, posing a potential threat to democratic freedoms, without necessarily promising to distribute the beneficence of government to all the people. One should not expect a simple story of triumphant public democracy in the pages ahead.

The meaning of civic life in these three cities almost 170 years ago, as today, was confusing and contradictory. Was it possible for so diverse a people, with such different beliefs and competing interests, to mold themselves into one public, even a harmonious circle of publics? Would the decentralized practices of democratic associations create pandemonium or a working coalition? Can a public composed of men and women separated by their different resources and flagrant inequities operate in a truly democratic manner? Can (must) democracy attempt to moderate inequality? Could democratic politics meet the needs of so many people living so closely together and yet often so culturally and politically apart? Can government administer to public needs without jeopardizing individual freedoms?

To address these basic questions I adopted a mundane empirical strategy that can be quickly recapitulated. After parting with the lofty aspirations of political philosophers who sought an Apollonian public realm, I come down to earth to explore the associated democratic practices of specific places. My research plan then takes on a tidy trinitarian shape. To explore a full range of civic possibilities, I set my story in three differ-

ent cities, each chosen to test the fiber of democracy under the most ri-
otously heterogeneous social conditions. Convinced that the quality of
civic life could not be measured or explained within the narrow compartments of historical specializations, I proceed on three planes of investigation—the social, the cultural, and the political. I have plotted the
history of the democratic public in an old-fashioned, linear narrative,
told from a single but hardly omniscient vantage point. Eschewing a
more fashionable posture, such as telling multiple or open-ended stories, I have indulged an irrepressible urge to make my own sense of
things and thereby give the reader a firm and fallible position to contest
against. (Such straightforward contention can be a useful mode of discourse in a democracy.) The narrative is divided just as predictably into
three parts. Part one describes the creation of a robust democratic political culture between the approximate dates of 1825 and 1850: It builds up
from the first chapter on city space, to a second describing civic ceremonies, to a third addressing politics in the conventional sense but as
conducted both inside and outside the electoral and legislative arenas.
Part two is but one chapter that recounts how, around the time of the
Civil War, the municipal public exploded into quite uncivil warfare. Part
three also contains three uneasy chapters that detail a sequence of critical
alterations in the organization of city space, culture, and politics. By its
termination, in the year 1880, civic life had quieted down significantly
and had been reshaped in some fundamental (not always democratic)
ways.

But in New York, New Orleans, and San Francisco the tidy plan ran
amuck and created some major disorder. Writing urban history, much
like touching down in a busy city street, can be a delightfully disorient-
ing experience. Early in the story the civic center splinters into a kaleidoscope of urban associations. Soon thereafter, and even before the outbreak of the Civil War, segments of the public went to war with one
another. By the end of part three, which reaches the year 1880, this account of municipal life will have earned and maintained its new title,
"Civic Wars." Running through the whole story of democracy in the city
is a spirit of public contention, which I will first report and then, in the
conclusion, attempt to come to terms with, if not explain. For now I
will only say that I have come to believe that the often uncivil history
that I am about to describe betokens something of a civic accomplishment. An indelicate balance between civility and belligerence may, in the
last analysis, be a precious contribution of the nineteenth-century city to
American democracy.

PART ONE

Heterogeneous Compounds and Kaleidoscopic Varieties

Creating a Democratic Public, 1825–1849

CHAPTER 1

People's Places

Visiting New York City in 1849, Lady Emmeline Stuart Wortley fumbled for words to capture a place "unlike every city ever beheld before." That a tourist was bewildered by "the cosmopolitanism" of Gotham and "the extraordinary stir and bustle and tumult of business going on perpetually" will surprise no one familiar with the place and its people. But Lady Stuart Wortley did provide one more original observation about civic life in the second quarter of the nineteenth century: In antebellum New York she saw "heterogeneous compounds and kaleidescopical varieties presented at every turn." With these two awkward pairs of words Lady Stuart Wortley compressed the life of the city into an image of variety and cohesion—a "heterogeneous compound"—and drew an unstable alliance between diversity and symmetry—those "kaleidescopical varieties."[1]

Part one of this book will describe how, in the second quarter of the nineteenth century, American cities indeed held the complexity and constant movement of urban populations together in an intricate but comprehensible and even pleasing whole. Before 1850 those who walked the busy streets of New York, as well as the lively promenades of New Orleans or the rugged pathways of San Francisco, were less likely to express anxious disorientation, so common in latter-day urban chronicles. Surely the antebellum city had its detractors, and historians properly point to growing apprehension of urban danger, especially as midcentury approached.[2] But the anturban bias that has pervaded American thought for the last century has cast a teleological shadow over a time of relative urban contentment. My reading of the historical record will, for the sake of balance, lean in the direction of a more sanguine interpretation. The people of these three cities managed to construct a mechanism that brought differences together into a colorful whole, something that resembled an urban kaleidoscope. This complex social creation was constructed from the ground up, on the concrete spaces of the city. These elemental building blocks of civic consciousness are the subject of this chapter, which will describe the particular arrangements of people and space that supported American democracy during a critical period between approximately 1825 and 1850.

No one could dispute that by the midpoint of the last century the cities of New York, New Orleans, and San Francisco were well supplied with the raw materials from which to construct a kaleidoscope or blend a compound. The human fragments numbered over half a million in New York and 110,000 in New Orleans. In each city, including the upstart settlement of San Francisco, the pieces of the kaleidoscope were very much in motion. The 35,000 residents whom the census takers found just within the Golden Gate in 1850 were almost to a man (and a very rare woman) newcomers to a village only recently claimed from the Mexicans (and the Spanish and Native Americans just before them). The city had acquired its name and corporate status only three years before. Meanwhile, in the relatively ancient cities of New York and New Orleans the population had grown fivefold in the two preceding decades. These two ports were, respectively, the first and second major points of entry into the United States. New Orleans saw an estimated 188,000 immigrants (one and one-half times its official population) pass through its port in the preceding decade. The diverse origins of these mobile thousands meant that unusually disparate languages, cultures, and peoples came together in these port cities. Over 40 percent of the residents of both New York and New Orleans had been born abroad, with the Irish and Germans constituting the largest immigrant groups. A full majority of San Franciscans were foreign born as of 1852. The population flowing into San Francisco and New Orleans was replenished from Asia, the Caribbean, and South America as well as Europe. Already in 1850 hundreds of immigrants from China were arriving in San Francisco. In New Orleans the balance between those of European and African descent was slowly stabilizing after an erratic half-century. In 1820 African Americans, free people of color as well as slaves, were a majority in the Crescent City. Thereafter steady migration from the Northern states and immigration from Europe gave Caucasians the demographic edge, accounting for almost three fourths of the population by 1850. From the perspective of New Orleans natives, the migrants from the Northern United States were as disruptive a presence as any: Just a few years after the French-speaking majority of New Orleans voted against enrolling Louisiana among the United States of America, they found that English had become the predominant tongue spoken in the city.[3] The "American" majority had shallow roots in all antebellum cities. As of 1850 over 55 percent of New Yorkers and New Orleanians had been born out of state if not out of the country.

These newcomers swept into the city at a time of frenetic economic expansion that splintered the polity along yet another axis. Social historians have demonstrated that the decades before 1850 saw the demolition of the bonds of interdependency that once linked master and servant, journeymen and apprentice, shopkeepers and clerks into joint households and under a web of deference and stewardship. It is equally clear that differences in wealth became more dramatic over the course of the antebellum period. Yet the shifts in occupational structure did not sort themselves into clear class divisions. The period between 1825 and 1850 saw both the expansion of independent wage labor and the continuing predominance of small-shop production. The militant producer consciousness of Anglo-Saxon Protestant artisans waxed its strongest just as unskilled foreign-born, often Catholic laborers came to dominate the manual work force. Finally, the whole motley marketplace was turned topsy-turvy by the prolonged depression that followed the financial panic of 1837. In sum the diverse and growing urban economies of these commercial cities tended to fracture the occupational structure, giving another bewildering turn to the urban kaleidoscope.[4]

The populations of these three cities were diverse in national origins, place of birth, lines of descent, and economic status and were composed of people who had resided together for only a short time. Such a population is unlikely to manifest the coherence of a folk, or common, culture or a singular and seamless community. Still, this does not mean that the coresidents of American cities were merely stray atoms strewn across the urban landscape. At the most basic level they were drawn into relations with one another by the necessity of sharing densely settled urban turf. During the second quarter of the century the physical arrangement of this common ground fostered public sociability and democratic association. Although the antebellum urban plan was a haphazard creation, to say the least, it was, to use Kevin Lynch's phrase, a readable city: Its basic spatial organization was clear enough that residents could comprehend where they were in relation to the whole urban polity (figs. 1–3). The social life of antebellum cities flowed along three spatial coordinates,

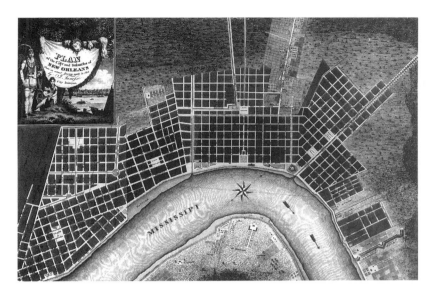

Figure 1. Plan of New Orleans, Louisiana, 1815. Courtesy The Historic New Orleans Collection, Museum/Research Center.

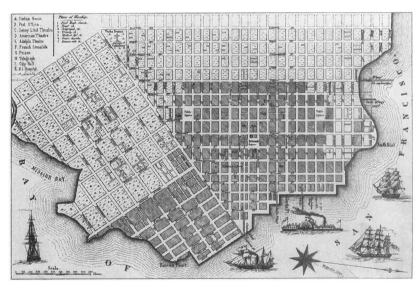

Figure 2. Map of San Francisco, California, 1853. Courtesy of the Bancroft Library.

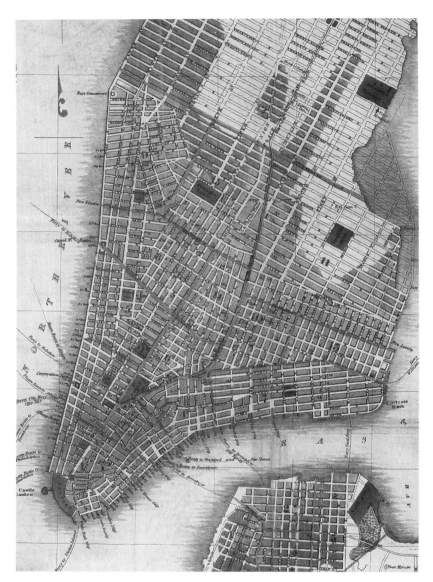

Figure 3. Map of the city of New York. Courtesy of the Bancroft Library.

which I have labeled centers, sectors, and arteries, that made the city intelligible to its inhabitants. After mapping these elements of the antebellum urban plan (all of which are visible in contemporary maps), this chapter will populate city space with some of the ordinary people who lived and created a public there.[5]

Grounding the Public in Space: Centers, Sectors, Arteries

In 1825 the peoples of New York and New Orleans, like the stray settlers in the village of Yerba Buena that would become San Francisco, still experienced their urban environment as a meeting place of nature and humanity, of land, water, and flora as well as buildings, pavement, and fences. Most New Yorkers resided below Fourteenth Street, where the densely populated but still narrow island bound them to rivers and bays. Waterfront borders served as recreation in Battery Park on the west and as a place of work and business on the docks of the East River. Place names such as Spring Street and Collect Pond still referred to the natural topography of the island. It was not until almost mid-century that the island became so densely and extensively settled that New Yorkers began to notice the absence of green spaces within the city limits. Ground for the first multifamily dwelling unit on the island was not broken until 1843 (the first proper apartment building would not appear until late in the 1860s), and even then the skyline was unscathed by buildings taller than a few stories. But closeness to the natural landscape and the small scale of construction do not necessarily create a bucolic habitat. The city of New Orleans, for example, confronted nature in a particularly abrasive mood. Built below sea level along the curves and twists of the Mississippi River and just below Lake Pontchartrain and its tributary swamps, the Crescent City marked the seasons with floods, torrents, and pestilence. Still, a brisk social life was conducted on storm-ravished streets and on fortifications against the temperamental waterways of the Mississippi Delta, especially the Levee, which served as a major promenade. New Orleanians took it for granted that the streets would be uninhabitable for much of the year and that epidemics would rage through the city almost annually. Off San Francisco Bay the forty-niners defied natural limits as they occupied a piece of bayshore whose sediments could swallow up their ships, whose steep hills constrained their mobility, where winds, fog, and sandstorms obstructed their view. One early settler dubbed her new home a "city of dust, not altogether gold dust." The lines on the real estate maps of early San

Francisco were a brash fiction superimposed on eroding sand dunes and a shifting shoreline.[6]

The locomotive powers of the human body as much as topography set natural limits on the conquest of urban land. With but a few rail lines and an occasional omnibus service, both prohibitively expensive, the residents of even the big city of New York knew much of the city in their very limbs. They could walk through most of it in less than six hours. Before 1850 only a small vanguard of houses extended very far to the north along a little-known street unpretentiously named Fifth Avenue. Downtown, in the heart of the city, the proud municipal center of City Hall Park and the eyesore of the Five Points slum were within a few minutes' walk of one another. In New Orleans settlement had grown both up and down river from the original French and Spanish settlements but not so far that any settled point was more than a short walk away. The pattern of land use in San Francisco as late as 1850 was extremely simple to describe: It was a few tents and rough-hewn buildings clustered around one plaza and just a few feet away from the spot where the new settlers had disembarked on the Pacific shore. Their dry-docked ships actually served as an early market street.

If the accounts of travelers can be believed, these rather ramshackle walking cities fostered an easy, ambulatory familiarity with urban space. In her *Letters from New York* in the late 1840s Lydia Marie Child reports having sauntered the whole length of the island in a leisurely afternoon and having spent an evening strolling Broadway and the Bowery without an escort. English visitors such as Lady Stuart Wortley and Mrs. Trollop might picture crossing the bustling Broadway as a harrowing adventure, but they seemed never to hesitate about making the trip. Local residents such as Philip Hone, a member of the affluent carriage-owning set, found it remarkable when he had gone a year without walking on the Battery. And then he and his wife walked effortlessly for an hour and a half. A humbler sojourner from Ireland also paced his diary to a pedestrian rhythm: "we begin the walking," "take our morning excursion," "much walking." Visitors to New Orleans in the 1830s and 1840s were also forever on the move through expansive patches of city space: a typical entry in the diary of Thomas Richards, who visited the Crescent City in 1839, charted his movements from a sidewalk auction sale where he met a friend, and the two proceeded to "walk together for more than two hours." Richards seemed to conduct his business while in transit through the streets and let chance encounters in public spaces set his daily schedule.[7]

Some of the pathways through New York and New Orleans had once been deliberately planned. Thomas Richards's itinerary through New Orleans, for example, followed streets that were plotted out many years before by the French. This plan, designed in 1721 by Adrien de Pauger, is a good example of the old-world assumptions that set the patterns for the quotidian peopling of America's walking cities. The French engineer, appointed by Governor Bienville, surveyed the land along the Mississippi and plotted a rectangular grid of streets hugging the shoreline. For all the symmetry and order of his plan it did not present a monotonous and unrelieved web of right angles. The rectangular blocks were arranged along a combination of broad and narrow streets sloping between the river and the lake and anchored by a central square. The whole city plan followed the gentle arc of the riverfront. The earliest plans marked that centering space with the spire of a church. Through periods of both French and Spanish administration of Louisiana, that central square and much of the surrounding territory was inscribed with military authority: It was called Place d'Armes or Plaza des Armas. A sense of medieval hierarchy and ecclesiastical authority mingled with the Enlightenment rationality of the eighteenth-century plan. The French set St. Louis Cathedral in the center of the Place and marked nearby streets with the imperial insignia of fleur de lys.[8]

It would take more than a century to furnish the Place d'Armes with the public buildings that made it a complete and enchanting focal point of urban space. The side of the square across from the river had been built up in the eighteenth century first with St. Louis Cathedral at its center, then with the French *presbytère* (or parish house) on one side, and finally with the Cabildo (or town hall) on the other side. The latter structure was erected by the Spanish in 1799 and gave an international balance to civic space. It was not until the 1840s that this triptych of colonial architecture was girded to the enterprising spirit of the commercial American city. In that decade the Baroness de Pontalba erected row houses with shops below on either side of the cathedral block. The iron galleries, wide verandas, and graceful balconies typical of the Pontalba buildings soon became the architectural trademark of the city. The city council picked up the spirit of improvement, put a new marble face on the Cabildo, fenced off and landscaped the square into a pedestrian garden, and added a third story to both the Cabildo and the presbytère, both of which were designed to echo the style of the Pontalba blocks. As a consequence New Orleans in 1850 was graced not only with a proper, enclosed city square but also with one of the most gracious public places in the nation.

By 1850 the Place d'Armes had been rechristened Jackson Square and the territory surrounding it had already been labeled the Vieux Carré— the old quarter and relic of the French past. But even as a confident American culture took hold over the Crescent City in the 1840s the pattern of land use laid down by the French and decorated by Spanish architects was maintained. When the Yankees moved upriver across Canal Street into what quickly became known as the American sector they conformed to the street plan that had been established by an eighteenth-century French planter. American businessmen and politicians proceeded to erect their own major private and public buildings around a central square that had been laid out in 1796 and named after Lafayette. Although Lafayette Square had a distinctly American character and was built up with banks, Masonic lodges, Protestant churches, and shaded private residences, all these Yankee institutions were still grouped around an unmistakable central space and anchored by the same symmetrical arrangement of intersecting streets to be found in the French quarter. When in the 1840s a humbler stock of immigrants, chiefly from Ireland and Germany, began to settle downriver in the third municipality they too were reined into a French faubourg. They shared a third central plaza, called Washington Square, with many French-speaking residents, including large numbers of African Americans, both slave and free. This bookend to Lafayette Square completed the trinity of centering urban spaces that still give a bold spatial definition to New Orleans.[9]

San Francisco's early history was enacted on a stage set by Spanish rather than French colonists. The Spanish colonial administration issued elaborate plans for pueblos in the New World that featured spacious central plazas and prominent edifices for both secular and ecclesiastical authorities. Long before the Yankees had been attracted to San Francisco Bay by visions of gold in the nearby hills, Spanish clerics had planted a mission on San Francisco Peninsula and Mexican settlers built a pueblo called Yerba Buena amid the fragrant fields of mint to the north. In laying out that village in 1835 a representative of newly independent Mexico, Francisco de Haro, created a central space called simply the Plaza. When Yerba Buena was surveyed by Governor Alvarado four years later, he further prescribed that houses "be in as good order and arrangement as possible, in order that the streets and plazas which may be formed may have from the beginning proper uniformity and harmony." When the Yankees sailed into San Francisco Bay aboard the *Portsmouth* in 1846 they planted the Stars and Stripes in that very plaza and summarily renamed it after the ship that brought them through the Golden Gate. Three years later, Yerba Buena, Alta California, would become the U.S. city of San Francisco, but for decades afterward Portsmouth Square was known locally simply as the Plaza.[10]

At the same time that San Francisco and New Orleans were taking on the qualities of an American city New York was moving uptown according to solidly American principles. The history of American urban planning is commonly said to commence with New York's Plan of 1811. This classic imprint of the gridiron street plan was both the act and the emblem of the early republican city. The plan was commissioned by the Common Council, whose elected members represented a political and social elite. The blueprint they accepted has been seen as the imposition of mechanistic, rational standards upon the earth of Manhattan Island. Its twelve avenues, 100 feet wide and intersected at right angles every 200 feet by 155 cross streets, defied the intricacies of the local landscape as well as the diverse needs of the inhabitants.[11] But, as Hendrik Hartog has demonstrated, the rectangular blocks also served as a more flexible blueprint for urban living. Like the U.S. Constitution, its abstract uniformity left the details of civic life to be decided by the people meeting in their republican institutions. The plan did not, however, specify that any of those identical blocks be reserved for public buildings, be rearranged into a network of public squares, or be ordered around a central focal point. Although it was drafted by a state-appointed board of street commissioners, composed of the elite stewards of the commonweal and pledged to create space "conducive to the public good," it laid out only one park and very few public buildings.[12]

Yet as that plan filled in over the next four decades it came to resemble the centered social spaces of New Orleans and San Francisco. Previous land uses and the practices of the local republican institutions, especially the City Council, did create and preserve a central space, called simply City Hall Park. In the more haphazard and parsimonious style that would become common practice for nineteenth-century city governments, the land for this civic project had been set aside for public uses long before, when it had little market value. This piece of land at the far northeastern corner of the town was first declared a commons around 1700. By 1785 it harbored a cluster of municipal buildings—the jail, a public school, the customhouse. The new city hall, commissioned by the

City Council in 1803, was finished in 1812. That stately yet intimate building gave new stature to the surrounding spaces, which the City Council ornamented, cared for, and modestly improved over the next decades. The city legislators routinely set aside funds for planting trees and tending the grass in the park and in 1830 appointed a full-time caretaker. The following resolution, from 1825, illustrates the homely, ad hoc ways New Yorkers provided for their central and integrating public space: "Resolved that the Committee of Public Lands and Places be instructed to cause the Manure on the Battery and the Park be spread and the ground prepared and sowed with grass seed if they shall deem it necessary." In another prosaic gesture of civic pride the New York Common Council voted in 1821 to erect an iron fence around the park. Without much overt, long-term planning, in other words, New Yorkers had filled one portion of the urban plan with the public functions and civic pride that would exercise a centrifugal force on the people's orbit through urban space.[13]

Quite early in their history each city created some central and privileged space, some public focal point. Ironically, the centrifugal pattern of urban space that would cradle urban democracy was founded on contrary architectural principles: The Cabildo housed the viceroy of a Spanish king in New Orleans, and New York's City Hall was a monument to the elite stewardship of New York's "natural aristocracy." The public buildings of the Louisiana capital were designed as pedestals for absolute authority, both the agents of the Spanish monarch who looked down on the people from the Cabildo's balcony and the representatives of the papacy who presided at St. Louis Cathedral. New York's stately City Hall was constructed between 1803 and 1812 by a corporate city council chosen under a limited franchise and expecting deference from the humble citizens who might assemble in their palatial quarters.

Still, when the leadership of these cities became more democratic in the second quarter of the nineteenth century, these central places served as the public arenas in which popular sovereignty could be exercised. The popularly elected governments of the antebellum era rarely constructed architectural monuments of the same grandeur. The early maps of San Francisco most always gave prominent space to the Plaza, and along one of its sides lithographers sketched an official-looking Greek revival edifice that was alternately labeled City Hall and the Jenny Lind Theater. This civic schizophrenia endured for some time, and it would be many years before the city could claim a proper city hall.[14] Until then the city government met not in a civic temple built expressly for the people but in secondhand quarters originally designed as a commercial house of entertainment.

The citizens of New Orleans made more progress on civic architecture in the 1840s. The "American" rivals to the authority of the French quarter drew public attention to their neighborhood by constructing a new city hall in Lafayette Square. Designed in monumental proportions and classic style by James Gallier, Municipal Hall featured a lofty portico and huge rooms for public receptions. Its high steps, massive columns, grand portals, vast interior spaces, and vaulted ceilings inspire even a twentieth-century observer with the lofty significance of the public sphere. The openness and spaciousness of Gallier Hall, completed in 1850, re-created the ambiance at New York's City Hall on a grander scale. The vast majority of floor space in both civic buildings was given over not to offices but to capacious, high-vaulted rooms, assembly halls and grand stairways, porticos and rotundas. New York's City Hall was dominated by its inviting circular stair, which led to the Governor's Reception Room and a public chamber of the City Council. Gallier Hall's broad corridors led to a massive public assembly room. These were palaces for the people, or at least their elected representatives, and spaces where citizens could congregate in groups the size of a routine public meeting.

In the quarter century after 1825 each city venerated public space with the simple gestures of civic caring. Fencing public ground, for example, was a kind of municipal fetish. In 1827 the New Orleans mayor announced that the fence in the Place d'Armes needed painting, while a few years later New York's Philip Hone took note in his diary that a wooden barricade had been erected around City Hall Park. Finely wrought iron fences cropped up around the squares of each city and were heralded in the public records with the same fanfare. By the 1840s public squares had become places for citizens' recreation, not military parade grounds, and accordingly were landscaped with grass, trees, and fountains as well as fences. City officials North and South also agreed that a public square was a place of alimentary refreshment and licensed the sale of food and beverages at these civic sites. Such municipal solicitude made the public square the heart as well as the stomach of the city. If they wished to listen to the pulse of urban life, visitors and citizens alike gravitated to City Hall Park in New York, to Jackson Square in New Orleans, and the Plaza in San Francisco (fig. 4).[15]

Viewed from a closer vantage point, these cities displayed a second order of spatial centering as well. Public squares, which were the major

Figure 4. City Hall Park, New York. Engraving by W. H. Bartlett. Collection of the New York Historical Society.

focal points of the cities, were not unique and solitary but often just the central hub in a whole network of more remote and smaller public spaces. As we have seen, New Orleans was planned around three squares. Everyday customs created yet others. The space just across Ramparts Street behind the French quarter and almost in a direct line from the Place d'Armes was officially known as Place du Cirque but had long been claimed by African Americans who used it as a market and a pleasure ground. Both free and enslaved, both women and men, congregated there on Sundays for music and dancing. Accordingly, this centering space was colloquially renamed Congo Square (and now bears the name of Louis Armstrong). In the 1830s the residents of the American sector developed another square called the Coliseum and talked of creating a classic forum, complete with a university on the site. Although such lofty plans were never realized, Coliseum Square was one of half a dozen secondary squares that dotted New Orleans and brought her residents together in smaller circles of sociability.

Such small spaces, preserved from private development and left open by haphazard planning processes, were to be found in other antebellum cities as well. The eclectic style of land use had similar consequences in New York. The early records of the Common Council harbor many petitions like this one dated January 3, 1825: "Freeholders and inhabitants from the East sector of the city" wish to take a "spacious piece of ground at the front of Corlears Hook to the East River to be laid out for a Park or open Square." The accidents of urban geography created other open spaces. Bowling Green and later Times Square, for example, took shape at the irregular angles where east-west streets intersected with Broadway along its diagonal path up Manhattan.[16] By such ad hoc procedures lower Manhattan had a fair increment of secondary public squares by 1850: Moving northward up both sides of the island, a pedestrian would encounter Washington Square, settled in the 1830s, Tompkins Square, opened in 1834, Madison Square, dating from 1847, and Union Square, opened in the 1830s and developed in the next decade. At the same time the city was converting land to squares, real estate developers were constructing another order of open but private space. St. Johns and Gramercy Park were the prime examples of park lands reserved for affluent property owners at the site of their domiciles. This exclusive practice was a variant on the more general custom of creating centering social space on a neighborhood scale. It was a practice found in New York and New Orleans in the years before midcentury and would later be adopted in San Francisco.

The concentric pattern of antebellum urban space often had an even finer grain. More recessed but often busier than the public squares were the public markets maintained by the city and lined with stalls that were rented to hundreds of venders and retailers. Some of these public spaces, like the French Market in New Orleans, were magnets to the whole city population. The French Market was only one of a series of commercial centers that grew in number as the city expanded. While New Orleans was opening new public markets as late as the 1870s, New York had suspended such construction by then. The active phase of creating such nuclei of commerce and sociability in Gotham had been the 1830s and 1840s, but by one account there were still some forty official public markets in the city as late as 1862. This species of public space was created by the same ad hoc, grassroots process as were small squares. The erection of Clinton Market in 1826, for example, was instigated by a petition to the Common Council signed by some 650 neighbors. By the 1830s the city had created a special commission to hear such petitions and regulate the growing system of markets whose operation brought thousands of dollars of license fees circulating though the city coffers. When in 1811 the City Council moved to create a centralized public market, it met effective resistance from the city's butchers. These barons of the neighborhood markets held steadfast to this localized way of doing business. Until midcentury the proliferation of squares and markets seemed to keep pace with the growth of population and the expansion of the borders of settlement. New York and New Orleans were honeycombed with places where city residents could meet one another elbow to elbow if not face to face.[17]

This spatial pattern was both cause and consequence of a certain meiosis of each city into separate sectors and neighborhoods, some of which corresponded with a social segmentation of the people. The most obvious, distinct, and actually de jure pattern of segregation was found in New Orleans, which between 1836 and 1852 was formally dissected into three municipalities, each with a separate municipal legislature. This was emphatically an ethnic partition. The first municipality was the French quarter, where one was also likely to find a concentration of slaves. The second was the American quarter, with fewer slave owners and almost no speakers of French. The third downtown segment housed a mixed lower-class population, including free persons of color and laborers recently immigrated from Europe as well as many French. In New York the spatial boundaries between different ethnic groups were more muted, but they were nonetheless visible in the minds of residents if not on the law books and street maps. A perspicacious observer walking up the Bowery in 1850 could reputedly detect the unmarked border between the Irish and German districts. Few would doubt that the mansions clustered around St. John's Park or Washington Square were the residences of Anglo-Saxons or a few scions of the Knickerbockers. In New York differences in economic status were probably more obvious than those based on birthplace or national origins. Five Points slum in the "bloody sixth" ward had become the spatial symbol of poverty well before 1850. New Yorker patois had terms for even more refined socioeconomic gradings of space: Gothamites divided Broadway between the "dollar and the shilling side." By that same date there were only a few hints of the functional division of urban space in the vernacular urban cartography. The clustering of dry goods stores around Stewart's Marble Palace of consumption on Broadway near Chambers Street formed the nucleus of what would become the "ladies mile" in years to come. Likewise only a few shopping emporiums on New Orleans's Canal Street hinted of central business districts to come. Wall Street was the prototype of the specialized financial centers that would locate among the bank buildings of Lafayette Square in New Orleans and on Montgomery Street in San Francisco.[18]

Urban architecture as well as street plans gave a physical grounding and cultural representation to these social distinctions. If the focal points of urban space found architectural embodiment in City Hall, the neighborhood had several centralizing edifices of a lower order, some as prosaic as the corner grog shop or grocery, others as majestic as the grand hotels epitomized by the lofty domes and rotunda of the St. Charles Hotel in the American sector and the St. Louis Hotel in the French quarter of New Orleans. These, along with a host of places of worship and sociability, still serve as neighborhood centers in American cities. What was distinct to the terrain of antebellum cities was a curious institution called the public hall, a generic term for buildings constructed for the explicit purpose of bringing populations together in units smaller than the civic whole but larger, more formal, and more novel in their social identity than the traditional groupings of church and family. The numerous public halls listed in the city directories for the period created another spatial infrastructure around which to sort out differences among the peoples of the city. The Merchant Exchange opened in New York in 1825 was among the most familiar landmarks during the antebellum period; it was renowned for such classic features as a towering portico and expanse of ionic columns. Travelers to New Orleans two decades later would find a similar grandeur in the American Exchange, which was designed by James Gallier and below whose classic rotunda not only merchants but all sorts of less prominent citizens regularly congregated. By the 1840s most cities boasted a Mechanics Institute as well as a Merchants Exchange, both of which extended the social breadth of the public hall at least as far as master manufacturers and skilled artisans. Mechanics societies erected structures in the same classic and imposing style as the merchants, but in the improving spirit of their class they seemed to prefer libraries to ballrooms and regularly reserved space for scientific exhibitions. Whatever their specific purpose, these buildings featured open interior spaces of grand dimensions and assembly rooms of approximately 50 by 100 feet; some of these rooms were reputed to accommodate several thousand people. They were a commodious stage for organizing the people into occupational units.

The many associated bodies of the antebellum city rarely acquired the prominence and lofty architectural pretensions of the merchant exchange or the mechanics institute. Yet the representation of social difference on the architecture and space of the city was quite catholic and extensive. While most humble lodges, artisans' guilds, or ethnic brotherhoods met in borrowed spaces—saloons, churches, rented halls, or street corners—a significant number of these plebeian societies had secured their own accommodations by midcentury. The city directory of San Francisco actually listed a special category called "public halls" in 1856, when such buildings numbered ten. Such structures numbered in the scores in New Orleans and were too numerous to count in New York. The Bowery alone boasted two halls devoted to the congregation of Irish associations, one named specially for the Ancient Order of Hibernians, the other called simply Hibernia Hall. Whenever a group succeeded in manifesting its identity in a line in the city directory or with a building on a public street it gave notice of its social integrity. When a lodge or association broke ground for its new building, it commonly mounted a public procession and won highly favorable notices in the press.

Despite the spatial definition given to ethnic and occupational differences, it would be a mistake to label the antebellum city a segregated space. The urban population was not divided into isolated urban encampments, be it in neighborhoods or separate public halls. In fact, pundits in New York and New Orleans, even at a time when the population reached six figures, audaciously called for the construction of halls capable of accommodating the whole citizenry. Most city residents shared allegiance to a set of larger landmarks, even if they could not occupy them simultaneously. Different local historians and travelers' guides had their own lists of these most notable sights, which in New York always included City Hall, Trinity Church, the Battery, and the thoroughfares of Broadway and the Bowery. New Orleans had two sets of public landmarks, the Cabildo and its architectural entourage in Jackson Square and the complex of banks and public halls rapidly growing up around Lafayette Square. Reputable San Franciscans might point to the Customhouse in Portsmouth Plaza, but the El Dorado Hotel, queen of the gambling houses that lined one whole block of the Plaza, was probably a more powerful architectural magnet in a city of fortune hunters.

In each city theaters served as another set of architectural landmarks and social centers. The St. Charles and the American in New Orleans, the Park in New York, and the Jenny Lind in San Francisco all drew highly mixed audiences through most of the 1840s. Not until the ominous opening of the Astor Place Theater in 1849 did anyone seem to doubt the capacity of the theater to bring races, classes, ethnic groups, even saints and sinners together in one building if not in the same box or tier. Antebellum purveyors of amusements—both hotel keepers and theater operators, and innovators such as P. T. Barnum, whose American

Museum provided entertainment for the whole urban family—all courted a wide and various, truly public clientele. The rotunda of the great hotels, for example, were like indoor streets in the inclement weather of New Orleans and were simply opened to the public from noon to three each day. Later in the day the city's many crowded dance halls provided yet other outlets for public sociality. The built environment was clustered with hotels, halls, and theaters that served as landmarks to a wide and mixed audience. These urban landmarks also reveal to historians, as they symbolized to contemporaries, some local nuances in civic culture. The wooden reproduction of the Goddess of Liberty atop New York's City Hall represented a homespun version of republican virtue; the bawdy houses and gambling casinos of Portsmouth Square suggested some antithetical priorities of gold-rush San Francisco; and beneath the classic rotunda of the St. Charles Hotel, New Orleanians brazenly conducted slave auctions.[19]

The Streets: Bedrock of Civic Mingling

It was not such civic landmarks, however, but rather the humble streets that brought most city people together on a regular basis. The spine of the walking city was made not of masonry or marble but of pavement—planks, cobblestones, macadam, or well-trod earth. Major urban arteries such as Broadway in New York became international metaphors for the cosmopolitan mixing of people. In 1849 Lady Stuart Wortley began her exploration of the New World at that site. "One of the first things that struck us on arriving in the city of New York—The Empress City of the West—was of course, Broadway.... It is a noble street and has a thoroughly bustling, lively, and somewhat democratic air." In the second quarter of the last century that street was more than an integrating metaphor: It could effectively link up the whole population of the nation's largest city on a daily basis. Nearly every house and shop in the city was within a few minutes' walk of this broad and busy thoroughfare, which spanned north to south at a conveniently sloping angle. Winding northward, it provided access to genteel recreation around the fountain at Bowling Green, admission to public business at City Hall, and just a short amble east a view of the slums of Five Points. You could take in all New York from Broadway.[20]

The settled terrain of Manhattan Island was marked off by not one but two major arteries, Broadway and the Bowery. Only a few yards apart and almost touching further uptown, they were like a divided highway for pedestrian traffic, moving a great mix of people efficiently on about their business. Unlike a modern freeway, these arteries allowed people in transit to take in something of one another's cultures along the way. A jaunt along the Bowery would give the fashionable set a taste of little Germany and Ireland and a more ribald set of pleasures than the shopwindows of Broadway. Yet for all the class and cultural differences that New Yorkers attributed to the patrician Broadway and plebeian Bowery respectively, both were easily accommodated in the same cosmopolitan stride. Lydia Maria Child happily walked between the two streets without losing a step, indeed almost dancing to the sounds of diversity that emanated from the Philharmonic and the Italian Opera on Broadway and the rougher music of the beer gardens of the Bowery. In New York, geography and planning came together to create a third, more truncated artery of urban sociability, a promenade called the Battery, slightly to the south along the East River. This leisurely analog to Broadway brought the same mixed population together for recreation rather than business. The City Council adorned the Battery and went to the expense of erecting an iron railing along a substantial stretch of the waterfront. This triad of arteries gave a sinewy unity to the elongated spaces of Manhattan Island. A street such as Broadway or the Bowery sponsored routine, everyday intercourse between a vast mixture of peoples.[21]

The especially bold spatial segmentation of New Orleans was also melded together by a set of renowned public arteries. One of these, the Levee, was an elevated dock upon the Mississippi and bulwark against its floodwaters. The festive locals characteristically converted the dock to a promenade and public living room. On the planks of the Levee ladies paraded the newest Parisian fashions while merchants conducted public auctions, peddlers hawked their goods, prostitutes negotiated their exchanges, children played, sailors made port, dock workers made their living, and New Orleanians together created their renowned urban ambiance. Out from the Levee sped other integrative pathways of the Southern city: Canal Street and Esplanade, which marked the boundaries of the French quarter, were as much meeting places as borders. These streets were referred to in the local patois as "promenades publique," while the islands of open space that divided them were called "terre commune" or "neutral ground."[22]

These terms were relics of the city's Creole days, when prominent strips of local real estate such as the Levee were officially protected from private development and reserved instead as open space for public enjoyment. The label "neutral ground" was attached to the space that divided Canal Street at a time when the French and American sectors were becoming estranged from one another. In the 1830s and 1840s that rivalry spurred both municipalities to make improvements in public space. Sparked by a private grant from a merchant named Judah Touro and assisted by city policy and the largesse of adjourning property holders, the neutral ground was converted into a kind of early urban mall; the wide boulevard was ornamented with gates, statues, fountains, benches, vases of flowers, and gas lights. As the newspaper reported it, the plan to beautify Canal Street "exudes a very tasteful and elegant arrangement which carried into effect would furnish the citizens with an accommodation which they have long wanted—an agreeable resort and public promenade, where all will meet for relaxation and amusement during the sultry heat of summer." This prized piece of public turf that marked a fuzzy border between the French and the Americans along Canal Street is a fitting example of a spatial arrangement that simultaneously differentiated and integrated the people, all carried off with that special style and whimsy of the Crescent City. The overt ethnic divide between the American and the French municipality was converted into an opportunity for decorous socializing in public space. The "neutral ground," which became the term for a central divide of any street, was not so different from the basic matrix of spatial organization in other cities of the time; the streets provided a place for the people to come together at the same time that they recognized their differences (fig. 5).

Because their function was transporting diverse people and a cornucopia of goods through a congested environment, the streets of nineteenth-century cities were preeminently places of promiscuous public sociability. At the same time, and particularly in the United States, these cities were not particularly well equipped to ease and enhance these functions. The public thoroughfares were, simply, a mess. Not until the very end of the century would municipalities have adequate sewerage systems; the streets of New York were often clogged with human and animal refuse as late as the 1850s. Waste removal was entrusted to the notoriously unreliable efforts of licensed cartmen or left to the pigs, some 30,000 of which still roamed the streets in 1820. As late as 1847 (decades after the first futile attempt to prohibit pigs running free in the streets) the New York press was still bemoaning the traffic problems created by these porcine pedestrians. At about the same time one paper issued this most alarming warning to its readers: mothers who do not protect their infants will have them devoured by foraging swine. Thoroughfares as el-

Figure 5. Canal Street, New Orleans, 1850. Courtesy The Historic New Orleans Collection, Museum/Research Center.

egant as Broadway were too dirty for promenading in the summer months, while the pedestrians of San Francisco were immobilized by the rainy season: "O the mud, it is dreadful, man and beast get stuck in the slush and cannot move. It is like glue, takes their boots off their feet. It is a foot deep." Those promenades publique of New Orleans were impassable from June through September because the streets were adorned with a "Green sluggish water serving imperfectly as a sanitary conveyor." None of the cities conquered regular epidemics before mid-century. Neither did they quarantine the germs of moral contamination. Sundry ordinances prohibiting indecencies in the public streets, from drunkenness to begging to gambling to prostitution, were hollow gestures at a time when few American cities had an effective police force. A handful of watchmen, constables, and citizen police neither tried, nor seemed to care, to morally sanitize their stomping grounds.[23]

Yet in these clogged and dirty spaces city people conducted myriad aspects of their daily lives. Thousands made their homes in the streets, and all manner of persons made their living there. Among the poor, of both sexes and all ages, streets were a place of scavenging, ragpicking, selling everything from newspapers to flowers to sexual pleasures. The newsboys and flower girls of New York were like bands of urban Daniel Boones surviving by their wits, "on their own hook," and thriving not on elbow room but the jostling of the crowd. The streets also served as places for more legitimate, adult activities. The middling ranks of the street economy were filed by public vendors who were licensed by city government to hawk their wares on streets and squares. The street vendor, selling anything from New Orleans's famed pralines to the hot corn that was a favorite snack North and South, was party to a symbiotic relationship between economics and sociability: he or (and probably more often) she simultaneously fed and fed off the appetites of street people. Vendors licensed by the city of New Orleans sold oysters on the Levee and ice cream in Anthony Square and operated fruit stands in the Place d'Armes. New York's Common Council approved setting up booths in City Hall Park for every species of refreshment, including alcoholic beverages. Then as now these street foods are a key index to the sociability and safety of street life.[24]

In the nineteenth century this political economy of the street was neither an illegitimate, black-market operation nor the exclusive vocation of the lower classes. City retailers everywhere stacked, advertised, and sold their wares on the sidewalks, and even major wholesale merchants relied on access to the streets in the operation of their businesses. Fortunes could be made off the dusty streets and shifting shorelines of gold-rush San Francisco, where goods were exchanged on shipside or sidewalk at exorbitant prices. In 1840 in New Orleans the mayor tried to block an ordinance that would permit businessmen to "Effect sales at auction upon the Levee, on the sidewalk, and in the streets." Still he had to acknowledge that the "very nature of the auction business, requires that it should be prosecuted in the most public streets of the municipality such, for instance, as Chartres Street, the banquettes of which already are too narrow for the passage of the crowds which daily throng there."[25]

The mayor in this instance was a Whig named Grossman who hailed from the American municipality and, although he was thwarted in this attempt to reorder the streets, probably represented the city's future. No sentient observer of his city in the 1840s could fail to see a contrast between the streets of the American and French quarters. Already in the winter of 1835 one visitor from the North made this report on the view across Canal Street: Downriver looked like a "decayed town of Europe. The streets are narrow, the buildings low and mean, exhibiting few signs of improvement and the population fixed wanting in enterprise, fearful of change." The American sector, as this visitor reported it, was more like "a growing city of the New World, with its wide thoroughfares, convenient walks, well-built houses, of three, four and five stories." Indeed, the contrast of cultures in New Orleans could be read off the streets. In the old quarter, those narrow streets were by law set up for pedestrians and their diverse activities: one third of the space was allocated to sidewalks. Those cherished banquettes were centers of sociability to Creoles who recalled spending evenings chatting there with neighbors. Easily accessible through French doors, the banquettes became an extension of the living room. By contrast the more exclusive sections of the American district boasted wider thoroughfares and more reclusive homes. Upperclass Americans moved upriver to the suburb of Lafayette and into single family homes, each withdrawn from the streets behind lawns and foliage, and tellingly named the garden district.

But if the French quarter looked backward in 1850, it nonetheless represented a distinct, not entirely extinct, pattern of organizing urban space. The pattern was reflected in the stylized forms of both urban plans and the bird's-eye views drawn by antebellum lithographers (figs. 6–7). It recalled a time when American cities were marked out by the following constellation of spatial features. First of all, antebellum cities in general boasted relatively ample centralizing spaces, especially public squares, prominent public buildings such as city hall, and local landmarks such as grand hotels, which provided a place for public assembly and symbolic civic attachment. Second, the vastness of the city was modulated by the articulation of smaller segments. These neighborhood sectors were anchored by a secondary set of spatial nuclei—public halls, smaller squares, public markets—that brought residents together in more intimate but not segregated places. Third, each city boasted spatial modes of connecting both people and neighborhoods—especially the great and well-recognized integrative arteries such as Broadway, Montgomery Street, or the Levee. Finally, all these spaces and all these people were joined together by the streets themselves. Clogged pedestrian arteries were the primary, almost exclusive, nearly unavoidable way of conducting everyday life. Ineluctably, street life sponsored a routine and casual intermingling people. These features set the spatial stage, the limits and possibilities, for people to come together, to view both the differences and the commonalties through which a public might find itself.

Everyday Uses and Meanings of Public Space

City people came together in public space in order to play as well as work. For some, the pleasures of the street were sedate and genteel. Grace King recalled the quiet sociability on the banquettes and in Jack-

Figure 6. View of New York looking south from Union Square. 1849. Colored lithograph. Artist C. Bachman. The J. Clarence Davies Collection, 29.100.1344, The Museum of the City of New York.

son Square; "the dining rooms ... open into the streets for all passers-by to see if they would the great family board ... the promenade after dinner, on the tree-shaded Levee, to enjoy the evening breezes and meeting with everyone one knew." To the old Knickerbockers, it was the Battery that stored memories of evening walks and summertime play amid the seaside benches or the white tables that circled Castle Garden. There "people could congregate in little squads, and take their uses between the acts." Even the San Francisco forty-niners could create an oasis of genteel sociability on the rugged pathways around the plaza. A pioneer such as E. O. Crosby anchored a reassuring memory in this characteristic observation: "When the girls appeared on the streets they were treated with the greatest respect and gallantry, the same as would be extended to the most respected women by men in general." Crosby was speaking of casual meetings with the fabled habituates of gold-rush streets, San Francisco's madams. The playful possibilities of the streets were usually rendered in more chaste but still ardent forms of public entertainment. In New York it was estimated that 10,000 people went to the theater and other places of amusement on a nightly basis in the 1830s. Be it at the famous Park Theater or the more plebeian Bowery, New Yorkers of many classes made a participatory sport of theater-going, engaging the actor in conversation, singing along, and mingling with one another.

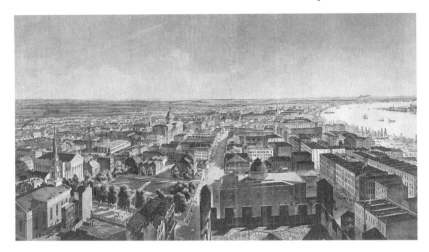

Figure 7. View of New Orleans, 1852. Courtesy The Historic New Orleans Collection, Museum/Research Center.

Pleasure gardens—private parks accessible for a small admission price and the cost of refreshments—were also gathering places for a broad spectrum of the population, affluent and humble, male and female. Be the destination the theater, a pleasure garden, or just outdoors, city people seemed to depart from their homes with alacrity in the expectation that pleasures awaited them in the streets.[26]

On the streets of antebellum cities, play could take on forms more organized than either random meetings or individual purchases of tickets to public amusements. City people often occupied the streets in groups and for the purpose of performance as well as pleasure. Each city was perpetually and cacophonously occupied by bands of marching men and sometimes women too. In New Orleans, that most rhythmic and irreverent of cities, the sounds of parades were heard even on Sunday, when they drowned out the sermons. Said the *Picayune*, "Drums, fifes and music break in upon the solemnity of the day...nothing is so spiritually stirring as a parade." This particular commotion was caused by a militia company whose spontaneous cavort through the city was described as "preceded, followed and hemmed in on every side by a motley collection of all colors, sexes, and conditions." Another observer of the streets of New Orleans estimated that ten such processions occurred on any random Sunday. Lady Stuart Wortley's walks through New York in the same era were so frequently blocked by parading militiamen that she estimated that they numbered in the tens of thousands. Although her figures were inflated, she had identified some companies that probably escaped the official tally: they bore such colorful names as Washington Market Chowder Guard, Peanut Guard, and Nobody's Guard. The spontaneous marching of these whimsical bands combined with the well-organized and elite units such as the Seventh New York regiment, with its haughty air, expensive uniforms, and precise ranks, to make New York streets a parade ground of many ranks and colors. Parading was so basic to antebellum street culture that San Franciscans formed militia companies even before they had a local government. In February 1849 the Washington Guards found a makeshift parade ground in Yerba Buena, Alta California: "turned out thirty-four muskets and it's orderly appearance and drill especially marching to the inspiring music of Gramma's and was highly commended." Such militia units, along with a second species of civic association whose identity was fabricated in the public thoroughfares, the volunteer firemen, testify to the all-American style of street culture.[27]

Yet the urban parade had far more diverse tributaries than these. In New Orleans the custom of parading was invented on the streets from a blend of French, African, and Native American folkways. The most renowned musical heritage of parading was the contribution of African Americans, whose funeral processions had already entered local lore along with the ritualized dances conducted on the Levee and in Congo Square. Repeated if rather desultory attempts to outlaw these potentially incendiary uses of the streets by the slave population could not deracinate an already entrenched street culture. In 1819 Benjamin Labtrobe found 500 to 600 persons in Congo Square gathered around two drums, one string instrument, and dancers of both sexes who seemed to have grouped themselves into an early formation of the second line. The streets were also a place where Native Americans expressed their tribal culture and contributed to an embryonic American one. The New Orleans press regularly (if condescendingly) recounted the public appearance of Choctaw Indians on the city streets: "a gang of ragged Choctaw were pow wowing and drumming about the streets yesterday, entering stores and coffee-houses, drumming citizens out of their small change. These vagrants have some ceremony to celebrate two or three times a year and tax the whites to raise funds in order to keep it up." Tyrone Power observed the Choctaw applying face paint in the Place d'Armes preparatory to such a procession; to them the public square was both a dressing room and a stage for public ritual.[28]

Although maligned by the *Picayune* editor, this mode of entering the streets was not a totally alien practice for the literate middling sort, in New Orleans or elsewhere. The Choctaws' noisy movements through the streets were one species of what was widely known as a "Cowbellion," a spontaneous, promiscuous, and festive example of street play. The *Picayune* described this custom on February 8, 1837: "a lot of masquerades were parading though our streets yesterday and excited considerable speculation as to who they were, what were their motives and what upon earth would induce them to turn out in such grotesque and outlandish habiliments." The paraders were costumed as Indians, animals, and circus performers and were joined "by Negroes, fruit women and what not . . . shouting and bawling and apparently highly delighted with the fun or what is more probable anxious to fill their pockets with sugar plums, kisses, oranges, etc., which were lavishly bestowed on them." The timing indicated a carnival was underway. Before 1850 this urban festival still had a spontaneous quality about it. It relied on the mingled customs of French and Native Americans and won the passive approval of the Americans as represented by the *Picayune.*[29]

Such casual fun was also common in New York, where it was a fixture of New Year festivities as celebrated by boisterous bands called calithumpians. One "calithumpian cowbellion" of 1843 was peculiarly rowdy and defiant of the forces of public order. It ended up in the "police intelligence" section of the *Herald;* "With pans for bass drums, and tin horns for trumpets, marched into the Tombs and notwithstanding two of the Justices were within calling distance, took possession of the officers' large room and began to discourse such music was rarely heard by ear of mortals." The slapstick scene that followed left the judges on the floor and the calithumpians in the calaboose until they were genially released on good behavior. The same makeshift musical instruments and rowdy antics were employed in New Orleans and by the most respectable of men. While doing business in the Southern city in the 1830s Edward Durrell joined with a cast he enumerated in the thousands in a noisy serenade, scored for steamboat whistles and cow bells and intended to express disapproval of a marriage between an old man and a young woman. This classic charivari was yet another variant on the street theater found in other antebellum cities and drew on a potpourri of ethnic rituals—Native American, French, English, Knickerbocker (fig. 8).[30]

Militia marches, firemen parades, cowbellions, charivaris, African American dances, and Native American encampments—altogether they

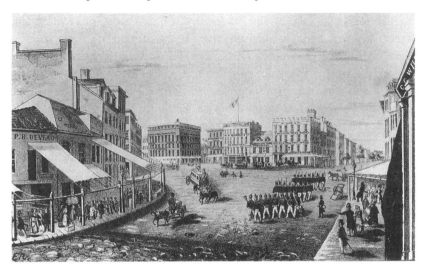

Figure 8. Chatham Square, ca. 1847. Publisher N. Currier. The Harry T. Peters Collection, 56.300.379. The Museum of the City of New York.

made the street a colorful and cacophonous theater. Other urban sensations stimulated the taste buds as well as eyes and ears. In the markets and squares of the Vieux Carrée the cries of street vendors mingled with smells of coffee and flowers. In one exemplary year in the 1820s the city of New Orleans issued twenty-three licenses to street vendors whose wares presented a mouth-watering bill of fare on the streets: strawberries, plums, and figs in summer; hot chocolate, wild duck, and other game in winter. Young women hawked "bouquets of Spanish jasmine, carnations and violets as boutonnieres for the old beaux" (an olfactory sensation no doubt especially appreciated, given the refuse decaying in the city streets). There, as in New York, the chant of "Hot corn!" was an especially savory urban association venerated in the memories of nineteenth-century folklorists: "Hot corn! Hot corn here's your lily white hot corn; hot corn; all hot; just come out of the boiling pot!" The fruits of the sea were hawked with this cry: "Here's clams! Here's clams! Here's clams to-day! They lately came from Rockaway. They're good to roast, they're good to fry, They're good to make a clam pot-pie."[31]

The sensual bounty of the streets—the foods and music and pageantry—were playful but hardly insignificant matters. The importance of street play was humorously registered in the press. For example, a New Orleans editor found this exuberant, besotted conversation between two immigrants newsworthy. A Scotsman and an Irishman about to be arrested for public drunkenness argued as follows: "Be carefu' Charley that you dinna' go ayont the bounds o'your duty: if I hen the constitution rightly, it says noething about the impropriety of folks crooning a song in the public streets." Another local songster named Miles West asserted his rights of patriotic and musical expression on the Levee, where he slept wrapped in the American flag. Hauled into court, he protested that his arrest meant that "The most sacred rights of a freeman were violated" and cried persecution again when he was silenced for singing the "Star-Spangled Banner." Even drunken and disheveled citizens seemed to know and claim the customary rights of the street.[32]

Stories such as these also reveal how city people more generally acquired a critical civic education in those same public spaces. The tales told above exploited certain stock urban characters, each identified by the manners, costumes, and accents that could be seen and heard in the streets, in order to draw the outlines of distinctive social groups—Irishmen, Scotsmen, Dutchmen. The sights and sounds of everyday public life projected silhouettes of social differences onto the city streets. Probably the most rudimentary and benign example of this codification of social differences was the construction of the individual street character who gave a human and reassuring shape to the urban caste of citizens and strangers. The antebellum cityscape was full of such personalities who were often remembered by name years later. The markets of New York were stocked full of memorable street characters. There was "Aunt Katy Barr" at her stall in the Union Market between 1818 and 1857 and known to work to midnight on Saturdays. Over at Washington Market resided two generations of the McCollech family purveyors of savory pickles, while the lovable Aunt Fanny operated a snug property over at Center Market. In the market of New Orleans a praline seller named Zabet dispensed advice along with her tasty morsels and was known for her refrain, "That's my philosophy." Although licenses for street vending were issued primarily to men, it was the women, often typologized by ethnicity and color as well as sex, who were overrepresented in the cast of street characters. According to New Orleans's elaborate scheme of classification, black women were consigned the sale of hot chocolate and coffee while "pretty quadroons" sold flowers. In San Francisco the street tossed up a different set of favorite street characters. The forty-niners vividly recalled the streetwalkers of gold-rush days. Some remembered Ay Toy, who operated a brothel for a respectable local clientele. Others spoke affectionately of "The Countess," reputedly of New Orleans origins, whose house on the north side of Washington Street on the Plaza was said to exude "as much politeness and grace as at the most select party in any Eastern City."[33]

These familiar presences lent a human patina to the city streets. They also represented and relied upon egregious if rather intricate typecasting. The street characters encountered so far were sculpted around sexual stereotypes. As female apparitions on the street, the vendors had a particularly unthreatening, sometimes titillating, but still rather variegated meaning. These urban extras, from prostitutes to market matrons, graded in color from white through shades of brown, and including bands of promenading ladies, provided a public school of social and sexual distinctions. Local street characters were drawn from an extensive catalog of social differences that was given quotidian definition in the street. Discerning observers of city life created more elaborate composite identities out of the social data collected in the public thoroughfares. This method of coding and decoding the city was described by the actor Tyrone Power in a transcript of a walk down Broadway in the 1830s: The street, he said, offered "most of the points needful to prove identity, from the monkey and hurdy-grudy of the Savoyard, the *blouse* of the carman and *Conducteur,* to the swagger of the citizen-soldier, and the mincing step and *tournure charmante* of the *belles.*" Another English visitor detected more signs of ethnic difference on the same street a decade later: "often to be seen a group of Irish or German immigrants, just as they come from the crowded packets, the latter looking very picturesque, with their national costumes." Travelers to New Orleans, from the Northern United States as well as Europe, quickly acquired the ability to read the wide spectrum of differences that paraded the streets: the linguistic clues to nationality, the status associated with skin color, the costumes that suggested class and region. The palate from which to paint identities and stereotypes was especially vivid in the Place d'Armes. "What a hubbub! What an assemblage of strange faces, of the representatives of distinct people! What a contrast of beauty and deformity, of vulgarity and grand-breeding! What a collection of costumes, from the habit of the German boor, just imported, to the toilet of the petit maître, à la Paris." The ability to discern social and regional differences was an especially important skill in the instant city of San Francisco, where newcomers scanned one another's costumes for signs of origin; Yankees were said to dress in

Figure 9. San Francisco view, 1851. Chromolithograph Samuel Francis Marryat, Courtesy of the Bancroft Library.

simple black suits while Southerners were clad in the latest Parisian fashions. An early lithograph portrayed the catalog of San Francisco's ethnic types with particular flair: It looked down on the cityscape through a chorus line of male figures in the costumes of China, Mexico, Chile, the wild West, and back East (fig. 9).[34]

Crudely but distinctly, the urban eye sorted street populations by region, nationality, class, racial, and gender differences. The kaleidoscopic stage of antebellum street life permitted a certain cavalier attitude toward social identities. At the very least, differences could still be reversed or toyed with in a carnivalesque fashion. When Edward Durrell went out on a charivari, for example, he always donned the same disguise: "(I) always dress a cock on such occasions." Calithumpians North and South more often crossed race and gender than species lines. Face paint could let a white man or boy frolic as an Indian or African, and the regulations at masked balls in New Orleans indicated that men and women, black and white, circled the same dance floors, momentarily oblivious of one another's skin color. Male citizens were not embarrassed by dressing as women. As the New Orleans *Picayune* put it in describing one festive procession in 1837, the principals "acted the part of women with particular skill." In New Orleans especially, but in other cities as well, the game of masquerading had not disappeared and was subject to only erratic regulation. If costume was a major mark of social difference on the antebellum streets, it could be taken on and off and played with, lending a certain whimsy to what under other circumstances would be oppressive stereotypes and ascriptions.[35]

This urban pageantry helped to maintain the differences among the people in a state of pliant tension that passed as a kind of ramshackle civility. No doubt the acceptance of difference was sustained by some conservative sentiments, the crude stereotyping and the expectation that each class and color and sex would stay in their places in the social hierarchy. But a leaven of democracy also seemed to have been introduced into the urban mix. Anecdotes of scattered encounters in all three cities support this interpretation. Lydia Maria Child saw something of this sort at work in the interchange between an Irish woman and a nativist male on Broadway in the 1840s. To the former's cry of "Get out of the way there, you old Paddy," she answered, "'And indade I won't get out of your way, I'll get right in your way,' said she, and suiting the action to the word, she placed her feet apart, set her elbows akimbo, and stood as firmly as a provoked donkey. She continued to stand and speak thus, for some time after the offending native American had passed. A polite word from a friend of mine soon lowered her elbow. 'Move' said she 'to be sure I will for a gentleman that speaks as pleasant as you do.'" All parties to this standoff—the nativist, the Irishwoman, Lydia Maria Child, and her gentleman companion—shared the street and a crude code of public etiquette. A similar kind of agreement to cohabit public space regardless of personal distaste is recorded in a complaint in the *Picayune* that the gentlemen at the Charles Hotel were regularly annoyed by "barroom loafers" who "if a man goes into a hotel or the arcade to take a lemonade or a wine julep he is forthwith crowded by half a dozen troublesome fellows who ask you how you are to make you treat them. Such fellows should be blacked and sold." As far as we know this sanction was never exacted, and the hotels as well as the streets of New Orleans remained open to gentlemen and loungers alike. At least a precarious détente reigned over the more contentious differences, and real inequities, that cohabited urban public space.[36]

Conversely, the antebellum streets were not quiet backwaters of unity and harmony. The real divisions among the people were openly displayed on the streets, and they provoked more than the cosmopolitan voyeurism of the flaneur. They sparked anger, conflict, and the assertion of raw power. Certainly, the Irish woman and the nativist in Lydia Maria Child's chronicle went into the streets of New York with a combative spirit and were prepared to do battle to claim their own turf. In New

Orleans the brutal power relations of slave society were exposed and sometimes challenged in the streets. It was the custom for "men and women of colour" to yield the banquette to those of European descent. One Felicité Durand defied this protocol when she encountered a white couple in 1813 and claimed the rights of the streets just as emphatically as those Irish immigrants in New York: "Je ne cedde jamais la pas à personne, le chemin est pour tout le monde." As long as this battle was a matter of street politics, it was a standoff, or even a victory of David over Goliath. The representatives of the master class prudently retreated with "Several abusive expressions made use of by the said woman of Colour" ringing in their ears. The white man, however, went directly to the police court, and the offending woman was imprisoned for twenty-four hours.[37] This incident was suggestive of the prickly peace that reigned on the antebellum streets. The combination of visible differences in common space and gross inequity in social relations dispels illusions of a simple civic unity.

But as late as the 1840s, American cities tended to tolerate the disorder that came from the public jostling of differences rather than resort to more coercive methods of enforcing civility. It was almost mid-century when American cities, first New York and later New Orleans, instituted proper police forces on the London model. The digests of local ordinances also reveal that city legislators were slow to enact laws that curtailed the uses of the streets. The fine line between tolerable inconvenience and disturbing the peace is illustrated by the New Orleans records in the 1840s. The city's mayors were reluctant to circumscribe even the rights of those called lewd or disorderly females. Mayor Montague of the First Municipality took the extreme measure of proposing a restriction on prostitutes' licenses to use the streets only when their business exploits interfered with the exercise of a most sacred right of respectable families, that of visiting their dead. He posed even this interdiction of street freedom very gingerly: "I ask you if it would be proper to order the numerous lewd women who established themselves in the vicinity of the cemetery a few years ago to move—I should regret it if a measure having so good a purpose should be disadvantageous to some personal interest, but this measure is justified by complaints made continuously by families who visit our cemeteries." Another move to limit the activities of streetwalkers, this one initiated by Mayor Grossman of the Second Municipality, was couched in similarly delicate terms: "I conscientiously believe that I am conforming with the wishes of the citizens and that I am asking in accordance with the public interest." Proposals such as these rarely were accepted in the 1840s. In New Orleans and elsewhere even "lewd women" were given considerable latitude in walking the streets. Edward Durrell, a Philadelphian whose urbane consciousness had been dramatically expanded by his sojourn in New Orleans, learned one possible lesson from this civic lenience: "a comparative view of the history of crimes proves mirth to be a better guardian of morals than the ascetic institutions of Protestantism."[38]

In the absence of repressive policies and police enforcement city people regulated their relations with one another in informal, customary ways, those ineluctable urban habits epitomized by the distinctive, predictable behavior of a New York pedestrian at a midtown cross walk. Along the Battery 150 years ago, New Yorkers had already taught one another some exacting rules of traffic—for example, to walk in two rows, one moving uptown, the other down, without jostling each other. Movement along major thoroughfares such as Broadway was also silently monitored to keep uptown and downtown pedestrian traffic in separate files. Other everyday urban customs were more conflictual and testy, like the habit of New York draymen (usually characterized as Irish) of cracking their whips at the passing ladies. Long ago the population of New York had come to accept the speedy, bantering, professional drivers as their natural predators on the public thoroughfare. Whatever the local etiquette, the social differences that lurked in the crowds along the Battery or characterized encounters between draymen and ladies, the people mingled together on the same streets and regulated their conduct by some tacit code of public conduct.[39]

Such familiarity and inescapable interaction on the streets educated urban dwellers to the myriad distinctions among them. Even painful encounters in public space were cherished by some cosmopolitan spirits such as Lydia Maria Child. Although she confessed that "I wish I could walk abroad without having misery forced upon my notice where I have no power to relieve it," Child would not have the human face of poverty swept off the streets of New York. In fact, because public space brought comfortable souls in touch with the misfortunes of their fellow beings, the streets could take on an almost sacred function. On seeing a group of gentlemen pay alms to a poor sidewalk musician Child observed, "The pavement on which they stood had been a church to them." While the streets were rarely honored as a sanctuary, neither were they imagined as the site of the American melting pot. One observer presented a more contemporary construction of urban demography in this depiction of a noisy Sunday in New Orleans: "no manners, no customs, no fixed habits:

all is unsettled, chaotic; the elements of society. as parti-colored as the rainbow but waiting the passage of years to blend them into one harmonious whole." This commentator, Edward Durrell, like so many others, painted New Orleans as a city of especially and often literally colorful differences; he described a marching band of militiamen, for example, as "preceded, followed and hemmed in on every side by a motley collection of all colors, sexes, and conditions."[40] A celebration of San Francisco's cosmopolitan population used the phrase "all races are represented." This term was extraordinarily capacious before 1850. It headed this list of social differences: Chinese, Maylays, Kanakas from the Sandwich Island, New Zealanders, Feegee sailors, Japanese, Hindoos, Russians, Turks, Spanish, Chilians, Peruvians, Mexicans, Americans from every state in the Union, Englishmen, Yankees, Germans, Italians, Frenchmen, and Jews.[41]

Long, rhythmic recitations of social categories such as this abound in antebellum chronicles of everyday life in the city. Another Yankee businessman rendered the street life of New Orleans in this litany: "such a scene. There were all kind of peoples there, Dutch, Spanish, French, English, American and white, black and all kinds of yellow—more shades than I ever before supposed could be in that color." If color and visual cues such as costume and manners offered one method of registering difference, sound was another, repeatedly rendered in the biblical reference to Babel. A walk on the Levee of New Orleans, for example, left this auditory impression of Babel on one European visitor: "A kind of music, accompanied with human, or rather inhuman voices resounded in almost every direction." Another visitor to New Orleans used the image of the street itself to linguistically accommodate the diversity of the city, calling the Levee "the main street of the world," "the world in miniature." Meanwhile a visitor to New York chose an image that was both mobile and extended to capture the city's fluid heterogeneity: It was, she wrote, a caravansary of the whole world. When it came to drawing the diverse populations of New York, San Francisco, and New Orleans together into some unified image, commentator after commentator resorted to some elastic trope like a babel of tongues, a caravan, or a street. Whatever the image or the literary cadence, the city was unified in space by people who came together in the momentary cohabitation of public places such as Portsmouth Plaza, Jackson Square, and Broadway.[42]

Nearly everyone was, of necessity, a street person in the antebellum city. They had very few places to socialize but public space. It was only in the 1840s that distinctly residential districts and expressly domestic architecture stood out in sharp relief on the cityscape, and then only in rare places such as Washington Square in New York and the garden district of New Orleans. Until then most buildings had mixed uses: They combined business, trade, and hand crafts with the work of family maintenance. Most households devoted very little interior space to intimate sociability.[43] Consequently, city people still conducted much of their social life in a public orbit, through the streets, in the squares, at places of public amusement. Their everyday comings and goings were guided by habit, conventions, and comparative ease. Only a few of even the most literate city people wrote of the anomie of urban life. Those who, like Edgar Allen Poe, mused about the lonely "Man of the Crowd" were apt to set their tales of alienation in vague or foreign locations.

Neither the consciousness of urban danger nor the distinction between public and private space were very well developed in antebellum America. One article in the *American Review* dated 1847 and entitled the "Physiognomy of Cities" documents the first halting attempts to map the social life distinctive to urban places. While the author, George Putnam, positioned himself in the classic stance of distrust toward the city, looking down on ant-sized beings in the streets below, he planted his easel in an unlikely and bucolic place—a hot air balloon launched from Niblos Gardens. From this buoyant vantage point the author sketched an urban view that was more picturesque than terrifying. The city of New York was arranged in a pleasingly variegated pattern: There was a discernible uptown and downtown, east side and west side, each with its own distinctive and appealing ambiance. "If any of us were suddenly transported to any street in either quarter, we fancy we should know by the general aspects of things (though we may not recognize the street) or else by some occult sympathy, the up-town and down-town feeling, what part of the city we were in." The author executed a smooth landing in a host of comfortable but stimulating urban sites: Union Square, the Battery, Grand, Canal, Broadway, and the Bowery. Everywhere he went he detected, respected, enjoyed, and inhaled a world of manageable differences. The euphoric sensation of such fine-tuned distinctions, all transmitted by some sensory osmosis while moving through public space, captures a particularly sanguine moment of urban history.

And it was not a passing moment. These hypnotic urban sensations, and many of the conditions that inspired them, still await the unwary on the streets of America's, and the world's, great cities. The pedestrian universe of densely populated cities can still offer an exhilarating education in social differences. What is distinctive about the antebellum period is the holistic spatial context in which these urban experiences transpired.

The distinctive spatial forms of the antebellum city—the centered, segmented, and connected features described in this chapter—made the life of public space a connecting tissue for hundreds of thousands of lives. The preeminence of the street in everyday comings and goings (and the converse underdevelopment of the spaces of private or exclusive sociability) invested everyday life with civic meaning. This spatial order was created largely through thousands of haphazard private decisions, not the result of conscious urban planning. It was rarely proceeded by a thorough and rational public debate. Yet once in place, the public city could be a staging ground for a more conscious and critical kind of civic practice.

Some of the civic possibilities of urban space were put on display in the summer of 1850 when the American people mourned the death of a sitting president. The city of New York and her citizens knew immediately how to respond in unison to the sudden death of Zachary Taylor. They simply took to the streets in a procession. The funeral procession wove for three hours up and down the island of Manhattan, from Chatham Street up the Bowery and Fourth Avenue to Union Park, and then down Broadway as it circled south from Park Row to its destination on the steps of City Hall. Most New Yorkers did not have to stray too far from their immediate neighborhoods to participate in the civic event: Their own familiar streets were anointed with public significance on this somber day. At the same time the route of the funeral procession inscribed some city places with particular importance to the civic identity. Those two key streets, the Bowery and Broadway, were the spine of the public procession and were etched in the minds and habits of the thousands of New Yorkers who walked them on a daily basis. The newspaper accounts also pointed to a series of familiar landmarks all along the route, from grand hotels to political clubrooms such as Tammany Hall. Most of all, antebellum New Yorkers gravitated toward an undisputed and singular center of civic action, City Hall. The procession moved single-mindedly to that distinguished piece of public architecture whose broad and stately stairway was adorned with flags for this occasion and festooned with memories of almost forty years of city history that had been enacted there. All these ordered and integrated public spaces set a sturdy and versatile stage for enacting civic ceremonies. The meanings of such civic rituals were as variegated as the streets on which they were written. These multiple cultural turns of the urban kaleidoscope will be described in the next chapter.[44]

CHAPTER 2

The Performance of
People in Association

When New Yorkers came together to mourn the death of President Zachary Taylor on July 23, 1850, they drew on more than a quarter-century of experience in designing civic ceremonies. As on many a public holiday, business was suspended for a day by decree of the Common Council, and much of the population took to the streets. Press reports of the event resemble a shooting script for an epic movie. They direct the reader's attention from a pan of the crowd to close-ups of individual mourners, cutting from marchers to spectators as they plot out each act in a multifaceted popular drama. The whole mise-en-scene was a study in difference as well as unity. The crowds that lined the route were composed of "All ages, sexes and conditions." Businessmen wore staid, black suits; washerwomen festooned sheets upon the nearby rooftops as their own humble gestures of public grief. Countless anonymous but acknowledged citizens labored to create a ritual of mourning as they draped hotels and shops with black banners — "the sable emblem of the nation's mourning." Other city workers hastily erected a special stand from which the funeral oration would be recited. Yet others labored for their own profit, hawking ice cream, lemonade, and portraits of the fallen hero to the crowd. The *Herald* gave an especially honorable mention to the selfless and stoic young ladies who waited hours in the hot sun for their cue to sing a funeral dirge.[1]

This was only the prelude to the major ceremonial event: a funeral procession that enrolled thousands and took three hours to wind its six-mile course through the city. The organization of this parade was described in the *Herald* as follows: "Forty thousand individuals, at least, took part in the procession. There were six thousand firemen alone, five thousand military, and an immense number of bourgeois who joined as such, besides all the organized institutions and public bodies of this great metropolis." The procession, in other words, ordered the people into prefabricated, readily mobilized affiliations. The first two groups noted by the *Herald,* the militia and the firemen, were easily recruited for this solemn rite; they had made a career out of taking to the streets, the one to parade their martial colors, the other to escort and display their engines. The reference to the bourgeoisie is more unusual but probably pertained to those groups of affluent citizens who often joined the rear of parades mounted in their fine carriages. But these isolated individual mourners were an exception to the general rule for constituting a procession. The line of march was composed, as the reporter for the *Herald* put it, of "All the organized institutions and public bodies of this great metropolis."[2]

This scheme for classifying the elements of public ceremonies was not just a journalistic convention. By 1850 most New Yorkers were experienced readers of that familiar prop of public ceremony, the "programme of the day." In fact thousands of ordinary citizens had written that program, not just in words but in their own actions and organizations. The program for July 23, 1850, scanned a long column of newsprint and listed almost 100 marching units grouped into some sixteen distinct divisions. By midcentury the grounds for forming a unit or establishing a division were various, eclectic, and sometimes a tad bizarre. Occupational groups, from the Medical Society to the city's boisterous cartmen, were followed by lodges whose conviviality was evoked by names such as the Universal Independent Order of Odd Fellows or the Independent Order of Faithful Fellows. Contingents of both Whigs and Democrats fell in line with a whole division of the cold water army, including the Sons of Temperance and a Roman Catholic Abstinence Society. The last division was, by some unspoken consensus, reserved for a mottled group of ethnic brotherhoods, benevolent societies whose names and patron saints suggested recent immigration from Europe, chiefly Ireland, Scotland, and Germany.

This particular procession was just one example of the many occasions when antebellum Americans claimed and exercised ceremonial citizenship. Interrupting their everyday, individual activities, they entered public time and space to represent themselves in a profusion of custom-made identities. Such diversified civic ceremonies were a distinctly urban accomplishment. The *Herald* scorned the small town of Saratoga, which greeted the president's cortege with a "sorry," "shabby" "failure" of organization in a community rife with "a miserable feeling of jealousy." In New York, by contrast, a committee of the Common Council had called into action thousands of citizens who promptly performed their coordinated roles in one civic drama. In the process public performances such as the funeral procession of 1850 brought a city's self-portrait into sharp focus. Antebellum cities came to present themselves not in the singular but the plural and as a veritable parade of social, cultural, and political differences. One method of classifying the public, now commonly called ethnicity, was a particularly powerful and inventive component of the polyglot civic exhibition of the antebellum period. Whatever the logic used to sort the population into the separate divisions of the parade, the citizens of New York presented their differences with one another in a relatively civil manner. There was only one hint of contention among the multifarious marchers, a rumored skirmish at the end of the march between self-proclaimed Native Americans and New Yorkers of Irish descent. As of 1850 the animosity that clearly existed on other planes, most especially in the bitter ethnic rivalries of electoral campaigns, could be contained at least for one solemn day.

The differences displayed in public space on public holidays were more motley and less inclusive than a simple pluralistic list of nationalities. The morphology of ceremony defied any simple pattern of differentiating the members of the public from one another. Neither was it specified just why some kinds of people (notably women and slaves) were denied a role in civic rites. On the surface of civic performances such as the funeral of Zachary Taylor, only one criterion of cultural citizenship was clearly visible. Public ceremonies assembled preconstituted and well-organized groups. Civic culture appeared on the street in 1850 as a procession of "public bodies," "institutions and associations," as those lodges whose members were both "independent" and yet "orders." Ceremonial citizenship, in other words, was the work of groups, not individuals; it displayed association as well as differences. The power of people in association will explain much of the vitality and the democracy of civic culture in the antebellum period. Yet as of 1850, entry into public civic culture was still restricted, and these limits must be addressed before this chapter ends. The story will begin, however, with a sketch of some rather patrician civic festivals of 1825.

Civic Performances: 1825

The year 1825 presents a particularly auspicious moment in which to begin a search for the ceremonial public. Both New York and New Orleans mounted fulsome civic celebrations in that year and set a standard of public performance that would prove very hard to follow. The New York festival was occasioned by the completion of the Erie Canal and inspired two days of exuberant celebration. In late November 1825 the citizens of New York performed what would be remembered as one of the most spectacular pageants of their history. This celebration is an example of that tradition of civic festivity that extended from the great celebration of the Federal Constitution in 1789 on to the extravaganza that feted the 100th birthday of the Statue of Liberty in 1986. The citywide party of 1825 took at least six weeks of earnest planning and culminated in a movable feast that traveled all along the waterway, from Lake Erie to New York harbor. The ceremonies in New Orleans in the same year, equally long in planning and extended in festivity, marked the visit of General Lafayette, the fitting impersonation of French culture in an American republic. These ceremonies were a high-water mark of civic and ceremonial creativity; they were rivaled but never bested, before or since, in the breadth of participation, range of celebrants, varieties of performances, and richness of unifying symbolism.

The standard of unity that marked these model ceremonies was built into their organization: Each was created by the official act of the mayor and city legislature and backed up by a generous expenditure of public funds. Almost two years later both cities would still be paying off the cost of their fete, which ran into five figures. The integral and integrating nature of these early republican ceremonies was manifest spatially. In each case several days of festivity radiated out through the city from a central public place. Place d'Armes in New Orleans and City Hall Park in New York were the central stages, and each permitted tens of thousands to share the same festive sights and sounds. The ceremonies spread to and from these focal points in a procession that meandered through "the principle streets" and along the waterways of these port cities. Lafayette was formally met and escorted down the Mississippi River, along the Levee, and into the Place d'Armes. The path of dignitaries at the Erie Canal celebration extended from Long Island Sound to the Battery, where it joined a larger procession that moved up Broadway to City Hall. In other words, both the central places and connecting arteries that integrated city space on an everyday basis were ceremonially anointed with civic importance.

The celebrants of these rites of 1825 also made ready use of a language of the public. The records of the Canal Celebration, which were published proudly and in remarkable detail, spoke assuredly of "our republic" and "the public good." The orator of the day had little trouble finding the terminology with which to unify the people: "So long as they continue to identify themselves with their fellow citizens," municipal institutions "will live in the grateful recollections of the Republic and of the People." The same political vocabulary was recited with a French accent in New Orleans. Lafayette fraternally addressed the people as "independent republicans, flourishing, covered with glory and forever united to the great American Confederation." The French hero assumed a shared history, a "common ancestry," with his audience in Place d'Armes and celebrated a political ideology that united "citizens of all classes" in a "happy republic."[3]

In 1825 the citizenry of New Orleans and New York was welded together not just by fine words but by far more substantial ritual ties, not the least of which were the practices of breaking bread and raising a glass together. Lafayette was feted with a parade of dinners and a seemingly endless litany of toasts. It was as if he was forced to play the centerpiece at the public dinner of every associated body in the city. In New York the food and drink so critical to communal bonding was laid out in a more inclusive and republican manner. On the evening of the Grand Erie Canal celebration, the *Evening Post* announced that no fewer than 3000 persons sat down at a common table in what they called the largest room in America, located in the Lafayette Theater.

The elected leaders of the Corporation of the City of New York put more than a rich repast before their fellow citizens. They commissioned local artists to embellish the ceremonies of 1825 with an unusual degree of drama and decoration. The New Orleans mayor held to a standard of courtly European pageantry on the occasion of Lafayette's visit. "We have no capital, no fortification, or navy, no arsenal for him to observe; no public establishment, no building deserving his attention." "It is the Theater where New Orleans can seem great." Although his first design, to reenact the battle of New Orleans and a whole military encampment on the original site, was never executed, his city did succeed in staging a splendid reception in Place d'Armes. The city commissioned two local artists, Messrs. Foliard and Pilié, to erect an Arc de Triomphe through which to receive General Lafayette. This hastily constructed monument was rendered in multicolored plaster, stood sixty-six feet high and fifty-

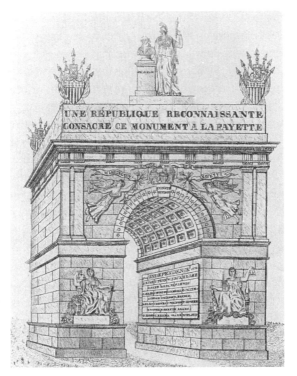

Figure 10. Lafayette's visit: engraving of Triumphal Arch. Courtesy The Historic New Orleans Collection, Museum/Research Center.

eight feet across, and was elaborately adorned—with Doric columns, classic statues of Justice and Liberty, two figures representing fame and an eagle, and the words (in both French and English), "A grateful republic has erected this monument to Lafayette" (fig. 10). Almost as much civic artistry and symbolism was employed to craft but one prop in the Erie Canal ceremony, the vial containing water from Lake Erie that was ritualistically poured into the Atlantic. This ceremony, enacted on Long Island Sound in the midst of a flotilla of ships, barges, and humble boats, was the opening act; the pageant next moved ashore at the Battery. There the notables who participated in what was called the water procession disembarked and linked up with a long parade through the streets to City Hall. These two pageants entailed extensive planning and demonstrated that city leaders were confident that they could represent the commonweal in some graphic and dramatic, unifying symbolism. In this determination, as in the constricted citizenship of a narrow franchise, these early American republican cities were in ways plaster replicas of predemocratic civic cultures of Europe that expended so much money and artistry on ornate, richly symbolic, civic pageantry.[4]

Like the earlier European models, moreover, these ceremonies included one important mobile element, a civic procession. In New Orleans this was a long entourage that joined Lafayette upriver and followed him down the Levee past the cheering populous and into the Place d'Armes. The program mentioned thirty-three discrete parts of this procession. Eleven of these were military, four were the general's personal party, and sixteen were public officials, from the governor's private secretary to foreign consuls to the committee of arrangements. Another division was given over to "the Ministers of the Gospel." At this point the procession looks much like a spectacle of European absolutism in which the state, clergy, and military passed regally before their subjects. In New Orleans in 1825 the procession of the powerful was expanded only slightly in a republican direction. A larger set of public actors was represented by the following units: members of the bar, presidents of the banks and other incorporated institutions, and finally "the Citizens." This last contingent, typical of the time in other cities as well, did not enroll the hoi polloi. It was an assembly point for propertied elites, those equipped with carriages, invested with property and votes, and entitled to join the procession independently of any associated profession or public office. In New Orleans as of 1825 "citizens" should not be confused, in other words, with the democratic notion of the people, who were still consigned largely to "the immense multitude" gathered on the Levee to watch, cheer, and make way for the procession of their betters.[5]

The civic procession in New York expanded significantly beyond this Southern parade. The contrast is testimony to regional differences in both political culture and economics. The New York procession of 1825 was a close facsimile of the republican spectacle that celebrated the ratification of the Constitution in 1789. Already in the eighteenth century New York put its artisan republic on display as part of an elongated representation of the citizenry. The line of march from the Battery to the Bowery in 1825 was called simply the "Procession of Citizens" and was given over almost entirely to a display of craftsmen lumped together as the "order of the Societies, Citizens, and Military." Of the fifty-nine units who lined up in no particular order, only fourteen represented something other than an occupational grouping, and these included such fixtures of civic life as the military, fire department, benevolent societies, and city officials. Among the occupational units the more elite groups (merchants, the bar, and medical society) lined up with skilled trades-men (sailmakers, chandlers, butchers, upholsterers) and those everyday lords of the streets, the cartmen. The civic procession had not swollen to embrace the whole of the people, but these bands of marching men, numbering in the thousands, were unprecedentedly inclusive and tellingly organized around the category of occupation. By common esti-mate that left some 100,000 New Yorkers to line the streets and fill the role of audience.[6]

Knit together of a variegated and rather homespun patchwork of oc-cupations, the civic culture of the Empire City defined the people in democratic, participatory, quite egalitarian terms. But ceremonial citi-zenship was far from universal in 1825, especially in a city such as New Orleans, where the majority of the population traced its ancestry to Africa and was cleaved by a brutal divide between the free and the en-slaved. Only the former class of African Americans was entitled to partic-ipate directly in public culture. On the second day of Lafayette's visit a contingent of "colored citizens" was included among those esteemed groups who held an audience with the general in his chambers in the Ca-bildo. Known in the record simply as "men of color," they were ad-dressed politely and honored as veterans of the Battle of New Orleans. The fact that Lafayette had "seen African blood shed with honor in our ranks for the cause of the United States" prohibited the exclusion of New Orleans's proud free persons of color from the ceremonial public.[7]

Select women, like some men of African American descent, found a niche in the civic pageants of 1825. Feminine images were in fact indis-pensable to the early ceremonial representations of the civic whole. These icons were, however, as much a study in class as in gender. Only "ladies" graced the official public ceremonies in both New York and New Orleans, and most of these were the consorts of members of the civic elite. A few privileged women of New Orleans were granted private audiences with Lafayette, who on his first day in the city met with the governor and the mayor and then a sequence of esteemed ladies—wives of congressmen, a sister of the governor, the daughter of Henry Clay, and one distinguished local writer. At the theater Lafayette was so over-come by the beauty there assembled that he reputedly "walked through the room, felicitating the mothers of so many beautiful daughters." At dinner he was seated in full view of "the six hundred ladies, who sat at the tables, forming the most brilliant and interesting spectacle ever wit-nessed in Louisiana." As customary, the last toast of the evening was raised to "The ladies of New Orleans—Never was a brighter reward; never did heroes better deserve it."[8]

In New York ladies were given an equally honorific and well-calculated role. One of the first acts in organizing the Erie Canal Celebration was to create the "select Committee of the Corporation, specially appointed to attend the ladies who were the invited guests of the Corporation." The ladies were provided with their own vessel (named the Lady Clinton, covered with flowers and equipped with bands of music) in which to travel to the water ceremonies. These select women, who included the wives of the governor, of canal booster De Witt Clinton, and of all the aldermen, were defined as "the matrons and daughters of the city." Whatever their vicarious credentials, they provided an aesthetic high point of the ceremony. "The barge was safely secured to the Commerce, and being superbly decorated, and crowded with ladies, elegantly attired, presented a most beautiful spectacle. The barge with the ladies proceeded to the ocean in the line of the fleet, and returned in its order. Such a sight was never before beheld." At this moment the lady was the only flesh-and-blood female to participate in the public's display of itself. And even then she was a curious representation of citizenship. She was always beautiful, or the mother of a great beauty, and inevitably attached to a man of elite social status. It was as if the republican leaders of 1825 held a hostage to a vanquished aristocracy in the personage of the lady. Aside from representatives of the refined species of lady, women were confined to the audience of early American ceremonies. They could be found only in perfunctory references, such as this from the *New York Post:* "The whole population of our city, male and female, lined the walks and filled the windows of the buildings of the streets through which the procession passed."[9]

Women might as well have been statues for all the self-determination and individuality they brought to the official report of civic ceremonies. In fact statues in female shapes, like the Justice and Liberty that had adorned the arch of triumph in Place d'Armes, contributed more substantial political meaning to the ceremonies than did living ladies. A retinue of classic allegories in female forms had been impersonating the republican philosophy of government for over a generation in western Europe as well as the United States. The invitation to the Canal celebration was embossed with such imagery. Feminine icons of every sort were carried through the streets of New York on the shoulders of rugged working men. The ropemakers carried a winsome, blind-folded justice. The chairmakers emblem featured a female figure standing behind

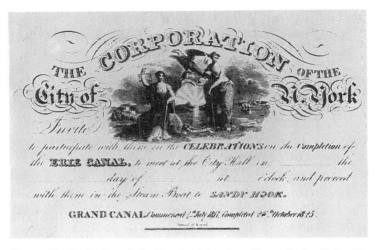

Figure 11. Invitation: Erie Canal celebration. From Cadwallader D. Colden, *Memoir of the Celebration of the Completion of the New York Canal*, 1825.

one of their products, clad in classic drapery and displaying no other iconography more revealing than her décolletage (fig. 11).[10]

Women, in sum, made only a phantom appearance at public ceremonies. They were not so much absent as present in disguise and marked for political exclusion. This representation of womanhood (to which female people bore only a remote relationship) lodged gender distinctions at an awkward place in the ceremonial architecture of the young republic. Amid all the republican language of the official ceremony, and even at a time when humble tradesmen as well as the bourgeoisie were taking up their places in the pageants of the republic, women's public personae were caught in some aristocratic time lapse. Women were not yet citizens in republican ceremony but remained bound, like ladies were to lords, to both their kinsmen and to a lifeless classic iconography. That female icons should embody liberty and justice at the same time that they were denied the active roles and rights of citizenship injects a jarring, ironic, and ominous element into republican ceremonies. The female allegory was a sign of the obstacles that lay in the way of a simple, steady, linear expansion of public ceremony to include all the people, "all the ages, sexes and conditions" found on the sidelines of the great processions of 1825. As of this date the ceremonial public had broadened its membership in a diverse and democratic direction, but it still paid homage to a certain hierarchical order and seemed quite unconcerned about the rights of ceremonial self-expression among both women and the majority of African Americans who were enslaved.[11]

Proliferation and Permutation: 1830s and 1840s

Over the next quarter-century urban ceremonies would retain some of these limitations even as they proliferated, expanded, diversified, and created a portrait of city people that was as brilliant, and as distorted, as a fun house mirror. By 1850 public ceremony had become a rather routine and predictable part of urban life. Residents of New York, San Francisco, and New Orleans found the calendar year punctuated by at least a half-dozen major holidays nicely spaced through the seasons and reflecting a variety of excuses for public jubilee. The winter holidays of Christmas and New Years allowed for the commemoration of both a Christian feast and a pagan saturnalia. Next on the calendar came national patriotic festivals, which were officially sanctioned by state and local governments in order to honor a national political heritage. The gray of winter was broken by the commemoration of Washington's birthday in late February, and the height of summer was marked by the July 4 celebration of Independence Day. Thanksgiving was also quickly granted public sanction in all three cities, despite its clearly New England Protestant lineage. Each city also set aside at least one day to commemorate anniversaries of more local interest, Evacuation Day in New York, Admission Day in San Francisco, and January 8, the Battle of New Orleans, in the city of the same name.

While all these holidays enjoyed some degree of official sanction— that is, public endorsement if not the actual appropriation of city funds—one holiday came without portfolio unto the public calendar of every city. This was St. Patrick's Day, the one major ceremony that originated in the second quarter of the nineteenth century and the handiwork of a newly prominent contingent of the people, Irish-Americans. In each city there was still an excess of ceremonial energy, which was released in quieter, less regular, more spontaneous ways. New Orleans had a surplus of ceremony, which added several holidays to the calendar, among them the Catholic commemorations of Mardi Gras and All Saints' Day with their French and Spanish origins. All Saints' Day, however, like the winter holidays up North, was customarily celebrated in quieter and more private ways, nearer the hearth and family. These were merely background noise to the major, most creative forms of ceremonial life during this period, the regular celebration of political anniversaries such as the Fourth of July and that new entry, St. Patrick's Day. The achievement of ceremonial citizenship remained a selective and a competitive process. Those units of society that joined the urban parade with special panache and consequence, first the political parties and second the ethnic brotherhoods, deserve special attention.

The origins of the patriotic holidays can be traced to specific political organizations, those "self-created societies" whose emergence in the new republic so alarmed George Washington. The Fourth of July began in New York as a parade from Tammany Hall. Soon the Federalist's Society of Cincinnati and a bit later the Whig opposition decided to join what they could not defeat and put their own mark on the public calendar by celebrating George Washington's birthday. By the 1830s New Orleans had its own variation on partisan holidays. The Whigs went all out for Washington's birthday, while the Jacksonians, for reasons of Old Hickory's local heroism and the inclemency of summer weather, moved their festival from July 4 to January 8. These occasions, which were first commemorated by partisan dinners, were translated into a truly public event by way of the military societies, which used patriotic anniversaries as a good excuse for taking the festivities to the streets.

By the 1830s city governments officially sponsored and financed these holidays. The process is illustrated by the nine articles of ceremonial etiquette endorsed by the Louisiana State Legislature and the City Council of New Orleans in 1833. They outlined a celebration of Washington's birthday that began with a Catholic liturgy (a Te Deum in the cathedral) followed by a multigun salute, an oration, a procession, and the illumination of the city square that evening. The concluding rite, as stipulated in article 7, linked the formal civic public with the famed informal sociability and capacious public space of New Orleans: All citizens were invited to view the illumination of the railing around the Place d'Armes and hear a band stationed in the middle of the square. In New York the city fathers also sanctioned the pleasures of the people. On July 4 City Hall was ringed with booths selling refreshments, including fermented beverages. For the time being the people could be festively represented by the jovial holiday observation that New Yorkers of "all ages and complexions were getting tipsy together."[12]

In the course of the 1840s, when patriotic celebrations would acquire a more sober demeanor, one other component of the ritual fare became especially pronounced. Both the first and last articles of the official program for the New Orleans celebration of Washington's birthday in 1833 revolved around a procession: What had been only one element of earlier civic pageants would become the centerpiece of latter-day celebrations. The first impulse of the organizers of George Washington's birthday was to invite public officials, clergy, foreign consuls, the "several corporate orders of association of the city, and citizens in general" to "attend in a procession which shall be formed at ten o'clock precisely." They also ordered that the official declaration of a public holiday be printed in the press along with the procession program, which would be "distributed to the citizens on the morning of the twenty-second." These rosters of the parade entries appeared in the press and on the streets of New York and New Orleans at least three times a year. They conferred an official imprimatur on some of the different identities that mingled daily on the public streets, and gave select urban difference the high definition of the parade.

Reading the pattern of differences inscribed on the programs of civic processions is no easy task, however, for the grammar, syntax, and vocabulary of ceremony changed rapidly in the 1830s and 1840s. The increase in the number of marching units, as seen by the sixteen divisions and more than 100 groups that joined Zachary Taylor's funeral procession, was the most obvious and linear change in cultural representation. Neither New Orleans nor San Francisco had the broad economic base on which to mount the full retinue of trades and professions that characterized a New York procession, but they experienced a robust growth in ceremonial citizenship in their own right. San Francisco was still too raw and rough-hewn a community to organize a proper Fourth of July procession in 1850. Yet the pioneers did manage an ad hoc march that included boatmen and draymen as well as two elite military companies and some volunteer firemen. Only a year later San Francisco officials managed to link a score of occupational and ethnic groups into a respectable looking parade. In New Orleans in 1837 the first fifteen units of the parade were set aside for the old elites, the likes of the medical society, the bar, and public officials. But toward the rear came both a society of printers and a mechanic society. By the 1840s the lines of entry in the New Orleans Fourth of July parade had grown to more than sixty. As New Orleans began to catch up with New York in admitting manual workers to its ceremonial public the latter city was also host to a newly assertive organization among the lower ranks of labor. On July 2, 1850, the press reported a meeting of the New York Industrial Congress that enrolled thousands of journeymen and apprentices in units consciously

Figure 12. View of the Plaza, July 4, 1851, San Francisco. Lettersheet. Courtesy of the Bancroft Library.

set apart from the master mechanics who marched at their helm twenty-five years before. Yet two days later these workers were not found in the Fourth of July parade, which had become a largely military procession in New York City. At midcentury, then, it appears that the process of admitting humbler economic ranks to the parade had, at least temporarily, reached an impasse. It did not as yet extend much beyond skilled workers (figs. 12–13).[13]

Still, the civic procession continued to grow, longer and longer, but according to a new principle of cultural incorporation. The new basis for forming parade contingents can be read from the programs of Fourth of July celebrations in New Orleans. In 1837 the line of march was joined by a group that represented neither old civic elites nor assertive tradesmen. It was simply the Hibernian Society. In a few years the Hibernians were joined by an association whose trademark was the Shamrock and another named simply after St. Patrick. By 1849 a whole division of the Independence Day Parade was devoted largely to ethnic groupings of the public: It included the Hibernians, St. Patrick, St. Andrew, Howard, German, and Temperance Societies. New Orleans produced a particularly clear record of the trend in other cities: As economic inclusion was

Figure 13. New York procession passing Brougham's Lyceum, July 4, 1851. From *Gleason Pictorial Drawing Room Companion*.

truncated in the 1840s, ethnicity and, to a lesser and related extent, temperance became the methods for pluralizing society and ceremony. This pattern was poorly disguised but not obliterated by the largely military celebration of the Fourth in New York where the two most notable marching units were the Seventh and the Sixty-ninth Regiments, associations of the Anglo-Saxon elite and of Irish-Americans, respectively. The same ethnic pattern could be found in the San Francisco militias: Yankees enrolled in the Washington Guard and the Irish marched under the banner of the Gaelic hero, Montgomery. Although the Irish regiments and the most prominent Irish societies tended to enroll the more affluent scions of the Emerald Isle, they nonetheless put a fresh ethnic face on the civic elite.

Yet other shapes of associations formed within the very fluid, mobile ranks of the parades of the 1840s. Ethnicity seemed to metamorphose into sobriety as scores of temperance associations joined the line of march under banners honoring St. Patrick or Father Mathew, the renowned Irish advocate of total abstinence. At times the whole Fourth of July celebration seemed given over to the cause of temperance. In 1841, when a prolonged economic depression still hovered over

Gotham, the *Herald* observed "temperance societies warring the rumshops" and seriously dampening the Independence Day festival. By 1844 temperance had installed itself in City Hall with the election of reform mayor James Harper, who banished the rumsellers from the park on July 4. Although temperance societies were a major contingent in the parades of the 1840s, they represented just one of many shifting foundations of public association. The following vignette, from July 5, 1849, illustrates the plasticity of public identities in the 1840s. A little after nine o'clock on the glorious Fourth, Father Mathew himself walked down City Hall steps amid a brilliant explosion of fireworks. Horace Greeley, editor of the *Tribune,* condescendingly tipped his hat to the sober representatives of the sons and daughters of St. Patrick who gathered around the Irish prelate: Greeley publicly acknowledged the first two persons who recited the temperance pledge to Father Mathew as: "Francis O'Connor and Mary Gan, both thoroughly Irish."[14]

This way of commemorating the nation's birthday, enacted by a humble Irish man and woman renowned for their temperate intentions, captures something of the chameleon quality of ceremonial citizenship in the 1840s. It shows, on the simplest level, that no one social group, not even native-born, Anglo-Saxon Protestants, could completely monopolize urban culture. It reveals, in addition, that categories of identity could easily merge and fade into one another, like the transmutation of religious and national affiliation into a primary allegiance to temperance. And, following from these first two points, it can be seen that the basic modus operandi of ceremony was to construct and reconstruct distinctions. All these ceremonial practices were capsulized in the ritual form of the parade. This ingenious civic institution allowed individuals to vote with their feet, electing to file into one slot or another on a mobile display of urban differences. Finally, looking just behind the scenes of the parade, one can discern the social methods behind the ceremonial madness. Francis O'Connor and Mary Gan were not anointed with civic significance just because they happened to trace their ancestry to Ireland, because they ardently pledged to practice the virtue of temperance, or because they won Horace Greeley's seal of approval. They made their ways into the parades through groups that organized for specific purposes at a particular time and place, probably one of those Father Mathew Temperance Societies. The meanings of public ceremony cannot be understood without reference to such organizations or associations.

The Infrastructure of Ceremony

New Yorkers seemed almost as proud of the organizational ability behind the Erie Canal celebration as of the great artificial waterway it commemorated. The City Council published a complete report of the ceremonies, recording for posterity the most minute details about the scores of committees that helped to create the jubilee. That record began with a set of resolutions attributed to "The Committee of the Corporation, and of the Committee of the Merchants and Citizens, appointed at the Coffee-House, held at the Recorder's Office, in the City Hall." This method of initiating a celebration, starting with a gathering of merchants, citizens, and officials at a coffee house, was but one element of an extremely intricate and effective infrastructure of public ceremony. The last resolution of the Coffee-House committee specified the most critical modus operandi of republican celebrations: "Resolved—That the Firemen, and all the other Societies in the City of New York, the Mechanics, Artists, Manufacturers, Tradesmen, Merchants, and citizens of all other professions be, and hereby are, respectfully invited to convene meetings of their representative bodies, and appoint on their behalf, respectively, a Committee of two persons, to meet the Committee on the part of the Corporation, and that the said Committee meet at the Session Room, in the City Hall, on Thursday, the sixth of October, at four o'clock, P.M." [15]

This rare documentation of the organizations that undergirded the rich ceremonial culture of antebellum cities exemplifies the organizational network that created civic ceremonies. Designated by a distinctive urban argot that included idioms such as "Societies in the City of New York," "citizens of all other professions," and "meetings of their representative bodies," this social process was largely in place before a ceremony was even imagined. The programs of the day that urbanites seemed to read so effortlessly off the streets were not just a reflexive perception of social "reality." Those images of the distinctive sectors of the people took form in, within, and around actual social organizations, not just through informal encounters on the public streets. These urban associations were not only necessary preconditions for civic festivals; they were also essential determinants of who would become visible, honorable, and powerful in public life.

Early in the nineteenth century, and with increasing velocity in the 1830s and 1840s, cities like New York, New Orleans, and San Francisco spawned legions of voluntary organizations, known generically as societies or sometimes, depending on their composition and function, labeled "associations," "lodges," "temples," or "institutions." The whole menagerie constituted a new and prolific species that crowded out the traditional social trilogy of church, state, and family and was crucial to transforming a people into a public. The fecundity of association can be read from the city directories of the period. Most of these publications, which were produced annually by enterprising local businessmen, offered their readers a more intricate and differentiated portrait of the city than a simple alphabetical list of names and addresses. The New York directory for 1825, for example, listed some ninety churches that were already vying for public attention with thirteen public amusements and three public buildings: City Hall, the Masonic Hall, and the Merchant Exchange. Another set of associations was found worthy of a category all its own: These "charitable and benevolent societies" numbered twenty-five in 1825, when they were joined by another twenty groups that were classified as "religious societies." The more august associations deemed worthy of special mention in the city directory—the Medical Society, the Historical Society, and the Academy of Fine Arts—were only the tip of an iceberg. Befitting the growing numbers of skilled workmen in New York, artisan organizations proliferated rapidly, if without acknowledgment in the city directory. Meanwhile, scores of fire companies and militia units enrolled thousands of all ranks and backgrounds.[16]

Cities to the south and west of New York joined enthusiastically in the propogation of associations and the consequent "pluralization" of antebellum "society." New Orleans, whose total population was a small fraction of New York's (and whose many Roman Catholics were supposedly immune to the Protestant disease of joining), boasted seventeen "societies" in 1832, including assemblies of more plebeian occupational groups such as the printers, whose association was named the Typographical Society. Two years later the New Orleans directory added the category of Masonic lodges, which numbered eighteen. By 1838 they were joined by twenty-nine units of the International Order of Odd Fellows. The forty-niners had no sooner landed in San Francisco than they set up a full collection of societies. The 1850 directory listed the basic institutions of the frontier town and clued historians to the battle of vice and virtue that was to characterize the city's history: the six churches were rivaled by an equal number of theaters, several of which were well-known houses of prostitution. By 1852 the directory added a listing that connoted Yankee respectability; the phrase "Benevolent and Social" was followed by the names of twenty-five "societies," outnumbering the nineteen churches on the list. The term *society* would be used in the plural through much of the nineteenth century, and the numbers would continue to grow. There were close to 200 societies listed in the San Francisco directory of 1871; an estimated 300 were found in New York in 1880 and 211 in New Orleans at the same date. But it was in the 1830s and 1840s that these associations experienced the most robust growth per capita and reshaped the whole organizational topography of the city.

Whenever a group succeeded in announcing itself with a line in the city directory, or with a building on a public street, it gave official notice of its cultural integrity. For example, when the Odd Fellows broke ground for their new building in New Orleans's Lafayette Square in 1837, they mounted a public procession and won this favorable notice in the press: "The music and banners and rich regalia all contributed to attract the attention of the looker on: but above all the faces of so many of our citizens well-known to all classes and the very general air of respectability and worth so conspicuous gave a guarantee for the efficiency and usefulness of this noble brotherhood." For the New Orleans Odd Fellows, the process of associating, especially when it acquired architectural embodiment, grafted a strong, selective, social identity onto the public mind.

Wherever they met, antebellum societies gave public notice of some specific characteristic that was common and consequential to those who assembled. The borders between these scores of associations can be plotted out so as to indicate the most visible social distinctions in the nineteenth-century city as it entered upon the industrial age. A superficial reading of these jagged borders created by the associated life of the city lends credence to most all the social categories to be found in the lexicon of social historians. They will be noted in only a cursory fashion here. First, a specific language of class was written on the city skyline by groups that met at places such as the merchant exchanges. Commercial and manufacturing elites met at these sites in New York and in New Orleans not only to make business deals and cement their class solidarity but also to act in the public interest, which they assumed to be their special province. "Public meetings" held at these sites not only organized civic ceremonies but often provided municipal services such as material relief for the poor. Urban elites, along with representatives of the learned professions, also gathered in rump meetings with names such as the literary club, medical society, historical society, or art institutes. In the early years of the century, and at least through the Jacksonian revolution of the 1830s, these patrician leaders assumed, like the principals in Habermas's bourgeois public sphere, that they were the natural custodians of the common good rather than the representatives of a single social group or "special interest." Long before midcentury, however, they were made well aware that many other humbler citizens had constituted themselves as "societies" and competed for public space and attention.[17]

The robust organization among working men and women in antebellum cities, especially New York, has been well documented. Out of the chrysalis of artisan associations grew a succession of class identifications—craft pride, hostility between masters and journeymen, workingmen's parties, and trade-union solidarity. Although only the most privileged and propertied of these associations of working men, notably the printers, were regularly listed in official directories of the public, their identities were duly acknowledged both in the press and, as we have seen, along the parade routes. Their organizational profusion was apparent to all by 1850 when a citywide industrial congress enrolled more than fifty different trades. But as of this date, worker consciousness was more a pastiche of craft associations than a phalanx of proletarian solidarity. Sean Wilentz counted more than eighty labor organizations in New York at midcentury, but more than three quarters of these were not unions but "societies" or "cooperatives" united around a specific craft or manual occupation. While most of these associations brought together the more skilled artisan groups, the growing class of common laborers, many of them recent immigrants, had also begun to catch the associational fever, forming collectivities of working men with such generic titles as the Laborer's Benevolent Association. The multiplication of organizations among artisans and laborers was one of the more robust examples of this general process of social differentiation through association, and it contributed mightily to the expansion in the ranks of ceremonial citizenship.[18]

Attention to the category of class should not, however, obscure other grounds of association. Religion remained a predominant and variegated rubric of American social organization. Not only were churches the most commonplace nodes of association in the United States, but religion, and most aggressively evangelical Protestantism, was a major catalyst of the volunteerism of the antebellum era. The prototype of the voluntary society was created by the Bible, tract, and Sunday school associations of the 1820s. In the 1840s it was another offshoot of evangelism, the temperance movement, that presented the heartiest new species of association. In San Francisco, for example, temperance accounted for three of twenty-five associations in 1852. But Protestants did not have a monopoly on association for purposes of either charity or moral reform.

In New Orleans one would find both a Roman Catholic Total Abstinence Society and a Catholic Boys Orphan Asylum. Perhaps it was a common allegiance to principles of petit bourgeois morality that brought Protestants and Catholics alike into the "society" of sobriety. Whatever its logic, if any, the creation of this panoply of organized societies was a frenetic civic project in antebellum cities: new societies arose, fragmented, bumped into one another, and defied an easy, rigid categorization of the differences among the people.

The Case of Ethnic Association

One mode of classifying ceremonial citizenship waxed particularly strong as the midpoint of the nineteenth century approached. At a time when elite professions had withdrawn from the line of march, and artisans' groups stopped replenishing the stock of ceremony, there was a growth in the number of parade contingents who identified themselves by a birthplace or ancestors in Europe. The principles of association mentioned so far were intercut with, and often eclipsed by, this matrix for classifying social difference. As Werner Sollors has pointed out with particular force, the conventional notion of ethnicity is largely the assertion of a common biological descent, usually tracing a lineage to some rather arbitrarily defined section of Europe. The partition of the antebellum city according to the national origins of immigrants from Europe provides a particularly interesting example of this anomalous process, for it drew on a combination of biological, social, national, communal, and religious characteristics. As such, the term *ethnicity* designates a particularly powerful, but in no way inevitable, point around which urbanites arranged themselves as a people. Be that as it may, groups that formed around a common point of debarkation for the United States, were the most aggressive and successful claimants for a space in public ceremony during the antebellum period.[19]

San Francisco was populated by so rich an ethnic mix that a demographer would be hard pressed to discern a majority. The 1852 directory listed seven ethnic brotherhoods among its twenty-five newly minted associations. These included organizations labeled French, Hebrew, and Hibernian, three German lodges, and one New England Society. The fact that the last group was organized like an ethnic association, rather than presumed simply to constitute part of the colorless WASP leadership of the community, speaks volumes about the culture of San Francisco early in the 1850s. The range of ethnic associations in New York

and New Orleans further refined the various possibilities of ethnic association and gave rise to a large number of societies of immigrants from
the Protestant sectors of the British Isles who met under the banner of
their various patrons, St. Andrew, St. David, St. George, and St.
Nicholas. Bound up with a national allegiance, a language, a religion,
and a whole set of rituals and traditions that separated recent immigrants from the host country, ethnicity fostered the creation of the most
intensely communitarian kind of urban association. Accordingly, ethnic
identities took shape in a distinctive social form, in small groups that
met locally, were united by mutual benefits and insurance plans, and
practiced a fervent sociability. By 1850 these more intimate circles of ethnicity had been organized on a grander scale. The Ancient Order of Hibernians gathered their lodge members into citywide groups numbering
in the thousands. If all the militia men who marched under the banner
of immigrant groups were tallied, they would, by one estimate, constitute 2000 of New York's 6000 citizen soldiers. The Sixty-ninth Regiment of New York, one of the city's oldest, largest, and proudest, was a
contingent of Irishmen.

As the largest single immigrant group in each city, the Irish presented
a particularly strong swatch of ethnic color on the cityscape. Immigrants
from the Emerald Isle had deep roots in New York, dating back to the
eighteenth century, when some of their number first began meeting to
celebrate St. Patrick's Day. By 1848 a whole spate of organizations met to
present the Irish colors on St. Patrick's Day, among them the Hibernians, the Shamrock Association, the Young Irelanders, and numerous
Irish benevolent associations, temperance societies, and labor unions.
Irish-American ethnicity became a visible public presence in New Orleans by the 1830s when the meetings of the august Hibernian Society
were recorded in the local press. In both cities Irish-Americans had their
own newspapers as well as leading editorial roles and deferential treatment in the press rooms of the major dailies. While the *Alta Californian*
noted on March 17, 1851, that "our Irish citizens and their descendants
have not as yet sufficiently organized themselves to make a very marked
demonstration," they had clearly brought the knack for forming associations with them from back East. Already a Shamrock Society was meeting at the Eagle Tavern.[20] In his study of San Francisco R. A. Burchell
has made a convincing argument that the Irish were the dominant and
peculiarly authoritative ethnicity of the instant city.[21]

The voluntary association of the Irish-Americans is a textbook case of
ethnic sociability. Irish-Americans gathered to practice the rituals of soli-

darity almost nightly in mutual benefit societies, fancy balls, Fenian brotherhoods, temperance and church groups. The *Irish American,* published in New York beginning in 1849 and speaking to a national audience, displayed the wide range of characteristics that could be orchestrated into an ethnic identity. Some of these seeds of solidarity were obvious offshoots of their native land. Nationalist politics, and its flip side, anti-British sentiment, were always a staple of Irish-American journalism. The traditions of the old sod, particularly references of a musical sort—to jigs and songs sometimes rendered in Gaelic—were also regular fare in the accounts of ethnic festivals that filled the Irish press. The meetings of Irish associations featured prolonged eating and drinking, scores of toasts after every meal, regular processions under flowery banners, through public halls, and past phalanxes of the daughters of Erin, all garnished with wreaths, banners, and yards of green ribbons. The earmark of all these congregations was the affectionate bonding of the members. One newly formed Irish brotherhood, called simply the St. Patrick's Club, stated this purpose very simply: "friendly association for purposes of social intercourse." There was a distinctly communal logic to ethnic association characteristically expressed in references to love, affection, and family feeling; "a bond of love and unity binds all our fellow countrymen on this side of the Atlantic." As of 1850 Irish associations like the lodges and Masonic temples that grouped Anglo-Saxon Protestants together seemed to exemplify that grand American tradition of joining, of coming together for the purpose of coming together.[22]

In the decades before the Civil War, however, the coming together of Irish immigrants was invested with other, more political meanings. Their association was first of all an act of cultural resistance, a counterforce to the experience of discrimination and virulent nativism. Between 1825 and 1850 the Irish were under siege from several flanks: nativist parties that sought to restrict their naturalization, Protestant educators who wished to set the curriculum of the public schools, and some evangelical reformers who did not disguise their anti-Catholicism. The Irish press, the archdiocese of New York, and the Irish man and woman in the street all rose in opposition to these assaults and gave positive definition to their ethnicity in the process.[23] On one level, then, the ethnic partitions of cities such as New York were constructed in the space between an Old World culture and New World discrimination.

As a by-product of this collision in urban space ethnic identity was of necessity an impure compound. The alloy of Irish and American attributes was visible in virtually every rite of ethnicity. At the Irish-American balls to which New Yorkers flocked by the thousands, the musical program read: "the merry jig and bustling reel interrupted the more modulated and disciplined moment of the cotillion and gallopade." The toasts at the conclusion of Irish dinners interspersed references to U.S. political institutions such as the presidency with insults to the British government and claimed George Washington as much as St. Patrick as a national hero. The Hibernians borrowed selectively from American political culture: they latched on to Evacuation Day, the anniversary of the British withdrawal from New York during the American Revolution, as a particularly congenial holiday and were especially fervent in their celebration of those clauses of the Bill of Rights that protected minorities. The Irish societies sang the "Star-Spangled Banner" with as much enthusiasm and more regularity than any Irish folk song, and they waved the red, white, and blue as well as the green. The march of an Irish voluntary regiment was described thus: "The green flag bending under protection of the stars and stripes and members moving to the measure of the beautiful music of the Star-spangled Banner, Patrick's Day, Hail Columbia, Garryowen, Yankee Doodle and the Bold Soldier Boy." Most often the lyrics of Irish songsters, like the news dispatches from the counties of Ireland that were found in the *Irish American,* were issued in English, not Gaelic. The Irish-American identity is an early and apt example of how, in Benedict Anderson's terms, language is but one of the very pliant elements that contribute to the construction of "imaginary communities." When it came to projecting an ethnic identity on the larger stage of city culture, it seemed necessary to prune off the more exotic branches of Gaelic, western, pagan, rural Ireland and resort to the fabrication of a more modern symbolism woven of green ribbons and banners of red, white, and blue.[24]

The pruning and grafting necessary to breed ethnic identity was also cut through with class differences. On the one hand, the cultivation of Irish-American identity resembled the cultural construction of an American middle class. The editor of the *Irish American* announced with the first issue that he intended to train "our people" to "thrift, knowledge, industry and enterprise...the prominent landmarks of American life." No less ardently than a petit bourgeois Yankee, the Irish editor praised the meetings and processions of his countrymen for their good order, punctuality, sobriety, and respectable appearance. On the other hand, all those extravagant balls and ladies in attendance point to the ways in which Irish-American identity was grafted onto the institutions and values of affluent citizens of more distant ties to prefamine Ireland. In fact the first formalized Irish associations in each city, the Sons of St. Patrick in New York and the Hibernians in San Francisco and New Orleans, were elite clubs set far apart from the poor émigrés of the 1840s. The class coloration of Irish ethnicity was in fact a full spectrum. The *Irish American* also defended the interests of Irish workers with special fervor. On St. Patrick's Day in 1850 the editor toasted "The bond of love and unity" with striking carpenters. On other occasions the *Irish American* called for public works to support the unemployed and championed the call of the Laborers Benevolent Union for a raise of twelve and one-half cents.[25]

The class gradation of Irish-American associations might be read simply as an ability to transcend economic differences for the good of the ethnic brotherhood. Or it might be seen as a case of false consciousness. The relationship of class and ethnicity was susceptible to different interpretations by contemporaries as much as by historians. While the *Irish American* cast class differences in an ethnic mold, the Laborers Benevolent Union of New York labeled ethnic solidarity as class unity. This group, like dock workers in New York, New Orleans, and other cities, was a kind of closet Irish brotherhood. The oldest, strongest union of skilled workers in New Orleans, the Screwmen's Benevolent Association, was composed overwhelmingly (but not overtly) of Irishmen and German immigrants. The cultural construction and social relations of these same groups were also intercut and overlaid with distinctions commonly called racial. The Screwmen's Benevolent Association was a product of the Irish takeover, accomplished by 1840, of jobs on the docks of New Orleans that once were claimed by free blacks. The unions of unskilled laborers and dock workers in New York could also be designated as ethnic or racial associations, composed disproportionately of those of Irish descent who often competed directly with African Americans for their jobs. Furthermore, this reading of Irish identity was not particularly off the mark of contemporary consciousness, for the Irish, like Anglo-Saxons for that matter, referred to themselves not as an ethnic group but as a "race." When the *Irish American* spoke of "the entire Irish race on this continent," it used a terminology that was more familiar in its time than any one of the series of flawed concepts in the dictionary of social science—from nationality, to subculture, to ethnicity, to identity and difference.[26]

To find some core Irish identity would also require disentangling the gender differences that adhered to every organization and representation of social difference. The *Irish American* spoke in a male voice and

adopted a courtly attitude toward women. Its editor, P. Lynch, acknowledged several critical ways in which the fair sex nurtured the ethnic
brotherhood. Ladies were the essential partners in the public balls that
accompanied the fraternal activities of militia companies and Fenians.
When it came to fund-raising, the press acknowledged that Irish servant
girls were the mainstay of many an Irish-American association as well as
of Irish families. At the same time the sons of Erin could show the other
side of their paternalism and scold Irish women for their failure to organize fairs and bazaars with as much energy as their Protestant competi-
tors: "Come together girls. Get a half-a-dozen beneficent matrons to assist you and try what you can do." Elsewhere in the public record we find
women enacting ethnic conflicts as well as soldering ethnic loyalty. An
Irish gal named Ann Kelly, for example, marked the explosive border between Americans of Irish and African descent with this street action:
"Kicked up a row generally and kicked a big nigger particularly." This
stationing of the virago at a place of violent racial mingling is all too
commonplace in the antebellum record of everyday city life. It is one
particularly ugly manifestation of the way gender differences riddle and
complicate social identities. The calls to manliness and cryptic messages
to women in the Irish press combine with the image of the Irish virago
to suggest that gender distinctions were a critical element in the volatile
compound of ethnicity.

The classification Irishman, which lisped so easily off the tongues of
antebellum Americans, was a complex and fragile construction. The
house of cards could and did collapse at the least provocation and at the
most untimely moment. St. Patrick's Day could be commemorated with
a donnybrook as well as a dinner party. The convention of New York associations that routinely met to plan the annual celebration disbanded
most unceremoniously in 1850. Suspicions that some of the organizers
were extorting funds for their own venal purposes led to a rancorous
meeting featuring the threat of a military assault from one Irish regiment, the dismantling of the platform by another, and the terrified flight
of the ladies. Irish solidarity dissolved quickly into vilification of ethnic
associations as "synonymous with idleness, money grubbing, platform
loquacity, blarney, big talk and cowardice." Irish-American solidarity exploded into something more than an exhibition of Irish temper. This
episode revealed the volatility of all the compounds to be found in the
extended catalogue of social history.[27]

These "heterogeneous compounds" still held together in a relatively
civil and playful way before 1850. For all the vehemence and energy that

surrounded the organization of differences, rival groups maintained a kind of camaraderie. When the organized public met in its different contingents, the revelers often raised a glass to "our sister societies." Even the competition between the French and the "Americans" in New Orleans was glossed over in the press with cavalier greetings to "our friends down town." Most of all, a full spectrum of different, often competing, even antagonistic groups did manage to line up and parade together in celebration of some common holiday such as the Fourth of July. The 1830s and 1840s would witness the invention of some novel differences that we can now call ethnic. At the time these associations were but one fragment in a very mottled mosaic of public urban culture. Urban associations and civic culture formed around such a variety of identities and interests that no single pattern of difference, be it labeled ethnic, class, gender, or race, can be given priority.

Separation and Exclusion

The newly defined differences, especially the sundry ethnic fragments of the polyglot urban culture, could not but have an effect on the integrity of the larger fabric of civic ceremonies. Even before midcentury it was clear that some of the assertive new contingents in civic culture were becoming restless along the line of march on July 4. Some of them coveted and claimed a holiday all their own. Ethnic differences in particular began to reshape the ritual calendar. Seeds of Irish-American identification that lay rather dormant in New York and New Orleans since the eighteenth century came out of hibernation on St. Patrick's Day in the 1840s when the more elite émigrés assembled to celebrate as gentlemen's clubs such as the Hibernians and the Sons of St. Patrick. Their characteristic rituals were of a subdued and private sort. The Sons of St. Patrick, for example, celebrated their patron's birthday in 1832 in New York's Bank Coffee House, whose "dining room was well-decorated with appropriate mottoes and emblems and a band from the third regiment." Their ceremonials continued over the years, altered only to reflect trends of American culture. In 1848, for example, the music was supplied by the "Father Mathew Band." By this date, when famine was depositing thousands of peasant Irish on New York docks, St. Patrick's Day had become a more popular and public festival. It was advertised and reported in the daily press, where it was labeled a "Roman Catholic Celebration." Indeed, the Catholic church was a major anchor for Irish-American identity. St. Patrick's Cathedral on Prince St. (not City Hall Park) was the destination of a parade on March 17, 1848, that snaked along the Bowery on its way to Mass. The Irish of New York carried the process of representing cultural differences to the extreme, mounting a separate parade, marching to a sacred spot of their own, and claiming their own date on the public calendar.

The Irish were not the first or the last ethnic group to covet a place on the civic calendar. It was not yet clear as of 1850 that St. Patrick's Day would be the grandfather of all ethnic festivals (bringing 150,000 marchers and 205 different groups onto Fifth Avenue a century and a half later). In the mid-nineteenth century one Irish tourist actually gave the title of ceremonial prominence to German immigrants. He described a German celebration of the anniversary of their victory over the French as intended to "show the whole world their strength as a great component part of American nationality" and found the Irish "beneath the Germans in this kind of thing." The measure of ethnic vitality was the size of the German procession, numbering 50,000 marchers, considerably less than the turnout the previous Paddy's Day.[28] Through the 1840s there was a ferocious competition for the prize of greatest "component part of American nationality." Candidates for that honor made themselves known by celebrating, usually with a convivial dinner, the anniversaries of St. Andrew, St. George, St. Nicholas, and even some Italian patron saints. During the first half of the nineteenth century immigration from other places in the British Isles—England, Wales, and Scotland—was as brisk as that from Ireland and Germany, and these groups were just as forthright about making their presence in the city of New York public knowledge. Figure 14 depicts a German-American festival in New Orleans and expresses the ethnic variety, geographic range, and general *Gemütlichkeit* of urban public life.

Immigrants from the British Isles were especially well represented in a parade organized in New York in 1842 to celebrate the completion of the Croton Aqueduct, a showcase of the urban improvement that carried water into the city from up the Hudson River. This citywide holiday was a replication of the Erie Canal celebration in many ways: in the special civic accomplishment it commemorated, in its pageantry (a water ceremony featuring the opening of a fountain in Bowling Green), and in its parade, which reputedly was four to seven miles long and packed full of the associated bodies of the city from elite professions to the humble cartmen. In 1842 some new contingents had joined the line of march, both temperance associations and ethnic brotherhoods, chiefly those representing the Protestant regions of Great Britain. Notably absent,

Figure 14. Volkfest, New Orleans, 1859. Courtesy The Historic New Orleans Collection, Museum/Research Center.

however, were contingents of Irish-Catholic-Americans. More direct evidence that a process of cultural exclusion as well as incorporation was at work here can be found in the names of some other contingents in the Croton Aqueduct parade, among them the United Americans, an explicitly anti-Irish and anti-Catholic society. The overt ethnic conflict that was played out in city politics will be considered in the next chapter. Suffice it to say at this point that there were not only differences but contestation at play in the public ceremonies of antebellum New York. The battle lines had not yet been drawn decisively along the streets of New York. Many groups vied for a place in the Fourth of July Parade; others scurried for a separate place on the public calendar; a few seemed intent on expelling others from the line of march. But these differences were still played out in public places and public time if not full public harmony.

A similar modus vivendi took a slightly different shape in New Orleans. The public calendar in the Crescent City had also become segmented by 1850 but in distinct and starkly segregated ways. When July Fourth celebrations died on the ceremonial vine in the heat of New Orleans summers, the affirmation of an American political identity was moved to two different and in many ways alternative dates, January 8 and February 22. The first holiday marked the anniversary of Jackson's

victory in the Battle of New Orleans and in addition to celebrating loyalty to the Democratic Party invoked a time when Creoles still held sway
over local culture and public ceremony. Through the 1840s January 8
featured oratory in French, a Te Deum in St. Louis Cathedral, and a parade of Catholic clergy in their religious vestments. It was, needless to
say, centered in Place d'Armes. Washington's birthday was a favorite holiday of the Whigs, in New Orleans as elsewhere, but it had a more emphatic ethnic meaning in the Crescent City. It was centered in the American sector, where its procession circled Lafayette Square and ended up
at Mr. Clapp's Presbyterian church. In general New Orleans's ceremony,
like her politics, was partitioned into the French and American quarters.
Even the most contagious citywide celebration, the holiday occasioned
by Zachary Taylor's visit to the city on return from his conquests in Mexico, acknowledged this spatial segregation of ethnic difference. The general was greeted with a salute from each of the three different city
squares.

By 1850 a certain spatial segmentation if not segregation was also apparent in New York celebrations. The fireworks displays that were becoming a central mode of celebrating the Fourth of July were now
mounted in multiple locations, in Bowling Green, Union, Madison,
Tompkins, and Harlem Squares, as well as City Hall Park. This spatial
pattern was but one of many strategies that city people had devised to
organize and express social differences among themselves. Be it the ingenious form of the parade, the division of the public calendar, or the segmentation of space, antebellum people seemed more intent on multiplying than melting differences.

The Limits of Difference

It would seem thus far that there was a strong correlation between the
social organization of the city and the representation of the people in
civic ceremonies. More precisely put, and more important, the freedoms
and opportunities of civil society that permitted citizens to form a
panoply of voluntary associations also served as vehicles for the democratization of urban culture. Through the power of association the humbler classes, more recent immigrant groups, and Catholics as well as
Protestants found an opening into the public ceremonies that defined
the city to its residents. This optimistic rendering of urban cultural history is true, critical, but not the whole story. The correspondence between organization and representation is neither that simple nor that

pluralistic. Not all organized components of the society found a place in the major public ceremonies; some groups that appeared in 1825 seem actually to have lost representation a quarter-century later.

At midcentury a curious discrepancy appeared between the organization of class differences and their representation in civic ceremonies. The occupational elites that had dominated the pageants of 1825 were mysteriously absent from the parades of the democratic era. This disappearance was hardly a sign that the upper classes had become disorganized or powerless, and it casts suspicion on the ability of civic processions to reflect social structure in all its dimensions. The fact that the ladies disappeared from the later ceremonies, while less suspicious and unexpected than the invisibility of men of power, reveals other irregularities in the ceremonial portrait of urban society. For the period between 1825 and 1850 had seen an explosion of societies founded and operated by women. Women's organizations, among the rich as well as the middle classes, accounted for a notable portion of those listed in every city directory, especially under the heading "charitable and benevolent institutions." Women had been mounting charities in New York since the eighteenth century and found new notoriety and power in the evangelical culture of the antebellum period. Thus, when hardly settled in San Francisco, the tiny minority of women could present a public presence that far outweighed their actual numbers. Societies of females accounted for one fourth of the associations listed in a local directory.[29] This organized phalanx of antebellum womanhood was not, however, a pure and natural crystallization of gender difference. To some the most critical identifying characteristic of a Ladies Benevolent Society was the religion, not the gender, of the members. Women's charitable groups represented the public face of Protestantism and were key backstage figures in the temperance associations and Protestant ethnic brotherhoods that swelled the ranks of paraders in the 1840s. Yet it is almost impossible to find a reference to any of these female associations in the records of public ceremony. The retirement of women from these civic ceremonies suggests that gender is a special order of social differences, one that would not be easily assimilated into the democratizing civic culture.

In fact, from a certain angle of vision, the democratization of the city appears to be a movement for cultural representation of white men. The processions of the 1830s and 1840s were reluctant to open ranks to even free men and women of color. The African American heroes of the War of 1812 were visible but never as prominent in New Orleans ceremonies after 1825. These muted and rare public appearances of free persons of color drastically underrepresented their organizational strength. In 1850 free men and women of color accounted for approximately one third of the nonwhite population of New Orleans. By virtue of this status, thousands of African Americans were empowered to organize their own contingents in the great voluntary army of societies. Free men of color fought beside Jackson and formed the first of the city's voluntary fire companies, their own churches, and countless benevolent societies in antebellum New Orleans. This is not to say that African descent did not mark these free men and women with social inequality as well as segregation in everyday life, be it in church, on sidewalks, and even in the fabled cemeteries of New Orleans. Similarly, the smaller communities of African Americans in New York were both well organized and supplied with their own rich ceremonial tradition. Yet their rites of solidarity were shunted to the side of public ceremony and virtually ignored in the mainstream press. In sum, although African origin was not a simple, prima facie reason to deny access to the civic avocation of forming associations, it did, like gender, exert a definite and singular constraint on the advance of democratic culture. These anomalies demonstrate that the changes in ceremony between 1825 and 1850 amounted to something less than a simple profusion of democracy and pluralism. Not every difference, no matter how visible in public space or how well organized, had an equal title to cultural representation.[30]

Any historian among the spectators at an antebellum procession would do well to heed the advice of Bertolt Brecht: "What we see is in the sunshine/Those in darkness can't be seen." The disorganized and least powerful citizens were virtually barred from the parade of civic differences. A sizable portion of New Orleans residents was simply excluded from cultural citizenship on grounds of abject social status. In 1820 the majority of the residents of New Orleans were slaves of African ancestry, and as late as 1850 the city's slave minority was a substantial 18,000. By virtue of the social death of enslavement thousands of African Americans were denied all title to a civic identity. Under French black codes and into the American era slaves were officially prohibited from gathering informally in public space, much less forming societies. Other minorities were worse than invisible; their images were manipulated and exploited by civic leaders. Native Americans were probably the most maligned personages to be found in American ceremony. Representations of noble savages turned up regularly in the iconography of civic pageants: on official seals and banners and in impersonations by white men in costume. This stage direction for the New York procession of 1825 is illustrative: "The corporation, preceded by the aborigines from Lake Erie, with their canoes, will fall in the rear of the City Procession, following it under the direction of the Grand Marshal to the City Hall where all will disperse." Demeaning representations of Native Americans adorned the embryonic doctrine of manifest destiny in San Francisco. General Montgomery reputedly rounded up a few Native Californians to witness and applaud his march into Portsmouth Plaza, and a few years later the city fathers ordered Chinese immigrants to take up servile stations in the audience to the celebration of California's admission to the Union. A perfunctory notice in the San Francisco press of 1851 illustrates the grotesque contortions of race and gender in the cultural practices of the American West. "Chinese women were imported and paraded through the streets in magnificent costume." People whose origins were not European were at best granted second-class citizenship in early American ceremonies and appeared, if at all, largely in subjugated postures.[31]

African Americans labored under multiple stigmata: their association with slavery, the gulf between European and African culture, as well as the often muted variations in skin color. New Orleanians of African descent conducted a separate and suspect cultural life, confined to Congo Square, the famed quadroon balls, or the slave quarters. Whether Christian or voodoo, the cultural performances of African Americans customarily brought out a crowd of white voyeurs. Frederika Bremer spoke less condescendingly than most when she described an African American worship as a "tornado." At the same time she also recognized that the African Americans had formed their own affective society in New Orleans when she noted, "Of the whole raging, exciting scene there remained merely a feeling of satisfaction and pleasure, as if they had been together at some joyful feast." Even such deprecating reports of African Americans' separate feast days, "black Saturnalia's" in "Grotesque Attire," appeared less frequently as midcentury approached.[32] However satisfying to the participants, however inventive this music and dance, such cultural performances were outside the bounds of official civic culture.[33]

A line of descent from Africa, Asia, and even America—anywhere but Europe—marked off a clear and pejorative distinction within the city population. When these differences were alloyed with the institution of chattel slavery, they signaled not only exclusion but the most ghoulish of public ceremonies. The public spaces of the city of New Orleans were the sites of bloody ceremonies of domination designed to give public support to the South's "peculiar institution." In 1845 a slave named Petronia

was sentenced to two hours in the pillory. She was chained to the fence
the master class had erected around the Place d'Armes with such civic
pride and draped with a placard reading (in French and English) "For
Kidnapping a white child." Petronia was acknowledged in the press for
bearing the lash and the jeers of the crowd "with the greatest indifference." Obviously, enslavement gave a distinct mark of difference to city
people of African descent.[34] That difference was more complicated, however, than a simple racial classification. The dramatic personae around the
pillory in 1845 were described thus: "Crowds of people, black and white,
were continually flocking around her, jeering and shouting." Scenes such
as this, which gathered the urban public in the dark carnival of exclusion,
subordination, and cruelty, tell us that civic ceremonies were far from
perfectly plural and fully democratic rituals.

The limits of legitimate difference expressed in the civic ceremonies
of antebellum cities posed an ominous question: Did the successful assault on formerly patrician public ceremonies (especially by the propertyless and foreign born) open the floodgates of a democratic public
culture to which everyone, even blacks and women, would eventually be
admitted? Or, in one integral movement, were some invited and others
excluded from ceremonial citizenship? Was this pivotal door to the public sphere opened a crack only to be slammed abruptly in the face of latecomers? As of 1850 it can only be said that both motions occurred at the
same historical moment. To optimists the newly opened doors might
offer some glimmer of full democratic ceremonial citizenship for even
patently subordinated people. This certainly was the case for African
Americans in New York City in 1827, when the end of slavery in the Empire State was celebrated with a march "through the principle streets,
under their respective banners, with music and directed by a marshal on
horseback." This ceremonial entrance into pubic life may have been
ridiculed by whites and was staged in segregated time (on the Fifth, not
the Fourth, of July), but, as Shane White has deftly argued, it staked a
claim in public culture for African Americans and would be remembered
as "a proud day...for those who felt themselves impelled along that
grand procession of liberty." The expanding ranks of the parade indicated
at least that citizens were not required to conform to some narrow standard of cultural sameness in order to practice ceremonial citizenship.[35]

This openness to difference, however unconscious or begrudging, becomes even more apparent when we consider the cultural strategies seldom deployed by New Yorkers, New Orleanians, or San Franciscans.
They felt little need to resort to one avenue that Claude Lefort finds an

all-too-common tendency of democracy—that is, a retreat from diversity and ambiguity into some transcendent, imaginary unity whose most extreme expression is a Nuremberg rally. The closest antebellum Americans came to this denial of specificity and difference was during the celebration of the conquest of Mexico. Throughout that war New Orleanians in particular were whipped up to a patriotic frenzy by public rallies and oratory that aimed its rhetoric at a loftier spot in the civic imagination than the mundane pavements of the parade. The patriotic fervor reached a paroxysm in December 1847, when General Zachary Taylor visited the city. The *Picayune*'s rhetoric strayed far from the prosaic ranks of the procession in its interpretation of this civic celebration. The editor turned to the crowd of spectators where "A thousand eyes grew brighter and wept tears of exultation and joy at the sight of a true hero." The crescendo lofted yet higher as "Tens of thousands were here congregated together, all breathing one spirit, all animated by a single desire to manifest to General Taylor their respect for his character and affectionate gratitude for his services." The editor of the *Picayune* seemed determined on this occasion to dissolve differences in mass psychology. He put it quite directly and presciently: "The streets were thronged with patient masses waiting for a sight of the old hero.... The people were one heavy mass of humanity." Perhaps even more revealing than this transcendent patriotism was this simple observation: "The military, as usual exceed the civic display in brilliancy; but we can recollect no procession in which so large a number of private citizens participated attached to no particular society or order."[36]

This militaristic imagining of civic homogeneity that issued from the Mexican War may have been an omen of ceremonies to come and is worthy of closer examination, but in 1847 and through the rest of the decade there was still little evidence to support the *Picayune*'s holiday forecast. New Orleans, like New York and San Francisco, continued to celebrate itself in organized units of difference. Moreover, not one of the three cities was particularly hospitable to a second, more benign method of transcending social and cultural differences: the invocation of some abstract and universal definition of humanity. The articulation of this basic tenet of the Enlightenment might be found in Fourth of July oratory but was surprisingly absent from most press reports of popular urban rites. A rare exposition of this doctrine came from English radicals such as Robert Dale Owen and Fanny Wright who sojourned in New York and formed the coterie of intellectuals who put out the newspaper *Free Inquiry*. Upon the opening of their own public hall in April 1829 these free thinkers extolled a "universal science of humanity": "In crossing its threshold, throw aside the distinctions of class, the names and feelings of set or party, to recognize in our selves, and each other the single character of human beings and fellow creatures, and thus to sit down as children of one family, in patience to inquire in humility to learn." The public response to Fanny Wright's New York lectures in the 1820s and 1830s featured catcalls, stink bombs, and sexual epithets and suggests that many people were neither willing to give up those "distinctions of class, set or party" nor particularly responsive to the symbolism of humanity as the patient, humble children in a family.

In fact the civic culture that countless Americans acted out on city streets honored the parade of differences more than either the transcendence of mass psychology or the abstraction of universal humanity. And they had crafted their own distinctive language in order to describe the makeup of their mottled and homespun public culture. An elderly New Yorker recalling a procession of 1825 described it as a "representation of every respectable class of society arranged in organized groups." In 1850 the democratic press used similar terminology in identifying the "various public bodies" who joined a civic procession. At that moment the public assembled in even less "respectable" contingents in San Francisco but under the same rubric of differences: "citizens in their various divisions." According to the *Alta Californian*, the sheer range and variety of differences were worthy of celebration: "Citizens and foreigners, Europeans and Asiatics, the civilized and the savage, the men of letters and the rude boor, with a splendid sprinkling of the young and fair of the fine sex lent their presence to celebrate the glorious day with becoming ardor."[37] In cultural performances that privileged the organized display of a multiplicity of differences, antebellum city people had created their own distinctive language of public life.

The origins of this language cannot be defined or duplicated. The multiple inflections of this tongue were supported by a whole sequence of societal structures: the limited size of antebellum urban populations, the centered and segmented space of the walking city, the social and economic integration of a commercial economy, the limited accumulation of power in this early preindustrial stage of capitalist development. This culture of differences was also rooted in a very specific political system that will be described in the next chapter. For whatever reason, one thing was clear: In the decades before 1850 the people of New York, New Orleans, and San Francisco not only devised a vocabulary of difference but put those words to music and paraded them through the streets.

CHAPTER 3

Public Meetings and the
"Principles of Pure Democracy"

In April 1834 a crowd gathered at Castle Garden in New York for "a day of general rejoicing." This festival, which brought an estimated 24,000 New Yorkers to a civic landmark on the tip of Manhattan Island, was the culmination of three days of boisterous activity on the city streets. The day before, two competing parades had clogged the downtown thoroughfares. The first formed when an open meeting of 20,000 adjourned into a procession and "rigged up a beautiful little frigate in complete order and named it the *Constitution*. As this moveable political symbol passed down Wall Street it met up with a second procession and engaged in a mock naval battle with a vessel called *Veto*. A special kind of public ritual was in process. These were partisan processions staged by Whigs and Jacksonians in the course of an electoral campaign. The meetings, processions, and drama continued until about 10 P.M. on the third day of the voting, when some 15,000 souls gathered on Wall Street to learn the final tally of votes."[1]

The vibrant publicness of civic culture described in the two previous chapters also characterized the formal political functions of the antebellum city. It can even be said that much of what is known as Jacksonian democracy was acted out on the same principles as the everyday sociability and holiday conviviality of the city. The meeting of October 1835 that launched the radical democratic politics of the Loco-Foco wing of the Jacksonian movement was recorded in the press as follows: "After the adoption of the resolutions a motion was carried that the meeting adjourn to the street in front of the Hall and form a procession with their antimonopoly Banners, Flags, etc., which was accordingly carried—and some thousands of the meeting bearing torches, candles, etc., marched up the Bowery cheering their Democratic citizens on the way." By the end of the 1840s the enthusiasm had spread across the land. Whigs and Jacksonians locked horns in New Orleans as early as 1837, and in the 1849 municipal election the Democrats marched "through some of the principle streets with a profusion of June torches, making a splendid display. The principle feature of the procession was an artificial chicken cock of gigantic dimensions, triumphantly born aloft, and which attracted universal attention." When San Franciscans elected their first mayor in 1850, their festivities included a band stationed on the balcony above the Plaza and a parade of carts pulled by teams of horses, adorned with flags and banners, and carrying voters to the polls. And this was just a primary election. The final polling featured a dashing equestrian display in the Plaza by one Captain Bryant, who carried off the office of sheriff. The Democrats also pitched a tent in the Plaza and named it "Tammany Hall." One of the first things that the forty-niners hastily unpacked on arrival in California were these rites of representation: ward meetings, parades, and partisan loyalties.[2]

Such public displays indicate that city people defined themselves not just according to the social groupings identified in the previous chapters but by the political status of citizen and by a range of partisan affiliations. Political campaigns were yet another example of the immense potential for associated activity in urban public space: They were staged, like civic ceremonies, in places such as Wall Street, the Plaza, "the principle streets of the city." But there was more at stake in these partisan gatherings than in those aspects of civic culture described in the two previous chapters. First of all, these partisan public events were a direct exercise of political citizenship and brought into play the doctrine of popular sovereignty, a title to rights, and a token of power. With his treasured (exclusively male) franchise, the citizen became an actual participant in self-government.[3] Second, when sovereign citizens came together for expressly political reasons, they did something more than display their cultural differences; they acknowledged and acted on their interdependency and agreed implicitly to work together to achieve some things, however circumscribed, that could not be trusted to chance, the market, or individual effort. Third, the political culture that is the subject of this chapter put urban heterogeneity to an extreme and decisive test. A partisan election placed different opinions in open competition: It was a declaration of civic war. A participant at the founding meeting of the Loco-Focos proudly described the event as "a struggle of gladiators on the platform around the chair; — the loudest vociferations are heard, and Tammany trembles with intestine war."[4]

The contentious urban politics of the Jacksonian era was also, as Tocqueville had divined, a major stimulant to the frenetic formation of voluntary associations during the antebellum period. "In all the countries where political associations are prohibited, civil associations are rare. It is hardly probable that this is the result of accident; but the inference should rather be, that there is a natural and perhaps a necessary connection between these two kinds of association."[5] Political events in New York, New Orleans, and San Francisco between 1825 and 1850 lend support to Tocqueville's inference. In fact the precise distinctions between politics, government, and more general urban associations are often difficult to determine. Antebellum citizenship was most always exercised in association with one's fellows: To the pioneers of antebellum democracy, the sacred civic act was not a private exercise of conscience or the individual practice of intellect but, in the words of the Loco-Focos, "speechifying and resolutions at political meetings." The political history of the antebellum city ran through a whole circuit of associated activities whose essential base of operation was a "public meeting." Innumerable assemblies in public space were the political equivalents of the fragments of the kaleidoscope or the divisions of a parade: They were the multiple cells of a functioning politics of difference. Hundreds of such meetings will be scrutinized in this chapter in an attempt to answer two essential questions: Who were the sovereign people? and What was done in their name? The changing ways the people of antebellum cities posed and answered these questions tell the story of democracy as a profusion of public meetings.

Public Meetings and Public Projects

A brief tour of the daily newspapers suggests the breadth and depth of meeting-place democracy. That itinerary can begin at about the time of the Loco-Foco meetings when a partisan city press had just begun to cultivate a market for local news. By 1835 the city pages in New York were little more than a series of calls to meetings. The new year was ushered in by a meeting at the Tammany wigwam, where "a punctual and general attendance is requested." The party faithful were called just a few days later, January 4, to meet in the third ward. Next, the Democrats, not surprisingly the party of favor at the *Evening Post*, would meet in units designated as working men and youth. Other partisans gathered to celebrate the Battle of New Orleans in honor of General Andrew Jackson. Rowdier and more eclectic meetings were interspersed with these staples of partisan organization. A riotous assembly of firemen, described as "a numerous body of native citizens and their antagonists only a handful of poor Irish," was followed one day later with a meeting at Firemen's Hall to explain the breach of the peace. In February the ward meeting became the vehicle of temperance societies, while mechanics were called to a meeting to protest the use of convict labor and the St. David's Society met to celebrate the common ancestry of their members. The city government was just one among many conveners of public meetings. The Common Council called a meeting that begot another meeting: it ended in an invitation from the mayor to "meet in front of the City Hall, to get aid for veterans of the Revolution." New York politics in the 1830s was an endless series of public meetings. In the next decade city papers began to combine all these notices into a regular column headed "Public Meetings."[6]

By the close of the decade the spirit of public assembly had animated New Orleans, and it continued to flourish a decade later. In truth the citizens of the Crescent City seemed to convene more often to party than for serious public business, and the calls to balls, dinners, and processions left less room on the calendar for ward meetings or self-improvement societies. Still, the festive public of the city was regularly called to meetings for such purposes as Irish relief, the Mexican War, reform of the inspection laws, to "express sentiments on current events in Italy," or in response to the seasonal epidemic. As early as 1837 and even in the South, Whigs as well as Democrats gave public notice of their conventions.[7] Whatever the cause or the segment of the community that congregated, the public meetings were carefully and formally constituted. Public notices included clauses that proclaimed them "In conformity with the universal wishes of the community." The etiquette of the public meeting had become rather complex at midcentury, as indicated by this notice in the *Picayune:* "It being pursuant to a call first made (by suggestion) through the *Louisiana Courier* of Wednesday evening, and seconded by a majority of the morning press of the city yesterday, a large, respectable and enthusiastic meeting convened at the St. Louis Exchange." This preamble was followed by a long list of resolutions, the names of scores of secretaries and vice-presidents, and a call to another assembly. As the 1840s came to a close, public meetings had become urban institutions, more routine and more finely orchestrated by the press.[8]

The population that migrated to San Francisco at midcentury used the custom of the public meeting as the basis for drawing up a social contract on the urban frontier. Calls to meet in Portsmouth Square were the only available method of governing in 1849, and at one time they had generated as many as three different sets of pretenders to the offices of town council. The pioneer variety of urban democracy was described in a public notice dated February 12, 1849. A crowd of men gathered in the Plaza and elected the secretary who read aloud the official call to the meeting and then heard a Mr. Hyde present a "plan of organization of the government." This roughly hewn constitution called for a legislative assembly, a justice of the peace, and another meeting in a nearby building called the "Public Institute." This second session of the founding public meetings would elect representatives to the territorial government forming in Sacramento. And then on February 22, another set of self-appointed agents of popular sovereignty gathered at the school house to send instructions to Sacramento, including the resolution to prohibit slavery in California. The legitimate government of the town of San Francisco remained a matter of dispute as late as June when the State militia was called up to moderate between the different claims to political authority. As far as the major and only organ of public opinion in the region, the *Alta Californian,* was concerned, the source of political legitimacy rested in a public assembly in the square called simply "The meeting." "The decision of the public . . . has sprung from a desire on the part of the prime movers to promote the public good."[9]

The busy civic schedules of all three cities seemed to mix indiscriminately rump sessions of the public mobilized around their particular interests (such as cabals of politicians and gatherings of philanthropists) with conventions of city officials to provide vital social services (such as public hearings on street improvement). It is within this checkered record, this mottled typography of private and public, that antebellum citizens established the boundaries of the common good, the range of responsibilities for the collectivity that might be assumed by the governmental body or overarching political authority. To put it in more legalistic language, the public meetings operated along the border of what was still known as the "police," the "administration and regulation of a city" that could entail quite broad actions to promote the general good.[10] During the antebellum period the provision of public needs was left neither to formal offices of government nor to the machinations of the free market but was met in the diffuse social space where public meetings were organized. Ad hoc, self-initiated public meetings were, for a time, the critical way stations between the government and the people. They provided the decentralized but preeminent domain of politics.

When San Franciscans wrote their charter in 1850, they codified the obligations of American city government or policing as they had evolved over the previous quarter-century. It was a short and simple laundry list: to tax, regulate roads, set the price of bread, police and regulate piers, streets, and fences, prevent riot and disorderly assemblies, and construct public buildings. This list, not unlike the table of contents found on the fronts of other cities' charters, can be sorted into the following categories: care of public land and protection of private property (the nitty gritty matters of pavements and potholes), provision of minimal public services (such as fire protection), and occasional projects of civic improvement (such as building a new city hall). Most of these essential, interlocking needs of the urban public were not met directly by city hall but by a wide social network that passed around and through the formal government.

In the antebellum years city people built their definition of the public from the ground up. The streets, the pavements, the sidewalks, and the gutters nearly monopolized the attention of magistrates and nearly filled up the municipal statute books and the minutes of the common council. The New Orleans street ordinances conveyed more responsibility to the public trust than was the case in most municipalities; this practice complied with the mercantilistic principles of land use inherited from the Spanish and French.[11] The digest of ordinances of 1852 still stipulated that the construction and care of the streets would be financed by a "Tax imposed on all the landed property within the limits of the city." The courts interpreted this law of 1832 in a spirit of public interdependency, designating "cases in which improvements are of so general a nature as to require payment of the expense by the whole community not only by the owners of property in the immediate vicinity who are especially benefited by the Improvement." The spaces that were so cherished by the citizens of New Orleans that they became a responsibility of the "whole community" included the port, the Levee, and the Place d'Armes. Private citizens, on the other hand, were assigned the entire responsibility for the care of the beloved banquettes. Even this private expense, however, was subject to public enforcement, which obliged all property owners to meet exacting standards for the care of sidewalks — right down to the size of the planks and precise placement of the gutters.

In general the street policies of New Orleans intermeshed public and private responsibility and placed greater emphasis on the former than did other American cities.[12]

The San Francisco charter of 1850 represents the other extreme: primary reliance on private initiative and enterprise. Article IV of the charter translated the relations of private and public into a mathematical formula that covered both the financing and the planning of the streets; the creation of a new street could be initiated by private citizens if three quarters of the owners of contiguous property agreed. Conversely, such a proposal could be countermanded by the expressed opposition of one third of the adjoining property holders. The formula for funding street repairs employed an equally baroque accounting technique. Once the neighbors had agreed on opening or improving a street, the city would foot one third of the cost and the property owners the remainder. Even this governmental responsibility had a loophole: It depended on the condition that "there shall be found in the city treasury funds not otherwise appropriated." New York, like San Francisco and many other American cities, minutely differentiated the governmental from the private side of the street improvements. They were all variations on the longstanding Anglo-Saxon practice (dating back as far as the seventeenth century in New York) called the special assessment or benefits assessment system. This practice made civic projects the financial responsibility of those judged most likely to benefit directly from them—that is, the contiguous property holders. What Robin Einhorn identified as the segmented system of municipal financing was the political institutionalization of the sectorial arrangement of antebellum social space.[13] The New York courts upheld such a procedure in 1831 and again in 1851 on the grounds that special assessments were preferable to a general tax that "burdens those who are not benefited and benefits those who are not burdened." The 1851 decision of the New York court of appeals used the revealing phrase "local public" to describe the community of property owners created by such special assessments.[14]

When it came down to matters of pavement and pocketbooks, the antebellum public operated as an intricate, specific, and local network of burdens and benefits. Neither magistrates nor citizens were willing to assume full responsibility for this mainstay of public life. They relied on something in between, a local public that, incidentally, required adjacent property owners to meet or otherwise come together to determine their common needs and assume mutual responsibilities.

This sectorial method of creating a public was only the beginning of the mundane civic project of laying out the streets. The actual digging and paving of the thoroughfares tested the relationship between city and citizens yet further. The municipal government of New Orleans relied on medieval methods of meeting its public trust. The report of the city engineer in 1831 could cite an energetic public works program: "repairing and paving city streets. repairing levees, transporting sick persons and burying dead animals." This labor was coerced from "79 Negroes in chains, 28 Negresses, 26 other condemned persons." These enslaved public servants were sometimes costumed in red.[15] New Yorkers, and later San Franciscans, employed a more modern method of public works: The tasks of opening, cleaning, and repairing the streets were delegated to private companies for whom public service became a lucrative private contract. Early in the century, contracts were awarded through a simple negotiation with the city council. By 1850 this civic function was delegated to a standing committee composed of aldermen, and a few years later it was entrusted to a street commissioner in New York and a surveyor in New Orleans. The former job was a coveted public office in San Francisco by the 1850s.

Work on the streets of America's fast-growing cities was also becoming a major source of employment for manual laborers. Some of these workers, like the New York stonecutters in 1835, also formed public meetings to protest the wages offered by city contractors. During the depression of 1837 yet another public meaning of street improvement was posed by a few forward-thinking men. In that year the *New York Evening Post* proposed that "The poorer classes will be left actively employed during the winter, providing us New Yorkers with the luxury of clean streets, and at such wages as will keep them comfortable. The contrary policy has neither lined the city treasury with dollars, nor contributed to the comfort of the greater number." Having presented this utilitarian formulation of public enterprise—midway between outdoor relief and the WPA—the editor came down to street level and directed the street commissioner to fix a particular pot hole that encumbered his walk to work.[16]

This is as good a symbol as any of the eclectic manner of providing vital services in the antebellum city. Several features of this system merit comment, as they reveal the distinctive contours of the work-a-day Jacksonian public. First, antebellum governments were not about to launch an elaborate system of public works. In fact the trend was away from such overall public responsibility and initiative, a tradition that endured only in New Orleans, where it was linked to the atavism of a slave labor force. Second, the street policies of all three cities usually converted civic responsibility into local publics and private enterprise; street openings were the initiative of property holders and street repairs were performed under private contract. Still, what distinguished this practice was how antebellum citizens wove together the public and the private. They wrought fine-meshed linkages—of citizens, neighbors, councilmen, workers—into a social continuum along which common needs were met on a largely voluntary basis.

This same diffusion of responsibilities characterized a second public function, that of maintaining public peace. Until 1845, when New York took the first reluctant and small steps toward establishing a professional police department, American cities relied on a combination of citizen vigilance and municipal contracts to patrol the streets. Before then New York hired a night watch to protect the lives and property of citizens, but they commanded only small salaries and little respect. The guardsmen, while described officially as "citizens of good moral character," were known privately for their lack of physical prowess and tendency to fall asleep on duty. The extreme repression required to maintain a slave system of labor prompted New Orleans to create a large *corps de garde* in 1817. To free white citizens, however, these officers presented a benign image. The three commissioners were required to live in their districts and place a sign on their front doors that gave their names and offices in "large and legible letters." The actions of the commissioners of police, constables, and nightwatch had no power independent of a circle of citizens and neighbors. Law officers—for instance, the commissioners of the New Orleans corps de garde—merely convened a self-policing public: "All constables, watchmen and citizens of the said city are hereby enjoined . . . to aid and assist the said police officers in the executing of their duties." In early San Francisco all members of the town council were declared conservators of the peace, without compensation. In New York in 1835 policing became just another subject for a public meeting. The newly reelected Democratic mayor Cornelius Lawrence organized the police in a familiar civic gesture. He placed notices such as the following in the press: "The residents of the tenth ward, are respectfully invited to attend a meeting for the purpose to adopt measures for forming a voluntary patrol." [17]

In sum the public function of policing operated all along that familiar political continuum between citizen, public meeting, and city hall. The

few, homely civil servants who were the special agents of this system—
the constables, watchmen, and members of the city guard—also assumed responsibility for much of the regulatory functions that remained
from the mercantile era. Like the commissioners of New Orleans, they
were assigned the jobs of investigating and enforcing all the city ordinances—rules for the operation of cafes, saloons, balls, markets, and
bakeries. In New York the beleaguered city inspector assumed the same
function in regard to what remained of market and price restrictions.
The provisions of the 1839 New Orleans statute on the assize of bread
stipulated that the mayor would set and announce the just price weekly
and then charged the mayor, assisted by police officers, watchmen, and
constables, with routinely examining, weighing, and pricing the bakers'
wares. Should fraud be discovered, the mayor or his agents could
confiscate the offending loaves and give them to the poor. What, if anything, sustained the assize of bread was not effective police surveillance
but a relationship of everyday social accountability that extended from
the mayor to the shopkeeper to the poor.[18]

The most illustrious example of this chain of municipal responsibility
was antebellum fire protection. Perhaps the archetypal public servant of
this period was neither an elected official nor a paid bureaucrat but the
volunteer fireman. New Orleans's first volunteer fire department was
founded in 1829, and by 1855 it boasted twenty-four engine companies,
four hook and ladder wagons, and seven fire houses. It also secured its
own date on the calendar of public celebrations, March 4, the annual
firemen's parade. This quintessential piece of Americana pulled up in
Lafayette Square in the 1840s and usurped the cultural and political
hegemony that the Creoles had once maintained in the Place d'Armes.
The New York volunteers were by this time a large and powerful civic
institution. They numbered approximately 1550 men in the 1830s and
were organized into contingents, whose unruly behavior provoked proposals to professionalize this public service. The Standing Committee of
the City Council that oversaw the volunteers managed to impose an appointed engineer above the rank-and-file firefighters in the 1840s, but it
did not get much further in its campaign to rationalize this public function. The firemen responded to one attempted reform in 1836 with mass
resignations and swift political action. They not only organized "one of
the largest processions ever seen in the city" in protest but elected one of
their own to the public office of register. The voluntary system of service
held power until after 1850 and steadfastly resisted the bureaucratization
of another civic function.[19]

Fire protection was only one public service performed in this voluntary fashion. Through most of the first half of the nineteenth century city charters and digests of ordinances also had no category equivalent to what we call the welfare bureau. This absence was attributable neither to the paucity of city residents in dire need of public assistance nor to citizens' utter indifference to the many poor among them. Rather, it was the product of an alternative system of caring for the needy. Until 1845, when New York created the office of Commissioner of the Poor, the city council maintained the indigent through institutions such as almshouses, which (in the fashion of the eighteenth century) provided for the "indoor" care of those who could not support themselves. Otherwise, the needs of the poor were met on an ad hoc basis. The Commissioner of the Poor, like New York's City Council before him, was charged with overseeing the flow of public moneys to benevolent institutions founded and operated by private philanthropists. For example, the New York House of Refuge, founded in 1824 in what its benefactors called an outpouring of "liberality and Public spirit," secured subsidies from both the state and the city. This civic practice can only be called a private project in the public interest. Such hybrids of public and private were germinated by women as well as men, most always of elite classes, and usually met with approval from the Common Council. Up until the 1830s appeals for city funding from groups such as the Female Assistant Society were usually granted with the rationale that they were "conducive to the good of the city."[20]

When, especially in times of epidemic or financial crisis, this method of coming to the aid of desperate citizens proved inadequate, further public relief was provided on an emergency basis. In 1829 ad hoc committees relieved some 3500 distressed New York families.[21] The depression years following the panic of 1837 provoked New York's mayor to call a series of public meetings in which funds for emergency relief were solicited ward by ward. Ad hoc public meetings in different districts of the city provided public assistance to as many as 100,000 New Yorkers in 1848. In New Orleans during one summer of a particularly virulent epidemic the city issued an urgent public summons: "a meeting will be held this evening in the screwmen's coffee house in the third municipality to hear the measures taken by the council at the meeting last evening for the relief of the sufferers by the epidemic, and then to take such measures as seem desirable. The cooperation of the municipality is earnestly requested." In this segmented Southern city the relief meetings were most often convened by private groups such as the elite Howard Association. During one epidemic summer they reported treating 371 cases of yellow fever during a period in which 427 persons had been interned as a consequence of the disease. The chronic epidemics of New Orleans brought the whole network of voluntary but public welfare into action. It was not just the Howard Association but also the poor afflicted residents of the third municipality and the ethnic contingents of the city that mobilized during crises. As if to re-create a somber analog to a civic parade, relief committees met in contingents representing the Irish, Hebrew, and German communities.[22]

The procedures for performing this particular urban function exposed some of the predemocratic aspects in this system of public service: It brought to the surface both the dire material needs of some city residents and the social hierarchy and economic inequities that crisscrossed the city. The members of the Howard Association, for example, raised funds for those in extreme need while dining and dancing in splendid opulence, but for charitable purposes. The system was gutted with paternalism as well. The benefactors of New York's House of Refuge, for example, presented themselves for public approval in 1832 not just as "agents of government" but as "fathers of the people" exercising "paternal care" as "guardians of Virtue."[23]

A similar sense of noblesse oblige propelled several other major civic projects. The most monumental examples of this third species of municipal policy, the initiation and completion of major public works, is found in public architecture and epitomized by New York's City Hall and the Cabildo and Gallier Hall in New Orleans. The city halls were major statements about public finances, revealing that in the early years of the nineteenth century cities had the will to make some major civic investments. The ledger of public projects in New York listed not only City Hall but also considerable expenses for public markets, institutions for the poor (such as Bellevue and Randall's Island), and the crowning achievement of antebellum public works projects, the Croton Aqueduct. By the time it was completed in 1842 this waterworks cost the city treasury over $20 million.

Such a massive investment, so atypical of the "private city," may seem a miracle, or an accident. In actuality it was the product of a fortuitous confluence of historical factors. At the outset the project was sponsored by the old elite, heroic stewards of the public welfare—people such as the Clintons, the Coldens, and the Hones. These gentlemen assumed civic responsibility for a service that had been provided previously by profit-taking merchants, Aaron Burr among them. The project was financed by the city well into the era of Jacksonian democracy, however, and was completed in 1842, after the Democrats and their laissez-faire philosophy had taken control of city government. In fact the Croton Aqueduct was on the agenda in the exuberant election in the spring of 1835. Amid all the hoopla the press casually noted that a bill to appropriate $12 million for the waterworks was soundly approved. Democrats and Whigs could agree that the Croton Aqueduct was necessary "for the general good, and the extension of this great and growing commercial emporium."[24]

The completion of public works, large and small, hinged on another political practice central to the era. The Croton Aqueduct—like the repair of streets or the opening of a market—began with a petition. Municipal records such as the Mayors' Papers in New Orleans or the Common Council Minutes of New York consist largely of a chorus of such petitions and responses. Groups of neighbors petitioned the cities of New York and New Orleans to open public squares. It was a group of partisan petitioners who engineered the erection of a monument for Washington in New York's Union Square and for Jackson in New Orleans's Place d'Armes (fig. 15). The latter project was endorsed by the city and funded by subscription at a minimum of $1 per citizen. The more monumental projects often bore the mark of civic elites and groups of philanthropists such as the men who petitioned for land on which to build such major institutions as the House of Refuge and the House of Industry: The latter appeared in the records simply (in meaning if not syntax) as an "Application of a committee appointed at a Meeting of Citizens to apply to the Municipal authorities for aid in the establishment of a House of Industry." The circuit from public meeting to petition to city hall was the pathway to many a civic project large and small. Perhaps the largest, most consequential, and most enduring creation was the American public school system, a product of the public political culture of the antebellum city.[25]

These public projects were undertaken at a time in urban history when the citizens were still grouped together in the manner of a public meeting. As neighbors or members of the same social circles or religious groups, active citizens bore direct and sustained relations with one another. Together they often shouldered some of the expense of these projects, from street improvement to erecting monuments. Assembled in their own social cells, these groups were neither remote from city hall nor distant from their fellow citizens. This relatively intimate public politics could still span social differences: The affluent assumed direct civic

Figure 15. Inauguration of the Jackson statue, New Orleans. From *Ballou's Pictorial Drawing Room Companion*, 1856. Courtesy of the Louisiana State Museum.

responsibility for the needy, fire protection was the work of the native, and the foreign-born councilmen planned city projects in response to petitions from every quarter of the city. Every one of the governmental functions noted above was at some time critically acted out in a public meeting. A call to provide relief in the winter, a meeting at the merchant exchange to consider building an aqueduct or a new city hall, a public meeting of New York's Private School Society—these were the grass-roots of antebellum public services.

Through much of this period this system also operated through a so-cial hierarchy. Patrician republicans broke the ground for the City Hall and the Croton Aqueduct in New York. At that time, in New York and in New Orleans, offices on the city council and even the right to vote re-mained the privilege of propertied white men. Even in the precocious democracy of New York, city government was a private corporation chartered by the state of New York until 1846, and the mayor was not popularly elected until 1834. Until then the meeting of the City Council resembled a private congress rather than a public convention of the people's representatives. Much public work and public expenditure of the early antebellum period was neither public nor democratic. It was often the handiwork of elites operating as exclusive associations. During these early years of the Republic everything from voting to street improvement was the prerogative of the minority of city residents who owned property. The political environment in which this public policy was conducted—a succession of meetings in public space—was, however, suffused with democratic potential. As we shall see, almost any one could convene a public meeting in the antebellum city, particularly after the political transformations of the 1830s and 1840s.

Democratizing the Public

Public meetings were part cause and part effect of a major campaign to dissolve the bonds of deference that wove through republican institutions and to build democratic procedures. As of 1820 democracy was a relatively limited component of municipal government. The municipal charter of New York, for example, entrusted the public good to a common council that was composed of and elected by propertied citizens. Elected council members in turn rarely consulted with the citizenry, before or after they entered office. The passage from deferential republicanism to "pure democracy" was gradual but ultimately decisive. In 1821 the city of New York removed most all property restrictions on the franchise (making a pointed exception for those of African descent). The same reform was accomplished in New Orleans when a statewide constitutional convention met in 1845. City charters and state constitutions alike were rewritten to bind legislators closer to the electorate. New York and New Orleans created bicameral legislatures—more than doubling the number of members—and thereby amplified and diversified the popular voice. The New York City charter of 1830 provided for a board of assistant aldermen adding sixty legislators to the twenty members of the Common Council. The creation of three municipalities in New Orleans in 1836 tripled the number of elected legislators and ensured the representation of the ethnic groups concentrated in different districts. Most of these representatives were elected on an annual basis, subject, that is, to frequent replacement by the voters. These regularly and popularly elected officials were in turn entrusted with the full burden of public authority. When the city required specialized work, the elected legislators commonly created "special committees" made up of aldermen and assistant aldermen rather than appointing outsiders. As late as 1850 only a handful of city functions, chiefly the basics of street repair and tax collection, were given over to special offices, and these were often elected posts.[26]

The purport of these reforms was to invest governmental legitimacy in representative procedures, whose advances in the 1830s and 1840s tell a familiar story: Elections became the critical act of a republican polity; the Jacksonians masterminded techniques of persuading voters; and electoral contests became a standoff between two principle party organizations. But neither the institution of representative government nor the creation of two parties was sufficient to create what the Loco-Focos would call pure democracy. That political ideal also reordered the relationships between voters and office holders, and among fellow citizens. Deference gave way to participation and converted harmony into opposition, which was the trademark of a public meeting.

Face-to-face congregations in public space were the most caustic solvents of the barrier between electors and office holders. As early as 1827, when the press had just begun addressing local issues, some public assemblages were defying the etiquette of deference. The *New York Evening Post* embraced direct democracy along with the party of Jackson in this account of a November rally: "The number who attended the late Jackson meeting in the park were so numerous and unprecedented.... Jackson is the favorite of the people." A Democratic meeting on March 28, 1834, illustrates the forward momentum of popular politics: It was called "The Great Meeting of the People—Triumphant Expression of Public Opinions." At about the same time the democratization of political institutions became a matter of debate in the Louisiana constitutional convention and moved candidates for office in New Orleans to announce themselves forthrightly as "Friendly to Popular Rights." Already in 1834 the *Bee* extolled the spirit that animated the Democratic public meetings of that era as "the power of the People when they declare their will."[27]

This was more than hollow rhetoric, and the partisan meetings of the antebellum period were more than a single volley of voter acclaim on the eve of elections. They were one part of an extended and systematic process of convening the electorate. The Jacksonians replaced the private and elite selection of candidates, the now tainted "king caucus," with a gauntlet of public meetings through which prospective representatives were required to pass. On March 12, 1835, the *Evening Post* hailed this process as "one of the most important objects that the people are ever called to act upon in their primary assemblies." The founding meeting of the Loco-Focos was mounted in defiance of the Tammany society, which was vilified as a "secret and select" association that chose its candidates by "private interview." To the Jacksonian editor the public nominating meetings of the Democrats, held that Wednesday evening in every ward of the city, were the lifeblood of the "great body of the democracy."[28]

It was through the circuit of the public meetings, furthermore, that the spirit of democracy was thrust into the annals of the American political tradition. Perhaps the most memorable public meeting of the era was that "Great Democratick Republican County Meeting" that took place in New York on October 30, 1835. Its claim to fame is the formulation of the major planks of the Democratic Party platform for well into the future— opposition to the national bank, tariffs, monopolies, and paper money. It is also justly famed for the flair of its democratic expression. This meeting made its historical mark after some party leaders, expecting a popular defeat, tried to terminate a nominating meeting by extinguishing the lights in the public hall. Then, as the story goes, "Total darkness, for a moment, prevailed; but in a twinkling of an eye hundreds of candles were pulled from the pockets of the people, which by the aid of Loco-Foco matches were immediately lighted and old Tammany, amid the cheers of the democracy blazed in her premature and resplendent glory."[29]

The "cheers of the Democracy" that went up from the public hall in 1835 thrust the name "Loco-Foco" into the American historical record and have rightfully captured the attention of historians. Other principles, proclaimed in a more reserved manner at that meeting, also merit comment. The single largest concern of the twenty-four resolutions passed that evening in October was the rights and procedures of the public meeting. Resolution 6 put it this way: "the people have the right and duty at all times . . . to assemble together to consult for the common good." References to an older construction of the public, as some larger good that stood above and apart from the mixed and mundane interests of the citizenry, were overshadowed by appeals to the "people" as they "assembled together." The members of a public meeting were obliged to "Give utterances to their sentiments, give instruction to their representatives, and to apply to the legislature for redress of wrong and grievances, by address, petitions and remonstrances." Subsequent resolutions went on to spell out the procedures of popular expression. free assembly, direct elections, reduced terms in office, and majority rule. Two weeks later the *Evening Post* put this vernacular political theory forthrightly: "to carry on to the fullest extent the principles of pure democracy."[30]

Local meetings of the democracy were quick to make their opinions known in the morning press. The fifth ward, for example, proclaimed opposition to the rechartering of the Bank of the United States: "As American freemen to declare our opinion and wishes without fear of control, of individual or corporation." The fourth ward was more garrulous, taking a stand "founded on the principle of Equal rights" and "with a view to the preservation of our rights as free and independent democratic republicans, and that the public may know the principles we profess and the motives by which we are activated. We feel it is our duty to give the public testimony." These democratic congresses at the ward level were the political analogs of the segmentation of antebellum urban space. The activist citizenry met in wards and neighborhoods, in those handy public spaces where the kaleidoscopic varieties of the city population could be assembled. In the spring of 1835 the Jacksonians convened simultaneously, thousands strong, in such places as the Richmond Hill Theater, Mr. Frederick's Bowery House, and the Ward Hotel and in spots organized for utterly partisan pursuits such as the seventh ward's "Democratic Hall." The public site of the democratic revolution, Military and Civic Hotel on Broome Street where the Loco-Focos first assembled, was remembered as nothing less than a "sacred" place.[31]

The "primary assemblies of the people" at the ward level formed one critical step in transmitting the popular voice to a higher level of authority and as such were subject to careful public scrutiny. In 1835 the system of vigilance was fully in place in New York. First, "The people met together in open and democratic assemblies to select delegates to nominating committees to appoint persons to represent them in a state convention with direct reference to their known views on the presidential question." At each stage representatives were reminded of their popular origins, that they were "chosen for their corresponding views, and thus when the body is assembled it truly represents the opinions of each of several counties in the state." Individual ward meetings always sent their nominations directly to the local press and reported any evidence of chicanery in the process. In the spring election of 1835, for example, those attending the fourth ward meeting notified the *Evening Post* that the published account of their deliberations as transmitted by Tammany Hall had omitted certain critical resolutions, most notably attacks on monopoly in general and a privileged local ferry company in particular. This offense provoked the editor to deliver a soliloquy on the sacred principles of popular democracy. "If the whole democratic theory of

Government is not a farce and a mockery, that resolution having been clearly and understandably adopted by the meeting" cannot be ignored by party officials. "When a public meeting is called, it is quite competent for that meeting to adopt the resolution which may have been prepared by those who called the meeting or to reject them or amend them or adopt part and reject part, or introduce new ones or take any word on the subject which may seem proper to a majority. The democratic theory is that the people's voice is the supreme law." Echoes of such ardent democratic sentiments could be heard in New Orleans a few years later. The Democratic *Bee* charged that one Whig meeting was "put forward by the aristocracy of the state" and that another was only an individual initiative and did not originate in "an understanding among citizens generally." The Whigs countercharged that the Democratic nominations were issued from a "private" meeting. Such charges and countercharges indicate that a truly public meeting was regarded as the temple of a self-consciously democratic citizenry.[32]

It took some time for the radical proposals of the Loco-Focos to be generally accepted. Even as late as the 1850s the word itself was a title of scorn to Whigs like Horace Greeley, who exclaimed simply, "We abhor Loco-Focoism."[33] When the opponents of Jackson put forward a slate of candidates for office in 1832, they couched their own action as deferential conduct in private space, "a large and respectable meeting of the friends of Col. Richard M. Johnson of Kentucky was held at the Masonic Hall to recommend him as a candidate for the Vice President of the United States." In 1835 even some Democrats still considered it demagogic to court popular opinion too fulsomely. One Jacksonian candidate for office presented himself to the voters in that year with considerable diffidence: "while inviting the appraisal of the humblest citizen," he owned that he "at the same time commands respect, the true characteristic of a republican magistrate." In New Orleans in 1840 a candidate for alderman was so zealous in avoiding demagoguery that he proudly reported, "This is the first time in thirteen years serving as your councilman that I have addressed you personally."[34]

Many antebellum politicians harbored a deep antipathy to the democracy of the public meeting. To James Brooks such political associations were hardly better than barnyard gatherings: "Men must be herded as cattle are herded. All classes, all parties, all occupations make use of societies for all purposes.... The societies of the day—not the thinking individual men who make them up—are the winds that often form the gale of public opinion." Others were still plotting to maintain

suffrage as a privilege of the propertied and to install presidential authority behind the fortress of a ten-year term. But such antidemocratic sentiments were rarely spoken in a loud public voice after 1840. In the words
of one historian the rivals of the Jacksonians maintained "An almost
deafening silence on the entire subject of political democracy." When the
political faction that opposed Andrew Jackson's attack on the Bank of
the United States found its name, "The Whig Party," during the New
York City municipal election of 1834, it entered the partisan fray on
terms set by radical democrats. By organizing publicly in order to object
to the policies of an administration sitting in Washington, they provided
the final solidification of a democracy of difference: They practiced and
legitimized open, institutionalized, popular opposition.[35]

Well before the presidential election of 1840, which heralded the second party system at the national electoral level, the Whigs had gone public in New York and New Orleans. In New Orleans in 1837 they claimed
"The Whig Party is actually the Democratic Party." And in New York
they adopted the official title "Democratic Whigs." Soon the opposition
employed the nominating procedures of the Loco-Focos, complete with
ward-level public meetings and primary elections. They had installed a
decisive, quite close, and cogent bipartisan political rivalry that would
endure for fifteen years. As a number of historians have demonstrated,
the Whigs and Jacksonians placed before the American people a clear set
of ideological and programmatic choices on everything from finance to
public investment, the judiciary, and the corporations. By the late 1840s
the Whigs had capitulated to popular procedure and created a foundation for democratic contestation in each city. The *New Orleans Picayune*
geared up for a "struggle" on election day; in San Francisco the *Alta Californian* endorsed a system of representation in which "everyone will
have the opportunity to express his wishes"; and the *New York Tribune*
published calls to meetings of "The Democratic Whig Party" in every
ward of the city.[36]

As the principles of democratic opposition spread from the Jacksonians to the Whigs and from the Northeast to the South and West, its
physical setting became more picturesque. In New Orleans in the 1840s
the haughty Whigs met at the St. Louis Hotel or the Exchange, while
the more populist Democrats assembled in the open air along Canal
Street. The first American-style election in San Francisco in the spring of
1850 revealed the range of spatial possibilities that had become available
for electioneering purposes at midcentury. The Whigs called the faithful
to deposit their ballots in a "Primary election" to take place "At the

house on Clay Street, three doors below Elleard's." The Democrats choose their candidate at a primary election held in Portsmouth Square from 7 A.M. to 7 P.M. and then ratified the nomination with a mass meeting in the same central location, where they called for yet another public meeting a few days later. This announcement—"The rights of the people will Not be Sold. Independent Mass meeting to rally the nomination of the Independent Washington Club"—includes a special invitation to "mechanics, workingmen, and all who are opposed to private clichés and hackneyed politicians." Democratic procedures of nominating representatives had become habitual by 1850: They were transmitted across the continent, available to third parties, and already associated with "hackneyed politicians."[37]

This aggressive public spirit was maintained through election day itself. The actual casting of votes (described so vividly by Jean Baker) reassembled the same people for a more prolonged, festive, and decisive public meeting. Ward meetings orchestrated this transition by appointing as many as 200 of their number to act as a "vigilance committee," pledged to stand watch over the poles for the duration of the balloting. At a time when municipalities restricted efforts to create a registry of voters as antidemocratic, the election was still a quite open convocation.[38] The ward assemblies, nominating conventions, and elections were transfer points in a relay of authority, a direct passing of the baton of power unto another representation of the people. Meeting-place democracy shared in the public character of the civic parade: It transpired in open urban space and was diffused through segments such as wards, centered in times and spaces such as election day, and invested with a festive and contentious sociability. In scarcely two decades the sedate and constricted republican form (fig. 16) had been stormed and supplanted by the boisterous politics of the public meeting (fig. 17).

The Political Definition of the People

The rhetoric of democracy seemed forthright: It proclaimed the rights of all the people to participate in the process of representation. But democracy as an actual political practice was something else again: It almost always came with strings attached and with specific provisos as to which people counted at any particular time and place. Of the cities of New York, New Orleans, and San Francisco between 1825 and 1850, at least this much can be said: The ranks of "the people who counted" had expanded significantly. In fact one of the major consequences of the cul-

Figure 16. Council chamber, New York City Hall, 1830–1831. From the Bourne Views of New York. Drawn by C. Burton. Engraved by H. Fossette. Courtesy of the New York Public Library.

ture of public meetings was to beg the question of who were, exactly, the people.

The Loco-Foco meeting answered this provocative question in the expansive language of "Equal Rights," ostensibly welcoming everyone into the democratic public. The first of the Loco-Foco's fabled resolu-

Figure 17. San Francisco election, 1850s. Lettersheet. Courtesy of the Bancroft Library.

tions proclaimed that "'all men are created equal'—that these United States are a nation—and that the national rights of every citizen are equal and indivisible." The third resolution elaborated, "That in a free state all distinctions but those of merit are odious and offensive and to be discouraged by a people jealous of their liberties." The principle was underscored again in resolution 4, which characterized all laws that would thwart "equal rights and privileges by the great body of the people [as] odious, unjust and unconstitutional." This notion of equal citizenship did not appear out of nowhere, however, or descend from high-minded universalistic principles of republicanism. It was championed by select social groups who had found in the public meeting a place to mobilize to claim their equal rights.

The notion of equal rights was the cutting edge (hardly the culmination) of a movement to expand access to democratic citizenship. In the early nineteenth century it was a political tool wielded most effectively by white males of the middling and lower social ranks. By the mid-1820s propertyless white men had secured the franchise, won the right to hold public office, and found a niche in the Democratic Republican Party. Soon this party of the "people" had booted the federalist "aristocracy" out of power across the nation. By the 1830s the ward-level meetings of Jacksonians styled their party the champions of the people against "the arts of the aristocracy" as practiced by the Whigs. The first mayor "ever elevated to that office by the suffrage of the people" was hailed in the *Evening Post* as a conqueror of "Besotted bank merchants" and champion of "the poor laborer who will not kneel at their footstool, who will not lay down his inestimable rights of equal political freedom, and consent to be their abject slave." By that raucous spring election of 1835 this rhetorical division of the people, between aristocrats and common men, had become a matter of electoral strategy. The Jacksonian press noted, for example, that although the fifteenth ward "is considered [in] an especial manner as the quarter of the aristocracy, yet there are enough democrats residing within it to secure the success of the democratic ticket if they will but exert themselves with spirit." In that year the Jacksonians lost the fifteenth ward, but by only a small margin.[39]

Under the principle of equal rights or, as one New York Democratic put it, "the perfect equality among mankind of legal, social, civic and political privilege," Jacksonians and Loco-Focos had not removed either class differences or issues of economic justice from politics. Rather, they made these differences legitimate matters of public consideration and magnets of political association. The Loco-Focos' founding manifesto excoriated "The odious distribution of wealth and power against merit and equal rights."[40] Loco-Foco William Leggett saw democracy as an endorsement of "combinations" of laborers against employers. Democratic platforms minced no words in attacking bankers and aristocrats. Even the Whigs were more direct in identifying their socioeconomic status. Around the mid-1830s they began to meet as "merchants" and at places such as the Exchange. In the process, however, the Whigs sacrificed the deferential prerogatives assumed in the past and in their former apparition as Federalists, or "natural aristocrats."[41] The wealthy classes who occupied two thirds of the council seats in New York City in 1826 had been reduced to three eighths by 1837 and one quarter by 1850. In New York, as in the cities to the west and south, this definition of the people was becoming clearer by the 1850s: The rights of citizenship, especially the franchise and office holding, would not be subject to a priori restrictions based on wealth or social status.[42]

Having dispensed with such invidious class distinctions, antebellum citizens faced a second political challenge: Should the foreign born be given full, equal, and swift membership in the political public? Despite the liberal naturalization laws (for Europeans) at the federal level, this test of citizenship had a long and divisive history in New York City, and the people whose political status was most often questioned had been born in Ireland of Roman Catholic parentage. As early as 1817 Irishmen marched on Tammany Hall demanding admission to the Democracy. The resistance to the foreign born at Tammany Hall was short-lived, but the Whig press felt free to publicly insult Irish voters as late as 1835, and there were a few organized attempts to restrict immigration and curtail the rights of immigrants in the next decade. The Irishman's title to full citizenship was fragile enough during the mayor's election of 1844 to give rise to rumors of an imminent nativist attack on St. Patrick's Cathedral. In New Orleans during the same period even the Democrats were still tentative about the political rights of the foreign-born Irish. In 1846 the mayor recommended that the period of ten years might be a prudent interval before immigrants were prepared to exercise the franchise. Such a term of residency would be "ample for the instruction of the most ordinary minds, for the divestment of all foreign prejudice and for the exhibition of that attachment to our government without which no man should be allowed an equal participation in our political privileges." M. Montegut, the hesitant voice for democracy, was defeated in the next election.[43]

The grassroots democrats of New York were grappling with the relationship between birthplace, religion, and citizenship in the midst of the tumultuous election of 1835. A report from a meeting in the fourteenth ward noted with "mingled regret and indignation" that American-born citizens were attempting to "draw a line of distinction between native and adopted citizens for purpose of kindling a hostile feeling and depriving the later of the rights secured to them by the constitution and the laws of their adopted country." The fourteenth-ward philosophers could take the high ground behind the Constitution and equal rights, proclaiming universal citizenship and at the same time courting Irish-American voters in particular. They resolved that "Although we are perfectly disgusted at any attempt to flatter and cajole the adopted citizens, still as friends of Equal Rights, we pledge we will oppose any unjust distinctions." The wisdom of this position would only become clearer in the years ahead when growing waves of immigration made the foreign born the largest single ethnic division in the urban electorate and a substantial voting bloc in every single ward of the city. By 1850 Whigs as well as Democrats had become cautious about disputing the rights of foreign-born citizens.[44]

Whatever their pragmatic or principled reasons, antebellum political parties had arrived at a quite sophisticated accommodation between democracy and differences and, in the case of the propertyless and foreign born, a relatively magnanimous one. From party leaders to the rank and file of the fourteenth ward they could juggle simultaneously the universal standard of equal rights and a particular attentiveness to specific groups that suffered from "unjust distinctions." This political pragmatics was worked out within a civic culture that made differences boldly apparent in the spaces and the ceremonies of the city. It might also be expected from a political system that had made democratic association an everyday habit. Once the broad electorate and sustained competition between two mass-based parties were jointly grafted onto the heterogeneous culture and social structure of American cities, it created a rather pluralistic portrait of the people. The outlines of that politics have been defined by the ethno-cultural school of political history, epitomized by Lee Benson's landmark study of New York in the 1840s. When the electorate was sorted out by the second party system, it appeared more like a vibrating pointillist landscape than a sharp-edged kaleidoscope, yet it made real social differences—in economic status, ethnicity, and religion—conscious, visible, and worthy of notice.[45]

This is not to say that the political hospitality to difference was without its clear limits as of 1850. Some barriers to being counted among the people were left intact, and others were even fortified during the age of Jackson. The political public, the whole representative circuit from the ballot box and its contiguous spaces—the parade, the nominating conventions, the rowdy congregation at the polling places—to public offices and legislative assemblies, was a pristinely white and decisively male universe. The political invisibility of both women and nonwhites coexisted with their often vivid representation in civic culture and their relatively easy access to public space. This contradiction suggests that participation in formal politics, the right to act as a citizen, was by no means an automatic translation from social and cultural publicness. This quandary requires attention.

The barrier to participation in the political public was particularly effective against women. The demand for women's suffrage raised at Seneca Falls in 1848 was seldom heard downstate, where women were seldom given even a symbolic role in partisan activities. The notice that a place for the ladies had been reserved among the Whigs gathered at New Orleans's St. Louis Hotel in 1849 was a novel appearance of women anywhere near the sites of party politics. Likewise, women seldom formed truly *public* meetings. The unusual assemblage given that title in the New York press in 1831 was a revealing exception. This meeting of the Female Moral Reform Society was a peculiar public performance. It focused on individual vices, preferred to work through private channels, and quickly receded from press attention into a more secluded network of female reform. The path of women through the temperance movement also followed this rather reclusive trajectory. When women appeared in the public jurisdiction, it was usually in the shadow of men or on behalf of children. In San Francisco, for example, respectable matrons stepped forward at an early date to support the cause of the public schools. They even organized a parade, albeit one in which their children did the marching, and acted out a surrogate ceremonial citizenship for their mothers and sisters. When the constitutional convention of the new state of California took up the question of suffrage in 1849, the exclusion of women from the franchise was just taken for granted. Women's suffrage was simply not at issue, despite the fact that the convention expanded women's rights to property beyond those found under the common law. California's constitutional convention wrote women out of politics, and the word *male* into the definition of citizenship, without consciousness, much less consideration. The thrust of democracy was not direct when it came to women; the twisted and divided path of gender repeatedly pulled them outside the orbit of public politics. The one case of bold integration of women into the politics of the public meeting sparked so much animosity and repugnance that it proves the rule of gender exclusion. When women appeared openly and actively at the antislavery conventions of the 1830s, they were greeted with charges of sexual amalgamation and violent protest in the streets.[46]

The status of nonwhites in the democratic public was equally anomalous and foreboding. But in this case, exclusion from citizenship was,
on occasion, posed as a public and political question. In New Orleans
the slave system placed the political status of all those of African American descent beyond the pale of citizenship. But once slavery was abolished in New York, democrats had to consider the meaning of citizenship for nonwhites. The constitution of 1821, the same document that
removed property qualification for whites, severely restricted African
American suffrage. It stipulated that only those New Yorkers of African
ancestry who possessed $250 of property were entitled to vote. By this
standard only 298 of almost 30,000 African Americans were granted the
right. Yet this small group of enfranchised citizens pushed the democratic possibilities to their maximum. In 1837 they organized to end the
property restrictions and succeeded (along with their white abolitionist
allies in the Liberty Party) in placing their demands before the electorate.
That referendum that demanded simply "Equal suffrage for Colored
Persons" went down to a crushing defeat, by a margin of 2.6 to 1.[47]

This mandate of the people made the hostilities to African Americans
harbored by so many antebellum Americans a public matter. The Democratic Party was particularly quick to exploit these prejudices, saying, for
example, that "Negroes are among but not of us" and vowing to "uphold our own race and kindred." The hostility broke out in vicious attacks on both African American neighborhoods and abolitionist conventions in New York in the 1830s. In the press this vernacular racism made
African American meetings the butt of sophomoric jokes. The *Evening
Post* in 1834 jested about the "curious piebald or checker-board appearance of one such congregation" being made up "promiscuously of white
persons and Negroes squeezed together in loving communion." But the
most ominous sign of the prospects for African Americans in the public
sphere was a street drama enacted by an antiabolitionist mob a year earlier. "The mob took possession of a room in the Chatham Street Chapel
and gave a Negro the name of an abolitionist and made him chair while
they passed absurd resolutions." This burlesque of the cherished procedures of public democracy was a vehement popular enactment of a major restrictive clause in the doctrine of meeting-place democracy.[48]

It would be a mistake, however, to read this exclusionary definition of
the people as a categorical racial division of the polity. "Men of color," as
they were denoted in the antebellum debates, were viewed through the
intricate and pragmatic lens of urban public democracy. During the 1846
election neither Whigs nor Democrats took a blanket and emphatic po-

sition against African American enfranchisement. They moderated or hedged their position in deference to local constituencies and electoral prospects. The issue was given over to the public in the form of a referendum because the members of the constitutional convention were divided and tentative about the whole matter and caught in the contradictions of their democratic ideology. The Jacksonians, for example, abhorred the property restriction in the 1821 suffrage rule but were equally affronted by the prospect of eliminating it and admitting all African American men to full citizenship.[49]

Attaching exclusionary clauses to the democratic definition of the people was a complex process requiring considerable casuistry. All its conundrums were placed before the forty-eight men who gathered in Monterey, California, in the fall of 1849 to draft a constitution for the new state. The majority of those assembled were from San Francisco, and most were experienced in politics as practiced back East. Fifteen of them, in fact, had recently migrated from New York. The document that emerged from this meeting allows a glimpse of the sophistry required to devise a logic for imposing restrictions on democracy. The prolonged discussion of suffrage was as notable for what it ignored as for what it mandated. Restrictions based on property were unthinkable in 1850; invidious references to place of birth were also anathema, given the far-flung origins of the forty-niners. Conversely, the disenfranchisement of women was taken for granted. Some antebellum facsimile of racial exclusiveness, on the other hand, was directly inscribed in the blueprint of government in California, but it took some doing. The word *white* found its way into the constitution of the Golden State following this motion: "to amend the original section, as amended, by inserting the word 'white' before 'males' and striking out the words 'Indians, Africans, and the descendants of Africans.'" For three days the convention struggled over these perplexing categories of the people. They came upon the word *white* as a definition of the voting populace only when they failed to find a single principle or coherent reason for judging such specific and varied groups as "Indians, Africans, and descendants of Africans" unqualified for citizenship.[50]

One delegate tried out the term *descendant* and the notion of blood as the standard for determining who was a voting citizen. He was immediately challenged by Mr. Sherwood: "What is meant by the descendant of an Indian, or the descendant of a Negro? Did the gentleman who offered the proposition mean to say that a man who has the least taint of Indian or Negro blood shall not vote? . . . The word descendant means a person who descends in regular line. He may be of mixed blood or full blood. There is nothing specific in the term 'descendants.'" To another delegate the category Indian, whether referring to full or mixed blood, was suspect: Mr. Wozencraft observed "many of the most distinguished officers of the Mexican Government are Indian by descent." Several other delegates attempted to associate the suspect classifications of the peoples of California with specific traits of character, distinguishing "wild" Indians from the civilized or noting with unusual crudeness that the Golden State "must exclude the low, vicious and depraved," meaning African Americans. None of these categorizations was left unchallenged: Delegates who hailed from New York and Louisiana could point to free men of color whose intelligence, wealth, and capacity to vote was indisputable.[51]

The recourse to the word *white* and the concept of color came in the eleventh hour of the convention and was perhaps the most peculiar classification of all. Sr. Noriega de la Guerra had risen to ask what is "the true significance of the word white." Noriega informed his fellow delegates that the gradations of skin color were very fine and a particularly poor indicator of lineage among Hispanic settlers of California. He hastily added, however, that if the word *white* was "intended to exclude the African race, then it was correct and satisfactory." An indirect rejoinder to this question came from Mr. Sherwood, who also found the category of color perplexing. "With respect to Africans, he believed that all after the fourth generation are considered white in most of the states," to which a Mr. More asked pointedly, "who is to determine, on the day of election, the various grades of color?"[52]

In the last analysis it was political calculation that resolved the semantic fine points of blood, descent, color, and stereotypes. Based on perceptions of their constituents' prejudices, and hemmed in by national sectional politics as well as by the Treaty of Guadalupe Hidalgo, which guaranteed the rights of Mexican residents of California, the delegates acted pragmatically: They tabled a proposal to bar free blacks from entering California, deleted references to Indians and Africans, and used the affirmative categories "white" and "male" to draw the limits of the voting public. The forty-niners had drawn a portentous line of exclusion across the landscape of democracy and scathed the topography of civic culture as well. Those who shared public space, participated in public ceremony, and even mounted their own public meetings could, if judged nonwhite, be turned away at the explicitly political border of the public sphere, the voting booth.

This was certainly a portent of a rough road ahead for what the Loco-Focos cherished as the "principles of pure democracy." But for the time being the intricacies of political differences in antebellum cities precluded the imposition of any simple and absolute "racial" designation of the qualifications for citizenship. The former citizens of Mexico, regardless of their skin color or line of descent, could vote in California, and so could African Americans in the state of New York, if they owned $250 in property. Furthermore, as the first half of the nineteenth century drew to a close, a more capacious invocation of public democracy also received a full airing. The voice was Edward Gilbert, a printer and native of Duchess County, New York, who had resided in San Francisco for two and one-half years. He spoke up at the constitutional convention in Monterey to say that to deny a man the vote "simply because he was black" was to "turn back the tide of freedom which had rolled across from continent to continent." To do so was a travesty to "the great public of the United States."[53]

As of 1849 the history of democratic political institutions seemed to be still advancing by precarious steps while dodging roadblocks such as race and gender. Perhaps Tocqueville's prediction of 1831 would prove right: "The further electoral rights are extended, the greater is the need of extending them: for after each concession the strength of democracy increases, and its demands increase with its strength." At the middle of the nineteenth century the progress of enfranchisement seemed to be moving onward and outward: It had leapt over distinctions of property, had beat back attempts to restrict the citizenship of the foreign born and Catholics, and had sidestepped the absolute racial standards of exclusion. Only the difference of gender seemed a categorical bar to full rights of citizenship. As of 1850 there was still a long way to go in establishing equality of citizenship, but the democratic project was set on a forward course.

What Is the Public Good?

The expansion of democratic participation does not, however, necessarily lead to a commensurate increase in public action in pursuit of the common good. In fact, by multiplying the different interests and causes for disagreement within representative bodies, the democracy of the heterogeneous city inevitably fractured civic unity and made it more difficult to act in the name of all the people. In addition, the democratic innovations of the 1830s might place in jeopardy those civic projects that resulted from the largesse of patrician republicans. Thus, to return to the question posed earlier in this chapter is still pertinent. How did the infusion of popular democracy into municipal politics affect the conduct of municipal policy?

If this question were raised in Portsmouth Plaza, the answer would be in the negative. The first issue of the *Alta California* had this to say about the pursuit of the public good in San Francisco, "perhaps the worst governed community in existence": "Her public funds have been expended in ill-directed and ill-planned schemes whose results are scarcely perceptible and of but little benefit. Her public domain has been parceled out and sold without the reservation of lots for public buildings, school-houses, hospitals or jails. She is without law, without proper executive offices and without the means of confining and punishing offenders." Certainly, the rush for gold in the California foothills put the common good to a severe test in San Francisco in 1849. But the erosion of the public domain was visible back East as well. If the ancient institution of the assize of bread is taken as the symbol of public control of private markets, free enterprise had been unleashed in New York long before. By the same period New York, like San Francisco, had suspended the creation and control of public markets and was selling off whatever remained of the public lands.[54]

Although the assize of bread and efforts to preserve municipal land would survive much longer in New Orleans, there too the notion of the public good had been undermined. In fact throughout the United States the same forces that drove the expansion of democratic participation seemed to erode the commitment to some overarching public good. The rapid growth of antebellum cities was itself testimony to the flourishing market economy, driven not by public morality but by private enterprise, which was rapidly converting the public domain into commercial opportunities for individual citizens. As Elizabeth Blackmar has demonstrated, even artisan republicans were grasping for commercial profit by subletting their domiciles to obtain cash income. This ethic of private enterprise was lodged at the very center of democratic political culture. The archetypal democratic public meeting, that of the New York Loco-Focos in 1835, alloyed Jacksonian democracy with laissez-faire economics. The twenty-four resolutions of the evening intermixed endorsements of participatory democracy with attacks on positive and improving governments—against tariffs, the Bank of the United States, government monopolies, and paper currency. Resolutions 9 and 10 spelled out the illusive meanings of private and public. They honored a government for the "whole community" as opposed to "the private interest or emolument of any one man, family, or class of men exclusively." To that end the Democrats disputed the grant of city monopolies and embraced open competition for city contracts. The representatives of the people tended to navigate a narrow estuary between private and public by either limiting government business or giving public services over to private contractors operating in the freedom of the market. By either selling public land or borrowing from bankers to meet the rising debts of the growing city, elected officials also made the public trust a source of private profit for the fortunate few who could purchase choice real estate or fund city loans at interest. When in 1844 New York City created a piece of municipal financing called the sinking fund, designed to retire the city debt by the sale of stock, they provided more handsome interest payments to financiers.[55]

It would seem that municipal democracies conform to the pattern that L. Ray Gunn has described so well at the state level. Gunn concluded that the democratizing tendencies in New York were both genuine and extensive, but they combined with administrative changes and market conditions that "drained political participation of much of its substantive meaning."[56] In fact the Jacksonian revolution would eventually deter even the Whigs from their program of positive government and "internal improvements," and by 1850 it had created a consensus around laissez-faire economics. As a number of historians have pointed out, an accounting of positive state provisions for the public good would fill a small ledger during the Jacksonian period. Richard McCormick, William Nelson, Jon Teaford, and Stephen Skowronek have argued that antebellum governments were quite inactive, especially in comparison to the high turnout of eligible voters and the amount of partisan excitement that orbited around both city hall and the presidency. These historians and political scientists provide various theories to explain this phenomenon at the national and state level, while others, notably Sam Bass Warner for Philadelphia, Hendrik Hartog for New York, Robin Einhorn for Chicago, and Gary Lawson Browne for Baltimore, have chronicled similar but more erratic developments at the local level. Warner saw laissez-faire eating away at Philadelphia's public good already in the eighteenth century; Hartog charted the paradox of how the city of New York moved from a private corporation to a city government whose state charter compromised its ability to act in the name of the public; Robin Einhorn shrewdly demonstrated how the special assessments of Chicago pruned down the public to segmented enclaves of property owners. Only Gary Browne charted a different direction of change. He saw Baltimore develop (between 1789 and 1861) from a town where "public services [were] performed by private individuals and groups" to a "public society" in which urban needs were meet by more formal, visible, and accountable civic institutions.[57]

The general consensus, that actions on behalf of the general public good declined in the antebellum period, is based largely on studies of governmental administration or party ideology at the local or the national level. They rarely take into account the full agenda of public goods as found in the circuit of antebellum public meetings. From the vantage point of urban democracy the measure of the common good was not just a matter of the municipal budget. Although one must concede that Jacksonian Democratic insurgents sped forward a fragmentation of the civic will and in their attack on monopoly encouraged a frenetic private competition for public contracts, the logic of meeting-place democracy actually multiplied as it segmented and democratized the provision of public goods. At the same time it would be myopic to regard the elite republicans who formerly dominated the "public sphere" as standing virtuously above private interests. The republican elite had always transferred public obligations on to individuals or companies by way of private contracts. All those projects undertaken in the name of the public good, even those jewels in the crown of the early republic, like the Croton Aqueduct and Municipal Hall of New Orleans, placed thousands of dollars of public funds in private hands. Furthermore, the benefits of those projects were distributed privately and unequally among the citizens. The gatherings in the elegant Governor's Reception Room at City Hall were likely to be patrician assemblies. The water brought into the city through the Croton Aqueduct at public expense did not flow freely through the city but was made available to private companies for purchase and resale at a profit. Not surprisingly, it streamed more readily into the homes of more affluent citizens.

The Loco-Focos and Jacksonians had not, in other words, misread the private interests that in fact undergirded the reputedly public good in the republican city. Their attacks on public projects like the Bank of the United States as hydra-headed tangles of private interests made sense: They presented genuine reasons to call a public meeting. Loco-Focos saw quite clearly that under the constricted franchise of the early national period what was called the public good was fashioned by a narrow class, however benevolent. The condition of the public sphere late in the 1840s might be better captured by acknowledgment that while the common good remained as ever an illusive goal, its determination had at least been subjected to public scrutiny by a more democratic though always imperfect procedure. While more people, in a profusion of public meetings, now had a hand in fashioning the public good, the Loco-Focos, no less than the board of managers of the House of Refuge, left the commonweal to be determined largely in a voluntaristic, associated, haphazard, pastiche political process.

As a result any change in the pace of public improvements is hard to gauge before 1850. The improvement of streets, opening of public squares, and building of city halls did not decline dramatically with the democratization of urban politics or the election of Democrats. Civic improvement proceeded at a sluggish but steady pace, as can be exemplified by the construction of New York City's waterworks. The Croton Aqueduct was first proposed as early as 1799 but did not get implemented until the democratic era of the 1830s and would continue to be funded by the Jacksonian municipal councils of the 1840s.[58] The major monument to New Orleans civic pride, Gallier Hall, was built amidst the contests of Whigs and Democrats and fed an urban beautification project that revivified the Vieux Carré as well as the American quarter. The minutes of city councils North and South found democratic aldermen treating the people to a fare of civic ceremonies with as much alacrity as the patrician organizers of the Erie Canal celebration or Lafayette's visit to New Orleans. Just what public projects would be implemented in San Francisco remained to be seen, once the dust of the gold-rush invasion had settled. For Jacksonians back East, meanwhile, the incentive of providing jobs for growing numbers of humbler constituents could only increase the incentives to undertake public works projects. In 1850, in sum, the condition of the public good was, like the expansion of public access, a young and robust democratic enterprise. Democratic assaults on monopoly, accompanied by the democratic expansion of the franchise, fractured public unity by bringing a broader, less elite political class into the public sphere, but it had not sapped the civic will or created municipal paralysis. Civic culture was not haunted by Habermasian doubt in 1850: The public good and the combative heterogeneity of democratic participation had not yet been proven to be incompatible.

Finally, it would be a mistake to assess Jacksonian urban politics solely by its record of public policy and administration. In fact the limited stakes of laissez-faire economics at the time of the democratic revolution can be seen as politically fortuitous. The absence of great economic pressure on the public sphere afforded the time and space in which to mobilize democracy and set precedents for the expansion of the citizenry, all at a relatively low cost. It permitted a rich public culture to grow outside the realm of formal governmental actions, in political institutions as diffuse and basic as the franchise, in practical political procedures as innovative as nominating caucuses and ward meetings, in the political routines and habits of citizens—such as attending and calling public meetings—and in the living political culture, exhibited, for example, in the almost reflexive action of forming a partisan procession. Public democratic politics could be practiced at almost any time, in a great variety of places and through a whole series of meetings, celebrations, and more meetings. In fact this collective and convivial exercise of democratic citizenship was an invaluable and enduring accomplishment of public life in the antebellum city.

These political creations of the antebellum city were significant in themselves and as schools of democratic public consciousness. If not virtuously focused on the common good, even if easily manipulated by professional politicians, the democracy of the public meeting did engage and invent a people. It placed the possibilities of public expression within the reach of more and more Americans and overthrew restrictions of birthplace and property on joining actively in citizenship. Invitations to full citizenship clearly were restricted by race and gender, but because antebellum democracy was practiced so aggressively at so many meeting places throughout the city, its borders would prove difficult to contain. The antebellum city had provided the conditions to challenge deeply held habits of political deference, for there a heterogeneous mix of people could come together in a commodious public space to form the associated opposition that propelled the democratic experiment forward.

The course of the democratic public through the 1830s and 1840s also ran roughshod over any refined notion of political protocol or decorum. The sheer number of what were called mobs or riots, disorderly expressions of public opinions on a panoply of issues, was higher than at any other time in American urban history. These minor civic wars were a fixture of antebellum democracy, and a goodly portion of them actually coincided with election campaigns. During the 1830s an election combined politics, ceremony, and donnybrook into one urban pageant and brought all sorts of civic differences jostling together in the streets. The processions through lower Manhattan described at the outset of this chapter and the ensuing battle between *Constitution* and *Veto* were classified as a riot in the great compendium of urban disorder collected by police chief J. T. Headley in 1873. The event, which Headley saw as "savage onslaughts" of the "mob" and filled the city presses with "rumors of bloody wars," was serious enough to bring out the forces of law and order for the first time in the rowdy history of New York elections. The mayor called up a special force of constables "to preserve the public peace." In the heat of the skirmish between Whigs and Democrats the mayor himself could be found "mounting the steps. He held up his staff of office and commanded the peace. But the half-drunken mob had now got beyond the fear of the mere symbol of authority and answered him with a shower of stones, and then charged on the force that surrounded him. A fierce and bloody fight followed."[59]

At the time, however, outbreaks such as this were taken more in stride, even reported in a jocular fashion. One contemporary observer of the rancorous election of 1834 reported that "A good temper prevailed" and provoked "nothing more serious as a black eye." Routine ethnic rivalries were often dismissed as "Irish shillelagh frolic" or "a furious fight...which resulted in sundry broken heads and bloody noses." Indeed, although riots were regular occurrences in antebellum cities, they caused few fatalities. (A total of two lives were lost in scores of riots that plagued New York in the 1830s and early 1840s.) The raucous election scene in New Orleans in 1847 was reported with the same equanimity: "municipal election yesterday passed off with little disturbance...some little squabbling" in the second municipality. Through most of the period this routine "high spirit" fell within the capacious range of civic tolerance. Not until 1845 in New York did rioting provoke a concerted attempt to establish a professional police department, and this initiative of a short-lived reform government resulted in only a minor buttressing of the old public-watch system. A mayor could take a blow to the face without taking undue offense. The pugnacious style of politics could even be excused when the perpetrators were recent citizens and ethnic and religious minorities. The *Evening Post* excused the aggressive political behavior of the Irish, saying, "they were quick, irritable and generous... and not particularly disinclined to a row...impatient of insult and coercion...no rational man would provoke them." This commentator reserved his apprehension not for the mob but for the specter of "armed soldiers" should they be called up to keep order. In general antebellum citizens treasured public assembly at least as much as public order. One anonymous source put the stakes of public democracy this way during the election of 1834: "has it come to this. Has a democrat no right to speak his honest opinion in the public street."[60] In 1834, and late into the next decade, the streets of cities such as New York remained open and hospitable to democratic speech even when it got a little raucous.

In fact a riot was not so much a breakdown of democratic process as its conduct by another means. The electoral contests that were the life of a democracy were from the first washed in the rhetoric of warfare. The Loco-Focos' offensive in New York in 1835 was heralded as a "struggle of gladiators," and the whole Democratic cause was one of "Warring not against individuals but against a system of wrong and oppression." When the Whigs joined in open democratic contention, their war cries, especially in the belligerent words of James Watson Webb of the *New York Courier and Enquirer,* were even more incendiary: calls to "armour, . . . fire and sword" against the "enemy." In other words the election "riots" condensed and gave a sometimes violent physical dimension to the conflict that was intrinsic to popular democracy. Any public meeting could cross over the border into a mob. The shouting and shoving match called the Anti-Sabbatarian riot of 1821, for example, was a battle of the public meetings. Two official notices of public meeting followed one another in the morning press, the first to inspire respect for the Lord's Day, the other to support the doctrine of separation of church and state. The classic bread riot enacted by New Yorkers in the panic of 1837 also began as a public meeting called by the Loco-Focos for April 3. "Again to the Park—To the Park. The People are Sovereign." And most way through the 1840s the protection of this public right against untoward governmental control was more precious than maintaining peace and quiet in the city. The Loco-Focos issued a public resolution on the question: "It was a constitutional right of the people to assemble for a redress of grievances. That to array the police or to order out the uniformed Militia for the purpose of intimidation was unconstitutional."[61] In sum, a riot was a species of political action not entirely unlike a public meeting. It was a congregation in open space to publish the collective opinion of a distinctive group. It was, like a partisan election, an act of civic warfare and an intrinsic part of what the *Evening Post* called "The great experiment we are making in popular government." Late in the 1840s this forceful expression of civic differences was still within the bonds of urban civility.

PART TWO

The Interregnum

1850–1865

CHAPTER 4

Civil Wars in the Cities

Within just a few years of the city's founding the people of San Francisco had mastered the urban art of displaying difference, and they proved it in the fall of 1855 by staging a splendid municipal party. The occasion for celebration was the victory of the French and English allies at Sebastopol during the Crimean War. On November 6 a "Great meeting of the French, English and Sardinian Residents of San Francisco" met in the Musical Hall, where, according to a call in the press and in compliance with the usual etiquette of public ceremonies, they planned the local commemoration, which included a Te Deum, 100-gun salute, procession, and a banquet for the benefit of widows and children. Three weeks and many meetings later, the committee of arrangements had collected subscriptions for the event from merchants of different nationalities, and the city was in a festive mood. The press estimated that almost one third of the city's cosmopolitan population turned out to watch a parade of 5000 men proceed through city streets to a pavilion that had been constructed in the park expressly for this occasion. After plentiful speechifying, all 5000 marchers sat down to a repast that would do the city's fabled gourmands proud: 100 roast pigs and twenty muttons were served along with champagne, ale, port, lager beer, and 2500 bottles of claret. The pièce de résistance was a replica of the Malokoff Tower, symbol of the Crimean victory. Rendered in cake, it mounted to a height of fifteen feet. What could more exuberantly proclaim the will to create a public out of the urban habitat of bachelors, fortune hunters, gamblers, and trickster politicians?[1]

But it was the finale of this festival that best prefigured civic life in the late 1850s. The Crimean celebration ended with a farcical overture to a tumultuous era ahead. Impatient with speeches, some in French, others in English, and all inaudible in the huge crowd, the diners stormed the dessert table and engaged in a slapstick battle: "Some vicious wretch got a rope around the platform and tumbled the whole affair to the ground, then the debris were attacked by the standard bearers of all nations, the American Flag being among those which were attempted to be planted among the rush. A general scramble ensued around this arena of confectionery." The combatants let fly with a festive fuselage; loaves, biscuits, trussed turkey and greased pork, as well as cake were hurled through the air. As the French, English and Americans fought one another to place their national standards atop the mound of cake, the opportunities for broad farce multiplied: the French standard bearer, for example, "rent his nether garment in a manner too shocking to relate."[2]

With their inimitable bacchanalian style, San Franciscans had forecast the civic strife that would storm across the United States in the 1850s and that would in turn serve as prologue for that most deadly season of warfare that ended at Appomattox in 1865. As the 1840s merged into the 1850s and 1860s urban differences seemed to become increasingly disagreeable and combustible. New Yorkers had a foretaste of civic fratricide to come as early as 1849. The setting again was a playful one, Astor Place Theater. Ethnic differences that had simmered for decades and were sporadically released in streetfighting erupted in a belligerent confrontation on the evening of May tenth. Irish American critics of British actor William McCready voiced their opinions with a virulence that overtaxed municipal tolerance. The Astor Place Theater riot provoked the first municipal recourse to outside military force in order to quell a riot—complete with heavy pieces of artillery, a squadron of infantry and twenty-two fatalities (fig. 18).[3]

It was not until the next decade, however, that the social and cultural divisions of American cities moved beyond the theatrical stage to become violent struggles for power at the very center of the polity. Nothing in the dictionary of American history quite captures the civic disorder that broke out in American cities in the 1850s and continued through the period of the Civil War. It is known largely by the specific episodes of urban conflict that struck each city independently but in such rapid succession that they could not be merely coincidental. The first incident

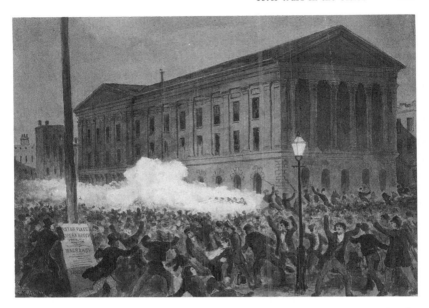

Figure 18. Astor Place riot, 1849. C. M. Jenkes, Watercolor over pencil, The Metropolitan Museum of Art, The Edward W. C. Arnold Collection of New York Prints, Maps and Pictures, Bequest of Edward W. C. Arnold, 1954 (54.90.222). All rights reserved, The Metropolitan Museum of Art.

was the Vigilantism that commenced in San Francisco in 1851 and erupted most explosively in 1856. This extralegal exercise of political force was soon picked up and used elsewhere, giving a name to the peculiar urban disorders of the 1850s. A vigilance committee went earnestly to work a few years later not just in San Francisco but in New Orleans, where it was run by the opponents of a nativist political faction. This second localized example of organized public violence was, like San Francisco Vigilantism, ensnared in the divisive electoral politics, much of it associated with the Know-Nothing Party, which was dissolving the vital glue of the urban kaleidoscope. The third species of urban convulsion, native to New York City, was actually a battle about the procedures for keeping the public peace. No sooner had professional police departments been installed in American cities than people and politicians tangled over their appointment and recruitment. On one occasion, in New York in 1857, two rival police forces battled one another right on the steps of City Hall. One newspaper called this incident a "Civil War in the Metropolis." This label echoed a depiction of the Astor Place riot as "thirty-six hours of civic warfare" and prognosticated the sectional conflict to come. The term *civil wars*—referring to episodic, localized, re-peated, and intently political outbreaks of urban violence—aptly denotes the public life and death of American cities in the 1850s.

The decade of urban cataclysm fed directly into the Civil War that commenced in 1861. The political conflict on the urban home front, like the national Armageddon, injected public life with a jolting dose of state power. These advances of military force into civic life between 1850 and 1865 are epitomized by the marching orders of New York's Seventh Regiment. Just one of many contingents of citizen soldiers who marched festively through antebellum streets in the 1830s and 1840s, the Seventh was called up to quell the incipient riot in Astor Place, marched off to war on the Southern front in 1861, and then was called home in 1863 to sweep the streets of civilian rioters. The five days of rage called the anti-draft riots were more like guerrilla war, complete with ferocious violence by the insurgents and draconian retaliation by the city police, state militia, and U.S. army. Whatever their location, these conflicts of the 1850s and 1860s created crippling divisions of the public sphere.[4]

It was difficult to discover the outlines of a coherent urban culture amid the carnage of these municipal wars. The streets were strewn with the shards of the old kaleidoscope; there was little order and no charm in this manifestation of urban differences. Amid debris left by the Civil War, however, one can find a few premonitions of the new public to come. First, the sectional conflict had taken social differences to a new plane of contention, situating them squarely in the center of political debate as orchestrated by new partisan institutions. Party factions fractured the Whigs, gave way to the Republicans, and developed into the third party system in the nation's short history. Second, in a process that achieved greater velocity toward the end of the 1850s and during the Civil War itself, local political struggles became swallowed up in the political discourse and policies emanating from the state and national rather than the local level. Third, the 1850s were the testing ground for some novel political practices that would challenge the sacred stature of the public meeting. These new political practices were entangled with a fourth portentous change in civic life, a reconfiguration of the principle borders between the people. Before 1850 and until late in that decade the primary fissure of the public, if indeed one can be singled out in the urban patchwork, was between the foreign born (especially Irish Catholics) and nativists of Anglo-Saxon descent (and Protestant faith). By 1863 the boldest and most vicious divide was between black and white, Americans of African and of European descent. Between 1849 and 1863 a new public and transformed people slowly took shape: The people were sorting themselves increasingly into racial rather than ethnic compartments.

Although the length, extent, intensity, and political consequence of the season of civic war took this researcher by surprise, the dominant narrative of Civil War era American political history paints much the same picture. Local stories mirror standard accounts of the political developments of the 1850s and 1860s: from party realignment, through sectional crisis, to Civil War. But viewed from a local urban perspective, this familiar story is stripped of its comforting teleology and appears as the stumblings and flailings of a fractious people. For those who lived in New York, New Orleans, and San Francisco there was no assurance about when and how the civic warfare would end. Even in 1863 the outlines of a new civil order had not been fully formed; they might have been only illusions in the haze above the urban battlefields. The story of part two is that of an interregnum only in retrospect. Civil wars seemed just to follow one after another. To contemporaries the civic tumult of midcentury only underscored, with more force than ever before, that urban democracy was a belligerent affair.

Civil War: San Francisco

Although the season of municipal warfare did not begin at a precise point, some extraordinary events enacted on the western margin of the continent in 1851 are appropriate places to start this narrative. In February of that year the settlers of San Francisco were called to a public meeting with an urgency bordering on panic: "All those who would rid our city of its robbers and murderers, will assemble on Sunday at Two-o'clock, on the Plaza." The call received a positive response: Somewhere between 1000 and 3000 citizens assembled and, according to customary procedures, elected a president and a committee of prominent citizens. The press was in the wings as usual collecting copy for the next day. The *Alta* endorsed the meeting as a routine exercise of popular sovereignty: "For the people are the fountain of all law." This public meeting did break with precedent, however, for it assumed the punitive function of avenging crime. Constituting some of its members as a jury, the meeting tried two transients, found them innocent, and dispersed, despite threats to "lynch them, lynch them." The delicate line between public meeting and mob rule had been drawn but not violated in the dusty plaza of San Francisco.

But in a few months this Rubicon would be crossed. The same cast of leading men, headed by a merchant by the name of William Coleman, presided in the Plaza in June when the assembled citizens ratified a constitution and claimed the name Committee of Vigilance. The vigilantes assumed the authority of "prompt and summary punishment" of public offenders. Before their extralegal but well-organized tribunal had adjourned in 1853, the first San Francisco vigilance committee claimed to have taken ninety-one prisoners, of which about one third were forcibly exiled from the city, about half were discharged, one was publicly whipped, and four were hung.[5]

Early in the 1850s something had gone awry in the politics of the public meeting. The principles of public assembly, popular sovereignty, and majority rule broke free of civic constraints as groups of willful men seized the power to punish and to employ force and violence in an extralegal fashion. Had the vigilance committee exposed the threat of coercion that undergirded every governing system, fulfilled Tocqueville's predictions about the tyranny of the majority, or broken faith with the republican pledge to respect the will of the people as entrusted to their elected representatives? Or was this just a fluke? In San Francisco in 1851 it was still possible to dismiss this incident as frontier excess, a pragmatic response to the disorder endemic to a city that had grown up overnight and harbored a rootless and adventurous population gathered from all parts of the globe. Perhaps such exigencies and such extreme measures would not be repeated, in San Francisco or elsewhere. In fact what the *Alta* called "the political cauldron...seething and boiling...filled with as many incongruous elements as composed the hodge podge of the witch's cauldron in Mac Beth" had cooled down considerably by the very next election. Public democracy seemed to be functioning smoothly once again. The turnover of city government in the 1850s was remarkably balanced: The Whigs won in 1851 and 1852, the Democrats in 1853, and a third party designated as a "Citizen's Reform Ticket" triumphed in 1854, only to be replaced by the Democrats in 1855. These elections, furthermore, were the culmination of widespread popular participation characterized by primary elections among the Whigs, the Democrats, and independent parties.[6]

If anything, San Francisco permitted a surplus of democratic political mobilization in the early 1850s. What the *Alta* called the hodge podge was created as "parties divided into factions, and those factions...subdivided into cliques." The election of 1854 is a case in point. In that year four tickets appeared before voters, including factions of Democrats with picturesque names like Rosewater and Pachouli and a Whig caucus called Bones and Sinews. The profusion of party factions was a by-product of widespread democratic participation, which had spread from the Democrats to the Whigs by 1854, when their nominating convention was constituted by ward meetings that deliberated until 1 A.M. to compile their slate of candidates.[7]

As it turned out, both the Whigs and the Democrats came out losers in the mayoral election of 1854, bested by a dark horse named Stephen P. Webb, who was affiliated with the Citizen Reform Ticket. Webb and his partisans were latecomers to the electoral arena. While the Democrats and Whigs had put their slates forward more than a month before the election, Webb's candidacy was only a matter of political speculation less than a week before the polls were to open. Just the day before the election another rumor surfaced in the daily press. "It is said," wrote the *Alta,* "that the Know-Nothing ticket is the one headed 'Citizen's Reform Ticket' and which will be extensively circulated through the city today." The rumored affiliations with a national nativist movement whose very name disavowed the standard of publicness foreboded a disquieting turn in local politics.

But this ominous sign seemed to dissipate in the course of a year. Stephen Webb spent an inauspicious, uneventful term in office, and when the Know-Nothings came before the electorate in 1855, their secret tactics and private nominating procedures were publicly rebuked. Even sympathizers such as the editor of the *Alta* owned that the "secrecy attending the councils keeps their deeds from coming openly before the public while plots and counter plots are carried on as successfully as in open convention. Secrecy was a cover from trickery."[8] With the Whigs moribund by 1855 the Democrats' prospects were excellent. They began convening ward meetings in the spring, each drawing 200 to 300 voting members. The delegates chosen at these "primary assemblies of the people" adjourned to "canvas their merits" and enacted procedures to guarantee full discussion. The Democratic convention of San Francisco was so wedded to popular participation that it ruled that no member could speak more than twice or for more than five minutes. In further support of publicness the Democrats also voted to continue weekly ward meetings through the campaign and to allow outsiders to sit in on their conventions. At the same time the Democrats held their party members to an uncompromising standard of toleration and openness. "One of the cardinal principles of our party is toleration in politics and religions." Against the Know-Nothing's "pernicious and proscriptive doctrines" the

Democrats proclaimed "Freedom, Equality, and Toleration," or, in more vernacular terms, appealed to those who "drank in Democracy with their mother's milk and not those recreants." And the Democrats took the election. The tally of votes gave the edge, by a small margin, to the Democratic candidate for mayor, James Van Ness.[9]

But less than a year after this robust exercise of representative process, the bodies of four San Francisco citizens, all of them publicly associated with the Democratic party and one who held a minor elected office, were hanging in the Plaza. They had been executed by a Committee of Vigilance, which summarily took power from the mayor, the judiciary, and the democratically elected municipal government. "The citizens whose names are here onto attached do unite themselves into an association for maintenance of peace and the good order of society. . . . And believing ourselves to be the executors of the will of the majority of our citizens, we do pledge our sacred honor to defend and sustain each other carrying out the determined action of the community at the hazard of our lives and fortunes." The violation of democratic procedure was in fact even more blatant than things appear. Not only were candidates who were rebuffed in the previous election prominent on the executive committee of the vigilantes, they actually held their meetings at 110 1/2 Sacramento Street, formerly the Know-Nothing Party headquarters. The vigilantes, as Philip Ethington has recently demonstrated, distanced themselves from the overt nativism of the Know-Nothings but were nonetheless a quite restrictive political movement. Irish Catholics were effectively excluded from the huge membership rolls of the committee, and Protestant merchants virtually monopolized the leadership positions in the new, self-appointed government (fig. 19).[10]

The vigilantes were in some ways just another example of the association and mobilization of differences in urban space. There were, however, two critical differences: This association disguised rather than displayed its social origins, cultural identity, and partisan concerns and then proceeded to usurp the power of coercion from legally and publicly constituted institutions. The vigilance committee represented its extreme actions as a defense of democracy: These extraordinary measures were required to rid the polity of the corrupt politicians and demagogues who had reputedly made a mockery of elections and left the streets awash in robbery, thievery, gambling, and prostitution. At times they employed the familiar language of the democratic public meeting, presenting themselves, like the Loco-Focos before them, as the protectors of the inviolable rights of voters. The term *vigilance committee,* after all, had a

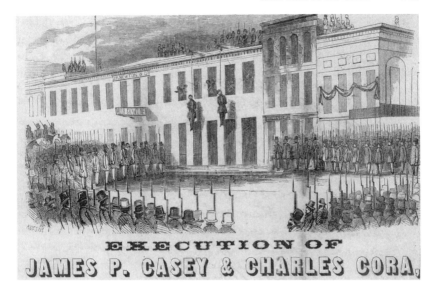

Figure 19. Execution of James P. Casey and Charles Cora. Lettersheet. Courtesy of the Bancroft Library.

long democratic history. Still, the vigilantes assumed power through the gun and noose rather than the word and the ballot and thereby emphatically rejected the politics of the public meeting. They did not attempt to mobilize for the next election through a sequence of ward meetings and primary elections. Rather, they adopted the practice of political secrecy. The committee's recruitment took place in an upstairs office on Sacramento Street, not in the Plaza or at ward meetings, and was anything but public: "Men were admitted only when they were personally endorsed as to character by well-known and respectable citizens" and were "compelled to pass a severe ordeal at the guards, one of whom was stationed at the foot of the stairs, another at the head of them and a third at the entrance of the committee room."[11]

Leadership of this closed membership was determined by consensus, not a vote. The executive committee, which exercised tight control over the paramilitary organization, never stood for election before the rank and file but was chosen from a small circle of friends and acquaintances, most all of them prominent, if economically insecure, merchants. Such methods of mobilizing a political opposition were at best a reversion to Federalist and early Whig principles of private deference. At worst they were the tyranny of a self-proclaimed majority. William Coleman actually boasted of his disdain for representative government: "No dictator could have it more absolutely than I.... It was always so in such matters."[12] Whatever its rhetorical embellishment, the San Francisco Committee of Vigilance practiced a politics of brute force and intimidation. The victims of the second campaign of the committee were not petty Western desperadoes but political offenders, indicted for alleged crimes against good city government: Charles Cora for buying off a judge who acquitted him, Supervisor James Casey for fleecing the voters of tax moneys, James Sullivan for being a notorious "ballot box stuffer." To the vigilantes James Van Ness was just "the aider and abettor of thieves and ruffians"; to others he was the popularly elected mayor. The vigilante terror drove countless Democrats either out of the state or into premature political retirement. Only a few tenacious public men such as David Broderick, who had served his political apprenticeship in New York's Tammany Hall, met the vigilantes head on, first attempting to organize countermeetings in the Plaza and then digging in for a long political struggle waged from state and national offices. The vigilantes, in other words, had transformed the conduct of government in San Francisco literally overnight, turning away from the public meeting and toward private organization and lynching under cover of darkness.

After a few weeks of zealotry, the civil warfare that raged in San Francisco in the spring and summer of 1856 quickly folded back into municipal routine. No sooner had the vigilance committee ceremoniously disbanded (in a stark recessional of armed civilians) than their leaders regrouped to plan for the next election. Naming themselves the People's Party, they called a "mass meeting" to endorse a slate of candidates chosen not by primary election but by a "committee." Their actions appeared in the press as follows: "We are told that the nominating committee appointed at the great Peoples Meeting held in front of the Exchange are actively engaged in the preparation of a ticket for legislative and municipal office which ere long they will present to the people for their suffrage." The *Alta* accepted this admittedly unorthodox process of choosing representatives, which replaced ward-level public meetings with the backstage deliberations of a small elite committee, followed by acclamation at a mass meeting. Their allies in the press were confident in the men rather than the method of the People's Party. "The characters of the gentlemen chosen to make the nominations to be presented for the ratification of the people at the subsequent mass meeting is sufficient to guarantee to us, the purity of their intentions."[13]

Opposition politicians and eligible voters apparently concurred. The Democrats could only put together a slate of political neophytes in the next election, and no one was able to drive the impervious People's Party from office for over ten years. Procedural reforms such as the abolition of annual elections further diminished the accountability of the People's Party to the public.

The extraordinary outbreak of civic violence in San Francisco in the 1850s opened up an alarming fissure in the still young and delicate tissue of public democracy. The contentious premise of electoral democracy, that a tally of votes would determine majority rule, was surely tested in the tumultuous campaigns and abundant opportunities for ballot box tampering found on the urban frontier. The response of the vigilance committee and the People's Party, their recourse to methods of secrecy, was a clean break with the Jacksonian tradition. It also served to suppress the cosmopolitan culture of difference. In its routine electoral strategies in the years to follow the People's Party never owned up to the social differences that informed its political position. Its strategy, unlike that of the Democrats and then the Whigs and even the Know-Nothings, did not acknowledge specific social identities or economic interests. The vigilantes posed as the "People," not as a political association that was top heavy with merchants, Protestants, and the native born. They seemed to imply that only the foreign born, the Catholics, and the manual workers who tended to affiliate with the Democratic party had such specific social characteristics as a birthplace, religion, or class interest, and only their opponents should be stigmatized as corrupted by the mundane associations they carried into the public sphere. Not just nativism, perse, or political violence but the vigilantes' obfuscation of urban differences violated the principle of public democracy.

This sudden and radical challenge to public democracy was predicated on San Francisco's short and volatile history. The city by the bay was detached from the political traditions of the Eastern United States by thousands of miles, settled at a time when corporate publicness had been eroded by the rapid advances of commercial capitalism, and admitted to the Union at a moment when the American party system was already in considerable disrepair. All these conditions made the transplanting of meeting-place democracy to San Francisco a difficult process. Yet with all its idiosyncrasies, San Francisco would turn out to be just an extreme and early example of an urban crisis that would soon be found to the South and in the East.

Warfare at Jackson Square

Scarcely two years after San Francisco's vigilantes disbanded, the *New Orleans Delta* reported that a "California Style Vigilance Committee" was mobilizing in the Crescent City. The cue for this political mobilization came on June 4, 1858, with this public notice: "Rally therefore citizens to the rescue and at once enroll yourselves in the committee whose head quarters is the state Arsenal at Peters Street opposite Jackson Square. Let the friends of law and order come at the signal of three guns." This self-proclaimed vigilance committee did not resort to lynching. Rather, it sparked a more conventional civil war. In response to the call to arms several hundred men gathered in the square, purloined weapons from the state arsenal, and constructed barricades of paving stones and bales of cotton. In an address to the "Citizens of New Orleans" this vigilance committee claimed that a temporary takeover of the city government was necessary to ensure honesty in upcoming municipal elections. They declared, "For the present the ordinary machinery of political justice is suspended." Many citizens begged to disagree and formed a second pole of outraged public opinion just to the north in Lafayette Square. There in the heart of the American quarter the city council called up the militia and requisitioned arms from a nearby hardware store. For five days two factions skirmished around these two encampments, while the indecisive mayor shuttled in between and was ultimately impeached by the city council. The two forces never directly engaged one another, but the fumbling process left four persons dead and scores wounded.[14]

The battle lines in this urban war zone were drawn along familiar lines. At the center of the conflict was distrust of the electoral process, which commenced early in the 1850s with the volatility in the second party system and charges of fraud at the urban polling places. In New Orleans, as elsewhere, the civic consensus was also cracking along religious and ethnic lines. Nativism, opposition to Roman Catholics, and appeals to extend the period of naturalization had been building since 1850 and came together in June 1858 in the armed force gathered in the central square of the American quarter. The encampment in the old Place d'Armes was composed largely of Catholics and immigrants, those of French, German, and Irish ancestry. There was also an ethnic dimension to the body count: Three of the dead were Irish, the fourth was German, but whether they died in enemy or friendly fire remains unclear.[15] The patterning of ethnic conflict had some unique features in New Orleans. First, in contrast to the ethnic alignment in San Francisco,

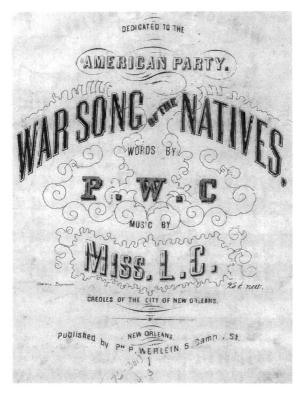

Figure 20. "War Song of the Natives." Sheet music ca. 1855. Courtesy of the Louisiana State Museum.

the faction that called itself a committee of vigilance was composed of the foreign born and Catholics who challenged a sitting municipal government that had been elected under the banner of native Americans. Second, the ethnic struggle was overt, not secret, in New Orleans. The ethnic stakes of this civil war, especially animosity toward Roman Catholics and opposition to political power among immigrants, were made explicit and public in the New Orleans. These bellicose strains of partisan warfare were even put to music, as in a ballad attributed to the American Party and entitled "War Song of the Natives" (fig. 20). The citizenry was so divided by 1858 that the center of the polity was illusive, the whereabouts of democratic authority was open to question.[16]

As in San Francisco the New Orleans civic earthquake occurred quite suddenly. Through much of the 1850s electoral combat seemed reined in by established public institutions and procedures. As late as 1856 the second party system was still installing monuments to itself in prime public spaces of the Crescent City: The Jacksonians finally dedicated the famed statue of Old Hickory dashingly astride his steed in the square that bore his name, while the Whigs raised a statue of Henry Clay in Lafayette Square. Both parties furthermore had made their peace with the heterogeneous electorate, and Whigs joined Democrats in supporting shorter waiting periods for the naturalization of immigrants and fewer restrictions on the franchise.[17] Both parties convened mass meetings, ward caucuses, and nominating conventions before the June election. As the Democratic press put it that year, "The Democracy seems to be getting wide awake in this city. Meetings and conventions are the order of the day as well as the night. We rather like this state of things. It tends to purify the political atmosphere and moreover throws more or less advertising in the way of the printer."[18] The campaign of 1856 was not, however, just a replay of partisanship past. The Whigs and the Democrats were joined by a tightly organized new political machine called the American Party. Two years earlier the nativist movement was no more than a rumor that a "reform" slate would present itself to the voters on the eve of the election. Then suddenly, with promises of fiscal responsibility, vows to clear the city of the public vice (which tended to concentrate in those downtown districts inhabited by the Irish, Creoles, and foreign born), and considerable intimidation at the polling places themselves, the nativists took the election.[19]

In 1856 the American Party came before the voters as incumbents. But like the People's Party, which made its debut in the same year in San Francisco, they posed as disinterested, nonpartisan citizens. They inaugurated the campaign with "A meeting of the citizens of New Orleans" to which "property holders and all persons interested in the proper administration of the affairs of our city and in taking the election out of the hands of politicians and political parties" were especially invited. Lists of prominent businessmen in their ranks, not the resolutions of ward meetings, were the favored political tag of the American Party. Among the espoused policies of the American Party, furthermore, were explicit checks on the broad franchise: a registry act for voting and the stipulation that election inspectors be citizens of ten years' standing and considerable property.[20]

The procedures of the American Party did not go unquestioned among New Orleans voters. One dissenter pushed the mayor off the American Party podium, while others made more genteel complaints against the party's unorthodox procedures. In the aftermath of the

American Party's nominating rally a number of citizens, several with French and Irish surnames, removed their signatures from the list of sponsors. They objected to the lack of "free speech and open discussion" at these party congresses. The final election results in 1856 suggest some interdiction of the right to vote as well. The tally of votes published in the *Picayune* was curious: the Americans won all but two precincts, and by unusual margins, typically 200 or 300 to flat zero. The American ticket had come to power promising to clean up the electoral process, especially by preventing ballot-box stuffing in the immigrant quarters. After a few terms in office they seemed to have tidied up the ballot count. In the eleventh ward, for example, the American candidate for mayor won 243 to 0. This pattern would indicate either an extreme degree of homogeneity by ward, tampering with the vote count, or intimidation of the opposition.[21]

If newspaper accounts and the governor's reports are to be believed, the elections of 1854 and 1856 were characterized by more than the usual level of disorder. In 1854 the reform slate entered office after a campaign marked by attacks on immigrant Democrats that left four persons dead. Three Irishmen were killed in a gun battle in front of St. Patrick's Church and a fourth was found dead right at his polling place. Two years later, the morning after the election found the *Delta* bemoaning the "most deplorable scene of disorder, rioting and bloodshed." The editor described a "bloody Saturnalia" on Orleans Street in the third district, where one challenge to a voter was met with death by bayonet, "while prostrate and weltering in his blood he was shot and stabbed some four or five times." This skirmish pit Sicilian immigrants and their French American allies against a gang of nativists that had mobilized in the American quarter. The vote recorded in this embattled precinct was 90 for the American Party and 0 for the opposition.[22] The governor tallied these numbers bluntly: he estimated that one in three New Orleans voters, especially large proportions of naturalized citizens, were deterred from casting their ballots in the elections of 1854 and 1856.[23]

By some nefarious processes the American Party in New Orleans had accomplished something akin to the triumph of the San Francisco Committee of Vigilance/People's Party. During the height of nativism between 1854 and 1858 they had obtained an electoral majority and silenced the opposition, especially in immigrant districts. The next municipal election, in the spring of 1858, would confirm the demoralized state of public democracy. The election had an eerie aspect from the outset. It was as if all the old venues of electioneering had become ghost towns while politics had been installed in the new quarters of the nonpartisan American Party. The party's executive committee met regularly and sponsored eleven ward clubs and a ward convention. According to the American Party procedures, the grassroots meetings had the power to ratify but not contravene the policies of the executive committee. As of late May, hardly a week before the election, no opposition had materialized. Finally, on May 27 an "independent ticket" came out of nowhere and put forth G. T. Beauregard as its reluctant candidate for mayor. This opposition simply presented a list of sponsors and proposed that on election day the supporters of Beauregard should march to the poles in united front.[24] The march in opposition to the American Party turned out to be the mobilization of the vigilance committee, whose goal was to ensure access to the polling places. More than four years of electoral irregularities and intimidation culminated in that armed display of political force in Jackson Square. The actions of the New Orleans vigilance committee also left their mark on the ballots: In the immigrant wards votes for the independent ticket were now a respectable size and in greater number than in the previous two elections. They were not enough, however, to dislodge the American Party from local office, where they would remain until ousted by a yet more powerful force, the Union army. Nonetheless, the New Orleans vigilantes seemed satisfied that electoral balance had been restored and quietly withdrew their forces from Jackson Square promptly after the election.[25]

The civil war in New Orleans was not as prolonged or as traumatically violent as that in San Francisco. The faction that claimed the title Committee of Vigilance in New Orleans assumed a more traditional and less extreme political function than its namesake in San Francisco: Its show of force on election day was for the immediate purpose of protecting voters from intimidation. Still, in both cities and within a four-year period, the delicate political balance of public democracy was toppled in a municipal coup d'etat. The coup operated by employing secretive political tactics as well as force of arms. In each city, segments of the polity had organized themselves behind closed doors and stood for election under titles such as Citizen's Reform Party, the American Party, or the Know-Nothings. By combining private methods with the claim to some transcendent and disinterested political identity, evoked by names such as "citizens" or "American" or "People's," these new political factions broke faith with the two basic premises of antebellum democracy, publicity and difference. In New Orleans the battle had been fought relatively openly and honestly, on overtly ethnic terms by the native Americans. In San Francisco the vigilantes strayed even further from the standards of public citizenship by camouflaging the specific interests and inevitable distinctions among city people under the name of the People's Party. In both cities the new parties adopted more reclusive methods of enrolling members and choosing leaders. In New Orleans and San Francisco the proponents of private homogeneous style of politics actually seized governing power, and they would then maintain it electorally for some time to come.

Civic War in New York City

The politics of social difference was made of tougher, more sinewy tissue in New York. Various anti-immigrant parties appeared as early as the 1830s but were never a major factor in the second party system. And although the secretive methods of the Know-Nothings had been devised in New York by nativist clubs such as the Order of the United Americans and the Order of the Star Spangled Banner, they were never very successful on their own turf. New York's nativists retreated into secret societies after the defeats of the 1840s and were only marginally more successful when they undertook another political campaign in the next decade. They secured less than one third of the votes in 1854, and their tally peaked in the fall campaign of 1855, when they won a plurality, totaling over 18,000 votes in a field of no fewer than sixteen tickets. By the municipal election in the spring of 1856 the Democrats had recovered their full strength and bested the nativists by a three-to-two margin.

The electoral defeats of nativism did not, however, save New York from its own season of civil war. As in other cities the path to New York's peculiar Armageddon—the battle of rival police forces—was strewn with the debris of an eroding party system in which nativism was one important element. The election of 1854 showed the confusing state of partisan alignments. There were four principle candidates for mayor and sixteen different slates of electors chosen through a dizzying array of representative practices. The Democrats divided into hard- and soft-shell factions (denoting the intensity of their position on slavery) and allied with either Tammany or Mozart Hall. Wherever they were, the Democrats deployed the old techniques of ward meetings and conventions. Ultimately, the Democratic consensus converged around the candidacy of Fernando Wood of Mozart Hall. The Whigs managed to set up their last slate of candidates in 1854, nominating John S. Herrick through the customary procedures and amid the usual charges of "wire-pulling."[26]

The two other candidates were selected in more novel, newfangled, and mysterious ways. The third pretender to the office of mayor, Wilson G. Hunt, was endorsed by several different factions, including the Temperance Party and the Ultra-Hard or Anti-slavery Party, which formed a generic City Reform Ticket. The public record suggests that Hunt's selection was largely the result of backroom negotiations. The formation of the City Reform Ticket was recorded in the press as a series of private meetings: "The Committee met last night and after a long session agreed upon the following ticket." Mobilized to clean the city of corruption, the reformers eschewed ward meetings and conventions and had difficulty finding a candidate, much less locating a rank and file. One nominee after another declined to run, pleading pressing private or business obligations. The nomination of a fourth candidate, James W. Barker, was propelled by a larger groundswell of popular support, mostly from the temperance and the nativist movements. Rumor had it that 10,000 New Yorkers had met in secret cells to press this nativist offensive forward. On the eve of the election, November 10, it was reported that 5000 to 6000 men rallied in support of Barker and what was now called the People's ticket. They marched up Broadway cheering for Barker and groaning at the mention of Wood's name, stopped to raise a Bronx cheer at the residence of Archbishop Hughes, and sang "Yankee Doodle" with particular vigor as they passed St. Patrick's Church. The Citizens Reform or People's Ticket was clearly allied with the nativist movement and avowed Know-Nothing James Barker.[27]

While equivocating about its ethnic identity and claiming the universal mantle of the American Party, the nativists' political energy was clearly fed by specific if negative signs of cultural difference, especially the rum and Romanism they saw lurking behind the facade of St. Patrick's Church. New York politics was a battlefield for real ethnic stakes, things such as Bible reading in schools, liquor laws, and foreign-born representation on city councils. Although such issues were often submerged in the universalistic rhetoric of people's parties in San Francisco and New Orleans, they were confronted squarely in the mayoral campaigns of New York. In 1854 the Democrats of New York, much like their stalwart native son in San Francisco, David Broderick, mounted a direct assault on the methods and ideas of nativism. "Who will stand here and say," said one Democratic orator, "that morals are to be enforced—that men are to be bounded to principles, involuntarily." Labeling nativists and moral reformers as trespassers on the Bill of Rights, the Democrats claimed the standard of "freedom versus fanaticism" as they marched off into their own torchlight processions. New York's Whig leaders, including William Seward and Horace Greeley, spoke out forthrightly against nativism. The 1854 contest was almost a stalemate, but Fernando Wood was elected by a small plurality. The next election made the issues even clearer. Wood stood for reelection in a small field of candidates and in open confrontation with a Know-Nothing Party that had all but dispensed with secrecy. This time Wood was clearly and solidly elected to another term as mayor. It would appear that neither a vigilance committee nor a civil war was imminent.

When civil war did break out in New York, it was not the work of a vigilance committee. Neither was it entirely a local matter. The assault on New York City Hall was actually mounted by a police force appointed by the state governor. In the spring of 1857 two different battalions of armed men vied for the title of city police. The first, called the Metropolitans, was newly appointed by the Republican administration in Albany. After the particularly unruly elections of 1854 and 1856, which featured street combat between gangs affiliated with both nativists and Democrats and ended in the election of the latter, the disgruntled opposition took their complaints to Albany. The resulting revision of New York City's charter removed responsibility for policing city streets from the hands of locally elected officials, vesting it instead in a state-appointed, and Republican-dominated, commission. But New York's elected mayor did not quietly surrender local autonomy. Fernando Wood refused to disband the police force he had appointed, known as the Municipals. The cast was assembled for perhaps the most bizarre civil war of all. Wood's opponents called it "the Mayor's Insurrection." [28]

On June 17, 1857, fifty Metropolitans were sent by the governor to arrest Mayor Wood for defying the state charter. An estimated 800 loyal Municipals promptly arrived to protect the mayor. The Metropolitans and the Municipals met on the steps of City Hall to begin what the *Tribune* called a "Reign of Disorder." But the two rival police forces were only a fraction of the combatants. One reporter claimed there were 10,000 "Burly ruffians," supporters of Mayor Wood, engaged in hand-to-hand combat in City Hall Park. An officer of the state militia threatened to call up nine regiments to support the governor. Before this could come to pass, however, an improbable but familiar deus ex machina appeared on the scene. The Seventh Regiment, by some suspicious happenstance, was marching through lower Manhattan at the time and struck up parade formation in front of City Hall. This seemed to have a sobering effect. A truce was declared while the state courts delib-

Figure 21. Metropolitan Police storm City Hall. *Frank Leslies' Illustrated Newspaper,* 1857.

erated about the legitimacy of the Metropolitan Police Act. When the act was ruled constitutional a few weeks later, Wood withdrew his forces from the field of municipal civil war (fig. 21).[29]

But not all New Yorkers were so compliant. Only a tenuous peace reigned as the city geared up to celebrate the Fourth of July. On the morning of the nation's anniversary the Metropolitans patroled the sedate celebration uptown, congratulating themselves on the good order but oblivious to what was transpiring in lower Manhattan. When some skirmishes erupted between rival political gangs—the Bowery Boys and the Dead Rabbit—a downtown alderman advised the Metropolitan police to lie low and not exacerbate the situation by raising the specter of a standing army mobilized in Albany. The appeal was not heeded: not only the Metropolitans but several regiments of state militia were called up to suppress the disturbances. A major urban conflagration resulted, spreading from Five Points in the sixth ward over to First Avenue and into the twenty-first ward. At this point a rumor surfaced that "a committee of vigilance was volunteering its services to keep the peace."[30]

The municipal civil war swept through New York with a ferocity surpassing the force of vigilantism elsewhere. It was more like a popular insurrection than a localized riot. The *Times* described the mayhem in Manhattan: "Brickbats, stones and clubs were flying thickly around and from the windows in all directions, while men ran wildly about brandishing firearms. Wounded men lay on the sidewalk and were trampled on." The street battles enrolled more than just bands of young men: "men, women and even children participated with an almost fiendish glee in the horrible work of destruction." Women made a prominent appearance in accounts of the violent politics of 1857. They were accounted among the most furious critics of Governor King and the Metropolitan police, and from Baxter Street came the report that mothers filled the muskets and loaded the pistols that their sons carried into battle. The *Tribune* called the turmoil in lower Manhattan "guerrilla warfare," a title befitting a rebellion that spilled over from the ballot box into the neighborhoods and recruited women as well as men.[31]

The police force used to contain civic disorder also escalated markedly in New York in the summer of 1857. Four regiments of the state militia were deployed with cool precision by General Sanford. Noting that the rioters were "driven by combinations of men, seeming to be under order of experienced policemen, and others of desperate character," the general ordered "the requisite force to restore order and arrest the civil force in presenting further havoc." When that countermarch led to several civilian deaths, the soldier retained his cool professionalism: "The appearance of the military on the street, with fixed bayonets and ball cartridges has had its usual salutary effect." During the summer of 1857 the level of violence sanctioned by the state rose to unprecedented heights. In August, for example, the Seventh Regiment of the state militia displayed a new set of procedures designed to control "street-fighting." "The regiment being on the ground in front of the mob and the companies formed nearly across the street, the first company after firing will face to the right and march down the right flank and to the rear. . . . A howitzer will be fired and the second company files on. By this new method a constant stream of ball is kept flying, the howitzer firing one hundred and twenty musket balls at each discharge and it is thought by the military men that very few mobs could stand against the fire of half a dozen companies."[32]

A political season that had begun with the relatively peaceful and rather even-matched electoral contest of a score of political factions ended in this confrontation between furious citizens and a well-armed state police force. While the political institutions of New York, especially her dense infrastructure of partisan politics, insulated City Hall from the ravages of vigilance committees such as those in New Orleans and San Francisco, it could not weather an assault on its autonomy from the state legislature. The show of force by the Metropolitan police sparked the tinder box of the big, heterogeneous city into the most heated urban warfare of all. The bloody rites of July 4, 1857, left twelve dead and over 100 wounded. A naive observer might think that the Civil War had begun in New York in 1857.[33]

In fact New York's civil war, if not federally organized like the great conflict that would erupt less than four years later, was part of a national phenomenon. In the space of just fifteen months New York, New Orleans, and San Francisco all saw the public come utterly apart. The loss of civic cohesion was punctuated by a bewildering proliferation of pretenders to the role of police force: vigilantes, volunteers, Metropolitans, and Municipals. It would seem that sometime around the midpoint of the last century America's urban democracies were losing their capacity to accommodate differences, especially of a partisan or ethnic stripe. The municipal crisis was attributable in part to the magnitude of social diversity and depth of economic divisions that wracked these three urban entrepots. In the 1850s three million immigrants entered the United States, and most of them passed through either New York or New Orleans. San Francisco was the most precocious and polyglot of the nation's "instant cities." The thousands of newcomers and transients increased the pressure on the cities' fragile structures for managing heterogeneity. In the 1850s New York had to compress its mixed population of over 800,000 souls onto a compact island; immigration swelled the old segmented order and crowded the old public spaces beyond capacity. Urban economics further taxed public good and private enterprise. Even New York's bustling economy could not accommodate the rising population. Between 1853 and 1856 the demands on the almshouse had increased by 240 percent. San Francisco, with fewer than 1500 industrial jobs, had even greater difficulty supporting the unemployed who were spilling over from the exhausted gold fields. In New Orleans the absence of industrial capital, stagnation of the once vigorous commercial economy, and the

shadow of uncertainty that hung over the Southern slave economy conspired to deflate even the boosterism of the American quarter. Then in
1857 the national economy, bloated by speculative railroad investment,
went bust. The fragile equilibrium of the democracy, balancing differences by means of an imperfect electoral machinery, was put to a savage
test.

Could such a large, mobile, mixed population file peacefully into the
representative process of antebellum democracy? Were segmented
spaces, parade culture, and public meetings capacious enough to accommodate all the newcomers? Were representative procedures (such as
popular elections and municipal contracting) too vulnerable to charges
of corruption to sustain public faith in the democratic experiment? The
answers to these political challenges of the 1850s were not always either
affirmative or public and democratic. These premonitions of another
kind of political practice were myriad: secretive meetings, homogenizing
political rhetoric, obfuscation of ethnic differences, a proliferation of
partisan factions, and the intrusion of outside institutions such as state
legislators and the state militia. It was under such pressure that the embattled urban democracies were swept up in a civil war of national dimensions.[34]

Circumventions of the Local Public

The municipal civil wars of the 1850s were harbingers of the great sectional conflict to follow. At least three premonitions of Fort Sumter can
be found at the local level by the mid-1850s. First, the municipal civil
wars had resulted in an early militarization of civil society. In each city
the forces that acted in the name of order were the major perpetrators of
violent death: those who held the noose in Portsmouth Plaza, patrolled
the ballot boxes in New Orleans, quelled the riot in New York. Predictably, a chief consequence of the urban civil wars was the buildup of
police authority. Under the People's Party, San Francisco installed the
most professional and politically insulated police force in the United
States. There, as in New Orleans and New York, the urban police would
grow more rapidly than the general population for the remainder of the
century. The links between the local conflicts of the 1850s and the Civil
War were sometimes discerned by contemporaries. For example, Charles
Royster has shown how General William Tecumseh Sherman saw the
destructive fury of the Union and Confederate armies prefigured in the
campaign of the San Francisco vigilantes, which he had observed years

before. In all three cities, furthermore, the expansion of police power would be under the jurisdiction of state or metropolitan, not local, authorities.[35]

A second and related consequence of the municipal civil wars was the erosion of urban autonomy. New York's revised charter was only the most draconian intervention of state government into local sovereignty. Albany had in fact taken so much authority away from the mayor and city council that the locally elected officials controlled only one quarter of the city budget. State intervention had also restructured the municipality of New Orleans: It was the legislature in Baton Rouge that ended the partition of New Orleans into three municipalities in 1852, unwittingly paving the way for warfare along the border between the French and American sectors only a few years later. Another local institution of authority, the county board of supervisors, was also introduced in New Orleans and San Francisco. State commissions, modeled after the governing Board of Central Park, provided yet another way of circumventing those messy democratic practices by which the urban public once operated. It was as if the municipal civil wars of the 1850s had anticipated both the militarization of society and the increasing centralization of the state that is conventionally associated with the Civil War proper.

Third, and most important, the same issues that brought the North and South to the battlefield had been coursing through local politics for at least a decade. A succession of political factions—Know-Nothing, Taxpayers', Citizens', Reformers', and People's Parties—cleared the way for the Republicans and with them the centrality of slavery and sectionalism in American political discourse. This political history, especially as it refracts upon the causes of the Civil War, is a familiar story. The critical role played by nativism and the Know-Nothing Parties in this process is well documented by scholars such as William Gienapp and Michael Holt. Nativism, as organized into a national political force by the American Party between 1853 and 1857, served as a transfer point along the way from the second to the third party system. The Know-Nothings' antagonism to both foreign-born Catholics and abolitionists served not just to undermine the Whigs but also to stave off the advances of the Republicans. This progression is exemplified in New York State, where Whig leaders such as William Seward rebuffed nativism only to be accused of "political Catholicism," all the while trying to placate proslavery voters. The strategy lost the Whigs votes to both nativists and Freesoilers. At the same time the newly minted Republican Party of New York made slavery its primary issue but was chary of embracing nativism. The Re-

publicans would not win a New York election until after they had made
concessions to nativists and anti-Catholics. Their compromises included
enrolling James Barker, former Know-Nothing candidate for New York
mayor, among their most popular stump speakers. The intricate unraveling of the old party system was dramatized in San Francisco by the tragic
career of David Broderick: The bane of the vigilantes had become a
pariah among many Democrats by the end of the 1850s because of his
adamant opposition to the expansion of slavery. The year after making a
poignant speech in the Senate opposing the expansion of slavery while
defending "my democracy," with its tenets of popular sovereignty and
local rule, Broderick would die in a duel in 1859, an early casualty along
the road from municipal to national civil war.[36] After the battle of 1858
the People's Party of New Orleans had also become more sectional than
nativist.[37] By this date the politics of urban differences were of more
than local interest; they were bound up in the whole tangle of factors
that contributed to the fateful presidential election of 1860.[38]

Indeed this shift in the center of gravity, from the local toward the national level, had been the key factor in the outbreak of civil war in New
York City in 1857. The Republican Party, which had recently obtained a
majority in the state legislature, had come into office in alliance with
many of the constituencies that made up city reform coalitions elsewhere, including nativists and temperance advocates. In addition to
modulating the representative power of immigrants by enacting registration laws and longer residency requirements the upstate Republicans
passed the city charter that drastically contravened the political sovereignty of residents of New York City. That legislation, enacted in April
1857, imposed on New York City a board of supervisors, a Central Park
Commission, and, most chafing of all, that state-appointed Metropolitan police force. To exacerbate the insult and injury, the charter set the
next election for December 1857, cutting Mayor Fernando Wood's term
in half. It was this extrademocratic intervention that sparked the most violent episode in New York's season of urban civil war. The partisan
source of that intervention, a new political party whose concerns were
sectional rather than local and evoked racial as well as ethnic differences,
was a harbinger of the Civil War yet to come.

Yet this melding of sundry political factions into Republicans was not
a simple, direct bridge to the third party system. There were many
treacherous steps between nativism and sectionalism, Whigs and Republicans; clearly, the issue of slavery and the impassioned and persuasive
political opposition to it was an essential element in local and national

politics through the entire decade.[39] The cityside view of the decade of the 1850s also demonstrates that it was not just ideology and partisan institutions but specific political practices that paved the way to Civil War. These rudiments of a new political machinery were all wrapped up in the pledge of "nonpartisanship," first clearly articulated by vigilantes and nativists and soon picked up by local Republicans along their way to national prominence. The nonpartisan parties practiced the secretive methods of mobilization and nomination favored by the nativists, excoriated professional politicians, elevated fiscal conservatism to the status of chief civic virtue, and, finally, tended to vault over local political affiliations and favor alliances at the state, sectional, or federal level. These practices are worthy of extended description, for they posed a challenge to the politics of differences that would eventually change the terms of democratic debate.

Each one of these principles of a new politics evolved slowly through local electoral practices. Most of them could be seen germinating in the People's Party of San Francisco as early as 1856 and had become the heritage of the Republican Party by 1860.[40] Although local opposition to the Democratic Party had coalesced into allegiance to Republicans by this date, the label People's Party was still used at the time of municipal elections. The New York mayoral contest of 1861, for example, was labeled a face-off between two factions of Democrats and a "People's Union Party." The latter ticket claimed to be nominated by "the spontaneous movement of the people without distinction of party." When the Yankees marched into New Orleans in 1862, they would find a "People's" or "American" Party still installed in Municipal Hall, and as late as 1863 the People's Party of San Francisco was still invoking the memory of the vigilance committee as champions of good government against "those who manipulate ward meetings, lay political pipes and stuff ballot-boxes at a pinch."[41]

The people's parties generally eschewed ward meetings. In San Francisco they continued to meet as a private committee. In the New York election of 1862 the opposition to the Democrats assembled an array of "committees," most under Republican auspices. There was the Fifth Avenue Organizing Committee, the St. Nicholas Organization, and the Tax Payers' Union, all of whom came together to form the Union Conference Committee. The report of the Republican convention noted only that "the Committee of twenty-two, it was stated, had appointed a Committee of Seven to confer with other organizations." The result of that conference was "agreement upon the following ticket."[42] The only notice of ward-level organization among the Republicans came after the nominations and on the eve of the election when an occasional assembly such as the "seventh ward ratification meeting" met to acclaim the people's ticket and hear patriotic airs sung by the Union Glee Club. The "committee meeting" and the "mass meeting" were the two poles of the new party organizations. Between the first, a small group of leaders that made formal nominations, and the second, whose loyal audience cheered its assent rather than chose delegates or formulated resolutions, there was little space for the old grassroots assemblies of public democracy.[43]

By the 1860s Democrats as well as incipient Republicans had welded a loyal rank and file to professional political strategists. Fernando Wood, the candidate for mayor of New York once again in 1859 and 1861, had secured the fealty of so many voters, enough of whom were members of political gangs and beneficiaries of municipal bounty, that the title "boss" was not entirely a misnomer. There is no doubt that Wood was dexterous about manipulating the loyalties of his lower-class and immigrant constituents.[44] By the 1860s partisan spirit was also orchestrated by campaign hoopla. Tucked away amid the calls to ward meetings in the advertising columns of the Democratic *Herald,* for example, was the notice, "Political Banners, Flags and Transparencies of every description on hand and to order. HOJER & GRAHAM, Artists and Manufacturers, 97 Duane street." Still, the extent of ward-level participation remained impressive and entrenched among city Democrats. On election eve in 1861 Democrats were holding regular meetings in sixteen of the city's twenty-two wards. Moreover, they occasionally passed their own resolutions and noted special constituencies such as working men, Germans, or youth as well as affirmed their party's nominations. Democrats, furthermore, were still a quarrelsome lot and remained divided between Tammany and Wood's Mozart Hall.

To members of the People's/Republican Parties these Democratic institutions were seen as the handiwork of venal, corrupt men. This was one of the most ominous and prescient consequences of the political strife of the 1850s: the casual and complacent acceptance of the notion that politicians were by definition morally suspect. New Yorkers calling for the independent ticket of 1854 "Resolved that we will commence this evening the work of reform by naming in open meeting, and without the intervention of Party wirepullers, an independent, capable, honest and energetic citizen, unconnected with and uncommitted to any political interest or faction, as the People's Candidate For Mayor." The reformers claimed that this was a simple rescue operation, taking government from "The clutches of the gamblers and ruffians who now govern it through the Primary election of all the great parties." The People's Party of San Francisco was less reserved and polite in its attack on this subspecies of humanity: Politicians were simply dubbed the tribe of "Rowdyism, violence and murder." When vigilantism came to New Orleans a few years later, its apologists used similar rhetoric against those in power: "Politics we repeat should have nothing to do with the administration of our finances, the appointment of an independent, honest and well-cosseted police, nor with the general superintendence of the various branches of our government."[45]

If the politician was clearly the heavy in the reformer's political culture, the hero was a bit more difficult to identify. The namesake of so many of the new party formations, "the people" was a purposively nebulous category that denied more than it denoted. Surely, the candidate of the people was not a political hack or wirepuller, neither a Democrat nor a Whig, certainly not an Irish Catholic or foreigner, not a member of any class. This pure citizen stood apart from those "Clickes" and "interests" that dominated the urban electoral arena. The *San Francisco Alta* defined city reformers against these negative apparitions in 1855: first, the candidate of the "silk stockings" who would improve the city by profiting in public land sales; next, the candidate of the "boys" for whom politics was the pastime of streetfighting; and third, the incumbents who fed on the spoils of office. Against these negative references the "citizen" and the loyalists of the "nonpartisan" or "People's Party" stood out for their personal virtues as "respectable," "responsible," "honest," and "capable," simply "the best men." In 1861, when the Republicans were well organized and fully professional, they still presented themselves locally as "The People's Union Ticket of patriotic citizens, without distinction of party," chosen "on the basis of personal integrity, capacity of their tried devotion to the union." The local Republicans were simply "men of character."[46]

The spokesmen for Peoples' parties were more explicit about one prominent and selective social characteristic of the party leadership. They were overwhelmingly merchants or businessman. James King's *Bulletin* employed a masterful casuistry in describing the political prerogatives of the businessmen vigilantes. "The public mind seemed ripe for such a demonstration, the public voice demanded it. Gentlemen of higher reputation in business circles, never prominent in political movements, above the suspicion of having merely personal or party ends to serve, resolved the measures calculated to give this public sentiment form and expression."[47] To be a businessman was somehow to be above political interest. By the 1860s the People's parties were blunt about the particular economic class they represented. The platform of the Taxpayers and Citizens Union Party in 1861 in New York was filled with the "most respectable and influential merchants." The rally for the Republican mayoral candidate in that year took place at the Merchants Exchange on Wall Street and was sponsored by "hundreds of the most prominent merchants, bankers and professional men of the city." In fact the long list of sponsors printed in the advertising section of the *Times* did more than name individual businessmen: In the majority of cases it recorded the titles of companies, from S. B. Crittenden & Co. at the top to Harris and Wyckaman at the bottom of the long column.[48]

It was the province of businessmen to enact one substantive plank in the People's Party platform—fiscal conservatism. In fact in all three cities people's reform parties were particularly zealous about limiting public spending. The short-lived Know-Nothing parties had anticipated this civic parsimony. In his maiden speech before the city council, San Francisco's Know-Nothing mayor, Stephen P. Webb, promised simultaneously to curb government spending and expand the police department. He was so concerned about the first priority, however, that he stinted on the second and never even considered more positive public programs. For the first decades of its history, San Francisco's civic functions would be located in rented quarters and in the converted Jenny Lind Theater, never dignified with the erection of a proper city hall. The story was much the same in New Orleans after midcentury when the Know-Nothing government maintained such a tight-fisted hold on the municipal budget that they would not even finance the police force to follow through on promises to clean up the streets and close the brothels. The interregnum would not support significant investment in public architecture in any one of these cities, the more public-spirited democracy of New York no less than the freewheeling private city of San Francisco. No major squares were opened in New York or New Orleans and only two in the ballooning city of San Francisco.[49] The development of grand parks (which will be detailed in a later chapter) was premised on the parsimonious use of cheap land on the city's periphery. New York public spending was hemmed in by state charters that reserved much of the budget planning to Albany and a stipulation that all civic expenditures be specified and publicly accounted for as well as awarded on the lowest secret bid of contractors. Similar combinations of policy and political expediency determined the miserly administration of the reform governments.

These strictures on spending are in many ways just a continuation of America's entrenched habits of public parsimony, in evidence since the eighteenth century and refortified by the laissez-faire standards of Jacksonian democracy. But under the guise of citizens' parties and people's reform tickets fiscal conservatism took on new meaning. It was no longer allied with the democratic meanings of the Jacksonian period, which scrutinized public spending with the end of curbing inequity and the concentration of power. The reforms of the 1850s were designed to root out another kind of public vice. They took aim first at the cost to property owners and taxpayers, and, second, they targeted not economic power but venal politicians. It was the politician, not a particular public policy or selective private interest, that was put on trial by the nonpartisans. If the prescient reformers of the 1850s eschewed Jacksonian populism, they also had lost Whig stewardship. As the People's Union ticket put it in 1861, "we insist upon honesty in every department of the government, economy in public expenditure, reduction of public burdens and a strict accountability on the part of public servants."[50]

After 1850 Democratic administrations were also hamstrung by these strictures on municipal spending. Even the generous public instincts of Mayor Fernando Wood were constrained after 1857. His expenditures on public relief, on opening Central Park, on engine houses and docks and his dreams of building a new city hall, even a municipal university and a women's free academy, were all shattered by the restrictions of the state charter. Wood took these complaints directly to the electorate. In his bid for reelection in 1861 Wood campaigned against the Republican opposition in the state legislature. "There is in the Legislature at Albany a great preponding power over us, exercised by men, too, in every sense of the word foreign to us, and opposed to us in every element and every characteristic which goes to make a great and free people.... We have been deprived of the right to appoint our own police; to build our own court houses; to lay out our public parks, or to say what shall be the legal observance of the Sabbath. (great cheering)."[51] Wood identified the ideological battle lines that divided the old Democrats and the new Republicans at the outset of the Civil War. First, his reference to the Sabbath called up the bitter ethnocultural rivalry of the Know-Nothing era between Protestant reformers such as the Sabbatarians and the immigrant Catholics of Wood's urban constituency. Second, the mayor's invocation of the rights of the people and popular sovereignty played on the sacred heritage of Jacksonian Democrats. And finally, his grievance against Albany identified a new faultline of local politics: between those who clung to the local base of civic life and those who attached themselves to state, sectional, and national centers of power.

Few local politicians would contest Wood by directly challenging the principle of urban autonomy. But neither could they elude the magnetic field of centralizing state power and the pull of sectional loyalty. For example, as early as 1856 both the Democratic and Republican Parties of California had enthusiastically endorsed subsidies for the development of a Pacific railroad.[52] The geopolitical order had shifted markedly well before 1863 when San Francisco's People's Party pledged that they would use their "influence to prevent extravagance or waste of the public funds or credit." They went on to say, however, "While we do not consider it sound policy for a state, city or county to participate in the construction of works purely local we do believe that a work of such magnitude and importance as the Pacific Railroad should receive the encouragement and support of every citizen."[53] In other words the same political faction that was so tight-fisted about local expenditures on streets and public buildings endorsed municipal funding of a transportation project that leapt the bounds of the city by hundreds of miles. And the funding was of an unprecedented size. The People's Party asked the voters to subscribe to a $1 million bond to subsidize the Western Pacific and the Central Pacific Railroads. The voters concurred, in every single ward and by wide margins. Clearly, urban politics and finance had vaulted over the city limits by the late 1850s and 1860s when the platforms of every California party, the Republican and several factions of Democrats, followed the lead of the People's Party in endorsing both railroad subsidies and municipal austerity. Civil war was lifting each municipality off the old political foundations.[54]

The Civil War in the City

The last and biggest episode in this long season of civil war would inscribe a new political topography on the cityscape: Republicans would replace the Know-Nothings as well as the Whigs, the differences of religion and birthplace would fade beside distinctions of "color," and the national "union" would hold more cachet than the local culture of difference.[55]

From an urban vantage point the years between 1861 and 1865 simply prolonged and sometimes intensified the period of civic conflict. Even in

San Francisco, the most pacific city in the 1860s, the civic order was rup-
tured by the sharply divided attitudes of citizens on national and sectional issues. Conflicts about the containment of slavery tore apart the
Democratic Party even before the war. By 1864 many Democrats had de-
fected to the Copperhead wing, which brought thousands of disgruntled citizens to rallies calling for the swift termination of the war. The
threat to municipal solidarity was severe enough to call together the veterans of vigilante campaigns under the name of Committee in the Aid of
Public Peace. A force of more than 3000 men, called a Citizen's Voluntary Police and paid for by the business community, patrolled the streets
during the fall political campaign. A week before the election, on October 27, the People's Party assumed its martial identity and paraded the
streets, executing several "bold, quick" military maneuvers, presenting
the police chief with a sword, and winning the cheers of a "large number
of spectators, including a number of ladies." By intimidation or the
magic sedative of the franchise, the Union was preserved in San Francisco. Lincoln was reelected and victory was celebrated in a military-style
procession: "four thousand men with flags and numerous bands of music, marched twenty abreast through the principal streets, singing patriotic songs, and the ladies, upon the sidewalks or in the window, waved
their handkerchiefs in congratulations." When Lincoln was assassinated
the next spring, the party wars broke out yet again in San Francisco: A
mob thousands strong besieged the offices of four local newspapers who
had not been unequivocal in their support of the war effort. The tattered
civic peace endured a few more weeks until the war finally ended in San
Francisco without other local causalities.[56]

The Civil War would also be relatively pacific on the home front of
New Orleans, which was occupied by the Union army in the spring of
1862. There was remarkable civility in the immediate aftermath of the
Union occupation. In February 1862, perhaps because of the city's half-
hearted and divided support for secession, the citizenry awaited the arrival of the Union army with stoic fatalism. As the Yankees marched into
the city on April 26 the *Picayune* and the Common Council urged the
populus neither to resist nor to surrender but to maintain an "eloquent
Silence" in the presence of their conquerors. The major battle was a symbolic one: The Confederate flag was removed from the U.S. Mint, only
to be unfurled again at Lafayette Square and finally stealthily lowered by
a Union soldier. Meanwhile, the City Council continued to meet in the
Greek revival citadel in Lafayette Square, urging cooperation and keeping order, hopeful that they could maintain civilian rule. The strategy

failed when the city police refused to pledge Union loyalty. The Union commander, General Benjamin Butler, promptly declared martial law and usurped power from the local civilians.[57]

Within days the Union army had occupied nearly every public site and symbol in the city, not just federal buildings such as the Mint and Customhouse but also Municipal Hall, Lyceum Hall, Odd Fellows Hall, the St. James and the St. Charles Hotels. In a stony assertion of his power General Butler had the phrase "The Union Must and Will Prevail" carved into the base of the statue of Old Hickory in Jackson Square. The conditions of martial law were austere. Public assembly was prohibited, respect for the U S. flag and insignia were required, local institutions such as the free market and French-speaking public schools were closed down, and a new metropolitan police force was enlisted, with a goodly number of black officers. Butler incurred the ire of the local citizenry with one particularly devious retaliation against assertions of Confederate loyalty. Notorious order number 28 made any woman found insulting Union officers in the street to be "liable as a woman of the town plying her avocation." This unusual exercise in martial law was in fact an apparition of sexual symbolism that was becoming familiar in municipal politics. It was reminiscent of how vigilantes and Know-Nothings used the promise of containing prostitution to win votes in both New Orleans and in Northern cities during the 1850s.[58] In some ways Republican rule in New Orleans was a license to enact the public policies favored by municipal reformers in the North. General Butler quickly professionalized the police force and put 2000 men to work improving the streets. Boards of health and hygiene would soon follow. Butler even inaugurated some reformed race relations. In 1862 a delegation of free people of color appealed to the general to integrate public places, and he responded with at least symbolic affirmation of racial equality.

Although Butler was relieved of his New Orleans duties soon thereafter, relaxing martial law considerably, one American city had lost its local sovereignty entirely. Through the war years public debate in the Crescent City was largely a charade, acted out in rituals such as the Battle of the Handkerchiefs, where women praying for the Confederacy in St. Paul's Church were assaulted by Union soldiers. The scene delighted Confederate propagandists who portrayed the Yankees in the unflattering pose of bayoneting ladies. In the long run, however, martial law was only an interruption of the process of reinventing urban politics. As men and women signed the oath of loyalty to the Union their rights were restored and they swiftly put forward rival slates for local office. By 1864 the new politics of difference in New Orleans promised to be more polyglot than ever, hinting, as we shall see, even that African Americans and even former slaves might assume the roles of citizens.

It was left to the City of New York to be the bloodiest urban battlefield of the Civil War. Even before the commencement of hostilities the question of sectional loyalty was a contentious issue in New York. In January 1861 Fernando Wood, long a defender of local rights as well as the city's commercial ties to the South, had proposed that New York declare itself a "free city" in any ensuing sectional conflict. But the attack at Fort Sumter changed Wood's mind and the Union rally of April 12 would find him at the podium. Soon a contingent from Mozart Hall would volunteer for battle.

Wood kept the municipal peace for about six months, or until the next election season.[59] By November the Union Party and Mozart Hall were engaged in a rhetorical exchange that was anything but pacific. Wood's campaign for reelection moved swiftly from a defense of the city against Albany to an offensive strike against the way the Republicans were conducting the war in Washington. "They will get Irishmen and Germans to fill up the regiments and go forth to defend the country under the idea that they will themselves remain at home to divide the amount of plunder." The attack was joined by the *Herald,* which supported the Lincoln administration in Washington but sided with the opposition at home. They painted the war effort as something less than the patriotic defense of the national union. One Union candidate was dubbed an "incendiary ecclesiastical nationalist of the Puritan character" and two others were called "radical amalgamationists." The *Times* and *Tribune,* firm supporters of the Republicans, shot back with a challenge to the Democrats' patriotism. They called Wood an "open sympathizer with the traitors of the South" whose supporters were "the baser portions of the population." Together they were held responsible for the "murder of our loyal citizens" and for holding "our best and brightest in pestilential dungeons." At this point the hostilities between the Union and Confederacy had only been underway for six months.[60]

By the winter of 1862 and 1863 devastating inflation and depressing news from the war front had worn away the veneer of Union solidarity. Mayor Opdyke, who had defeated the incumbent Wood by a small margin in the election of 1862, presided over a tense municipal peace. The *Tribune* called a rally marking the anniversary of Fort Sumter and proclaimed the event a "Glorious outpouring of the People." The most reassuring sign in the crowd was painted by the ladies: "a sea of upturned faces beaming with patriotic devotion." But within weeks the city was the site of dueling rather than unifying political rallies. While Republicans continued to stage loyalty meetings the Peace Democrats or Copperheads, led by Fernando Wood, called the public to endorse a quick end to hostilities and a disavowal of a "War for the Negro." Sometimes the opposing factions met within days of one another at the very same site, Cooper Institute. The Peace Democrats raised a barrage of charges against the Lincoln administration. Federal policies violated the free trade principle of elite Democratic merchants, angered the prosperous with their taxes, and exploited the poor with a conscription policy that offered relief only to those who could pay $300 for a substitute. The call to a "Grand Rally of the Democracy at the Cooper Institute" on April 7, 1863, said it all. "The people will assemble in their might to express their sentiment on the public questions of the day. Let all come who are Opposed to the Conscription Act Opposed to War for the Negro. In favor of Constitutional Rights of the Poor." Among those scheduled to address the people were "eminent men such as Fernando Wood." In rapid counterpoint the next Loyalist meeting was set for April 21 and festooned with flags, bands, cheers, and ladies in attendance. The Union offensive continued on May 1 with a day of fasting declared by Mayor Opdyke in support of President Lincoln. May 19 and June 4 found Wood addressing 4000 to 5000 people in a peace meeting. So it went until July 4, when the nation's birthday was celebrated in an understandably subdued spirit.

The tense quiet continued through Saturday, July 11, when the draft lottery was to commence in an Upper East Side armory.[61] The violence began as an organized protest at the site of the lottery by working men objecting to a grossly inequitable conscription law. As it moved through the industrial districts it picked up venom and spread throughout the city. Gestures of protest gave way to grotesque acts of personal violence perpetrated on human targets, especially the persons of African American men and women. The pogrom against blacks made this qualify as a vicious race riot. But the human targets of public rage were more various than these. Rich men identified by their fine clothes were among the early victims. Bodies of white women, presumed consorts of African American men or reputed prostitutes, were also assaulted. One of the most grisly accounts of personal mutilation involved Colonel O'Brien of the New York Police Department, whose torture and murder were recounted with sick fascination in the press. As one sensational newspaper account described it, O'Brien was pummeled to death, dragged through the rough pavement to his own backyard, mangled, trampled, and finally left a bloody gore on which women reputedly "committed the most atrocious violence." A repeat performance of horror occurred at Third Avenue and Forty-sixth Street, where a band of women allegedly gorged a soldier with a bayonet and assaulted Police Chief Kennedy. Representatives of the army and the police evoked particularly intense personal violence from a wide spectrum of the community.

In this the mob enacted a morbid retribution. The chief cause of death in the preceding days was the gunfire of the police and military. By riot's end some 10,000 troops were stationed in the city, bivouacking in Gramercy Park and Madison Square and patrolling Manhattan with a terrifying arsenal. "The howitzers belched forth on the crowd, the soldiers leveled their pieces, and the shelling of mince-balls was heard on every side. Men and women reeled and fell on the side-walks and in the streets. One woman with her child in her arms fell pierced with a bullet. The utmost consternation followed. The crowd knew from sad experience that the police would use their clubs but they seemed to think it hardly possible that the troops would fire point blank into their midst." This gruesome account was not issued as a criticism of the police action. Rather, it was one of many press homages to a "great victory," to "order restored." Another account began with the bombast "By the right flank company front, double quick charge" and ended with the observation "Broadway looked like a field of battle, the pavement was strewn thick with bleeding, prostrate forms." When the bodies were counted a minimum of 106 persons were dead, the vast majority felled by police or army bullets (fig. 22).[62]

Rescripting the People

Such ferocious civil warfare intensified rather than suspended the process whereby citizens formed associations, identities, and divisions among themselves. The middle decades of the century found the people of New York, New Orleans, and San Francisco still gathering in the streets, parade grounds, and city council chambers to piece together a civic mosaic. In the three years of political contention that preceded the draft riot New Yorkers had been sorting out their civic differences into the categories that would battle one another in July 1863. The simplest way of summarizing this excruciating process is to say that ethnic divisions were reconfigured according to a scheme of difference that was

Figure 22. Charge of the police at the *Tribune* office. *Harper's Weekly*, 1863.

now often called racial. Indeed, it could be argued that the principle thrust of American politics from municipal interregnum to the Civil War was to reconfigure the issue of race slavery into a political culture of racial dualism.[63]

Through most of the 1850s, as in the decades before, racial differences had certainly entered urban politics in the North. A number of historical investigations have identified the virulent racism of everything from the minstrel shows of the 1830s to the Democratic campaign rhetoric of the 1850s.[64] While resting at the foundation of the American political system—in the constitutional compromise with slavery and statutory limitations of the franchise—this racial divide had been but one among many elements of the fervid urban politics of the antebellum period. Racism thrived in theaters and workplaces without coming front and center on the stage of political debate. Unskilled workers, the poor, and immigrant Irish had battled blacks for jobs on the docks in New York for years. San Franciscans also dealt with race, in the persons of Chinese immigrants, as an economic conflict, the curse of cheap "coolie" labor. There, as elsewhere on the national political map, race was most often an attribute of slavery, coded either as competition with free labor, free soil, and free men or as the seed of sectional division. Even as the rise of the Republican Party made slavery the primary national issue, partisan loyalty was still more reflective of local ethnic and religious rivalries than purely racial animosities. The rage of Irish Catholic immigrants during the draft riots was in part a deflection of anger against the nativism of

Whigs, Know-Nothings, and Republicans onto African Americans. Democratic publicists put it aptly during the New York election of 1861 when they recited this Republican genealogy: "Schooled in Whiggery, graduated in Know-Nothingism and but just opened its eyes to Democracy."[65]

At midcentury slavery and its handmaid race encroached on the center of partisan discussion and then eclipsed and transformed more immediate local issues. With the presidential election of 1856 race entered political discourse on the shirttails of Republican efforts to curtail the expansion of slavery. During the fratricidal spring of 1857 New Yorkers heeded a call to "Assemble in the park" and "rally for the Freedom of the City" against the intrusions of the Republican legislators in Albany. In the process the proponents of home rule for New York City also unveiled a new logic and a new language of politics that would have corrosive effects on city democracy. This call to meeting attributes the restrictive city charter passed by the Albany legislature to the work of "Black Republicans." That phrase, which linked an upstart political party to a racial group, would be heard throughout the country in the 1850s. As early as 1854 the *New Orleans Delta* churned race into the volatile ethnic politics of the decade, chiding the North, "Mingle! Mingle! the proofs of a thorough amalgamation of the nigger-worshippers and the Know-Nothings in the free states are multiplying daily." In 1858 the *Bee* updated the roster of racial partisanship by labeling the "nigger worshippers" meeting in Philadelphia "Black Republicans."[66] This political triangulation, yoking blacks, Republicans, and the circumvention of local political autonomy, presaged the course of the municipal civil wars into another decade of even greater strife.

But even on the eve of Civil War the politics of race remained guarded, even suspect. In 1860 the right of suffrage for nonwhites was placed on the ballot once again in New York, but both Republicans and Democrats hesitated about embracing the issue and relegated it to a minor theme in that electoral campaign. One Republican procession was attacked from the sidelines by an anonymous charge of being "negro steelers," but party regulars skidded away from even discussing racial themes. Republicans in particular tried to disassociate themselves from the cause of Negro suffrage, which, yet again, went down to a quiet but crushing defeat.[67] Just a few months later, when the issue of slavery was magnified by the hardship of Civil War, racial differences became the center of angry attention. The ascendancy of race as a political category in New York closely follows the developments Philip Ethington has described for San Francisco.[68] Some New York Republicans posed the issue of race as a forthright call for equal rights. From his podium at the *Herald* Horace Greeley stated simply that "This is not Richmond but New York and here the Negro is a citizen, with rights which white men are bound to respect." But most Republicans presented the war as a defense of the Union, rather than the liberation of African Americans, and were reluctant to champion even the cause of emancipation, much less the civil rights of former slaves.

It was left to the Democratic opposition to make race and slavery a local issue, and they did so with deadly venom. In the winter of 1861 the *Herald* was calling the war effort the work of a "nigger worshipping faction" conducted "for the sole end of raising blacks to a level of the white race." By 1863 Copperhead rallies in New York were singing refrains like this: "Go in for the nigger/The sweet scented nigger/The wool-headed nigger/And the abolitionist crew." Other lyrics by Democratic wit and maverick Mike O'Reilly, himself adamantly opposed to the Copperheads, were no less cruel to African Americans. In support of enrolling African Americans in the military O'Reilly composed "Sambo's Right to Kill" in these rhymes: "Some tell us 'tis a burnen' shame/To make that naygers fight; And that the thrade of bein' killt/Belongs but to the white;/But as for me, upon my sowl/So liberal we are here/I'll let sambo be murthered instead of myself/On every day of the year."[69]

Meanwhile the press continued to advertise the Republican friendship for the Negro with notices of colored Republican meetings, celebrations of the Emancipation Proclamation, a Protestant fair for the colored orphan asylum. The draft riots were the crest of this wave of race consciousness, which did not ebb once order was restored on the streets of New York. In the wake of riots, the Republican elite of the Union League Club pointedly formed a Committee of Merchants for the Relief of Colored People, raised a black regiment, and honored it with a parade through Union Square. For Democratic loyalists, especially among immigrants and the urban poor, the sight of their traditional political enemies in ranks with African Americans only intensified their acrid racial consciousness. As slavery occupied the frontline of national government, race moved from the periphery to the core of local politics.[70]

For race to assume this prominence required some modification of the whole skein of urban difference. Occasionally, the press would display reproductions of the old kaleidoscope, such as this account of a rally of the Peace Democrats on June 4, 1863: "The crowd was such a one as can only be seen in New York. All classes of the community were represented, Irish laborers, longshoremen, members of the bench and the bar, dry good merchants and their clerks, clergymen, members of both branches of the common council, returned volunteers and large numbers of ladies who evidently viewed the proceedings with considerable interest." Democratic rallies throughout the era still jocularly bandied about the images of "Teutons, Celts and Sabbatarians" in their playful characterization of their constituents. Even the People's Party set up stands in English, French, and German at the campaign rallies of 1862.

But at the same time sectional and Civil War politics tended to draw lines of unity around these European ethnic distinctions. Fernando Wood seemed to anticipate a new American identity in 1861 when he entered a rally along with what was described as "a large accession to the meeting, in the shape and form of his Celtic supporters." Yet Wood promptly affirmed, "I have ever regretted any attempt to continue distinctive nationalities and national prejudices. I have always held and believed that when once the man merged with the citizen he merged his nationality and he became, as it were, dissolved into the general community, without any other appellations, rights or privileges than those which appertained to every other man in the community. (cheers)." Wood's invocation of universal citizenship was an act of either myopia or hypocrisy, for it drew a blunt line of exclusion around Europeans and between those he called "blacks and whites." Another Democratic rally of 1863 pointed awkwardly in this same direction. The speaker was a Professor Hitchcock who seemed a bit unsure of his audience. He began, "This continent has been peopled substantially by one race. Two-thirds of the inhabitants of the present states of our Union are Englishmen in blood." He was promptly challenged from the crowd: "Irishmen are not." Hitchcock went on: "The other third in the providence of God has been gradually distilled into one blood, and this grand amalgam that we hail as the new American people of history is the gift of God and the continent." After continuing to banter with the genial Irish contingent of the audience Hitchcock proclaimed, "There will be no more Englishmen, no more Irishmen, no more German . . . but they themselves bless god that they are American [loud and prolonged applause]."[71]

The distinctions between different European nationalities would not be easily or quickly forgotten, particularly not the category Irishman, and particularly when he was Catholic and of lowly social and economic status. Yet these categories were inevitably blurred by the rising significance of race in the war-torn city. The course of the sectional politics led New York's most expert interpreter of ethnic politics, Fernando Wood, to assert the priority of race, or more precisely, the political distinction between "Negro" and "white." He concluded in 1864 that "The Almighty has fixed the distinction of the races; the Almighty has made the black man inferior...and you cannot wipe out that distinction."[72]

In the heat of the Civil War, these newly prominent racial divisions among the people were more than semantic or ontological distinctions. In New York in the summer of 1863 they became raw civic wounds around which deadly prejudices festered. Some of the protagonists in Manhattan's civil war denied one another any semblance of human dignity. The mob denied human standing to the police and the Negro. "Kill the dammed nigger" was the infuriated howl raised at the sight of any unfortunate black man, woman, or child that was seen in the street, in the cars, on the omnibus. Even the most civilized gentlemen, such as the writer Nathaniel P. Willis, applied humanistic doctrine selectively. Of a crowd attacking a gun factory he said, "The lewd but pale and sickly young women scarcely decent in their ragged attire were impudent and scattered everywhere in the crowd. But what numbers of these poor classes are deformed, what number are made hideous by self-neglect and inferiority, and what numbers are paralytics, drunkards, imbeciles or idiotics, forlorn for their poverty-stricken abandonment of the world!... The female forms and features are made so frightful by sin, squalor and debasement." Although Willis took pains to discriminate between Irish American rioters and all their countrymen, he concluded with this tirade: "Dirty half drunken, brutal rowdies who are the leprosy of that fair-skinned race. They were the filthy pustules of an eruption on the Irish skin."[73]

Race and ethnicity may have been the divisions of the New York public that evoked the most vitriol and rancor in 1863, but they did not exhaust the popular imagination of differences. Politicians, voters, and the men and women of the streets were also struggling to define the economic distinctions among them. On the most immediate level the Civil War had exposed and dramatized the distinction between rich and poor that had been growing bolder throughout the interregnum. The escalation of municipal civil war in the late 1850s coincided with economic dislocations created by an expanding industrial economy and the fits and starts of railroad construction.[74] The year 1857 brought both a financial panic and a proliferation of trade-union organizing and strikes. With the outbreak of the Civil War, New York City became the central base of operation for the financiers who traded in arms and war supplies and profited from the rising national debt. The war-induced inflation and competitive labor conditions led the working poor to some serious thinking about their economic position. In March 1863 striking employees of the Erie Railroad Pier "gathered on the dock and discussed the condition of their families in a style that showed that they were really in need of increased wages. They refrained from actions of violence," said the *Herald* reporter, who went on to speculate that the striking dockworkers "perhaps would not have occasioned any serious disturbance were it not for the injudicious action of the railroad company, or their foremen, in subsequently employing negro laborers." This small skirmish was but a prelude of things to come. A popular spotlight was turned on wealthy New Yorkers in 1863 when the conscription law permitted those with $300 to buy their way out of military service. Class differences were on open display in the glow of the gunfire that summer. While riots spread through the industrial districts a group calling themselves simply "merchants and bankers" met at the Exchange and proceeded to form patrols of 100 men each to protect their property.[75]

Wartime also induced politicians to ruminate about the increasing economic distances between their constituents. Mozart Hall resolved at public meeting to resist the "infamous distinction between rich and poor." One Edmond Blankman told a Democratic rally on May 19 that when his boss was buying out of his patriotic duty he "would be d——d if he answered the Presidents call to go and carry on a war for the nigger." Characteristically, Fernando Wood had an astute analysis of the situation. Already in 1861 he planted a class interpretation of the war in the minds of the public, saying that the Republicans were an abolitionist party bent on bringing "black labor in competition with white." By 1863 he was arguing that the war was not just "for the nigger" but in the interest of the bankers who funded the rising federal debt. Wood was clearly fumbling for an economic explanation of the municipal chaos around him. He resorted to such terms as *classes, interests,* and *ruling element* to describe the realignment of power at the nation's financial center. Horace Greeley, perhaps the most perspicacious social commentator among the Republicans, stuck with classical economic theory and dismissed the grievances of the working poor with the comment, "if longshoremen or any other class of laborer do not choose to work with Negroes they need not. No law compels them. But the Negro, as well as the white man, has a right to work for whoever will employ and pay him, and the law, and the courts, and police, and public opinion, ought to protect him in that right and will. Dislike the Negro if you must, but you and he are equally under law [which] expects your obedience, and will require it by force of necessity."[76]

In sum the Civil War had sponsored this crash course in the study of those differences that social scientists have variously labeled class and race. Contemporaries used these concepts in a tentative and pragmatic way, suggesting that city people were straining to find names for themselves, one another, and the differences between them. They were, in the process, reaching beyond those more motley and particular social variations that could link up along a parade route and were beginning to grasp at more abstract and hierarchical distinctions in status and power. In 1863 in New York this was not a very civil project. The new categories became rhetorical cannon fodder in a grisly war at home. And the most decisive consequence of this recharting of the boundaries of the public was brutally clear in New York: Those of African American decent were not only denied full and equal citizenship, they were driven out of town in fear for their lives. In New York the political language of race had been used in the most destructive, now all-to-familiar way, the way of scapegoating.[77] New Yorkers of African origins were made to bear the onus of deep social divisions and real conflicts of material interest, equity, and justice among Euro-Americans. These racial differences, which were constructed politically by both Democrats and Republicans, simultaneously obscured the more various divisions among the people and converted them into the most virulent civic animosities.

The social differences that became more prominent during the Civil War were more than eruptions of hatred and vindictive warfare. After all, race came to occupy the center of American politics as part of a movement to end slavery: It was a civic distinction that emerged in the process of attempting to remedy a grievous affront to the principles of democracy and equality. In other words racial distinctions could also operate as levers of emancipation and standpoints from which to demand equal rights. In New Orleans, long a city where relations between those of European and African descent were intricate and entangled, the occupation of the Union army brought racial difference directly into democratic public discourse and decision making. Free people of color, some of whom were slave owners or supporters of the Confederacy, began the difficult process of building a political alliance with ex-slaves. The first challenge came from free *gens de couleur* who raised the demand for the franchise on behalf of their relatively privileged group. By 1864 they had collected 5000 signatures on a petition to confer the right to vote for those of "African descent," provided they had served in the Union army, paid taxes, and showed "intellectual fitness."[78] Although such a restrictive suffrage was more stringent than even the voting rights of non-whites in New York State, it was a first step in a long march toward full citizenship made by African Americans of the South on their own behalf.

Augurs of a more optimistic future could be seen in the streets of New Orleans during wartime. Parades were described as rainbows of all colors, ages, and sexes, while racially mixed public meetings formed in Lafayette Square and City Hall as well as Congo Square. In January 1865, for example, a young and vigorous black press invited "All colored citizens and societies" to assemble in Lafayette Square "in full Regalia" to celebrate emancipation in Missouri and Tennessee. By 1864 elite free men of color began to entertain alliances irrespective of previous conditions of servitude. Edward H. Durrell, a wealthy free person of color, enunciated this policy clearly: "We are to work no distinction of races, no distinction of color." When men and women of African descent could assume a standpoint of their own in the public spaces of a city such as New Orleans, race had become a doubled-edged political category; it was another one of those democratic distinctions that simultaneously decried discrimination and built on social differences. The work of revising the racial restrictions of public life was under way at the same time in San Francisco, where the black newspaper the *Pacific Appeal* demanded simply that the word "white" be erased from all guarantees of constitutional rights.[79]

Many "white" Americans were also casting about for a new political identity during the 1860s. The war had fully exposed the fissures in ethnic identity. The Irish would find their compatriots arrayed all along the political spectrum in 1863, not just among the Copperheads but in the Sixty-ninth Regiment, which fought loyally to preserve the Union. Not just the archetypal rioter but also the commander of the police forces, Commissioner Kennedy, bore an Irish name. In the heat of the urban battlefield both ethnic and racial identities seemed to splinter along class lines. The rioting Irishman or woman was likely to be among the poor. It was a working man with a distinct interest who called for "White only docks" in the 1860s. The rioting concentrated, furthermore, in the east-side factory district where the scale of production and the proximity of work, home, and neighborhood were forging something of a self-conscious proletariat. Already in April 1863 "working men" had claimed the central public podium of Cooper Institute and prepared to form "a grand central organization." Their expressed purpose was to ensure that the "rights of labor" be "properly protected from the ravages of Capital." In the wake of the riots the press was full of signs that New York trades were mobilizing: "Umbrella Sewer's Strike," "railroad strike," and "a labor movement" that enrolled "marble manufacturers, lithographers, iron-molders, carpenters, clothes-cutters, working-women, plumbers and laboringmen, in various places in this city and Brooklyn." According to the *Tribune* this mobilization bore no relationship to riots past, for "The best of order has prevailed." This incipient class consciousness of New Yorkers was not especially precocious. The war had sped up trade unionism in New Orleans as well, where working men became major allies of the Radical Republicans. The Civil War may not have forged a class-conscious American proletariat, but it did expose the cleavages around which it might take form.[80]

Finally, as a trail of evidence winding through the foregoing pages have anticipated, gender had a new currency in city politics at the end of the interregnum. The familiar political manipulations of feminine symbols were deployed with a special urgency during wartime. A Union general drummed these chords to the desired effect in May 1863: "it is very cheering to see so many Patriotic faces here, and more especially the patriotic face of the ladies (Applause). I am sure that we are all right when they are present with us. I rely as much on their patriotism as I do upon that of the gentlemen, and perhaps a little more (laughter and applause)." But the war also brought women into the public in their own name and in their own right. April 1861 found Southern as well as Northern women forming their own public meetings: The headlines spoke of "mass meetings of the Ladies," "another Ladies Movement," "Patriotic Meeting of the Ladies," and "Ladies Military Faire at the Odd Fellows Hall." When New York was heating up toward riot in the spring and summer of 1863, the meetings of Copperheads and Union men were interspersed with calls to attend convocations at Cooper Institute of the National Loyal Woman League. This was not only an organization of women but also the source of one of the most radical Republican contributions to the heated debates of 1863. The LWL was the most vocal champion of emancipation and enfranchisement for African Americans in New York City. The public meeting, which the *Times* misnamed "The Ladies League," used the wartime opportunity to do something even more radical: It placed the demand for women's rights directly before the urban public for the first time. This bold assertion could be read right off the front page in the words of Elizabeth Cady Stanton and Susan B. Anthony. "If the wife or mother cheerfully lays her loved ones on the altar, she must be impelled to it by a living faith in the justice of her cause." These relative latecomers to the urban public stage claimed the "Rights and privileges of equal citizens" not only for blacks but for the sex that would no longer be "placed at the mercy of a legislation in which they are not represented."[81]

Between 1850 and 1865 the citizens of New York, New Orleans, and San Francisco had ricocheted from one civil war to another. They had barely a chance to catch their breath before local conflicts were caught up in the whirlwind of a national politics that would forever alter the terms of democratic contention. A look around the urban battlefield near the close of the Civil War shows not only women's rights advocates but also radical white men, newly empowered blacks, and militant workers assembling around the borders of the public sphere. Granted, the center of public life was occupied by a vast war machine, fortified police forces, and suspended civil liberties, but sometimes the most outcast of the people won a skirmish in this increasingly high-powered politics. Some less powerful New Yorkers won an ugly Pyrrhic victory during the New York draft riots. They prompted a week-long public discussion of the costs of war to the poor, secured a municipal appropriation of $2.5 million for purchasing substitute soldiers, and established the principle that the city could expend funds for the direct remedy of social inequality. The process of recasting the people, contesting their interests, and rediscovering the public did not end at the urban Appomattox. The interregnum may have culminated in a more militarized state and disciplined city, but city people were also quickly finding ways to combat and manipulate the new political structures. In the process they began also to redraw the lines of difference among themselves and to create new vantage points from which to confront the modern municipal organization of power. Not only the politics of the state but the public outlines of race, class, and gender were setting the terms for a new urban drama. Civil war had battered the democratic process and incurred staggering human cost, but the indomitable urban public also spawned some new political possibilities.

PART THREE

"The Huge Conglomerate Mass"

Democracy Contained and Continued,
1866–1880

CHAPTER 5

The "Vague and Vast Harmony" of People in Space

The myriad political possibilities released by the civil wars of the mid-nineteenth century would be played out in an altered urban space and a revised civic culture. The map of this distinctly modern setting of urban politics was drawn with a new precision after the Civil War, not just in words and sketches but through photography. In 1877 one of the most accomplished masters of the new art, Eadweard Muybridge, set up his camera atop Nob Hill in San Francisco and created a 360 degree panoramic reproduction of the city. At the time San Francisco harbored less than a quarter million residents. It was not much larger than New York City a half-century earlier, when lower Manhattan was a relatively readable space, furrowed with integrating public thoroughfares such as Broadway and the Bowery and linked to the central space of City Hall Park. From Muybridge's vantage point atop a hill in the compact sun-drenched city of San Francisco one might still expect to capture a sparkling, transparent urban vision.

Muybridge's camera picked up the sharp lines and intersecting planes of thousands of structures laid out on tidy thoroughfares. Not a cloud in the sky, piece of refuse in the street, or a stray human being marred this silver-plate image. The cool serenity of this urban view, and many like it produced in the 1870s, would seem to banish all memories of vigilantes and civic wars and reassure citizens that civility had returned. Still, one can easily get lost in the vast expanse of uniform housing along the hillsides and feel at sea in the undifferentiated private spaces. It takes a magnifying glass and considerable patience to find a commodious public

183

space in either Muybridge's panorama or the city itself. Portsmouth Plaza was out of sight, in disrepair, and threatened with being sold off for tax revenue. Plans for a new city hall had not gotten much further than digging a foundation and leaving piles of upturned soil, "the sand-lots" that would become a major site of conflict just about the time Muybridge closed his shutter on San Francisco. The index of places attached to Muybridge's panorama is no more helpful in sighting public urban spaces. The list of significant buildings consists almost entirely of the private addresses of rich businessmen. The preference for private over public space is taken to an almost ridiculous extreme in Muybridge's photographic strategy: He set up his camera not just among the elite on Nob Hill but in the bedroom of Mark Hopkins's mansion, thereby conferring upon this classic example of panoramic photography the unlikely name "boudoir view of San Francisco."[1]

This chapter began as a search for a postwar public vantage point on the cities of New York and New Orleans as well as San Francisco. It was propelled by the expectation that even the most anonymous city offers its residents some more comprehensive perspective than the bedroom window in the mansion of a railroad tycoon. Somewhere in the sea of residences bounded by thin streets, city people found their way to common ground on which to rebuild the public life that had been eroded by years of civil war. Surely, at street level one would also find some of the variety and color of the urban kaleidoscope. It was difficult but not impossible to get from the civic heights occupied by Mark Hopkins and Eadweard Muybridge to the city sidewalks. The everyday life of city people in the late nineteenth century was obscured as much as it was represented by the growing number of professional interpreters of urban life. One journalist, writing in 1883, called the urban ambiance of the late nineteenth century a "vague and vast harmony." The people who inhabited this space were no more than a "huge conglomerate mass."[2] The perception of order in the city was often purchased at the price of increasing remoteness from the everyday life of the people, be it the heights at which photographers positioned their cameras or the professional distance assumed by journalists and bureaucrats. Sometimes, in some cities, such reassuring images were not available at any price. The popular photographic genre of the panoramic view was never successfully imposed on the full expanse of New York or even New Orleans. The sprawling growth of these cities during the late nineteenth century could not be squeezed into one comprehensive image, not even a neat sequence of photographs such as Muybridge's mosaic of San Francisco.

Thus, the following chapter will consist largely of a pastiche of snap-shots, each attempting to order the modern city by an act of intellectual abstraction and selection. These glimpses will include, in addition to photographs, the urban views drawn by statisticians, architects, urban designers, writers, and journalists. These cognitive schemes (no less than the linear maps and bird's-eye views of the antebellum period) do not present a realistic urban portrait; but neither did they conjure up the ideal type of centered and segmented spaces imagined in urban plans drawn before 1850. When the civil wars of the 1850s and 1860s had sub-sided, they left only scattered rudiments of a new way of seeing the het-erogeneity of the city. This vast and vague harmony deserves attention as a record of changing urban consciousness and as the essential context for the postwar reconstruction of public life. The civil wars, followed by the rapid growth of the urban population, disrupted the spatial foundations of meeting-place democracy. The city of the late nineteenth century turned out to be more compacted than centered, more a conglomerate than a segmented whole; it challenged urban residents to find new places in which to express themselves and confront one another (figs. 23–25).

Counting the Masses and Mapping the Spaces

The people of New York, New Orleans, and San Francisco might well suffer a kind of civic vertigo after the civil wars. Still reeling from a decade of municipal conflict, and sharing city space with tens of thou-sands of newcomers, they lacked the cognitive and social mechanisms for ordering the metropolis many of us rely on today, not the least of which are class and racial segregation, specialized land use, and urban planning. In the absence of some spatial containment of differences ur-ban chroniclers often spoke of the city population as simply a "motley multitude." One of the most assiduous attempts to order the urban masses was the work of fledgling social scientists at the U.S. Bureau of the Census. It was under the direction of veteran New York City re-former, George Waring, that the bureau compiled two comprehensive volumes on the nation's cities in 1880.[3] The 1870s had marked a water-shed in the flow of peoples into America's cities: New York for the first time topped one million in population, having grown by a rate of 25 per-cent in the preceding decade. New Orleans and San Francisco were much smaller, not even reaching the quarter-million mark as of 1880. Yet their rate of growth was more dramatic than New York's. San Francisco grew at a rate of 163 percent in the 1870s. After the Civil War New

Figure 23. Panel from the Muybridge panorama, San Francisco, 1877. Courtesy of the Bancroft Library.

Figure 24. Panel from panorama of New Orleans, ca. 1870. Courtesy The Historic New Orleans Collection, Museum/ Research Center.

Figure 25. Panel from panorama of New York, 1876. Collection of the New York Historical Society.

Orleans jolted back from the stagnation of the 1850s with an inundation of migrants that continued through Reconstruction.[4]

In the 1870s and 1880s the Bureau of the Census surveyed these great cities looking for ways of reining the masses into categories based on such characteristics as occupation, national origin, and previous condition of servitude. Much of the growth in cities conformed to preestablished patterns of population movement, flowing chiefly along the Atlantic route from northern Europe. The foreign-born portions of the population had stabilized at high rates in the 1860s and 1870s, and most immigrants hailed from the now familiar places, Ireland, England, and Germany. As the immigrant population matured and produced a second generation, the cities' sex ratios also became more balanced. Even the demographics of San Francisco had become somewhat domesticated by 1880, when there were at least two women for every three men. In all three cities most of the women had also assumed a settled domestic position in the urban maelstrom. Only a small proportion of the female population, overwhelmingly young and unmarried, reportedly left their homes to enter the paid labor force. While the majority of these working women joined the feminine ranks of domestic service or laundry workers, they constituted one third of the industrial work force in New York.[5]

The occupations of men alerted the census takers of the 1870s and 1880s to more dramatic changes in social structure. Measured by their dominant sectors of employment, New York and San Francisco were maturing as industrial economies. The manufacturing sector represented the single largest employer in both these cities by 1880. The garment industry remained a major worksite, while heavy industries such as rails, steel, and machines grew up in and around the metropolis. Although the size of firms remained small, it was growing and averaged over twenty workers in New York, where some factories employed hundreds. Although the census takers would not use the terminology, they were tabulating the creation of an American proletariat, a mass force of wage laborers. The single largest unskilled occupation among men was "laborer," an undifferentiated, probably unstable job category that the Census Bureau classified under professional or personal service. It harbored around 35,000 in New York, 15,000 in New Orleans, 9000 in San Francisco. The most populous work places in the industrial sectors involved some level of skill, jobs such as the cigar and tobacco workers and the city builders themselves, the carpenters and joiners. In the big city of New York the undifferentiated and massive quality of occupational classification had come to characterize the nonmanual labor force as well. In 1880 over 45,000 citizens of Gotham were identified simply as clerks, this in a total labor force of 513,000 where fewer than 3000 could claim the skilled and prestigious nonmanual job of doctor. The rapid growth and numerical domination of jobs with generic labels such as laborer and clerk suggest that occupation was losing its more precise social moorings in traditional skills or small-scale business. Work was, in contemporary terms, increasingly "massified."[6]

Reading down the columns of census figures for New Orleans conveys the impression of a relative economic backwater. In this Southern city the category of manufacturing accounted for only about one in four jobs, and the modern industries—railroads, steel, iron, and machinery—employed fewer than 500 workers. Yet however undeveloped New Orleans's manufacturing sector, its postwar economy was undergoing a wrenching transformation. In 1870 the census takers registered this rupture statistically as the inundation of over 15,000 simple laborers—almost twice the number in the smaller labor force of San Francisco and almost one fifth the city's workers (as opposed to fewer than one in ten in New York). The source of this influx was obvious: the migration of former slaves off the plantations and into the city seeking employment. This sudden transition from servitude to a wage economy was one of the most cataclysmic changes an urban economy could experience. Moreover, New Orleans, like the rest of the nation, could not escape the juggernaut of American industrialization now in full swing. If nothing else, the depression of 1873 would notify citizens as well as census takers that the economic well-being of every city was hostage to massive dislocations in a nationally integrated manufacturing economy.

The demographic shift in New Orleans was more than a simple matter of economics. The Census Bureau also registered this transformation under the column headed "Colored." New Orleans's colored population climbed sharply after the war and continued to grow for the rest of the century. Before the war New Orleans had become a predominantly white city with only one in seven residents of African origin, the majority of whom did not compete in the free-labor market but were enslaved. The colored population of New Orleans doubled in the 1860s to more than 50,000 and by 1870 accounted for almost 27 percent of all residents. They were all free men and women. The African American population in New York and San Francisco was, by contrast, numerically small, accounting for under 5 percent of the total. The latter city, however, made a distinctive and sizable contribution to the new category of colored. The 1880 census report specified that the colored included persons of Asian as well as African descent. The population of Asian ancestry was almost all concentrated in California, particularly San Francisco, where the Chinese numbered 12,000 or 8 percent of the total. The publications of the Census Bureau for 1880 found this tiny portion of the national population significant enough to provoke some new strategies for sorting out the American masses. In the table headed "Population by Specified Age, Sex, and General Nativity" it inserted the term *race*. This ominous word replaced the prewar classification called "Population by Color and Condition," under which the people were divided into categories denoted by the social terms *free* and *slaves* as well as three gradations of complexion, black, mulatto, and white. Before the Civil War and the Emancipation Proclamation had undermined this system of categorizing the people immigrants from Asia had a rather ambiguous status: In one chart the Chinese were enumerated by "nativity" in the same tabulation as other immigrants, and in another they were identified by color. By 1880 they were simply placed in the tabulation of the "races" and in the column labeled "Colored," which included Chinese, Japanese, and civilized Indians.[7]

The Census Bureau was searching for ways to classify people after the Civil War. The charts of differences once based on place of origin and condition of servitude were being reconfigured in terms of race and pigmentation and increasingly polarized into two classifications, white and colored. This stratagem expressed more than the mental gymnastics of statisticians or transparent variations in physical characteristics. It reflected new practices of constructing urban differences. The Chinese, for example, were a tiny population, small even in San Francisco and almost invisible elsewhere. Yet they were the magnet of intense public scrutiny. "Chinatown" was the only segment of the city singled out for intense observation within the relatively monotonous panorama of San Francisco.[8] This pocket of dense settlement near the city's center also captured the attention of journalists and writers. Benjamin Lloyd, surveyor of the "Lights and Shades in San Francisco," placed the Chinese decidedly in the darker quarter of the city and estimated their numbers at 60,000. The exaggerated importance given to the Chinese immigrant and the prominence of the vocabulary of race are clues to the transformed meaning of difference after the American Civil War.[9]

The inordinate attention given migrants from Asia was due in part to their concentrated settlement in a highly visible urban setting. Chinatown was like a cognitive anchor amid the tides of urban growth. The Far East may have been one of the least crowded points of debarkation for the United States, but San Francisco's Chinatown gave a clear geographical representation to at least one of the myriad differences that characterized the big city. Benjamin Lloyd's map of San Francisco devoted eight full chapters to the Chinese minority. Without traveling outside a small radius of the old urban center of Portsmouth Square he found an unusually pure distillation of ethnic and racial difference. Not only were most of the city's Chinese squeezed into one small readable space, but they held almost exclusive title to this urban turf. Recent arrivals from the Far East also branded the pavement with their own habits and manners of using urban space. To the outsider the first sign of Chinese urban geography was population density. Lloyd estimated that an eight by ten room in Chinatown could harbor a family of five or six or bunks for six to eight lodgers. He and others noted that these domiciles were arranged in an equally economical fashion, knit together not just by the usual grid of streets but by a fine tissue of alleys. The alley became a kind of material synecdoche of Chinese character: "vice and abomination, the filth and misery, are not prominently visible but are hid from public gaze in the dark alleys that beset the broad public streets." Another account of the "Mysteries and Miseries" of American cities read a similar moral message off the same spatial pattern. After seeing the alleys and inner courts where the Chinese cooked at iron boxes, James Buel penetrated into rooms where immigrants slept on shelflike cots and moved on through narrow halls to opium dens and cubicles of prostitution stacked together like egg crates. He pronounced these physical spaces of Chinatown "Cauldrons of Offensive rottenness which simmer and evaporate" (fig. 26).[10]

Chinese leaders did not dispute that theirs was a distinctive way of organizing city space. When asked to report on their living arrangements in San Francisco, a committee of Chinese merchants issued a map of social geography that was indeed foreign to most Americans. They estimated that all but a handful of immigrants belonged to one of six Chinese companies, each of which provided hundreds of men with living space and domestic necessities along with employment. These large, barracks-like structures, sometimes ornamented like Chinese temples, featured common kitchens, dining rooms, and sleeping chambers for male laborers. The sympathetic Protestant minister, the Reverend William Speer, explained that these structures were called "Ui-kun," or company house, and were "evidently of Chinese architecture." The Chinese immigrants had occupied a central portion of the Western capital of the United States in so distinctive a way that they lent an unusual spatial clarity to the urban mass. The Chinese pattern of segregation was in fact so clear and self-contained that it could be called a "town" unto itself.[11]

The attempt to give a spatial order to ethnic difference rarely yielded such clear boundaries after the Civil War. New Yorkers, for example, spoke of places such as "the American Ward," "Nigger Hill," and "Dutch Hill." Yet these categories were quite vague and flaccid: A hill or even a ward was something less than a town, and such ethnic labels for urban space were inexact if not downright misnomers. The so-called American ward was the ninth around Greenwich Village, which still harbored over 15,000 foreigners in 1870, almost one third of the total population of that election district. Dutch Hill was also a misnomer: It was neither Dutch nor German but, if anything, dominated by Irish residents. In smaller cities attempts to map the city by ethnicity were even more imprecise. In New Orleans ethnicity and race were less readable than in the past. The unification of the once-divided municipalities, followed by Yankee occupation, blurred the once-stark boundary between Americans and Creoles, slave quarters and poorman's hovels. In San Francisco the only patches of ethnic or class concentration outside Chinatown were

Figure 26. Chinatown alley. M. Blaisdell ca. 1880. Courtesy of the Bancroft Library.

also vague and mottled: the association of the poor, workers, and Irish in the region south of Market, for instance, as well as the huddling of some native-born citizens in a middle-class development on Rincon Hill.[12]

Signs of class or economic differences were becoming clearer than the ethnic borders of city space. In New York the "Americans" of Greenwich Village were middle class, and the "Nigger Hill" dwellers were poor squatters whose hovels would be bulldozed away to create Central Park. Perhaps the most dramatic signal of social differences to appear on the city skyline after the Civil War was the erection of ostentatious mansions for the rich. Nob Hill in San Francisco was the most garish example, unmistakably home to the zenith of San Francisco wealth and society, the railroad tycoons of Huntington, Stanford, Crocker, Hopkins. The Big Four competed with one another to build the largest, best-fortified mansion atop the city and then fenced their properties in granite, brownstone, or brass. James Flood, whose fortune was made in mines rather than rails, won the height contest, erecting a tower of thirty-four feet alongside his palace. In New York as well the map of wealth that would endure a century appeared as the rich began to build their mansions on Fifth Avenue and line their facades with marble, which eclipsed brownstone as the insignia of an affluent neighborhood. The opulent Fifth Avenue mansion of dry goods merchant A. T. Stewart covered a space sufficient for the tenements that housed hundreds of the poor downtown. The chiaroscuro of class grew more dramatic in the late nineteenth century, be it measured in figures on the distribution of wealth or in contrasts between Fifth Avenue and Nigger Hill. But symbols of class differences were not the same as spatial barriers between the rich and poor: Few city people could erect granite fences between themselves and the masses. Pockets of wealth and poverty dwelt side by side in every city. The dispersion of zones of impoverishment throughout the city was reflected in increasing use of now-familiar terms *slums* or *tenement district*. This urban argot indicated a simultaneous concentration of poverty and its dispersal beyond any single fixed and centralized place such as Five Points a generation earlier (figs. 27–28).[13]

As late as the 1870s the polyglot population of America's great cities could not be sorted out into tidy niches. Kenneth Scherzer, an assiduous historical geographer of New York City, has concluded that although the class and ethnic patterning of city space became perceptibly more segmented after the Civil War, residents were seldom afforded either homogeneous neighborhoods or a cushion of distance from people different

Figure 27. Stewart's mansion. From Frederick Lightfoot, ed., *Nineteenth-Century New York in Rare Photographic Views.*

from themselves. The native born, for example, never found a perfect refuge in Greenwich Village, and the Irish immigrants never barricaded themselves inside an urban village all their own. The people of late nineteenth-century American cities still lived close together in a world of obstinate differences.[14]

Building toward Modernity

Yet the turf on which they encountered one another was changing in undeniable ways. The transformation of the built environment took off in the real estate boom after the war, stagnated in the prolonged depression of the 1870s, and sped up dramatically at decade's end. In New York and San Francisco builders and businessmen found a way to expand the boundaries of urban settlement. Slowly the shape of Gotham began to swell in a vertical as well as a horizontal direction. By 1864 half the city's population resided north of Fourteenth Street and pressed up the island on both the east and west side. Driven by the power of steam to move the granite that covered much of the island and propelled by the ambi-

Figure 28. Five Points, 1875. From Frederick Lightfoot, ed., *Nineteenth-Century New York in Rare Photographic Views.*

tions of real estate entrepreneurs, development on the west side of Manhattan began to rival the earlier northward expansion along Fifth Avenue in the east. By April of 1868 no less than $6 million in property was sold along the Park in the Upper West Side.[15]

When real estate investment resumed in the late 1870s, this premature speculation began to pay off and further transform the cityscape. The tenements numbered more than 15,000 by 1865, when they were joined by their high-rent cousin the apartment house. Late in the 1860s plans for something called the Parisian Dwelling Building appeared among requests for building permits in Manhattan. Also known as French Flats, these were the first examples of multifamily dwellings designed to be shared by middle-class families. They were not only more spacious and sumptuous than tenements, they towered above them, rising to six, eight, and then ten stories by 1876, when more than 200 such modern edifices dotted the island.[16] By 1880 the plans were set in place for what contemporaries called scientific compactness in residential architecture. The designs of Henry Hardenbergh, including the Vancorlear, completed in 1880, and his more memorable Dakota, occupied square blocks, were equipped with passenger elevators, sat close to the street, and turned inward around a private courtyard. The new multifamily buildings presented a rather daunting face to the public: The Dakota, built in 1884, rose nine stories and occupied 200 square feet flush with the sidewalk on Seventy-second Street. With a facade of rusticated masonry and brick it stood like a medieval tower uprooted from the countryside and glued to the urban pavement.[17] Buildings of less architectural authority but similar scale were advancing steadily over the cityscape: Fewer than one in ten of the thousands of new dwellings constructed in New York were single-family houses. The majority, numbering more than 5000, were multifamily units designed for the middle classes and were now called apartment buildings. The rest were called tenements, the older, more plebeian species of the now quintessential Manhattan residence, a single edifice that housed multiple families in their separate compartments. The plan of the typical apartment building kept public entries and lobbies purposefully small, provided separate service stairways, and funneled residents quickly into their separate spaces. It was an ingenious method of imbuing shared space with a sense of privacy.[18]

The rise of apartment houses and tenements prepared the way for an architectural assault upon the heavens. By 1880 the built urban environment was not yet scraping the sky, but residential and office structures of ten stories were not uncommon in Manhattan. The business as well as the family life of New Yorkers began to be boxed up and piled high by the 1870s, when structures such as the Western Union, Equitable Life Insurance, and New York Tribune Buildings punctured the sky at Wall Street and midtown. The skyline was lower and more uniform in San Francisco and New Orleans, where frame houses rose one to three stories and whose major expression of architectural fashion was a flourish of Italianate trim. Still, each city regarded the formidable facades of apartment house and office building as the symbol of urban progress. In San Francisco it was the Palace Hotel on Market that presented this lofty ambition of man over urban space. There and on Canal Street in New Orleans, the tall, uniform, commercial facade became the clearest sign of the new scale and authoritative manner of building the city.[19]

One of San Francisco's more formidable highrise buildings, a six-story granite structure erected on Montgomery Street in 1876, was the office of a corporation called the Real Estate Associates. TREA was a relatively modest example of the large corporate developers, including John Jacob Astor and Company in New York, that were reshaping cities across the country. This small San Francisco company alone built some 1000 residential units during the real estate boom of the 1870s. Constructed at least a block at a time, of uniform style and prefabricated materials, these expanses of single-family dwellings would become the typical housing stock of the Bay City by the 1880s and would be counted as one of the city's great charms a century later. Similar forces were at work in New Orleans, where spatial limits spawned another compact form of residential architecture, the shot-gun house. These structures lined up rooms from the front to the back of narrow lots and filled up the constricted spaces of the old city with tightly packed rows of small, single-family dwellings. The architectural changes of the 1870s—San Francisco's Victorians, New York's apartment houses, and the shot-guns of New Orleans—all converted large sectors of city space for concentrated domestic uses.[20]

The necessary handmaiden of this new architecture and developing pattern of urban land use was a new technology, especially elevators and rail lines. In 1880 the Census Bureau was adding up the length of urban rail transportation to over 100 miles in New York and New Orleans. In all three cities hundreds of streetcars carried tens of thousands of passengers along hundreds of miles of pavement. Plans for a rapid transit system that were drafted amid the technological hubris of the Civil War began to reach fruition in New York soon thereafter. By the 1860s no fewer than six railroads were carrying passengers up and down Manhattan. The elevated, which opened in 1868, was moving three million passengers a year as far north as 129th Street in Harlem by 1880. The march of progress also gave other cities their signatures: By 1880 four cable car lines defied the steep grades of San Francisco streets, and in New Orleans the St. Charles Line was soon winding its picturesque way from downtown through the garden district and on into the newly annexed town of Lafayette.[21]

But the structural and technological innovations were more the signs of things to come than the parameters of everyday existence for most city people in the 1870s, especially outside New York. Even there most architects and builders seldom scaled above six to ten stories, despite the availability of the elevator for over twenty years. Preferring what Thomas Bender and William Taylor have called a "horizontal civic style," New Yorkers left the higher reaches of the sky to be developed by the corporate business sector in the next century.[22] As of 1880 the outlines of the city changed in less visually striking but critical ways. Expanded territory, compacted residential buildings, and rapid movement of more people and more goods was creating a dense, fractured, and frenetic life in the streets.

Although the everyday public life of New York, New Orleans, and San Francisco was not yet shadowed over by skyscrapers, neither was it anchored in the old centering civic landmarks. The rapid propagation of private dwellings put the old integrating elements off center and in the shadows. San Francisco's Portsmouth Plaza and New Orleans's Jackson Square were clouded in civic gloom. Police Chief Hiram Ellis said of the former, "the old-time center of town is surrounded almost entirely by the Chinese" and has become a "great reservoir of moral social and physical pollution." References to the Vieux Carré are extremely rare in the press after the war; Lafayette Square and the American quarter were also uninviting to many. The Confederates found these public spaces draped in the shame of defeat, occupied by Yankees, Radical Republicans, and freed men and women. The latter had ventured from the confines of Congo Square and stood their ground in Lafayette Square and the Federal Customhouse on lower Canal. To former slave owners, this apparition in the civic center was a sacrilege. The monuments of antebellum democracy suffered further indignities: photographs of Canal Street in the 1880s find the statue of Henry Clay lost in a snarl of traffic and electric wires (fig. 29).

New York's traditional center of civic identity, City Hall, was just too far south of the center of new settlement to be a real spatial anchor after the Civil War. In 1870 George Ellington dismissed the once-cherished grounds outside as just the lounging place for the human refuse from the noxious concert saloons and dens of vice nearby. The points of sociability and the arteries of traffic that formerly moored the flow of people also lost some of their luster after the war. The Battery was placed in the darker region of Matthew Hale Smith's *Sunshine and Shadow in New York*. Already in 1869 he pronounced the old promenade a ghost of its former self: "The grass has disappeared, the iron fence is broken, the wall promenade near the sea gone to decay, freshly-arrived foreigners, ragged, tattered and drunken men and women set under the old trees and the Battery is now as unsafe a place at night as can be found in the city." Broadway was the most resilient civic symbol and remained a spatial magnet for visitors and residents alike. Still throbbing with the vitality of the cosmopolitan city, it was the "Reflex of the Republic" to the usually dour city cartographer Junius Browne and a place where George Ellington said you would meet everyone in the course of a year. Yet there was a certain taint of alienation in descriptions of Broadway in the

Figure 29. Canal Street, Clay statue, 1884. Courtesy The Historic New Orleans Collection, Museum/Research Center.

1870s. George Ellington warned that your chances of meeting up with prostitutes were very high on the Great, not-so-White Way. To Browne, Broadway was the touchstone of urban America's frenetic pace: "hustling, feverish, crowded, ever-changing." "How the ranks and antagonisms of life jostled each other on that crowded pave! Saints and sinners, mendicants and missionaries, priests and poets, courtesans and chiffoniers, burglars and bootblacks, move side by side in the multifarious throng. They touch at the elbows, with all the world between them." (Tellingly, Browne's catalog of urban differences featured pairs of moral opposites, not the omnibus of variation common in antebellum urban chronicles.) Browne was even more suspicious of the Bowery, the other renowned New York artery that once joined Broadway in a spatial gesture of diversity and commonalty, movement, and connection. On the Bowery, he said, "the order and form, and cast and deference, shaken and confused in Broadway, are broken into fragments in the Bowery and trampled under foot." (These fragments did not strike Browne as the makings of a kaleidoscope.)[23]

With the old landmarks and arteries that once knit the city together showing such wear in the 1870s New Yorkers looked elsewhere for a spatial ballast. The 1876 guidebook *New York as It Was and as It Is* did find a few notable improvements in the open spaces, such as a new monument in Union Square and a fountain in City Hall Park. It ignored City Hall itself, however, and looked to the police department as the nerve center of a dangerous city, whose crime statistics were duly noted. Similarly, the only public buildings listed in the directory of San Francisco were the Mint, the Post Office, and the Customhouse, all products of federal, not municipal, policy. When Benjamin Lloyd provided a more extensive and popular map of San Francisco, he also turned not to City Hall but to a melange of private and recreational spaces: the Palace Hotel, the Barbary Coast vice district, the Cliff House, Chinatown, and Golden Gate Park. Similarly, the photographic genre that replaced the panorama, high-angle views, tended to give prominence to hotels and post offices.[24]

Private visitors to these cities set their compass by a similar set of landmarks. A young English businessman arriving in New York in 1872 was guided through a route that commenced at the St. Nicholas Hotel, proceeded to the offices of the Equitable Life Insurance Company (billed as "the finest building in New York"), stopped to applaud Wall Street and Stewart's Department Store, and tarried in a saloon where, to his shock, he and his young mercantile friends were served by "girls." He found one bucolic interlude at Greenwood Cemetery. The young businessman's itinerary through the city—from the citadel of the capitalists to the venues of love and death—was similar to the path on which Horatio Alger placed Ragged Dick. Alger's hero had a intricate mental map of the city, but its landmarks—chiefly private amusements, hotels, dry goods stores, transportation routes—were dispersed quite randomly along a grid of streets. City Hall is only a signpost along this mechanical partition of space. "About a mile from the City Hall the cross streets begin to be numbered in regular order." Women of the middle class measured this territory by a slightly different standard. They were more likely to stop at Barnum's American Museum, Central Park, or the Academy of Music, landmarks of propriety, femininity, and family entertainment.[25]

Male or female, these pedestrians were enticed by private enterprise more than guided by public arteries and landmarks. By the third quarter of the nineteenth century commercial places not only charted the flow of individuals in space and time but also vied for the title of city center. Christine Boyer's map of Manhattan real estate marked off Fourteenth to Twenty-third Streets at Fifth Avenue as the "spatial center that distilled all the sentiments of New York's cultural and political Life." In that space were concentrated such major institutions as Stewart's Department Store, the Fifth Avenue Hotel, endless varieties of commercial amusement, and a public ceremonial ground, Union Square. Unlike City Hall Park, Union Square had no formal political function and was defined by the commercial and residential space around it. Moreover, this appendage of a central business district, the Ladies Mile, sprouted yet another commercial branch after the Civil War. A new phalanx of shoppers wove their way along Fourteenth Street, keeping time to the jingle "Westward the star of Fashion takes its way." The Pied Piper of this movement, R. H. Macy, used convenient shopping and modest prices to stretch the Ladies Mile into a housewife's haven that extended as far west as Sixth Avenue. The advances of commercial space could also be found on Canal Street in New Orleans and Union Square in San Francisco. With the proliferation of stores like Macy's commerce occupied space with new authority. No longer just a fancified dry goods store, Macy's featured some twenty-two retail departments by 1877 plus such amenities as a ladies lunch room. To keep pace with this change Stewart's had to relocate to the north and increase its labor force to some 3000 employees, becoming a city within the city. The concentration of retailing of such massive scale marked out the rudiments of a central business district and the leading edge of the modernization of urban space.[26]

Under the aegis of rapid economic growth and urban expansion city people were free to chart their own course through relatively undefined spaces. Some visitors such as Englishman John Tunstall were drawn to such spaces as "Chinatown," a "nigger performance" at a local theater, and the private, suburban homes of fellow businessmen. San Francisco locals such as the young Chester Gunn, son of a Republican editor, recalled that his routine movements stayed within a narrow circuit of his middle-class refuge on Rincon Hill. He moved from home to school, to church on Sunday, to a sylvan glade for fishing, to a local grocery for the daily news and nourishment. By contrast his peer Lucy Jones, who lived above Market Street, filled her diary of the 1870s with a much richer stock of street knowledge. Her lively movements, however, had a certain uniformity to them. They were mapped almost entirely by a compass of commercial leisure. Her routine circuit went through theaters, pleasure gardens, picture galleries, mechanics fairs, Sunday schools, lectures, concerts, boat races, the opera, and endless shopping. During the same period the unemployed iron molder, anxious father, and future labor leader Frank Rooney also found spots of commercial leisure irresistible. Like many working people of San Francisco, Rooney was a regular patron of Woodwards Gardens. Soon after absenting himself from a labor picnic because he lacked the entrance fee, he dined out with male friends, saying, "Poor as I am, I try to be sociable." This sampling of individual routes though city space is consistent with more systematic studies of public and private records that have traced extensive but seemingly random patterns of diurnal traffic among immigrants and natives, rich and poor, eastsider and westsider. Even recent immigrants from Ireland charted an urban course that extended far outside their neighborhood and even into the suburbs, while the affluent assumed a haughty distance as they promenaded through city streets, ensconced in ostentatious carriages.[27]

The modern city was a space in which individuals could sidestep the old civic centers and integrated spaces. The socialite, the young businessman, the matron, the young lady, the enterprising Irishman had each taken different courses through an increasingly large and diffuse urban space. Many found this freedom, choice, and anonymity exhilarating. The perspective from Mark Hopkins's window as photographed by Eadweard Muybridge was just one Olympian example of myriad personal angles on city space. Yet one can proffer a few generalizations about these diverse and fragmented itineraries through the city. First, public and civic space was occluded by larger expanses of concentrated residential land use. Second, the massive investment in standardized and compacted residential architecture shifted the balance of the built environment from street, square, and public space toward more private, interior zones. Third, the magnets that drew people outside their homes were increasingly places of business—Woodward's Garden, the St. Nicholas Hotel, Barnum's Museum. Fourth, these commercial spaces often dispensed organized and packaged entertainment: a concert, a play, or lager beer from the hand of a bargirl. Commercial space, in other words, sponsored a less public form of sociability. It was often prefabricated for the masses and available only at a cost, a kind of sociability for hire. In sum major spatial innovations of the 1870s were located in neither exactly private nor fully public spaces but in a border territory marked by the apartment house, the houses of public amusements, and streets defined by the shop windows that lined them. This pattern suggests that the changing built environment was channeling everyday urban life and imagination in a private direction, away from associated or civic consciousness. The physical center of the modern city took up its position among the office buildings of corporate capital: Equitable Life Insurance and Western Union, for example, loomed high above both City Hall and St. Patrick's Cathedral.

Public Space as Open Space

Late in the last century the heterogeneity of the city seemed not to lessen but become more diffuse and boundless. As population outgrew the old segmented forms it was left largely to competing commercial interests—transportation companies, real estate developers, department store managers, amusement entrepreneurs—to provide the citizenry with new urban accommodations. Between the period of civic warfare at midcentury on through the 1870s each city made do with the old city halls, now located off center along the receding margins of an expanding cityscape. Neither New Yorkers nor New Orleanians bothered any longer to punctuate the urban plan with public squares at regular intervals, while San Francisco never appears to have opened a single public market and only two small squares for its 200,000 residents. In New Orleans civic building was neglected through the troubled period of Reconstruction while the public works of New York and New Orleans were stuck in a quagmire of municipal malfeasance. In the case of San Francisco the quagmire was actually made of sand and called a lot. The project of finally building a proper city hall commenced in 1870 but was hamstrung by the municipal charter, which prohibited municipal borrowing and kept the city from spending a nickel more than it collected in taxes annually. Consequently, the ambitious building program lumbered along slowly. It got as far as a lively ceremony to lay the cornerstone in 1872, the opening of the hall of records a few years later, and its final completion in 1892, in time to be destroyed in the earthquake of 1906. Hence, the decade of the 1870s would close with only the debris of the "sand lots" to show for the progress of public building beside the Golden Gate.[28]

By this time New York had gotten somewhat further in its projected annex to City Hall, called the Municipal Courthouse, and actually more an office building than a public hall. First proposed in the 1860s, it was nearing completion in 1880 but crippled by the same suspicious and niggardly schemes of public financing. The County Board of Supervisors doled out the payments to a snarl of contractors for every painful and expensive step in erecting the monumental brick structure. In 1870, when William Tweed became the president of that board, the building was renamed in his dishonor. The erection of "Tweed's Courthouse" was tied up in litigation and scandal as its civic function was reduced to symbolizing political corruption rather than public pride. The Tammany governments associated with Tweed were actually relatively foresightful providers of public space, creating a public works department and initiating plans for a modern sewer system in the late 1860s. But his tarnished public image excused the curtailment of such public investments thereafter and elsewhere. The snail's pace of public building in the late nineteenth century was most often testimony to the miserliness of taxpayers. The outgoing mayor of San Francisco put it in the language of political calculation in 1871: "While I am always in favor of a liberal expenditure of money for enterprises of real public utility, I am opposed to taxing the people for the erection of these costly edifices which are more for glory than for use." [29] Municipalities were slow but a bit more generous in providing basic services. Before 1880 each city struggled with essentially the same inadequate methods of providing water and waste removal through private contract. Although, as Jon Teaford has shown, the nation's expanding cities would make major investments in new streets and public transport by 1900, these public goods were delivered haltingly in the 1870s and by a shadowy, scandal-infested network of private contracts, development schemes, and government bureaucracy. The few innovations in street construction and the provision of smoother surfaces such as macadam had the result, furthermore, of speeding vehicles along the public arteries and past opportunities for urban sociability. [30]

One space offered relief from this record of public complacency. Significantly, that bright spot on the urban landscape was not a public building but actually a lack of building—that is, the preservation of space for the development of parks. The allocation of land for New York's Central Park was one of the last feats of antebellum public politics, accomplished in the heat of municipal civil war in 1857. Crusading editors, abridging property owners, city Democrats, and upstate Republicans all took a hand in shaping the final legislation that set aside over 800 acres for public use. This creation and development of park land signaled the troubled future as much as it recalled past civic glories such as the Croton Aqueduct or Gallier Hall. Real estate profits were prime considerations in the decision to locate the public reserve not in the center of the city but far uptown. In the same decade similarly inexpensive spaces were reserved for the later development of Riverside and Morningside Parks in New York, while New Orleans set aside the land in Metairie Ridge for its "city park." [31] Finally, San Francisco acted to reserve its own park land immediately after the Civil War. The actual laying out of the parks was a slow process in each city, encumbered not only by financial limits but by repeated investigations of the commissioners entrusted with the public funds.[32]

San Francisco's Golden Gate Park, although less renowned than its New York counterpart (whose history has been told in detail by Roy Rosenzweig and Elizabeth Blackmar), illustrates how public space became redefined as open space. First of all, like its predecessor in Gotham, San Francisco's great park was the product of a kind of political miracle birth, conceived and brought to life in a municipal atmosphere of civic warfare, administrative inefficiency, and niggardly taxpayers. The project was sold to the public as a profitable enterprise, "a direct moneyed return on investment." The Park Commissioners report of 1872 attested that "In all other cities where public parks have been made the increase in the amount received from taxation, on the enhanced value of property resulting from Park improvements is largely in excess of the interest on the money expended." The first essential step in financial strategy was to settle for some marginal and remote location—the distant granite fields of the Upper West Side in New York, an abandoned plantation in New Orleans, and uninviting sand dunes in San Francisco. San Francisco's entrepreneurs did New Yorkers one better by using the park project as a way of securing private titles to adjacent public lands. For decades voracious San Franciscans had fought one another and the city to secure ownership of territory called the outside lands, which happened to border the proposed park site. These enterprising urban frontiersmen seized their chance when park developers came courting and agreed to give up 10 percent of their disputed holdings to the park in return for outright title to the rest.[33]

Civic parsimony and private profit set the course of park development in all three cities. A collusion of interests, from the poor beneficiaries of public works jobs, to the calculations of middle-income taxpayers, to the profits of shrewd real estate investors, determined the tempo of public landscaping. In the process the space was inscribed with private identities. The wealthy James Lick wrote his name on Golden Gate Park in the glass fantasy of the conservatory. Having accrued tax benefits from his public beneficence, Lick died while the project was still in the red and bequeathed title to this public works to Charles Crocker. Ornamental gates erected in the parks in the 1880s and 1890s bore the names of yet other business leaders. By this date, as Rosenzweig and Blackmar have vividly demonstrated, Central Park was becoming a more demo-

cratic space, taken over by more plebeian New Yorkers for their own social amusements. But even here everything from refreshment stands to
erecting statues of ethnic heroes were basically private initiatives. In sum
the great parks, the major oasis of public space in America's cities of the
late nineteenth century, were a patchwork of private interests and ad hoc
measures, under a loose public surveillance. The cityscape remained an
alloy of private enterprise with public meeting place, but the balance of
power was shifting to the former.[34]

This expedient blend of public and private also characterized the day-
to-day operation of the new open spaces. In accordance with the proposal by Frederick Law Olmsted, Golden Gate Park, like its New York
predecessor, was to be run not by politicians but by experts and disinterested professionals. In both cities the park management was removed
from the messy urban political scene and vested in the state legislature.
The legislative enactment passed in Sacramento in April 1870 established
three park commissioners to be appointed at the state level. Still, the political ties of the appointees were a source of constant suspicion. One investigation lamented their "crude opinions...with equal ignorance and
dogmatism, substituted for and made paramount to the well considered
and deliberately formed opinions of engineers of acknowledged capacity,
attainments and experience." While such commissioners came and went
with shifts in political winds, the professionals stayed in place. At the
helm of Golden Gate Park was William Hammond Hall, an engineer
hired from Maryland and linked to a circle of experts like Olmsted rather
than to the general public of San Francisco. The nascent bureaucracy of
the parks also provided a power base for Olmsted and his successor, Andrew Green, the New York City comptroller who reigned as city planner
without portfolio until late in the century. Under the management of
offices such as that of park engineer the city's public spaces became the
turf on which careers were made and bureaucracies became entrenched,
thus marking another prescient shift in the center of public gravity.[35]

The changing balance between public and private was also visible in
the design and use of the great urban parks. In the eminent pronouncements of Olmsted the park was designed to provide a spatial base for
utopian social relations.[36] The San Francisco park commissioner put the
social theory of parks in terms that had become civic cant by the 1870s.
Great parks would provide a "quiet and salutary effect" on the "rush and
turmoil of urban life" and exercise a "potent influence upon the moral
condition of the society," "guiding the emotions and regulating the
habits of members of society." Andrew Jackson Downing offered a suit-

ably bucolic wording of this social function of the park: to provide a "green oasis in the arid deserts of business and dissipation for the refreshment of the city's body and soul." By the late nineteenth century the moral benefits of great parks had become such a cliché that officials regarded it a "waste of time to advert to the hygienic and esthetic influences of pleasure grounds."[37]

Probing the rhetoric of park design a little deeper reveals the altered meaning of public space that grew up along with the bridal paths and great meadows. The San Francisco commissioners recited from the catechism of urban landscaping in 1874. "With drives and rides for the rich, and pleasant rambles for the poor, and quiet retreats for the gaily disposed; sheltered nooks for invalids, and open grounds for lovers of boisterous sports; tracks adapted to the special wants of children, and arranged to insure their comfort and welfare, the modern urban park is indeed the municipality's open-air assembly room, acceptable alike to all, and pleasing to each of her citizens." As a place of public assembly in the modern city the park held a meaning very different from that of its predecessors, the square or the street corner. First, an assembly in a park connoted a fragile social relation: It was almost an antisocial place, devoted to "quiet retreat." Neither "sheltered nooks," nor noisy playing fields, nor busy roadways were places of mingling and meeting; rather, they fostered separate, individualized, or competitive cohabitation of public space. The bucolic natural landscape was above all designed for solitary or intimate relations, it provided "views to contemplate" and "walks" for quiet conversations (not "promenades" for social exchange). Political meetings were prohibited outright. Even posting public bills or congregating in large groups was interdicted in the park. Section 7 of the Golden Gate Park regulations stipulated, for example, that picnics or parties over ten persons should inform the gatekeeper of their intentions, while groups over twenty-five could not assemble without securing a special permit the day before. Section 6 could not be clearer: "No public meeting, and no public discussion or debate shall be held within the limits of the said parks, avenues and grounds"[38]

The large urban park was also tenuously public in its accessibility. Not even democratic paeans to parks, like that quoted above, were particularly attentive to the diversity of the people they served. The classifications of the citizenry employed by the San Francisco Park Commissioners in 1874 were rather curious: rich, poor, invalids, and children. The latter category denoted an especially favored parkgoer. In San Francisco as in New York the "children's quarter" or "dairy" was one of the

Figure 30. Shelter, Golden Gate Park, ca. 1874. Raymond H. Clary, *The Making of Golden Gate Park.*

most hallowed spaces within park territory. Described as "a warm, sunny, protected nook with a decidedly rural air and fitted with the appliances for children's games and entertainment" (and often dispensing milk), these precursors of playgrounds both served an important, often neglected segment of the public and at the same time beat a retreat from the more menacing of urban differences. Neither children nor their assumed caretakers, women, were tainted by the aggressive manners of adult male citizens, veterans of the years of municipal warfare. In fact women, like children, were treated with extraordinary deference by the architects of parks. The park was a gift of good health, open-air recreation, and childcare, especially designed to acclimatize women to big city living. In turn it was expected that an infusion of feminine sensibility in the rural decor of the urban park would exert a salutary moral influence on husbands as well as sons. If the social imagination of the park designers and managers extended beyond the image of the solitary user, it rarely saw beyond a small family, whose Sunday picnics made the great park a domestic rather than a promiscuously public space (fig. 30).[39]

In point of actual use the parks fell far short of meeting even these narrowly public goals. The statistics of park use in 1872 tell the tale. In that representative year the commissioners happily reported that 255,000 individuals used Golden Gate Park. This respectable figure represented a very narrow portion of the population, however, for almost 225,000 arrived "by vehicle"—mainly by costly forms of transport such as carriages or streetcars. With another 15,000 arriving on the equally expensive mount of horseback, that left only a few thousand pedestrians—persons of modest means—to enjoy access to the park. Until cheaper public transportation became available the great parks remained compromised as public space.[40] Accordingly, the big parks, despite their vast acreage and potential for distributing urban amenities in the next century, left a relatively small imprint on the everyday life of most urban residents and even visitors before 1880. Golden Gate Park shared the sunshine of commentator Benjamin Lloyd with such private recreational spaces as Woodward's Gardens and the Cliff House or with the relative wilderness across the bay in Oakland or Alameda. A foreign visitor, William Laird MacGregor, missed it entirely in 1876, saying, "Beyond some half dozen insignificant little squares, no provision was made by the projectors for public parks or gardens."[41]

By 1880 the provision of open spaces in densely settled cities had become an object of desire and concern nationwide. The U.S. Census Bureau reported, however, that American cities provided less open space per capita than was common in Europe and favored large parks over the smaller squares that offered wider access and more salutary effects on the masses of the city. Any bird's-eye view of New York, San Francisco, or New Orleans would reveal that this limited and asymmetrical provision of open public space had deformed what remained of the segmented and centered pattern of antebellum urban space. The former arrangement of quadrants of marketplaces and squares, linked by prominent thoroughfares and anchored in public landmarks, was becoming obscured and bypassed by the sweeping contours of new business districts, rapid transport lines, apartment buildings, office towers, and great parks. Only on the margins of the dense and poorly differentiated streets could one find a space set aside by public mandate for public sociability. But this public initiative, the reservation of large open spaces for popular amusement, shaded into privacy. It offered limited access by class, catered to more passive citizens—middle-class women and children—and valued solitude over sociability. Such shifts in urban space presented obstacles as well as distractions for the congregation of the people (fig. 31).

Life and Literature of the Streets

The public record seldom detailed the everyday life that transpired in the smaller nooks and crannies of urban space. Only a few stolen glances into the lives of ordinary people suggest the finely textured sociability

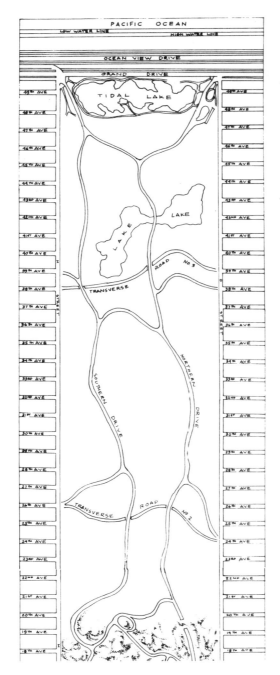

Figure 31. Map of Golden Gate Park. Raymond H. Clary, *The Making of Golden Gate Park.*

that formed around such spatial nuclei as corner groceries, fruit stands, saloons, and street corners. But surely these nodes of neighborliness abounded. In 1880 the census takers recorded the numbers of licensed drinking places in the four figures, counting over 9000 in New York. These more intimate social centers replaced the old public markets, which survived principally in New Orleans, where they numbered seventeen. Grog shops and sidewalk retailers were friendly sentinels along the everyday routes of individuals through the city. Occasionally, we get a glimpse of the ways that these semipublic institutions provided a glue for the localized community. The heroine of everyday neighborly sociability in San Francisco, for example, was a fruit dealer south of Market Street who intervened to protect and care for stranded children.[42] Mean streets were also humanized by old familiar sounds: the cries of rag sellers, tin menders, food sellers, and newsboys still made the usually dyspeptic Benjamin Lloyd say of San Francisco, "What a human Medley is the City." If we are to believe another professional street monitor, Charles Loring Brace, a city even as large and anonymous as New York could be very cozy at street level. In Brace's eyes even children could make the city streets into a comfortable home. "The children I saw everyday in the streets, following organs, blackening boots, selling flowers, sweeping walks, or carrying ponderous harps of old ruffians." New York's newsboys found shelter in old boxes under stairs, in harbor barges, under bridges, and in a burned-out safe on Wall Street. In San Francisco an enterprising journalist followed the adult version of the street savant, called simply the tramps, through an elaborate itinerary along the docks and in back allies, revealing how the darkest and most remote corners of the city could sustain a comforting sociability. Brace, the newsboy's guardian, was more uneasy at the thought of young girls making a living on the streets and thus skating close to prostitution. But George Ellington confessed that even streetwalkers found social comfort in their workplace. "They are anxious to gossip to each other about their affairs the same as the virtuous world. At night they may be seen in groups of three, four or half a dozen, standing on certain corners and holding friendly chat as to their affairs."[43]

If even the underworld of prostitutes and street children could elicit images of urban hospitality, surely the typical working families of the city found ways of staving off anomie. Amid the pathologies of the big city one also finds icons of neighborhood cohesion. An English visitor to Manhattan in 1879 could anchor city sociability on the "stoop": "In the summer evening the whole indoor population of New York seems to overflow on the stoops of their house." The custom was common in the "best neighborhoods and the poorest." It was found North and South, among blacks and whites. It still flourished in Congo Square in New Orleans after Emancipation, when former slaves revived for a time the African American community of song and dance in public spaces. Vernacular elements of urban architecture, the roofs as well as the stoops, were easily converted to neighborhood living rooms. The roof became the place to celebrate the Fourth of July, as tenement dwellers mounted the stairways to watch the fireworks together. City people routinely came together on rooftops, on stoops, in neighborhoods, in the local and everyday uses of the streets. The question is not whether the city sidewalks could provide opportunities for human contact and social pleasure but how far these human links extended, what social differences they spanned, and whether they integrated the people into a public. Were they moves toward a civic center or a modern recessional, not unlike a middle-class picnic in the park, into more intimate, homogeneous, and narrow social space? [44]

More highly educated observers of the late nineteenth-century urban scene often suspected the latter. Observing the modest city of San Francisco, a street preacher named Taylor observed, "In all old-settled communities each member, however humble, is a link in a chain of association which runs through the whole community. . . . But here the links are nearly all separated, and where they are connected it is generally by open links which can be slipped at pleasure." Many educated commentators showed similar symptoms of being ill at ease in public spaces, among them William Dean Howells, who made a literary excursion through New York in 1871.[45] "The Wedding Journey" recounts the tour of Basil and Isabel March, commencing with the familiar promenade down the old artery of the republic, Broadway. Some familiar literary devices can be found along the route: like the diurnal schedule of occupying the thoroughfare, beginning with early morning cordons of working men followed by businessmen and shop girls, then finally the late-sleeping fashionable ladies. And from the mouth of Basil March came some venerable notices of urban attractions, especially the "Niagara of people" that "transformed a shabby stretch of pavement into a stunning spectacle." To his bride, however, Broadway was something less appealing. The parade of democracy was illegible to Isabel March, for "like all daughters of a free country Isabel knew nothing about politics." The passage down Broadway to refuge in the hotel became a disagreeable obstacle course. Isabel's posture to the city was at best primly disdainful, "catching up her skirt, and deftly escaping contact with one of a long row of ash cans." She passed through images of "decrepit children and mothers of the streets...clawing for bits of coal." The reputation of the city seemed to have decayed considerably since the days Lydia Maria Child and Walt Whitman walked so happily down Broadway. The Marches left Broadway for a trip to Niagara Falls and found greater spiritual nourishment in nature. New York was just one rather unpleasant memory, buried in the exquisitely private communication between husband, wife, and reader. Writers such as Howells had not deserted the city, but they began, even before 1880, to divert the literary imagination away from symbols of democratic association and toward a landscape of intimacy.

By the time Henry James made a literary excursion to *Washington Square* in 1879 this public space was becoming a barricade around middle-class privacy. His characters almost never ventured beyond one anothers' drawing rooms and took to the streets largely for secretive and nefarious rendezvous.[46] This ambivalence toward the city and urge to domesticate public space was common among American intellectuals of the time. Olmsted rested his urban ideal in an intimate and domestic scene. He closed his argument for *Public Parks and Enlargement of Towns* with a fantasy of a husband telling his wife to bring the children to meet him after work "under the chestnut tree" in the park.[47] Olmsted's social vision was often even more confining than domesticity: It could be reduced to atomic individualism. He projected the sensibility of a city resident in images of men who "have seen thousands of their fellow-men, have met them face to face, have brushed against them, and yet have had no experience of anything in common with them." Or consider this refined street calculation: "to merely avoid collision with those we meet and pass on the side walks we have constantly to watch, to foresee, and to guard against their movements.... Our minds are thus brought into close dealings with other minds without any friendly flowing toward them."[48]

Despite their apparent discomfort in the city streets, writers such as Olmsted, Howells, and James made it their business to interpret and rehabilitate cities for the middle classes. Another growing class of writers trafficked in outright libels against the city. The relatively upbeat sensationalist chronicles of the 1850s (typified by George Foster's wide-eyed views of the city), which provided literary accompaniment for the civil wars of the 1850s, were eclipsed by a meaner spirit of urban commentary in the 1860s. After the war this literature become more abundant, more lurid, and a more relentless libel against the city streets. Scores of authors hawked sensationalist tours of the city, painting its sunshine and especially the shadows in flamboyant detail.[49] A master of the genre, Junius Browne, whose *Great Metropolis* appeared in 1867, painted the chiaroscuro metaphor with characteristic hyperbole: "Clouds and sunshine, corpse lights and bridal lamps, joy anthems and funeral dirges contrast and mingle in New York." Such literary portraits so polarized the population of cities between the super rich and abysmal poor that there was little room for a reader's empathy.[50] Even the children of the poor were liable to such urban ostracism. Browne found them everywhere on the streets exercising "semi-savage independence," "strange little creatures who flaunt their rags and make grimaces in the face of the Hudson." In 1872 *Appleton's Journal* gave an inhuman ancestry to some 30,000 desperate street children of New York: Their "unnatural parents" cast them into the streets to "beg and steel and minister to their vicious appetites." Matthew Hale Smith traced the genealogy of human refuse to little girls "picked up from the streets, found in the gutter, taken from dens of infamy, brought to the mission by drunken women—many of whom had never known father or mother."[51]

Perhaps the most maligned person on the streets of New York was the negligent mother whose absence of maternal traits banished her from the feminine sex if not the human species. Images of drunken and hence inhuman mothers abounded in this genre, part of a systematic desexing of a certain class of city women. Hankins found a vagrant woman at the city police court and "shuddered at the thought that such a creature bears the name of woman." Browne went deeper into the demimonde to find "wretched females (all the woman seems to have gone out of them). . . . The distinction of sex is purely physiological." The animalistic metaphors ran riot when journalists encountered prostitutes. George Ellington came up with some especially imaginative zoological labels for harlots: "three different classes of localities devoted to prostitution, as distinct from each other as the flea is from the bedbug and the vampire and all of the same intrinsic immoral character—just as all the three animals named are bloodsuckers, and differ only in degrees."[52]

Clearly such a population warranted a quarantine. The favored trope for the spatial confinement of unsavory urban populations was a reference to animal habitat. Urban chronicles of the postwar period placed poor families and prostitutes in dens and herds where they came together by animal instinct. Edward Crapsey despairingly conceded that "every vast city must have a vile population, and it will herd together." Matthew Hale Smith aimed his compass at the Jews and Chinese in

New York who "herd together without the decency of cattle." Other writers expelled the dangerous classes from the body politic with images of coalescing waste products. To Benjamin Lloyd the "putrid mass" of San Francisco was concentrated in the Barbary Coast vice district, like a "stagnant pool of human immorality and crime." James Buel, writing of the same urban site a few years later, called it a "cauldron of offensive rottenness."

This historical moment also produced one of the most commonplace metaphors for the moral decay of the city. An essay written in 1873 used this synecdoche when it lamented how the children of the poor "are absolutely brought up in the gutter." By 1880 the term was standard and versatile. A writer for the *New York Tribune* in 1880, for example, pictured corrupted children "skating on the gutter." References to the whole infrastructure of urban waste removal, the sewer system, provided a more extended metaphor for evacuating the city of its unsavory population. A visitor from France, speaking of great cities such as Paris and London as well as New York, observed that "new, hideous and terrifying aspects of reality are uncovered everyday. Whenever we get beneath the shining mask of the city's public face we discover what is squirming about in the depths of the sewers."[53] The decaying social matter of the city was represented by a whole litany of terms for contamination: poisoning, curdling, ulcerating, and stinking. This literary rendition of germ theory could find a breeding ground of vice among the more harmless and passive city residents, poor women, children, and bathetic beggars.

One entry in the dictionary of street types was more aggressive and demanded a more urgent exercise of social control. Known sometimes by more exotic names such as street corner bummer, rough, or hooligan, and a relative of the antebellum fireboy and corner lounger, this urban type was christened "the hoodlum" in the late nineteenth century. Reporting from the streets of San Francisco in 1876, Benjamin Lloyd offered this etiology of the hoodlum: "It is really wonderful this growth of hoodlumism. A few years ago it was unknown; now it is met in every department of social life." Junius Browne aimed a full blast from his rhetorical arsenal at this archetype: "until we kill him outright, until the Metropolis is purified, he may awake us at midnight with his mingled hiss and roar and strike and strangle us in the arms of Love, and in the very breast of Peace."[54] Browne drew on the familiar menagerie of labels for the new urban personality: "social hyena, a rational jackal," "A more despicable, dangerous, detestable character than the New York rough does not exist." The hoodlum's age was somewhat indeterminate: Not a boy, not a man, he was a youthful "graduate in vice and crime." His habitat was "dimly lighted street corners; in front of the corner grocer (in fact he is a fixture here); on vacant lots; in dark alley-ways and nooks; at the entrance to suburban public halls and on public conveyances, during excursions and picnics." Ellington found a similar species called corner loafers in New York who "hang about the avenues, in front of cigar stores and rum shops, and who make it their business to insult ladies as they pass along the street." The New Orleans press might have been speaking of similar phenomena in the late 1870s when it reported on "the crowds which congregate on Canal Street on matinee days. The outlet to the theater is jammed by loafers whose only object is to stare at ladies."[55]

The hoodlum exemplified a new way of classifying the people: according to negative associations with the street. The sensationalist literature of the late nineteenth century, not unlike urban reformers and the popular press, often marked urban space with such negative references to alleys, gutters, sewers, "dimly lighted street-corners." This literature did not picture the city population as citizens in all their occupational, ethnic, or cultural variety. Neither did it populate public space with the colorful street personalities found in earlier tales of the city. Rather, the most popular cityscapes were stocked with marginal figures—poor women and children and young, apparently jobless, nonvoting men. In other words the inchoate space of the big city became the imaginary habitat of aimless and voiceless, yet dangerous, people. These alterations in the imagination of urban space can be seen in the form as well as the content of this literature. The sunshine and shadows were not only polarized spaces, they were brought together in a haphazard and fragmented fashion. Authors of sensationalist literature rambled the city as if in a state of delirium that could last through upwards of fifty chapters. The literary guide to the city was truly a map—that is, a transcription of the city that relied on filling in abstract space with specific labels, recording each street and building with little recourse to summary images, dramatic plot, or a central purpose. George Ellington's compendium *Women in New York City* illustrates this strategy. The single category "women of ill fame" wound through many chapters and up and down the city. In lower Manhattan Ellington stopped at houses of ill repute on Mercer Street, Water Street, Baxter Street, Greene Street, Prince Street, Amelia Street, Crosby Street, Broome Street, and West Broadway. Working northward to Canal and Church Streets, he made his way past brothels in Washington Square and on Lexington, Madison, Four-teenth, Twenty-third, Thirty-fourth, and Fourty-second Streets and of course Broadway. While Ellington typed these enterprises by class, color, and degree of moral bankruptcy, he did not have at his command a neat pattern of segregation, specialization, or spatial containment for this or any other urban menace. In fact the scrupulous mapping of New York's vice district by historian Timothy Gilfoyle was no more successful in confining prostitution to one area of New York for the period before 1880. The actual spaces of the big city continued to defy simple patterns of segregation.[56]

In the absence of such an orderly arrangement in space, the vast ur-ban population of the 1870s could seem overwhelming: "a huge con-glomerate mass of people." This terminology comes from George Ellington and resembles Junius Browne's metaphor of the urban people as "the Motley Multitude." Others emphasized the aimless mobility of the urban mass, "driftwood in the current of Metropolitan Life." More often the movements of the masses were simply called tides. Browne en-countered this natural force at a city newsstand where "the human tide descends; the heaps of papers rapidly diminish. There is no conversation between buyer and seller." The "mass," the "multitude," the "tide" signified some uncontrollable force that splintered bonds of association and reduced citizens to "strangers in a strange land." This language of alienation was not confined to the jaded hacks of the press room. The more respectable journalists at the *Nation* magazine resorted to even more jaundiced epithets for New York's people: "the vast hordes who swarm here to make a living" being just one example. By the 1870s the streets and public spaces of the city had acquired their all-too-familiar reputation as places of danger.[57] A whole genre of writing redirected the civic imagination away from the old social centers, deserting squares for parks and meetings for offices, and populating the streets in between with menacing strangers. Is this what lurked in the shadows of the panoramic urban view?

Order in the Streets

This negative portrait of the city, although made only of words and a gross exaggeration, offered a way of conceptualizing urban space that exerted potent cultural and political force. By codifying urban reality in fearful terms these jeremiads influenced voters and policy makers. At the very least they sanctioned accelerated efforts to maintain public order and discipline the occupants of public space. In the late nineteenth century the municipal police grew to be the second largest urban expenditure after the public schools. The professional police force had been firmly established during the period of municipal warfare and was reinforced thereafter. More precinct houses, call boxes, telegraph links, and manpower made the police department an ever more formidable monitor of life in public space. Matthew Hale Smith praised New York's finest for "the ease with which the police controlled the masses" and arrested the suspicious persons found on their beats. Statistics bore him out as each city rapidly increased the number of officers patrolling the streets. As of 1880 they numbered 400 in San Francisco, 300 in New Orleans, and 2500 in New York. They compiled an impressive record of street control, arresting 21,000, 18,000, and 67,000 in the three cities respectively. The masses who were arrested were not quite the heinous predators described by sensational literature; most were simple drunks, beggars, and a sprinkling of other public eyesores such as transvestites or nude bathers.[58]

After the Civil War cities created increasingly bizarre and refined lists of urban transgressions. The *Digest of Ordinances* for New Orleans proscribed indecent language, soliciting for prostitution, and disorderly picnics. San Francisco enforced curfews for dance hall girls, forbad beggars from displaying unseemly deformities of their limbs, and permitted the arrest of children found idle and unattended in the streets. New York City statutes regulated all these activities and more routine matters as well. The state liquor law passed in Albany at the same time as the Metropolitan Police Act patrolled and controlled such spaces of lower-class sociability as saloons and corner groceries.[59] The municipal code required licenses for street merchants, and the Tenement House Act permitted police inspectors to enter suspicious private homes. The Board of Health reported in 1873 that the tenement act "continued to require constant supervision and frequent inspection" in order "to educate the people in the densely populated part of the city as to the necessity of cleanliness and obedience to the sanitary regulations of the board."[60]

The local policeman was not the only force of order on city streets after the Civil War. In New Orleans the U.S. army became the ultimate authority during the Reconstruction period, while in the North the National Guard was given new stature and license to intervene in civil disorders. New York's Seventh Regiment grew even more arrogant in its parades through the city. In 1879 the Seventh dedicated a new armory on East Sixty-sixth Street. It took up its new quarters with President Hayes presiding and proclaiming that "behind the policemen's club glistens your bayonet worthy of an imperial state and the imperial city." That building spoke for itself. It featured battered concrete walls, narrow windows, a looming tower, heavy iron gate, thick oak doors, iron bars, and shutters. The Sixty-sixth Street armory was the prototype of the new castellated style of architecture that would soon proliferate across the country and install a brutal symbol of police force on the cityscape.[61]

Be it the force of the state or roughs on the street corners, threats of violence seemed to loom over the city, not just in war and riots but on an everyday basis. Although there is little evidence that cases of assaults and battery grew disproportionately with the city population, they did mount to the thousands annually and thus became newsworthy. The police report was now a regular feature in the daily press and sent images of violent crime into drawing rooms all across town. One sample report from the San Francisco press recorded everyday incidents of street violence such as these: A man named Sullivan stood outside his Sansome Street boarding house and knocked down a passing stranger. Some "scamps," the oldest age eleven, beat another unsuspecting pedestrian. A gang hanging out on Mason and Vallejo threw cayenne pepper at a vegetable vendor. For some "trivial affront" a man was hit with a "cudgel over the head." Two men came up behind an unsuspecting victim on Clay Street and "inflict[ed] a deadly blow with a cobblestone or heavy club." All this grisly street business was conducted between 1867 and 1873. Thereafter, arms are mentioned increasingly in the police reports. This report of July 15, 1876, is typical: Some "over grown hoodlums," fourteen to twenty years of age, accosted a twelve-year-old and held him down while they pounded his face. The victim drew a pistol and got away. The city did indeed seem to be a dangerous place, its streets rife with personal violence.[62]

These particular assaults, however, were neither routine nor likely to target those members of the reading public who showed the most trepidation in the streets. The victim in each instance was an immigrant from China. These particular examples of street crime were ferocious but hardly random. They were part of a sustained campaign to rein in a specific segment of the people. The hoodlum patrol enacted a kind of de facto segregation by terrorizing any Chinese-Americans who ventured out of their ghetto. The community south of Market seemed to endorse their actions: "A considerable portion of the population in California especially the lower classes are not disposed to interfere in behalf of the Chinaman." The anonymous vigilantes who patrolled the Chinese had other more legitimate weapons as well. They secured support in the Board of Supervisors, who enacted such eccentric and xenophobic street regulations as the ordinance that prevented carrying goods on poles or wearing hair in queues and ordinance 666, which called for rounding up and arresting prostitutes of Chinese descent.[63] A second public agency was quickly enlisted in the campaign against the Chinese. The Board of Health enacted a policy designed to see that the prostitutes of Chinatown and "other wretched occupants of these tenements, which are so productive of crime and disease, may be driven to some locality where they may be herded by themselves and not offend public decency." Under the auspices of the Board of Health, claiming to act to contain venereal disease and prostitution, the city of San Francisco attempted the first instance of de jure segregation: The ghetto was Chinatown.[64] The violence on the streets of San Francisco after the Civil War was part of a spatial reordering of the people in the name of public order. In San Francisco immigrants from Asia and prostitutes were singled out as the kinds of people whose place in the city demanded spatial confinement. This bold outline of social difference in urban space was to have powerful political consequences in the decades to come.

The politics of Chinatown linked race, gender, and spatial segregation in ominous ways that were not unique to San Francisco. The period after the Civil War produced rudimentary attempts in all three cities to order the "Vast and Vague" urban spaces through de jure segregation. These attempts advanced the furthest in the case of prostitutes and non-Europeans. Concerted attempts to confine prostitution to special districts were made in all three cities and were moderately successful, laying the groundwork for the development, later in the century, of separate vice districts such as the Barbary Coast in San Francisco and Storyville in New Orleans. The other major form of segregation was based in distinctions we now designate as racial. The streetcar was where these impulses of racial segregation played themselves out with the greatest venom: In 1873, for example, a man named Calhoun attacked a Chinese immigrant on the Folsom Street cars in San Francisco, saying "he had no right to sit beside a white man."[65]

More often it was African Americans whose place in public cars was disputed, especially during Reconstruction, when discriminatory local customs were challenged by a Radical Republican Congress.[66] In 1867 New Orleans blacks made a forceful stand at the front of the public cars, much to the displeasure of the former rebels who expected vindication under the Reconstruction plan of President Andrew Johnson. Amid "public anxiety" provoked by attempts to desegregate theaters and restaurants as well as public transportation New Orleanians experimented with new formulations of racial differences, public place, and gender. First, the mayor declared that these spaces were private, and thus entry could be denied at the inclination of the owners. After referring to freedmen by such various terms as *classes, races,* and *portions of the citizenry* the press rested much of its arguments for spatial distancing on gender. On May 16 the *Picayune* proposed that "even colored nurses be excluded from the white cars." The editor also suggested an ingenious way of avoiding overt racial segregation: "can't we have street cars exclusively for ladies and small children. A lady who went up town the other day, complains that one of the dirtiest and filthiest Negro men sat himself down in the midst of a number of ladies, nor would he rise when it filled up with them and some had to stand, even for a little child. We propose no distinction of color, but as to sex. Ladies and male escorts can ride other cars but let us have some in which none but females ride or such with young children accompanying them."[67]

A week later the *Picayune* abandoned this curious strategy and called for simple segregation between "the two classes . . . black and white." But even then it made its case in gender terms. "We would again suggest as relief from the annoyances which ladies especially experience in the crowding of street cars with freedmen, whose bodies and clothes have a hydrophobia which shudders at the use of water, that certain cars be set aside for the exclusive use of colored people and certain others to the like use of white people. Certainly this is equality and justice." The black press was not adverse to returning these insults and using gender as a political weapon. They taunted "white ladies" with images of proximity with freedmen and charged the fair sex with drunkenness.[68] At a time when cities still remained heterogeneous, relatively unsegregated, and even more crowded places the images of "natural" and dichotomous social differences such as gender and race were acquiring particular prominence on the streets and in the minds of the "masses."

Urban geography was not a simple transcription from demography, the built environment, popular prejudice, or middle-brow literature. The order of social space would have to be worked out in the formal political sphere, where, as we shall see, African Americans would defiantly resist segregation. The postwar transformation of space would, however, set the stage—but not the terms—for public debate. Neither Civil War nor its aftermath had reduced the streets of San Francisco, New Orleans, or New York into the journalists' topography of unrelenting danger and disease. Neither had the reformers' dreams of antiseptic order been realized. Not even the installation of powerful methods of public surveillance (the modern, militarized police force, for instance, and intrusive state bureaucracies) could subdue the diverse peoples of American cities. Despite all the anxious attempts to draw boundaries around groups deemed dangerous, or reserve open spaces for a middle-class retreat from the heterogeneous mass, the urban patterns of difference seemed to persist and became, at times, even more annoyingly diffuse. Some city residents were so ill at ease that they took advantage of the new transportation networks and deserted the city entirely for the growing suburbs.

Other people found exhilaration in the heterogeneity and liberating confusion of the modern city. Already in 1871 *Appleton's Journal* articulated this cosmopolitan point of view. In arguing that a French flat had some advantages over a suburban cottage, the journal argued that "A rich, specific, and munificent life arises from the compactness of settlement in cities" and that "men and women, moreover, often like the stir and bustle of cities."[69] One thing was clear as the people were massed together in ever greater numbers and buffeted about on street cars and railways: the old central places and segmenting arteries lost some of their power to sort and contain a multitude of differences. In 1871 some prescient urbanites imagined a campaign "to scientifically provide for the compact neighborhood of conditions that make up cities."[70] Proceeding more historically and politically than scientifically, cities did devise a number of new mechanisms for patching their habitat back together again after the season of civil wars, among them apartment houses, park commissions, police forces, statutes on public order, and the cognitive maps through the urban morass supplied by journalists and writers. Taken together these ad hoc measures altered everyday life in the city in a vague but uniform way: They infused the streets with a stronger dose of coercion and authority, a greater degree of abstraction from the immediate social relations, and a growing tendency to cast urban differences in more dualistic terms—sunshine and shadow, black and white, or male and female. To see this increasingly dense and opaque public more clearly requires another chapter that will examine how the "masses" exercised cultural citizenship and were represented in public ceremonies.

CHAPTER 6

The People in Ceremony

Multiply, Divide, Explode, Transcend

An uncharacteristically solemn procession filed through the streets of New York on April 25, 1865. Less than two years after the mayhem of the draft riots the citizenry managed to organize themselves into a dignified demonstration of a staggering array of social distinctions. An estimated 100,000 New Yorkers set out from the old urban center, City Hall Park, and wound through the streets until they quietly disbanded in Union Square. The procession was composed of eight orderly divisions, each packed with hundreds of different organizational units, and enrolling a full spectrum of classes, from bankers in the third division to longshoremen in the sixth. The ethnic continuum encompassed both the fifth division, which was devoted entirely to Irish organizations, and the sixth, containing members of the American Protestant Association. Finally, the parade opened its ranks to African Americans: 2000 of the "colored population" marched in the eighth division and were "vehemently applauded by the crowded assemblage." This reclamation of public space was prompted by the assassination of Abraham Lincoln. In the face of tragedy, after the carnage of civic warfare, and amid the frenzy of industrial growth New Yorkers seemed to have regrouped in the old ritual of a heterogeneous but associated democracy. In 1865 it would seem that America's biggest, most menacing city could still, if the occasion demanded it, represent itself in public space as a democratic assortment of social and cultural differences.

More than a decade later, the centennial of the Declaration of Independence called forth more lighthearted parades in New Orleans and

223

San Francisco as well as New York. Although federal troops were still stationed in New Orleans, suggesting that the wounds of prolonged civil wars had not entirely healed, the headlines read: "Fourth of July Brilliant Procession." The five divisions that celebrated America's birthday in New Orleans included a full range of ethnicity—French, Portuguese, and Cuban as well as Irish and German—and spanned the classes from clerks to screwmen. The parades in New York and San Francisco outdistanced the Southern patriots, boasting nine and sixteen divisions respectively. In New York the ethnic organizations alone totaled more than 130, including forty associations of the Ancient Order of Hibernians. Such events demonstrate the tenacity and resilience of the democratic institutions that had been devised in the antebellum city.

But such grandiose civic ceremonies were relatively rare after 1865. Between the funeral procession of 1865 and the centennial, parades seldom put such a full replica of the citizenry on public display. The rare public holiday was more often commemorated with less participatory if more spectacular rituals. On a routine Independence Day in San Francisco the spectators' attention would turn to a reenactment of a battle of the Revolution or tableaux such as this reproduction of a mining camp in the early days of California. "A bark hut was strung around with camp utensils. Miners were occupied in digging and washing for gold. Eureka with helmet, spear and cat-of-mail represented by Miss Kate Thorp, was seated upon a mound of earth and rock. The car was drawn by four horses." To compete with such splendors a New Yorker could point to a Fourth of July pageant featuring forty-eight illuminated windows at police headquarters, ornamented with 380 flags. Just one corner of Union Square could rivet public attention. "The piece on the Northwest corner was entitled 'Rock of Liberty.' A shield surrounded by an eagle formed the central point. On one side stood a soldier in continental costume, holding in his outstretched hand a national flag with the figures 1776 inscribed upon it. Over against this was the form of a modern soldier, grasping a flag with the devise '1876' upon it." In the late nineteenth-century city, people came together in this public gallery of sensual delights: the panorama of colorful bunting, dramatic tableaux vivants, cascading fireworks, and the timpani of firecrackers, brass bands, church bells, and artillery salutes. Such spectacle eclipsed the relatively homely gesture of filing through the streets representing social differences. Even the Lincoln funeral procession was construed in these more abstract, mesmerizing, and ephemeral ways. The *Herald* gasped at "what a spectacle that procession was," "such a sight," a "moving mass of men," so

Figure 32. Lincoln funeral procession, 1865. *Frank Leslie' Illustrated Newspaper,* 1865.

"magnificent," "wonderful," and "sublime." The *Herald* portrayed the different units in the procession in universalizing terms: "All classes, conditions, creeds, and politics" of New York "represented the universal sentiment of the country" (fig. 32).[1]

Such civic ceremonies were possible—stored in memories and available in emergencies—but rare. A more hardy survival of antebellum civic culture was the parade of separate ethnic groups, which in fact seemed to multiply after the Civil War. But all was not well along the parade routes of the late nineteenth century. In fact public civic culture was in crisis by the 1870s. The chords of civic unity that sounded in April of 1865 were soon followed by sounds of explosive division. In 1871 a parade of Protestant Irish colors along the West Side of New York provoked the "Orange Riot," which left sixty-two men, women, and children dead—the worst urban violence since the draft riots. In the face of this crisis of ceremonial citizenship postwar cities resorted to the more abstract and spectacular forms of public display such as those found in the patriotic celebration of 1876. By the end of the 1870s these new ceremonial forms had recast civic identity in a new scheme of difference, within which dualistic representations of male and female were particularly prominent. The public ceremonies of the late nineteenth century featured a surfeit of gender symbols—the "modern soldier" and "Eureka" as played by Miss Kate Thorp, for examples.

These renovations in civic ceremony, like the reordering of urban space during the same period, did not restore the old urban kaleidoscope but did show that city people were as inventive as ever in exercising cultural citizenship in public places. The construction of a ceremonial mosaic out of the spatial segments and voluntary association of the antebellum period was difficult to replicate in the congested and undifferentiated social geography of the postwar city. The characteristic ceremonial forms of the later period were more often worked out in private meetings, by city bureaucrats or by commercial sponsors. The whole process can only be captured by a sequence of verbs that evoke the disparate actions that transformed civic culture: multiply, divide, explode, transcend, and, in the process, recast the differences among the people.

The Sum and the Parts of Ceremony

A look at the annual civic calendar reveals that the field of official public ceremony was not overcrowded after the Civil War. The Political Code of California recognized only Christmas, the Fourth of July, New Years, and Sundays as public holidays. The urban press was only slightly more magnanimous with public time: In 1865 the *San Francisco Examiner* had conferred its imprimatur on a full five public occasions, adding Thanksgiving and Washington's birthday to the registry of holidays. The press, the legislature, and the people concurred in deleting from the calendar such local political anniversaries as Admission Day in California, Evacuation Day in New York, and January 8 in New Orleans. Other omissions and additions to the public calendar were matters of dispute and created rival schedules of celebration in the same city. Without public sanction St. Patrick's Day would continue to be celebrated across the nation and in fact reached its apex in New Orleans only after the Civil War. Conversely, the homage to Washington's birthday was a bow to the more Anglo-Saxon Protestant and Republican constituency that few Irish Democrats mimicked.[2]

Although it was increasingly rare for city people to agree on the occasions for celebration, urban festivity itself had hardly become extinct in the last quarter of the century. The sheer volume of urban festival continued to grow after the Civil War and to this day shows little sign of slowing in pace and imagination. Ceremonies proliferated, however, not under public aegis but according to more selective impulses. For example, a compilation of San Francisco's ethnic festivals for the year 1939 contained approximately forty entries, from O-Sho-Gatsu, the Japanese New Year marked with feasting and visiting, to December 13, Santa Lucia Day, when Swedish citizens met in Stern Grove for games and refreshments. If we look to the inauspicious date of 1877, a year of depression and labor unrest in the city, private ceremonies had already filled the calendar almost to capacity. In January the fetes included the Caledonians, who represented Scottish immigrants, the Pioneers, the badge of Anglo-Saxons, and that elite and flamboyant men's club called the Bohemians.[3] February brought the Turn Verein out for a masked ball and found the Swiss Philharmonic Society tuning their instruments for a public fete. The spring picnic season found the Germania Rifles, the Garibaldi Guards, the Typographical Union, the Unitarians, the Orange Society, the MacMahon Guards, and the Slavonic Society all frolicking in the open air. All these groups had made their ceremonial mark before Memorial Day, which was followed by a picnic of 4,000 Chinese in June. The pace of festivity seemed to slacken a bit over the summer and fall but not before the representatives of the Welsh, Chileans, Mexicans, Hebrew Orphan societies, and the German Lutheran Church celebrated their anniversaries. The Italians meanwhile had chosen Columbus Day as the date for a procession through the streets of San Francisco.[4]

The press of a city of more than one million like New York was not likely to record urban festival in such detail, but one would expect that the over 100 societies that turned out on July 4, 1876, had busy festive calendars of their own during the rest of the year. The record of ethnic festival, culled from the pages of the daily press, is clearly incomplete even for the small city of San Francisco. It failed to publicize, for example, an occasion worthy of fervent celebration after the Civil War, the anniversary of the Emancipation Proclamation on January 1. That day was recognized by the African American newspaper the *Pacific Appeal,* which reported in 1866, for example, that a procession of African Americans, complete with brass bands, banners, military companies such as the Corps d'Afrique, and marching tradesmen snarled through much of central San Francisco before it adjourned for dinner at the Methodist church. The African Americans of New Orleans found the period of Reconstruction a season for many public celebrations, not just of emancipation but of the French Revolution of 1848 (which granted suffrage to those of African origin) and the death of John Brown (which warranted a special High Mass). In New Orleans the press reports of ethnic ceremony are not as extensive as in San Francisco, but if measured against the Crescent City's prewar record it amounted to a veritable explosion of festive energy. The winter social season of 1877 was ushered in by celebrations of Jewish, Swiss, German, Portuguese, and Italian ethnicities. St. Patrick's Day became a major fete in postwar New Orleans, and St. Joseph, St. Cecilia, St. John, St. Theresa, St. Alphonous, and St. Aloysius were all recognized on the city's cosmopolitan calendar. Clearly, the recessional of grand public rituals of the antebellum period had not left American cities bereft of festivity. Rather, constituencies of the public divided off and multiplied the number of ceremonies, creating an open civic calendar to which a panoply of groups, especially those identified by their national origins, including those who traced their roots to Africa, could find public access.[5]

Civic culture cannot be measured by the simple arithmetic concept of pluralism. The transfiguration of ceremonial culture after the Civil War was not just a matter of adding new or formerly marginal social groups. It was driven by contest, struggle, loss, and gain, and it remained riddled with inequities and productive of violent disagreements. At the simplest level the multiplication of ceremony was produced by the unauthorized and uncoordinated assertion of separate cultural identities. Such fragmentation of civic culture were already evident in public performances before the Civil War. The celebration of the completion of the Atlantic cable in New York City in the fall of 1858 was not a seamless community ceremony. In fact it was a poorly disguised celebration of Anglo-Saxon origins. The gallery of decorative art was draped that day with the slogan "Anglo-Saxon Twins"; on Laura Keen's Theater the transparency read, "There is no such word as fail for Saxon Blood"; at the La Farge House it was written, "Severed July 4, 1776, United August 12, 1858." Most Irish Americans read such slogans as something less than an invitation to join a public party. Only the associations of Protestant Irish joined the parade. The *Irish American* spoke for the Catholic majority, saying, "The mass of the people will not run in open-mouthed glorification" of such affinity between America and Britain. Other partisans of home rule for Ireland called the event "A gigantic debauch at public expense" and branded the building of the cable itself as the exploitation of manual labor. Throughout the tense decade of the 1850s such ethnic and religious rivalries maintained a chilly ceremonial separation. For example, the Irish Sixty-ninth Regiment refused to march in a parade welcoming the Prince of Wales to New York in 1860, and, needless to say, the Seventh did not parade on St. Patrick's Day.

But this polite and civil disengagement in public space did not put an end to ethnic hostility. After the Civil War Americans would learn that celebration, even a parade route, could become a deadly battlefield. The most explosive civic ceremony occurred on the anniversary of the Battle of the Boyne, an event of July 12, 1690, in which Prince William of Orange defeated King James II and proclaimed Protestant rule in Ireland.[6] The day had been a minor, mildly contentious American holiday since at least 1820 when some militant anti-Catholic groups used the occasion to parade the Irish Protestant colors. The Orange Loyal Association originally intended to mark the anniversary in 1870 in a relatively quiet, not quite public way. Several lodges of Orange Irish planned to gather at Cooper Union and march in a casual entourage of families to a picnic site on the Upper West Side. One observer described it as "A Pic-nic Party" and as a "procession accompanied with banners and music [that] made quite a gay appearance along the streets." Even the Orange parade the following year, which was organized with great fanfare and fore-thought, was a rather modest and familiar rite: a "parade flaunting their chosen colors, and marching to their own favorite music, under the protection of the constitutional authorities." This would seem to be a routine urban event, about which much of the public was complacent if not jaded by the 1870s: "There is nothing that some classes of our foreign citizens like better than a procession. Stick a band of music and a few banners before them, fit them out with a pair of white gloves several times too large and a long black coat dragging on the ground and they will march all over the city and be as proud of their appearance as a pea-cock is of his tails."[7]

This parade of Orangemen, however, acquired public notice in a menacing new way beginning in 1870. The holiday that year kindled a long smoldering religious conflict. As the Orangemen passed through Irish Catholic neighborhoods and among gangs of Catholic immigrants at work on Central Park and the Croton Aqueduct, they provocatively waved their banners and sang some frankly offensive lyrics. One verse went "Water, water, holy water/Sprinkle the Catholics everyone;/We cut them asunder,/And made them be under/The Protestant boys will carry the gun." The refrain of this sadistic song evoked a torture called crop-ping, whereby the Protestant Irish had pitched and torn the scalps of their Catholic enemies almost 200 years before. It went: "Croppies lie down;/Croppies lie down:/We'll make all the Catholic Croppies lie down." Some Irish Catholics in earshot of these fighting words responded with fury: They attacked the picnic party, pursued men and women into the West Side streetcars, hurled paving stones, fired guns, and left eight persons dead. Some of the Orangemen also came to the picnic armed with pistols and ready for a fight.[8]

The consequences of that small parade had only begun to unfold. The violence of 1870 inflamed public opinion, and the press in particular, igniting a febrile debate about the legitimacy of parading ethnic identities. A quintessential ritual of public democracy was in jeopardy. The discussion was haunted by the inevitability that the events of July 12 would recur the following year, after both parties to the already bitter antagonism had nursed their wounds, hardened their hatred, and pressured public authorities to take sides. The press lost no time fueling the controversy. The *Tribune* championed a ritual they had long considered a puerile foreign sport. The *Times* concurred, propounding the simple doctrine that "associations, of whatever nationality, have the right to meet and celebrate their festivals provided they do not violate the law."[9] Newspaper readers expressed divided but strong opinions. A German correspondent wrote, for example, that both the Orange and the Green had a "public right" to parade. Another reader differentiated the rights of the two contending nationalities on the principle that the latter were not celebrating a patron saint but rather gloating over a humiliating defeat suffered by the forefathers of their fellow citizens. Other correspondents had race and section on their minds. One questioned the absolute rights of ceremony, citing the precedent that Confederate rebels had recently been prohibited even from placing flowers at the graves of their war dead. Another noted that while the "colored" had been permitted to celebrate the passage of the Fifteenth Amendment it was unlikely that the Confederates would be allowed to gloat publicly over their victories in the late war. Meanwhile, the *Herald* stationed its reporters in the quarters of the Irish Catholic laboring poor, where they overheard quarrymen and longshoremen vow to stop the parade, with violence if necessary. As July 12, 1871, approached, it was rumored that Catholics were arming themselves for battle and that Orangemen were defiantly mapping out their parade route in a manner more public than ever before.[10]

City officials appeared to squirm in the privacy of their offices trying to find a way out of an impossible political dilemma. The mayor, Tammany Democrat Oakey Hall, was already under attack for catering to Irish Catholic voters and feared loosing his electoral advantage, whatever he did. Just two days before the scheduled parade, City Hall made its decision public with a proclamation deftly issued above the signature of the Protestant Police Chief, James Kelso. The order outlawed the pa-

rade called for July 12, 1871. It went to some lengths to argue that a procession through city streets was not an inalienable right.

Assemblages of any kind in places of public access, and public street processions of every character, have never become matters of popular right. In accordance, however, with the operation of free institutions, they are generally
permitted, and usually enjoy by popular assent, much freedom of action, although often submitted to at considerable sacrifice of public comfort. They
therefore became subjects for police regulation and supervision. If not an
impossible, it is nevertheless a delicate task for the authorities to decide
when this regulation and supervision shall begin, or how far it shall extend.

Given the volatile conditions of July 1871, the police chief asked, "would
it not be more politic to forego any popular or public demonstration?"
Without pausing for a response to this rhetorical question the police
chief denied permission to parade.[11] This municipal ruling did not settle
the matter. Another Democratic politician, Governor John Hoffman,
read the rights of parading and the winds of public opinion (as expressed in the press, from the pulpit, and at meetings on Wall Street)
differently. Scarcely an hour before midnight on the eve of July 12
Hoffman countermanded local authorities. Noting that New York
officials not only tolerated ethnic processions in the past but also protected them with a costly police presence, the governor ordered that the
parade could proceed. Acceding to requests from the Orange Societies
made weeks before, the governor called up the National Guard to ensure its ceremonial safety.

　What ensued was a procession like no other. Its location on the city
map gave the first warning that this ceremony was not to have an integrating public effect. Rather than winding along the main public arteries
to the civic center, its route began at an inauspicious street corner,
Twenty-ninth Street and Eighth Avenue, followed a plebeian path down
the West Side, and then took a sharp turn at Fourteenth Street toward
the more elite residential quarter of Union Square. The units that lined
up for this procession removed any expectations that this was to be a
convivial display of urban differences. Behind a phalanx of mounted
New York Police filed the whole Seventh Regiment; then came the
Orangemen, with a contingent of the press in tow and flanked by the
Twenty-second and Eighty-fourth Regiments. Taking up the rear were
the Ninth and Sixth Regiments and more mounted policemen. On the
sidelines, barricaded by this major show of military force, stood the
masses: "on sidewalks, doorsteps, windows and roofs black with people

Figure 33. Attack on the Orange Societies' parade. *Harper's Weekly*, 1871.

all around." The small band of Orangemen had commandeered a central position in the public limelight. The *Times* calculated the demographics of this strange parade as follows: 160 citizens, 800 police, and 2200 soldiers of the state. Twyford's twelve-piece band and a bit of orange bunting were the major festive touches in this display of force and defiance (fig. 33).[12]

This parade was a military action, not a democratic display. It began early with reports of the soldiers clubbing the bystanders "left and right," both near the parade route and at Hibernian Hall. The major violence erupted at the chaotic intersection of Twenty-fourth Street and Eighth Avenue. Provoked, some said, by a sniper's bullet or, according to others, just by a woman throwing a piece of cork, an unknown soldier in the ranks of the Eighty-fourth Regiment fired into the crowd and triggered a volley of gunfire. The first reports counted the deaths in three figures. The *Times* was inspired to the most sensationalist war reporting: "the sight of women and children in the throes of death at their own doorsteps." "The side walk was drenched with blood. A panorama of blood, a vista of gore, an arena of agony." Images on the field of battle included lifeless bodies left to be claimed in the street, "women making the night hideous with their cries," and the senseless death of ten-year-old Mary Anne York, felled by a bullet in the back of the head.[13] The hysterical descriptions of how this parade ground turned into a battlefield were interlaced with cool calculations about methods of riot control. The *Times* headline read: "Order Restored. The Disaffected Classes Completely Subdued. City Seldom so Quiet." Veteran nativist Joel Tyler Headley excused the carnage, saying, "Soldiers cannot be expected to discriminate in a mob between women and children. The taking of a life is a serious thing, but it is not to weigh a moment against the preservation of authority and the supremacy of the law." The *Herald* reported in one line that a child's head was blown off and in another that the police action was "mercifully cruel," "the deaths of so many comparatively innocent beings is an event at which humanity shudders, but the responsibility rests not on those who defended themselves and the cause of law at once, but on the reckless imbroglio." The headlines for July 13, 1871, most often exonerated the military and the police of responsibility for the slaughter, exalting that "Law Reigns, Order Triumphs."[14]

Behind the editorials and beneath the headlines in the mainstream press were mute signs of popular response to this macabre ceremony. For example, a crowd reportedly gathered in Union Square to receive the triumphant troops and Orangemen. As the marchers arrived at the square, the customary place of sedate ceremony associated with the Protestant middle classes, the crowd broke into applause for the champions of law and order. There was also a report of sniper fire upon the crowd. Another reporter noted that amid the cheers an Irish woman and some Negroes were heard talking angrily on the margins of the crowd.

The Irish Protestant anniversary of 1871 began with a parade but ended with a horrifying display of police and military force. The militia was the largest unit in this parade, and their gunfire was the primary cause of death, responsible for at least fifty-five of sixty-two fatalities.[15] This transfiguration of democratic representation into a display of military force was not entirely unanticipated. American parades in general had been acquiring a more military aspect since the Civil War. They usually were preceded by long deliberations about "police arrangements," began with a platoon of uniformed officers, and in some cases (New York's Fourth of July parades in the 1870s, for instance, and the few remaining Washington's birthday fetes) were entirely military in composition. By the summer of 1871 it was clear that the city's fractious and fragmented citizenry could not always be contained within the old ceremonial forms. The Orange riot unveiled one innovative method of unifying the divided city—the use of armed force to keep order. Accordingly, the culture of ceremony itself would acquire a more militarized aspect in the late nineteenth century. Not only were uniforms and weapons more prominent, they were paraded not by a festive array of voluntary companies but by regiments of the Grand Army of the Republic or the mounted police at the front of the procession.

This bloody ceremony revealed the difficulties of celebrating differences in the more congested and incoherent space of the modern city. It issued an excruciating reminder of the civil wars of the past and would haunt civic culture long after the episode receded from the headlines. The last major incident of crowd violence in New York until the race riots of the twentieth century, it marked a historical watershed: a loss of innocence about public ceremony. No longer could citizens casually take to the streets parading their favorite colors. Once a parade had ended in the loss of human life, citizens, journalists, mayors, and historians had some second thoughts. Who would second guess the fateful public and private decisions made on that day in July 1871? Could the violence have been prevented? Is there an absolute right to parade? Had ugly ethnic antagonism simply been unleashed, or was it conjured up by the press and manipulated by the politicians? Whatever the case, in July 1871 the architects of civic festivity not only lost their innocence, they curtailed their tolerance. Permits, police arrangements, and restrictive ordinances increasingly surrounded such potentially dangerous public performances.

Recede, Transcend

Understandably, the most inveterate paraders of the past began to mark their anniversaries in more constrained, less public ways. St. Patrick's Day had become a quiet and defensive affair after the nativists attacks of the 1850s, its organizers nearly obsessed with "decorum," "sense of responsibility," "general sobriety." It resumed its exuberant form and indeed became the quintessential Americana parade in the 1860s, but estimates of the size dwindled from as many as 60,000 in 1870 to as few as 1000 marchers by decade's end, these consisting largely of undifferentiated units of the Ancient Order of Hibernians. The more elite and Yankee holiday of Washington's birthday receded quickly from public attention. By 1876 New York's Seventh Regiment stopped coming out for Washington's birthday as well as for the Fourth of July. At that time thousands still turned out on Washington's birthday in San Francisco, but the ceremony had been removed from the city center to the Presidio, a military site on the outskirts of town where the hillside was covered by a "black mass" of spectators. Elsewhere, Washington's birthday was likely to be observed inside and behind closed doors, at banquets and balls that were often organized by the ladies.[16]

As the traditional civic commemorations vacated public time and space the more private feast days of Thanksgiving, Christmas, and New Years acquired new prominence. These holidays had never been marked with public performances. The one official aspect of New Years in New York, a mayor's reception at City Hall, disappeared in the late 1870s, leaving only a Martha Washington Reception, private fetes, and disorderly street processions of young males to mark the day. Christmas and Thanksgiving became even more emphatically private in their meanings. Their centerpiece remained family conviviality at the dinner table and the gluttonous consumption of turkeys. These celebrations were not convened by public meetings but by an alliance between housewives and shopkeepers. Shopping became the major public behavior associated with the winter holidays. In 1875, for example, the *San Francisco Chronicle* described Christmas in images of the promiscuous but antisocial occupation of the streets: It observed rich and poor mothers jostling one another on the sidewalks as they went single-mindedly in search of gifts for their own children. The winter holidays were also the occasions for one more public ceremonial gesture, the rite of feeding the poor at the "Public Institutions." The columns of newsprint reporting on this ritual revealed, however, that the sites of this ceremony were private, usually Protestant charities. Public action was only a fall-back position to the *Chronicle*, which advised on Christmas 1872, "If we can find no personal charity send a gold note to some public institution."[17]

The public calendar, in short, was acquiring a private aura, one that even began to color the political anniversaries. Increasingly, July Fourth was celebrated as a family holiday when kinfolk retired together into nature. Taking excursions into Central or Golden Gate Parks, or resorts on Lake Pontchartrain, families celebrated the newly popular and intimate rite of a picnic. As early as 1871 the *New York Tribune* mused that "The time seems to be coming when the Fourth of July shall be a holiday plain and simple, devoted to rest and recreation and some sort of civic observance which will recall for ever the beginnings of the republic." The *Tribune* noted that "Men had promised their families weeks before hand an excursion." The *Tribune*'s favorite adjective for a successful holiday was "quiet." In 1878 it proclaimed a "Quiet Celebration in the City.... The Rush to Coney Island and Other Resorts." July 5, 1880, warranted this headline: "Quiet Keeping of the Fourth." In San Francisco in the same year the newspaper featured an article entitled "A Lady's Fourth." Although this particular story was datelined Sutter Creek, women were putting their own stamp upon the holidays in the cities as well. In New York, New Orleans, and San Francisco they took up stations at public institutions delivering charity and ice cream or bedecking the public stage in flowers.[18]

The retreat from parade routes, the patrol of public ceremony, and the practice of a more retiring style of celebration constituted the mainstay of civic performance in New York and San Francisco. But the last quarter of the century was also a time for inventing some novel civic rituals, especially in New Orleans. In the city that the Civil War had divided, occupied, and vanquished, cultural survival virtually demanded some ceremonial creativity. In 1865 the *New Orleans Bee* translated this civic imperative into a call for an old-fashioned Fourth of July celebration: "May the day mark a new era of true peace, of reconstructing in heart as well as in form, of people of all parts of the common country bound together on principles of justice and acknowledging one future and one destiny." Scarcely a decade later the city's ceremonial calendar had been almost totally rewritten.[19]

The *Bee* or *Abeille,* one of the few remaining bilingual institutions in the city, used the phrase "Liberty, Equality, and Fraternity" to evoke one set of common values for the city. Neither fraternity nor unity would be easy to achieve in a city where liberty and equality had so long been denied to those of African descent. And the Fourth was not to be a unified ceremony. Secession had rent that holiday in two. In 1865 the *Picayune* noted a clear fragmentation in a generally lively Fourth. The Mechanics Institute was the site of a familiar if subdued ceremony complete with reading of the Declaration of Independence, music, and a benediction. A second ceremony, identified as a National Republican event, was conducted at the Customhouse, the seat of federal authority where both "whites" and "colored" honored the nation's birthday. Yet a third ritual was enacted on the periphery of these two divided ceremonies: a torchlight procession of the voluntary fire department. This last rite, performed in darkness, punctuated with fire crackers, and located on the outskirts of town, drew the largest of the three audiences. The flickering lights of the torchlight procession failed to illuminate the political and social divisions displayed in the daytime celebrations of the past. But the very opaqueness of postwar ceremony augured fundamental changes in how the people represented themselves.[20]

In the following years the prospects of civic harmony rose and fell through Presidential Reconstruction, Radical Republicanism, and finally the Redemption of the old Confederate elite. Each political change jolted the performance of civic ceremony. In 1866, when President Johnson's lenient policies of Reconstruction seemed to augur an easy restoration of white power, a small and quiet Fourth of July ceremony was held at the Mechanics Institute. According to the *Bee,* many "colored" were in attendance, suggesting that this traditional fete was a Republican affair. The *Picayune* was bold enough to scoff at this official ceremony of the Reconstruction government as a harbor for every color, "from Caucasian to full-blooded African." Another "novel" festival was more to the *Picayune's* taste. This was a firemen's celebration that featured a parade and picnic and occurred not in the center of civic space at Lafayette Square but outside the city at the fairgrounds. It featured an apolitical program of sporting competitions. To the *Bee* this ceremony was nonetheless "in a sort the official representation of the municipal government in this regard."[21]

Something peculiar was happening: Civic ceremony seemed to have been kidnapped from its central and official site and held hostage among the firemen on the outskirts of town. The *Picayune* noted another firemen's parade in 1866 with effusive praise and unbridled mirth. Of one gaily bedecked horse in the procession the editor noted that the ladies were "Sorely humbled by the vastly superior exhibition of the noble charger Jeff." This sophomoric joke aside, the convivial outfitting of the engines and steeds of the voluntary firemen had become the focal point of civic pride. It was enacted not on July 4, however, but on March 4. By grafting local civic identity onto the annual fireman's procession the former rebels had effected a ceremonial coup: It was a spatial move (from city center to fairgrounds), a ritual innovation (from the traditions of reciting the Declaration of Independence and parading the streets to ornamenting firemen's equipment), and an alteration of the ceremonial calendar (from July 4 to March 4). The charm of the firemen's procession, said the *Picayune,* was "enhanced from local causes and home influences.... It is a New Orleans Holiday." It was, in other words, a circumvention of federal authority at the level of ceremony.[22]

It was also a sentinel of the ceremonial creativity of the postwar city. In future years the Fourth of July would recede from the headlines and become a private ceremony for Republicans. In the 1870s the local conservative press noted with scorn that only the metropolitan police (a force appointed by Reconstruction authorities and including a conspicuous number of African Americans) marched on that day, through largely deserted streets. Meanwhile, the fireman's festival day became the centerpiece of the ceremonial calendar, the occasion for banner headlines and effusive self-congratulation: "Grand Display, The procession, the Companies, the Engines." This depiction of the Brooklyn Company No. 2 in 1874 gives a flavor of the pageantry. "First were the engines, a central delight ornamented with a deer head, mounted on a crimson velvet base with gold lace against a backdrop of flowers." Then there was the favorite horse named Billy. And of course there were the "boys," numbering fifty, uniformed in red shirts, firehats, and black pants. The glowing report on the firemen of Brooklyn Company No. 2 closed with the notice that the banner adorning their engine had been presented to them early that morning by "their lady friends." This was only one of some forty fire companies who paraded before a congregation of spectators that was described as large, ardent, and as ecstatic as any Fourth of July crowd in the North. Amid all the play and pageantry the press did not lose sight of a certain civic seriousness that surrounded the firemen's parade. Unlike the Fourth of July or January 8, the firemen's anniversary was a ceremony for secessionists, unsullied by allusions to federal or Northern institutions.[23]

While the firemen's procession was an evasive ceremonial action, mounted outside Yankee jurisdiction, other ceremonies practiced a kind of cultural camouflage. At least two spots on the New Orleans civic calendar disguised the resurgence of Confederate power in mourning clothes. The ceremonies of the lost cause found a fitting place on the calendar of the once largely Roman Catholic city, All Saints' Day. The practice of visiting the graves on November 1 acquired new solemnity and status as well as explicit political references after the war. The *Picayune* orchestrated this transition by singling out the graves of "fallen soldiers" for homage and giving explicit directions on how to find the tombs of rebel heroes. A second date for Confederate mourning was the ritual handiwork of the Ladies Benevolent Association, founded in 1874 to honor the men who gave their lives for the Confederacy. They chose the date of April 6, commemorating the 1862 Battle of Shiloh as the Southern Memorial Day. By 1875 the female architects of public ceremony came out of hiding. Calling themselves the Ladies Confederate Association, they convened as many as 5000 people to place flowers on the gravestones of rebels. Soon the mourners dared to carry Confederate flags, and by the end of Reconstruction their memorial day featured a full military parade. Other women and men of New Orleans worked through the 1870s collecting funds for a statue of Robert E. Lee that would not be unveiled until 1884. In the meantime they filled the public records with bathetic images of defeat, "Bitter regret to the past... prayerful and chastened aspirations to the future," to a time when "all virtue is not dead."[24]

As the 1870s progressed resistance to Reconstruction took an overtly political and defiant form. Ceremony and politics worked together, hand in hand, and on many fronts. St. Patrick's Day parades, for example, construed "home rule" as a policy for the American South as well as for Ireland. When, through most of the period between 1872 and 1877, Reconstruction divided Louisiana into two rival governments, the factions jousted with one another on local ceremonial turf. The rivalry reached its zenith in 1877. That year opened with two inaugural ceremonies. The supporters of Confederate General Francis T. Nicholls where so confident of their imminent resumption of power that they invited women and children to attend the ceremonies at St. Patrick's Hall. The triumph was premature. The Union army outlawed this elected government and, with minimal pomp, installed Governor Packard nearby at the statehouse. Due to the undecided presidential election of 1876, the legitimate government of the state remained in dispute until the spring. On April 6 the impatient Redemptionists organized another ceremony in Lafayette Square. With an estimated 20,000 attending, "The whole people seemed to be enthused with the spirit of the day." Some had entered by procession and then adjourned in the old ceremonial form, a parade led by a band of music. "The people were there in force, black men and white men, old men and young men, rich men and poor men, men of all nationalities and interests were there." And ladies and children joined in the reception that followed in St. Patrick's Hall. With this local rite citizens of New Orleans added their endorsement to the partisan bargain that would end Radical Reconstruction. In exchange for a promise to withdraw the federal troops that were protecting Louisiana's Republican governor, Rutherford Hayes secured the congressional votes that made him president. On April 25 New Orleanians gathered behind a cordon of police to watch the federal troops, in dress uniforms and accompanied by a band, march back to the North. Ladies waved handkerchiefs from the balcony and Confederate veterans fired a 100-gun salute.[25]

Public ceremonies such as these had gone beyond the call of civic duty to foster the redemption of Confederate political culture. Ceremony served as a chrysalis in which a new politics came to life. When the anniversary of the attempted coup against Reconstruction came around in September 1877, the restored Confederates proclaimed a new public holiday. The relatively Spartan celebration featured a procession of rebels dressed in civilian attire, but bearing arms, before an audience of admirers. "Indeed the people did not merely gather—they thronged and swarmed and came out in myriads." The Redeemed population resumed its status as "mass." Only one distinguishing identity stood out from the crowd: "An immense concourse of people assembled on Canal Street, young ladies in white dresses, and activated by the utmost enthusiasm, being in the majority."[26]

The civic reunion around a new set of symbols was complete by 1877. But one especially creative avenue to that ceremonial end remains to be described. It is of course Mardi Gras. New Orleans Carnival had begun to take on its modern form late in the 1850s when a group of businessmen from Mobile formed the first elite Carnival Club, the Mystic Krewe of Comus. But it was after the Civil War that Mardi Gras became the most lavish festival of this or any American city. By 1880, when an estimated 100,000 persons gathered in the streets of New Orleans on Shrove Tuesday, Carnival had assumed many of its characteristic ceremonial elements. A spate of new carnival clubs, the figures of Rex and the *boeuf gras,* elaborate parades of allegorical tableaux, and a carnival queen rendered Mardi Gras a capacious and movable receptacle of symbolism, a stage for extended enactment of civic parables. Rex and his queen brought the whole city under his royal authority, and the parades took the elite out of their private balls to write their opinions in the streets and engrave them in the sensations of the dazzled masses.

Mardi Gras exemplified a major formal innovation in public ceremony accomplished after the Civil War, the turn away from didactic self-representation to a more spectacular style of civic expression. The Mardi Gras pageant clearly emphasized the reception of visual and audible stimuli rather than the participatory construction and display of identity found in antebellum parades. As spectacles they unleashed the colorful and musical aspects of ceremony from their moorings in concrete social differences and specified political ideals. Mardi Gras, with its surplus of symbols, ornate moving allegories, opulent costumes, excess of color, song, and sensation was the zenith of spectacle. As the *Picayune* put it, "Comus personifies the pleasures of the senses and presides over the revel and the festal board." The spectacle in New Orleans was an extreme form of a more general development in civic ceremony that had been

Figure 34. Mardi Gras, 1872. Courtesy The Historic New Orleans Collection, Museum/Research Center.

underway for some time. The glimmer and shadow of torchlight parades were progressively effacing the direct mottoes and variegated costumes that once represented specific urban constituencies, just as the words of the Fourth of July speaker were lost in the phantasmagoric impression of a fireworks display (fig. 34).[27]

Mardi Gras also presented an especially elaborate rendition of the second thematic innovation in postwar civic performances, the enactment of authority. In 1872 Carnival season witnessed a kind of ceremonial revolution, a ceremonial coup d'etat that installed a new monarch called Rex. Organized by a club of conservative businessmen, this carnival krewe decreed that one of their number would preside over the entire civic festival. When Rex appeared in 1872, he did not come quietly into the divided city. He trumpeted his entry, not just with pomp and ceremony and noblesse oblige but with a full retinue of edicts. By 1877 they numbered thirty. With each proclamation Rex dictated elaborate regulations of public behavior. The old democratic methods of convening ceremony, through public meetings, elected delegates, and argumentative meetings, were satirically replaced by quite another order of cultural citizenship. Cabals of businessmen made plans in secret and published them as unassailable royal commands. The language was a hyperbole of authoritarianism: "proclamations" were issued to "our loving subjects" or "our loyal subjects"; "edicts" were "hereby ordered and decreed";

maskers were "ordered" to "immediately report to the War Department"; "All places and businesses both public and private [were] hereby ordered to be closed." Even the democratic offices of government were "ordered" closed. In 1877 the *Picayune* explicitly endorsed the authoritarian streak in Mardi Gras; "There is at the bottom of the public heart of every people, no matter whether the government be despotic, monarchical or republican a firmly rooted though sometimes inactive predisposition to yield allegiance to centralized authority when exercised by a person or persons surrounded by the attributes which exalt humanity."[28]

The coronation of Rex was a rehearsal of the tumultuous impositions and reversals of state power that wracked New Orleans during the Civil War and Reconstruction and just one of many references to national politics played out in Mardi Gras.[29] The great carnival themes of the 1870s were undisguised burlesques of Radical Reconstruction government. In 1873, for example, carnival presented Republicans such as General Grant and Benjamin Butler as caricatures of Darwin's "Missing Link." Of the 1877 pageant the *Picayune* surmised that Comus "was immeasurably diverted with the campaign of 1876 . . . What a rich fund was there for ridicule and badinage." Against a backdrop of headlines forecasting the removal of federal troops from the South, Republican leaders were paraded across the civic stage in gorilla costumes (fig. 35).

The final irony and signature inversion of carnival in late nineteenth-century America was that it ordered mirth and presented Saturnalia as submission to authority. Most civic ceremonies clothed state power in a velvet glove of spectacle. This dual aspect of modern ceremony was found in all three cities. In New Orleans after Reconstruction the glove was an especially ornate spectacle, the pleasing sensual enjoyment that surrounded Rex, the glow of torchlight and of fireworks, all of which seduced the audience into the role of passive receptor of impressions manufactured by the Confederate elite. This merging of authority and spectacle was evidenced in New York's Union Square in 1871 when the triumphant regiments returned from the Orange massacre. According to the *Herald's* report of July 13, 1871, "A curious crowd looked out upon the glistening bayonets and waving banners as the procession moved in from Fourteenth street. . . . Bright and buoyant moved the column of infantry men one on either side of the guilty-looking men, wearing the emblems of British monarchy, and the sun whose rays were yet unchilled by the evening breeze lent a halloo to the whole. Well and fair the militiamen marched with arms at the right shoulder shift, and wheeled round."[30] San Francisco in the centennial year added a sham battle of the

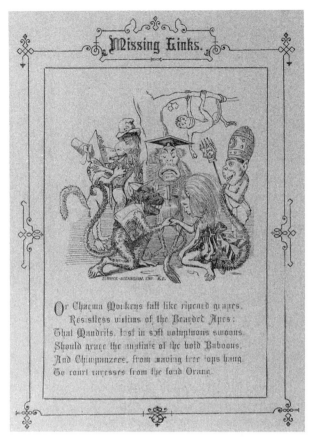

Figure 35. *Missing Links.* Comus booklet, 1873. Courtesy The Historic New Orleans Collection, Museum/Research Center.

Revolution to the spectacular elements of the modern Fourth of July ceremony. Its fireworks were equally spectacular. The same period found the field of American ceremony propagated with stars and stripes, a profusion of flags presenting a spectacle of patriotism. San Francisco's Fourth of July celebration of 1871 featured a "wilderness" of such banners, "the seeds of patriotism sown in the American household blossomed out in flags." In New York in 1870 the pyrotechnic display had already reached maximum symbolic excess by featuring a "Grand temple of Liberty," "Chinese and Egyptian wheels," a "radiant fire like a kaleidoscope," emblems of Washington, Liberty, Justice, the seals of city and state, and—the finale—"a grand union battery of red, white, and blue stars and stripes." This was advertised as "one of the grandest and most expensive" pyrotechnic displays ever attempted covering "over thirty thousand square feet of fire and the most brilliant and beautiful colors known in art."[31]

Such spectacles could not always disguise the authoritarian side of public performance. Authority assumed concrete and brutal forms as well. In the spring of 1877, after both Rex and the Union army had vacated the streets of New Orleans, white power was displayed in another public ceremony. On the evening of June 14 "the theme everywhere" was "Hangman's Day—A Terribly Assuring Evidence of the Restoration of Law and Order." While an "immense throng of people, white and black," massed outside, three persons were hung and their bodies left suspended for approximately thirty minutes before they were carted away. The public presentation of authority, be it enacted by a hangman or impersonated by Rex, was a critical element of public ritual in postwar New Orleans. Such performances were deadly serious matters to an urban population whose civil war was so prolonged, so tumultuous, and so revolutionary in its consequences.[32] But the ceremonial apparition of authority was not unique to New Orleans. About the same time a hanging was also staged in San Francisco. "The body swung to and fro ... the morbid crowds in the street lingered on until after the body was removed from the jail." Both public executions inflicted civic violence on similar human targets, representing increasingly suspect social categories. The bodies that swung in New Orleans were of two Mulatto women and one native of Manila, while in San Francisco the hangman's noose claimed a Chinese immigrant. Although no such hangings were staged in New York City, the press was not lacking in morality plays that foregrounded state violence. The bloody aftermath of the Orange riot was interpreted, like the hangings elsewhere, as a brutal but legitimate use of public authority, enacted on another often racialized other, the Irish poor.[33] All these ceremonies augured new meanings of social difference being conjured up by urban spectacles. Most were products, furthermore, of a different social process; fiats of government bureaus, schemes of businessmen, and backstage designs of private clubs were replacing the coordinated actions of sundry public meetings.

Recasting the People: The Illusions of Gender

These formal elements of the postwar ceremonies—authority, spectacle, and private manufacture—went against the grain of democratic tradi-

tions such as the parade. Rex was not a man of the people, and a pyrotechnic explosion shattered the urban mosaic of differences. The
bright lights of the spectacle were, however, well adapted to capturing a
third ceremonial motif—more abstract, high-contrast distinctions such
as those between male and female. Icons of masculinity and femininity
were given new prominence during Mardi Gras and in other ceremonial
creations of postwar New Orleans. Just as Rex took a queen, other civic
performances employed a gender division of labor. The firemen's parade
was the play of boys and men, while Memorial Day and All Saints' Day
were the work of women. No one questioned this gender logic. The
Picayune said of All Saints' Day, "the female mind originated the practice,
the female had perpetuated it and keeps the custom green. The ruder sex
with its ruder occupations and secular thoughts could scarce think of
anything so beautiful and mindful."[34]

The firemen's parade was stocked full of gender stereotype, sometimes to the point of the ridiculous. Consider Mrs. Jacob Leidner
mounting bouquets on the smokestack of the fire engine or another lady
acting as "god mother" to a fire engine. Or recall the stallion named Jeff,
whose decorative accessories rivaled those of the finest lady. Flowers and
smokestacks, femininity wedded to masculinity, were the starring duet in
the firemen's anniversary. The 1871 account in the *Picayune* was written
from a gendered viewpoint: "the eye will linger delightedly upon long
lines of galleries freighted with the loveliest women in the land—all eager to express their admiration for the noble men who through so many
years have kept watch and war over their houses and over the vast city."
Because male and female differences seemed such basic symbols, they
could provide anchors of allegiance in a city whose identity had been
shaken by the conquering Yankees. Gender provided symbolic ground
on which the defeated Confederacy could culturally regroup. White
ladies in white dresses waving white handkerchiefs were the essential audience to that celebration of September 14, 1877. and they would remain
key motifs in the cult of white supremacy.[35]

Gender distinctions, and especially apparitions of femininity, were
also prominent in Northern spectacles. If the detailed accounts of fireworks in the morning papers mentioned human icons, they were likely
to be drawn from "George Washington and his Galaxy of goddesses."
The chief female deity was Liberty, who appeared not just in the fiery
skies but also in the tableaux mounted on wagons in the rarer but more
spectacular parades of the late century. The organizers of a San Francisco
parade for July 4, 1870, for example, loaded a wagon with "the goddess

of liberty and amazons." This same line of marching spectacle included the Garibaldi Association's car decked with a beautiful girl wreathed in fruits (the precursor of the Goddess of Agriculture who came to reign over Columbus Day later in the century). Indeed, it was as the spectacular representation of nationality, be it Irish, Italian, or American, that the female allegory was most often pressed into ceremonial service. This iconography was nothing new in American ceremonies. It appeared as the emblem of civic virtue in the early national period. Even Mardi Gras had its full house of female images, including a Marianne who patrolled French Liberty in a circle of monarchical authority figures: Charlemagne, Louis XIV, and Napoleon.[36] Icons of femininity became increasingly prominent during the season of municipal civil wars. Both vigilantes and nativists were enamored of gender symbolism. When the former disbanded in 1856, it was with a parade of military manhood complete with "the glistening bayonets observed from an elevated position." The streets were filled with masculinity and "lined with female attendants" whose ceremonial contribution was "so profuse" that "thousands of the muskets in rank were eventually ornamented with flowers placed in the muzzle."[37] With such genuflection to gender, the Protestant middle classes largely deserted the public stage of ceremony, in San Francisco and elsewhere.

The appearance of gender symbolism after the Civil War was updated and inflated, such that projections of the difference between male and female assumed an unprecedented centrality in civic culture. Female allegories, for example, were now presented in the flesh. The roles of Liberty, the Maid of Erin, and the Goddess of Agriculture were usually played by the daughters of leaders of voluntary associations who wore white gowns accented by their national colors. In Irish green or red, white, and blue, women wedded ethnicity to spectacle. The *Tribune* described this novel apparition of the 1860s as two women on horseback at the closing of the St. Patrick's Day parade. The young woman in green represented the genius of Ireland and the other, in red, white, and blue spangles topped with a liberty cap, portrayed the Goddess of Liberty. In 1869 San Francisco's goddess had acquired a court of girls representing the counties of Ireland as well as the states of the Union, giving the opportunity for scores of ingenues to appear in the streets and be recognized by name in the newspaper.[38] Accompanied by marching men, the living female allegories dramatized masculinity and femininity, much like the duos in the New Orleans firemen's parade. The ethnic pas de deux was danced on July 4, 1875, in San Francisco by the Maid of Erin and

Figure 36. St. Patrick's Day, Union Square, 1870. The J. Clarence Davies Collection, 29.100.2658, Museum of the City of New York.

"Adjutant Abraham Newman . . . the handsomest officer without any exception in the entire line, and the hilt of his glorious saber was generally reported to be studded with costly diamonds." The *corps de ballet* consisted of thirty-six women in white representing the states of the Union and partnered by a "solid appearance and well composed fine specimen of vigorous manhood" as played by the members of the Irish American Benevolent Society (fig. 36).[39]

The appearance of femininity in the ceremonies of the latter half of the nineteenth century was something more than visual ornamentation. The press began to actually print the speeches written, if not delivered, by the women who had long been presenting wreaths and banners to militia units or fire companies. Perhaps because of the urgency of ceremony in the conquered South, this practice was especially common in New Orleans. Just after the war, for example, a Mrs. Sancier delivered "A pretty little speech" as she bestowed a wreath upon the Sons of Louisiana. The voice of female ceremony became more audible at the St. Patrick's Day parades of the next decade. A Miss Donnelley was allowed to be positively loquacious in public: "knowing as I do that you have always practiced that spirit of toleration and fraternity which these emblems indicate, I feel no hesitation in entrusting them to your care. Take them now and proceed to the pious mission which has called you out today.... Act your part like true sons of liberty and the women of your race will cheer you to victory." Responding for the Mitchell's Rifles, Captain McCooney gallantly replied: "Your words have sunk deep into our heart.... In future camp grounds we will see them and know that the true and beautiful daughters of our race are cheering us on." In San Francisco in 1873 a Mrs. O'Brien called Irish men to the same nationalist duty, and in a less pacific but equally gendered style. She asked that the members of the nationalist corps "never be forgetful of your manhood or the claims of your far off brothers."[40]

The physical and audible appearance of women in ceremony conformed to a sharply binary division between the sexes. The ceremonial woman was not only feminine in demeanor but also supportive of a militantly masculine political position, be it a warrior for Irish nationalism or fighter for white supremacy. The feminine side of gender antinomy was a convenient support for ethnic identity, evoking as it did the ties of blood, marriage, kinship, and reproduction, which gave definition to different descent groups. An orator on St. Patrick's Day in 1854 invoked this symbolism when he spoke of "the hope that this good brotherhood may often meet together on this day to do honor to the mother from whose wearied womb they came."[41] Frail femininity was also readily adaptable to the enactment of the lost cause. New Orleans ladies organized Memorial Day as a flourish of demure femininity: "there were no noisy demonstrations, no parades, no gatherings," just a quiet laying of flowers and whispering of prayers for the dead. Even the male orator that year dealt out images of victimization, of "weary, sick wounded" men coming home in defeat. Wreaths bore the words "to some dear dead one to a lost cause." (It should be noted that all this docile prose was issued "by order of Mrs. C. M. Pritchard, Pres.")

The ladies of the North also found new roles to play and opportunities to exploit in modern ceremonies. Their forte was not the Civil War memorial but the charity benefit. By the 1870s the image of the benevolent woman was emblazoned all across the winter holidays and installed in the rites of noblesse oblige performed at the public institutions. In San Francisco the presentations of the "little Sisters" objectified the recipients of female charity. In 1869 the Roman Catholic Sisters of Mercy conducted the usually Protestant rite of feeding turkey to the needy. Their objects were the inmates of the Magdalen Society, numbering seventy-eight, who were treated to "lectures on religion" as they feasted. On New Years 1868 the Ladies of the Larkin Street Presbyterian Church and Sunday school staged exercises for children whose behavior was "commendably orderly." Elsewhere, charity women decorated the "Orphan Christmas Tree" and escorted Santa Claus to the poor and deserving. This editorial homage to the San Francisco Orphan Society sums up the philosophy of public welfare in a laissez-faire political economy: "This associated maternity that stands before us to-day with open arms, offering a shelter and a home to the orphaned life of this city, it is a fond maternity, gentle in winning, skilled in nursing, tender in cherishing, patient, affectionate, faithful and pious. . . . This corporation has not only a soul of intelligence, but a warm woman's heart a most motherly charity."[42]

The impersonators of benevolence presented themselves in especially ingenious ways and elegant costumes in New York. A Miss Huntington made a winter ritual out of her method of instructing poor girls in housekeeping. Holiday season at the public institutions was an opportunity to display her "kitchen garden method" of domestic education, set to music and performed by poor girls. Other women organized balls and soirees to benefit their favorite charity. During the depression years of the 1870s the custom of conspicuous display of dress, dance, and dining as a way of collecting alms for the poor offended many New Yorkers and prompted even the New York Tribune to rebuke the lady organizers of these ceremonies. The charitable rites at a girls' industrial school in 1879 were considered in better taste. They featured 260 girls being fed 200 pounds of turkey. "The girls pick ciders and wood in the streets in the morning and attend school later in the day. They always have a substantial dinner and are given warm clothes to wear if they earn a certain number of credit marks. On Wednesday their parents and many of the other deserving poor persons in the neighborhood called at the school with baskets, which were filed with turkey, potatoes, pies, etc."[43]

In such rituals as these women of the middle and upper classes spelled out an elaborate social and political theory: They honored free enterprise, self-help, class harmony, and female altruism all at once. Such extended metaphors of class and gender wove in and out of the neighborhoods of New York in the late 1870s. The Tribune's coverage of ceremonies of public and private charity for the winter of 1880 consumed two columns of small print and included rites such as these: Miss Huntington demonstrating her housekeeping method at the Wilson Mission for girls; a ritualized feeding of an orderly file of poor children at the

Howard Mission and Home for Little Wanderers; the provision of 6,535 pounds of turkey to children housed in state institutions; and a dinner at the Girls Lodging House No. 27 in St. Mark's Place presided over by Mrs. John Jacob Astor. Clearly maternal charity could not mask an increasingly condescending and cavernous gulf between the classes in modern America.[44]

These female rites of class were only one of the myriad projections of gender difference on the public calendar of industrial American cities. During the winter holidays images of nurturing femininity—mothers around the Christmas tree and the charitable matrons at the public institutions—monitored the more private boundaries of urban culture and class privilege. When women approached closer to the public stage, it was usually in a gendered phalanx and trailing allusions of privacy—voluntary benevolence on Thanksgiving, domesticity on Christmas, abjectly mourning for a lost cause on Confederate Memorial Day. This feminine construction of social welfare as somehow marginal to the public sphere was illustrated vividly by the Ladies Evangelical and Philanthropic Society of the First Congregational Church of San Francisco. On September 14, 1877, they appointed a "Flower committee," "The object being to carry flowers to homes where they are seldom, if ever, seen." After visiting families and assaying their needs, however, these ladies reconstituted themselves into an "Employment Committee," a mode of recruiting domestic servants. Completing this recessive, privatized picture of women's place in the civic ceremonies of the late nineteenth century is the figure of the female allegory. The Goddess of Liberty or Maid of Erin did offer some women a central place in a genuinely public ritual. But masked as a symbol of nationality or ethnicity, these living icons represented some transcendent femininity or served as the objects of voyeuristic desire. They did not represent themselves as active citizens.[45]

Maids of Erin, Goddesses of Liberty, and the whole repertoire of feminine imagery served at least two symbolic functions. The first was to transmit meaning beyond and above the field of social difference and political conflicts to a plane of spectacle and abstract civic unity. Second, and somewhat paradoxically, female symbols unified the separate ethnic groups by weaving cultural bonds around common national origins, biological descent, or class position. In neither case did women represent themselves. By appearing in public as transcendent symbol and a species of spectacle herself the female icon was a synecdoche of the innovations in cultural performance after the Civil War. She served to evade and obscure the fissures in the urban population—class interests, demands for justice, the claims of participation for excluded minorities—even as she gave symbolic shape to other identities such as Irish nationalism or whiteness. Female gender symbols represented civic order, not warfare, but order at a price.

The ceremonial performance of gender operated by a dialectic all its own and peculiar to its time. Within the context of Victorian gender categories, women were admitted to civic ceremony carrying intimations of privacy and passivity that tended to disguise the interests specific to their gender position. Thus, the ceremonial apparition of femininity in public ironically turned in upon the women who impersonated it. The female historical actors behind the scenes of these ceremonies, the likes of Miss Donnelley, Mrs. Huntington, or even Mrs. Astor did not lead a female assault on the public sphere. They may, in fact, have even diverted women from demanding full citizenship in their own right. The apparition of femininity in public was not, for the moment, the beachhead for a mobilization of women's rights or feminism. It would take more than another generation for women to assemble in significant numbers and on their own behalf in city streets. Even the boldest advocates of women's rights were still rather shy of public spaces. When Susan B. Anthony scorned the gender exclusions of the centennial celebration of American Independence she called her sex to a rather secluded demonstration of their disapproval: "In meetings, in parlors, in kitchens wherever they may be, unite with us in this declaration and protest."[46] Women had hardly begun to imagine the suffrage parades of the next century, and not until the 1960s would they appear alongside and equal to men in a few Mardi Gras clubs. As long as women represented some transcendent other and projected ideals of domestic seclusion onto public ceremony their civic actions had the dialectical effect of affirming exclusion from the sphere of democratic participation.[47]

The Articulation of Race and Class

Another construction of difference that came into sharper focus after the Civil War, the division connoted by the term *race,* operated according to a different and equally complicated dialectic. First of all, racial differences resembled gender dimorphism in that they were readily adaptable to spectacular display. In fact the quintessential spectacle of Mardi Gras was one of the first and most elaborate public stages for the racial theories that were becoming prominent at midcentury. Tableau 3 in Rex's procession was captioned "Delicate satire on the disposition of the

Aryan race." The entry of His Majesty Rex into the city a few days before had in fact been advertised as "a compendium of the 'Aryan Race.'" The oldest and most prestigious Carnival club, the Mystic Krewe of Comus, presented a vernacular enactment of a new language of race as the theme of its tableau in 1877. This eclectic text rattled on about the descent lines of Noah, "Aryan Anthropology," and the etymology of the word *Caucasian* and prefigured the carnival representation of Radical Republicans as the missing link in evolution. New Orleans was neither alone nor particularly precocious in employing the new language of racial difference. The iconography of the Orange riots in New York had featured apelike depictions of the rioters, epitomized by Thomas Nast's drawings of the hairy visages and protruding jaws of Catholic rioters. Some Irish Catholic sympathizers took up the same symbolic weapon. A cartoon in the *Irish World* pictured the parade of July 12, 1871, carrying banners like "Orange-outans" and "APA-pes, Darwin's missing link."[48]

This racial scheme of classification led to a second parallel with the ceremonial attention to gender distinctions: It grounded social differences in biology. To shore up the biological bonds of human communities required attention to matters of marriage, bloodlines, and descent. Tellingly, carnival tableaux, from enactments of Spencer's *Fairie Queen* to an exegesis of Darwin, focused on parables of mating. One text that accompanied a parade entry told how "some of the Aryans became fossilized by isolation and corrupted their blood by constant intermingling of close relatives." Another bemoaned, with tongue in cheek, "the Aryan tendency to seek alliances and admixtures which elevate, and hence an earnest and marked progression is visible in their morals and intelligence." In the spirit of carnival inversion the revelers from Rex's club added some gender ideology into the spoof on Aryan anthropology in 1877 by posing the comic King of Carnival as a champion of women's rights as well as the Aryan Race.[49] A cartoonist for a California periodical even found materials for punning in the emerging language of race. He pictured the progeny of an Irish man and Chinese woman in the same frame within equestrian competition and labeled his creation "Coming Races" (fig. 37).

Under the masks and disguises of Mardi Gras, New Orleanians played with serious, politically charged questions about human descent. In attempting to chart clear lines of what we now call "racial" differences within the multiple and intermingled bloodlines of the New Orleans population, Mardi Gras pageants stumbled upon perplexing gender issues. Rex may not have been an Aryan feminist, but he did point out

Figure 37. "Coming Races," *The Wasp,* 1880. Courtesy of the Bancroft Library.

correctly that gender was key to constructing racial difference in the aftermath of slavery. Sexual contact between blacks and whites took on new meanings when they were no longer contained within the power relations of master and slave. Race also resembled gender in that it was deployed primarily as a way of excluding certain people from full and equal participation in public life. But here the parallels between the two diverge. For, while women did not storm the public sphere after the Civil War, African Americans and their powerful Republican allies mounted a major challenge to racial exclusion.

By claiming full citizenship as a right of manhood African Americans placed themselves in direct line to inherit democratic civic traditions. In New Orleans in particular they began to march proudly into public urban space under the mantle of Reconstruction. Freedmen claimed title to civic stature by enacting time-honored American rituals, parading the streets as organized and associated groups. The movement of African Americans onto the public festal stage in New York began even before war's end. In 1864 the Republicans of the city pointedly inserted race into civic ceremony by forming a black regiment and seeing it off to war with full pomp and circumstance in Union Square. This glaringly public display featured even a ceremonial presentation of a banner by white ladies to African American troops. This act provoked the expected outrage from some New Yorkers and incurred charges that the promiscuous ceremony was endorsing miscegenation. The attempts of African Americans to integrate public ceremony in San Francisco were only slightly more successful. A contingent of colored citizens secured the right of entry into the 1866 Independence Day parade, but not without difficulty. In that year blacks had been excluded from the parade in nearby Marysville and were admitted in San Francisco only against concerted opposition. A convention of African Americans voted to boycott the press and merchants who had opposed their ceremonial rights and to shame any of their fellows who failed to march on July Fourth by publishing their names in the newspaper. This protest was effective and brought a contingent of 300 African Americans into San Francisco's Fourth of July procession, where they won accolades for being well dressed and orderly. Even then the African American contingent was placed at the rear of the procession. In subsequent parades the issue of black participation would continue to produce conflict at the meetings of the committee of arrangements, and when blacks were admitted they were pushed to the back of the line of march. The programme in the *San Francisco Call* for July 4, 1871, for example, placed African Americans in the last division, number fourteen.[50]

In New Orleans the fate of African Americans in public ceremonies was tied to the roller-coaster history of postwar race relations. After the Union army marched into New Orleans the African American population jumped at the first chance to enroll in the ceremonial public. The radical newspaper, the *New Orleans Tribune,* began the offensive with stirring words: "Let us organize as one body and let us one of these days not only have public meetings in the open air but march in procession through the streets with unfurled banners floating to the breeze and tell the inhabitants of the city: Here are the freeman who claim their rights under the constitution of the United States and true principles of the re-public." In fact neither freedmen nor slaves were shy about taking to the streets in parades. Early in the war it was rumored that they marched through the streets and past their masters celebrating the Yankee victory at Vicksburg. As early as 1862 African Americans proceeded to parade openly in Lafayette Square. They would hold tenaciously to this beach-head in the public sphere. Even as the Union troops left the city in 1877, 1500 black Odd Fellows could be seen parading in the streets. When a full ceremony was mounted in 1881 for President Garfield's funeral, African Americans still paraded, and not just in the last division but a few paces forward, clad in the regalia of the society of masons.[51]

African Americans often practiced their newly won rights as workers as well as citizens. In 1866, for example, the dock workers of New Orleans led by the skilled and proud Screwmen's Benevolent Associa-tion "marched up the Levee" in contingents of "Black and White, on strike."[52] Following the Civil War the identities of the laboring classes were written in the streets all across the country, where their rising mili-tancy had a cultural and ceremonial as well as an economic flank. In the 1860s the offensive of organized labor formed around the campaign for an eight-hour work day, a demand that was paraded through the streets. The offensive in San Francisco, where the parade was still a prominent form of public ceremony, was especially impressive: A torchlight proces-sion of 1868 reputedly enrolled 3000 marching workers. A year later the labor movement had all but taken over the Fourth of July parade, con-trolling the committee of arrangements and dominating the line of march with twenty-four labor associations in attendance, including many eight-hour leagues, construction trades, and shipping workers. The *San Francisco Chronicle* was disgruntled by this "turnover" of the holiday festivities and rejoiced at a countercoup the next year when the procession featured ethnic assemblies with their goddesses and juvenile contingents but no representation whatsoever of organized labor. By 1875 ceremonial politics had turned over yet again: A full division pa-raded behind the banner, which read, "Labor Organizations."[53]

By that time the word *labor* had become a part of the vocabulary of urban ceremony. The same year Henry George was chosen to be the Fourth of July speaker in San Francisco, and one need not look very hard, anywhere in America, to find the signature of labor and capital on the public streets or podiums. In 1877, when the great railroad strikes consumed smaller cities and towns, a variety of workers took to the streets of big cities for a common cause. Cigar workers announced their militancy on the streets of New Orleans and New York with particular vehemence and solidarity. The New Orleans press reported that they assembled in Congo Square and heard speeches in Spanish, French, and English. Similar work stoppages in New York won favorable notices on the sidewalks and in the press. Of "The Cigar Makers Street Parade" the *Tribune* observed, "The faces of the striking cigar-makers beamed with smiles of triumph as they assembled yesterday in front of Concordia Hall, to take part in the procession of the organization. Men, women, and children came singly and in groups from shops, each bearing a flag and banner with inscriptions. Those flags included the colors of Germany, Bohemia, and Austria and, like the language groups assembled in Congo Square, signaled a new mobilization within the urban public, that of "labor" in multiethnic array.[54]

The labor movement wrote one of its most impressive public proclamations on the streets of San Francisco in 1877. On Thanksgiving Day the Workingmen's Party of California took over the streets in a major ceremonial coup. They claimed a sacred American holiday, one customarily observed in private, as their own public possession, marching through all the principle streets and radiating out from city center before 50,000 spectators. The working men retired after a polite and formal reception by the mayor. An estimated 8000 to 10,000 marching men, and a few women in carriages, won the applause of even skeptical journalists for their good order and respectable appearance. The message of the Workingmen's Party of California was broadcast on the streets and in the press. The banners read "Uphold the Dignity of Labor," "Workmen to the Front—In Your Hands Is the Nation's Future." One even proclaimed that "The Right to Revolution Is Sacred."[55]

Such a vocal presence of workers of sundry nationalities in the streets in the late 1870s bespoke a major development in urban culture. Working men had found a way to come together even within the compacted and confusing spaces of the industrial city. As the major summary ceremonies of industrial America assumed a more universalizing and transcendent aspect, and because the public calendar was less open than in the past, those excluded from public culture became more aggressive and forceful in their ceremonial offensives. Accordingly, in the 1860s and 1870s, in an industrializing nation and an altered civic context, processions of workers in the North and African Americans in New Orleans took on the demeanor of the "demonstration" or "protest march." They defied the culture of transcendence and unity as they mobilized on two fronts, at once political and cultural, both to proclaim their identity and to make demands on the polity.

After the Civil War organized workers and former slaves had commandeered the open public spaces of America's cities as a place not just to display their separate cultures but also to make demands upon the state. Workers demanded such things as an eight-hour day, and African Americans demanded the full rights of citizens. Both would be partially successful. At any rate they had managed to use public ceremonies as opportunities to construct identities around differences that were only dimly visible in everyday life or social statistics. The language of race and class heard in public ceremony would acquire even sharper definition in the political arenas.

Yet before departing the realm of civic ceremony, it is important to recall that not all the residents of the city would make this transition. In fact the very people who had acquired such attention among city cartographers, the residents of Chinatown, never even won access to the parade route, much less the guarantee of civil rights. On the centennial of American independence, when Reconstruction sponsored the ceremonial citizenship of African American men, and when women at least were honored observers or icons in the civic arena, Asian Americans were ostracized or worse. In San Francisco, for example, they were absent from the Fourth of July parade but visible on the sidelines. The *Examiner* reported that a Chinese American had been physically assaulted in the crowd, while a letter to the local press reported that only those committed to the restriction of immigration from China were invited to apply for the post of Fourth of July orator.[56] The signs were even more explicit and more sinister in that Thanksgiving Day parade of working men. Among their banners were mottoes such as this: "This a country for free white labor, not coolie labor."

Invidious distinctions among the people stained the urban festivals of the late nineteenth century. Hatred of Chinese Americans, antagonism to those of African descent, bitterness between Irish Catholics and Irish Protestants blemished parades across the country and throughout the calendar of ceremony. Not even the most splendid civic spectacle, not all the flags and fireworks in the municipal stockpile, could disguise or resolve these bitter divisions. But the ceremony had, for better and for worse, given some bolder names and clearer shapes to the differences that had been spectral antagonists in previous civil wars. The murky, increasingly insidious terminology of race was being applied to Africans, Asians, and sometimes Irishmen. Those proclaiming themselves the privileged citizenry sometimes took on names such as Aryan or white. Audacious titles such as Labor and Capital announced sharper lines of economic and political conflict. The dialectic of feminine symbolism was entangling and distorting the representations of race, class, and gender. The public ceremonies of the 1860s and 1870s spoke a new and ambiguous language of social differences. To understand their full power and meaning requires moving closer to the formal public sphere and directly onto the contentious terrain of city politics.

CHAPTER 7

Publicity and Democratic Practice

T he crowded and amorphous spaces of the modern city were less hospitable to public meetings and parades, but they still served as stages for civic contest, sometimes violent, uncivil wars. New Orleanians engaged in deadly battles in 1866 and 1874, both of which were fought around the old civic center of Lafayette Square. The riot at the Mechanics Institute in 1866 left forty-five dead; a confrontation at the Clay statue in 1874 claimed thirty-six lives. New York's Orange riot left upwards of 100 bodies along the route of the parade. The hostilities in San Francisco were less costly, but there too violent civic warfare continued well after Appomattox. The militant labor struggles of July 1877 created so much tension in the city by the bay that the vigilance committee reassembled yet again to patrol the streets with 4000 armed civilians. Keeping peace in the cities after the Civil War remained an arduous process. It would require major alterations in political practice and some compromises with the "principles of pure democracy" that dated from the antebellum period.

The general trajectory of the changes in urban politics can be drawn along four poles, from differences toward dualism, from representation toward bureaucracy, from a citizenry toward a tax base, from voluntary associations toward social movements. Taken together, these changes plot the transformation of meeting-place democracy into the politics of publicity. The enactment of this transition was not so tidy: It unfolded according to the plodding, disorderly, unpredictable pace of urban public life. The story proceeds from one urban crisis to another, notably the

New Orleans race riot of 1866, New York's Hibernian riot of 1871, and the labor struggles of San Francisco in 1877. Through the whole cycle of conflict city people created a kind of interurban public discourse and found ways to challenge, contest, and share the concentrated power of industrial capitalism.

Race, Riot, and the Reconstruction of Difference: New Orleans, 1866–1877

The unfinished business of the Civil War was taken up not just in Washington but in the cities, most especially in New Orleans. In fact it was in Lafayette Square that a critical early battle of Radical Reconstruction commenced in 1866. On July 25 a racially mixed group of about 200 persons gathered at the Mechanics Institute to revise the state constitution. Before this sacred rite of popular sovereignty could be called to order, however, shots were fired upon the congregation, vicious hand-to-hand combat ensued, and forty-five persons, thirty-seven of them African American, were left dead. News of this Confederate insolence traveled quickly to Washington, where it was a major catalyst for the national ascendancy of Radical Republicans and a heroic effort to achieve political equality by and for African Americans. The local riot that provoked Radical Reconstruction was not a spontaneous racial combustion. The parties to the combat at the Mechanics Institute were locked in a decisive and deliberate political contest that had been building since before the end of the Civil War. The war's termination brought considerable uncertainty and mixed expectations in New Orleans. To the leaders of the Confederacy the succession of Andrew Johnson and his increasingly conciliatory gestures to the South raised expectations that they might return promptly to power. For ex-slaves and freemen of color peace promised something else, perhaps a place in the American public sphere in which to exercise the full rights of citizenship. As a consequence the period between the spring of 1865 and the summer of 1866 was marked by energetic and expectant public mobilization, but by several opposing camps. Both vanquished rebels and emancipated slaves were poised to make claims on the public sphere. In between many others, including white working men and freed men and women of color, were alert to possibilities of heightened status under liberal Republican government. All parties joined in translating the vague categories of difference that wafted over postwar civic ceremonies into a dualistic racial classification.[1]

On one side the forces that would restore the status quo of the antebellum South came boldly forward in 1865. The *Bee* welcomed the return of "liberty, equality, and fraternity" and told its readers frankly, "don't be outvoted by colored people." The conservative press in general wasted no time in summoning rebels to sign up to vote. In the next spring election rumors of secret meetings of the Conservative Democrats gave way to open political rallies, ward elections, and full mass meetings complete with fireworks, torchlight processions, and bands playing "Dixie." The reports on Conservative meetings pointedly noted that blacks were welcomed and sometimes even present at these reconventions of the Confederacy. In May, buoyed up by liberal reinfranchisement standards under President Johnson, the Conservative Democratic Party won the municipal and state elections. They brought some old notions about race into public office.[2] The Redemptionists began by polishing up the old paternalistic language they had employed under slavery. They posed as the "Natural guardians" of ex-slaves and even welcomed African Americans "within the Caucasian family." The *Picayune* explained the paternalistic notion of race relations this way: "The past history of this class and their inferiority in many of the qualities which are possessed by those who have grown up in the full exercise of civic and personal freedom, gives them special claims upon our generosity, our care, our kindness and our justice." Citizenship, social status, and paternalism were among the terms for differentiating the ex-slave from the ex-master in 1865.

As African Americans began to mobilize and demand the full rights of citizenship they challenged the Conservatives to devise a more concise mode of addressing these new political actors. Those African Americans who dared engage in political actions independent of their former masters earned the most offensive press notices. The *Picayune*'s description of the crowd at a radical meeting in May 1866 used a full palette, from "coal black rose and a number of cream-colored lilly-whited pomatumed damsels" to "tan colored, long coated barbers." When a month earlier an African American militia unit disbanded in Washington Square, the reporter acknowledged the marching men as "kinky heads in uniforms."[3] Still, the bigotry of the Conservative Democratic Party was constrained both by the need to placate Radical Republicans in the U.S. Congress and by the complex and variegated notion of race acquired while living among free persons of color for generations. To complicate things further, the forces that would expand the rights of ex-slaves included white radicals and free men of color and many persons of mixed racial background. Subtle gradations of skin color and even intersecting lineages wove through the whole political spectrum in New Orleans. Just after the war the Conservatives of New Orleans played out these various political possibilities of the racial spectrum. Both the *Bee* and the *Picayune* warned ex-slaves against being manipulated by untrustworthy mulattos and free persons of color who had not welcomed emancipation. On the other hand the conservative press invoked the example of Haiti to warn the lighter-skinned Negroes that the deeper-hued African Americans would turn on them in the end.[4]

Men of African descent often took the lead in reshaping the language and politics of racial difference. The central characters in this near revolution included African Americans of Protestant affiliations such as Lieutenant Governor Pinchbeck and French-speaking, Paris-educated free men of color such as Louis Charles Roudanez. Together they forged an alliance between ex-slaves and free blacks and across a spectrum of complexions. The Radical leadership also included men of uncertain lineage such as Jean-Charles Houzeau. Although often presumed to be of African descent, Houzeau was a native of Belgium who imbibed the French Enlightenment and the revolutionary tradition of 1848 while a student in Paris. According to the most reliable calculations, nearly half the Radical leaders with African origins were mulattos, well over 90 percent were former free men, and a few were former slaves. These leaders would, however, invite ex-slaves and former free men of color to adopt a common political standpoint. Conspicuously, as in a call to a meeting of January 1865, they named this political creation a "Convention of Colored Men of Louisiana."[5] A common identity based in color did not come naturally or easily in New Orleans in the 1860s, where the African American community was rent by differences in status, religion, even language. The fact that some prominent New Orleanians of African descent (the patrician Frances Ernest Dumasz, who disdained speaking English, for example) had actually been slave owners precluded automatic acceptance of race as the template of radical politics. Hence, the classification of "colored men" was a deliberate political construction, designed to create a broad political alliance, which encompassed both former slaves and former *gens de couleur* and demanded full citizenship for both.

This political identity, like many others before it, took form within the democracy of the public meeting. Soon after emancipation, by November and December 1863, New Orleans was hosting regular meetings of the National Equal Rights League. At the beckoning of the militant bilingual black newspaper the *Louisiana Tribune* eager citizens of African descent gathered in Economy Hall, the African Methodist Episcopal Church, and spaces renamed Schools of Liberty. One of the first meetings of the Equal Rights League, called for December 27, 1864, announced their goal in the opening prayer—"to bind colored people together."[6] Mass meetings of African Americans posted their demand for the right to vote as early as 1863, without the sponsorship of Union governors or the Republican Party. At first the colored suffrage movement proposed small steps across the racial border of the franchise: votes for former freemen of color, for quadroons, Union soldiers, taxpayers, men of property, or those of "intellectual fitness." One group called the Friends of Universal Suffrage, led by the *Louisiana Tribune* editors Paul Trévgine and Jean-Charles Houzeau, was far less hesitant. Meeting every Thursday, they proposed that racial restrictions on the franchise be simply rescinded. These radicals moved to create a political identity and African American solidarity in the same gesture. Some, like Houzeau, took the principle of universal suffrage to its outer limits. "The United States is a great hospitable land open to immigrants of all nations. May it be the common land where not only all white people will melt together but also all races—the 'Caucasian,' the black represented by the African, the Yellow Chinese and the Red Indian." Anything seemed possible after the Union victory and in a city of such unusual diversity.[7]

The same conditions made it practicable to mobilize these diverse groups so as to exert political power. Public meetings called by the radical press in the city of New Orleans played a major role in moving the Republican Party and the nation beyond emancipation and toward civil rights. The Louisiana constitution of 1864, dominated by moderate Unionists, did not issue an appeal for African American suffrage. It was left to the public meetings of New Orleans to push that demand and foster the democratic insurgency of the spring election in 1866. In turn this democracy of the public meeting, African American style, demanded that the 1864 convention be reconvened and get out the vote of masses of ex-slaves and free men of color to support their appeal. By one report 20,000 men of color participated in a mock election to demonstrate their potential political clout. It was said that the people came lame, barefoot, and blind to cast their votes. "All were on hand, eager and panting from freedom's boom." The Union Republicans elected the first major black officials, including half the delegates to the convention in Mechanics Hall. Meanwhile, a delegation of the Creole elite pushed moderate and white Republicans toward universal suffrage and made alliances with radicals in Washington. On the eve of the convention radicals in congress had been alerted to the possibility of racial violence in the Crescent City.

This, in sum, is how things stood on July 25, 1866: In the center of the public sphere stood a racially identified political movement, led by mixed-race free men of color who had mobilized the ex-slave majority; they squared off against former rebels who were organized as the Conservative Democratic Party and were intent on restoring the antebellum social hierarchy.[8] In the public spaces of New Orleans after the Civil War race entered politics in the time-honored democratic manner, as a positive assertion of difference and demand for political participation that met organized opposition. This classic battle of meeting-place democracy even began with a parade: On the morning of July 25 groups of African Americans formed a procession that filed down Burgundy Street across Canal and on to the constitutional convention in Mechanics Hall. Some said they were led by a young boy beating a drum and hoisting the stars and stripes. The mob did not tarry in the streets but stormed into the chamber of government and inflicted its rage on the elected delegates to the Louisiana Constitutional Convention (fig. 38).

The news that this procession was greeted with gunfire undermined Andrew Johnson's conciliatory policy to the South and helped usher in Radical Congressional Reconstruction, including a constitutional amendment that guaranteed African American men the right to vote. Under the protection of national military authority, the Louisiana radicals would create the most racially integrated government of the nineteenth century. The state enacted five civil rights bills and elected a biracial government whose lieutenant governor, nineteen sheriffs, and one third of the legislature were of African American descent.[9] The radicals of Louisiana also resumed the constitutional convention that had been interrupted by the riot of 1866 and created a document that outlawed racial restrictions in public space as well as the halls of government. Article 13 of the new state constitution is especially pertinent to this history. "All persons shall enjoy equal rights and privileges upon any conveyance of a public character and shall be opened to the accommodation and patronage of all persons without distinction or discrimination on account of race or color." This act had an immediate impact on the everyday public life of New Orleans. The spring of 1867 brought "riotous demonstrations of portions of the colored population insisting on the rights to enter private establishments against the will and consent of the owners thereof." No place of amusement or recreation seemed inviolate. On May 17 came reports of "attempts of turbulent Negroes to force themselves into confectioneries and restaurants." Congo Square was a major site of resistance, where hundreds gathered to cheer as African Americans

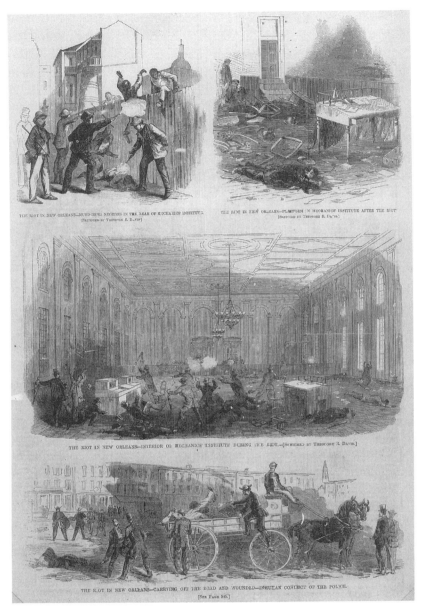

THE RIOT IN NEW ORLEANS—MURDERING NEGROES IN THE REAR OF MECHANICS INSTITUTE.
[SKETCHED BY THEODORE R. DAVIS.]

THE RIOT IN NEW ORLEANS—PLATFORM IN MECHANICS INSTITUTE AFTER THE RIOT
[SKETCHED BY THEODORE R. DAVIS.]

THE RIOT IN NEW ORLEANS—INTERIOR OF MECHANICS INSTITUTE DURING THE RIOT.—[SKETCHED BY THEODORE R. DAVIS.]

THE RIOT IN NEW ORLEANS—CARRYING OFF THE DEAD AND WOUNDED—INHUMAN CONDUCT OF THE POLICE.
[SEE PAGE 546.]

Figure 38. New Orleans riot, 1866. *Harper's Weekly,* 1866. Courtesy of the Louisiana State Museum.

paraded triumphantly by in once "white only" streetcars. Although these private businesses remained segregated, spaces whose public status was more difficult to dispute were proclaimed open to all. It was the mobilization of men and women of color in the squares, on the streets, and on the streetcars in 1867 that desegregated public transportation for at least a generation.[10]

Just the same year, after similar public actions and with support from Radical Republicans in the U.S. Congress, the color line was also erased from the street cars of New York and San Francisco. The Radicals, black and white and across the nation, had cause to celebrate with the *Louisiana Tribune* in New Orleans in 1871. Some five years after the racial violence of 1866, with "no riots to report, or any massacres of men on account of race or color," the *Tribune* could make this remarkable observation. "The grand principles enunciated by Jefferson, 'All men are created equal'... enlarged, defined, and liberalized by the genius of the last decade with regard to race, color or previous condition have come gradually to be received and accepted as established facts." This first act in the postwar reconstruction of the public ends at a scene of euphoric democratic expansion in the city of New Orleans.[11] The peoples of New Orleans had witnessed the mobilization of African Americans and radicals into a successful social movement. Beginning with the hopes for justice and democratic participation, one group of Americans took the political initiative away from government officials and established parties. With creative methods of engendering solidarity and pressuring the public sphere, which had heretofore ignored them, the grassroots radicals of New Orleans became the driving force behind a movement for social and political change that went all the way to Washington.

Reconstruction's extraordinary accomplishments in New Orleans were only the beginning of a long, still unresolved civic struggle. Once Americans of African descent had placed the demand for full citizenship on the public agenda, an opposition quickly formed, in the North and in the South. That opposition would also come to define itself in racial terms, fading much of the diversity of urban politics into the identity of white men. The assertion of the "white" political identity was initially retarded in postwar New Orleans by the continuation of military government under the Radical Republicans. But as Northern vigilance relaxed in the 1870s the forces of white supremacy came into full public view. By 1872 Conservative Democrats and the white majority had reclaimed local offices but not state government and prepared to do battle against Radical Republicans nationwide.

The opponents of Radical Republicans in New Orleans went into the second civic war of the Reconstruction period carrying a banner embossed with the title "White League." They gathered at the Clay statue, a landmark that would be renamed Liberty Place, in September 1874 and took up arms in a bloody but ineffective coup against the state military government and what they called a "blindly obedient league of blacks." But as late as 1873 even these conservative Southern Democrats were still somewhat uncomfortable with this crude political identity. Those who enrolled in the White League of New Orleans felt the need to explain the adoption of this new identity. The prologue to the League's Platform began: "'The Crescent City Democratic Club' of 1868 having changed its name to that of 'Crescent City White League,' has thought that an explanation was due alike to its retired members and to the people of New Orleans of the motive of a change so seriously and so sadly suggestive." The insurgents claimed to be acting reluctantly and defensively against the "league of blacks, which under the command of the most cunning and unscrupulous Negroes in the State, may at any moment plunge us into a war of races—a conflict in which we are resolved that we and ours shall not be the victims." This forecast of race war was not provoked by a real and immediate threat but born in the arrogance of long-standing white supremacy. The members of the White League condescendingly reminded the black citizen that "We would demonstrate even to his understanding that the predominance of our race in government is indispensable to his well-being." Having embraced their racial identity, the members of the White League proceeded to construe color as the primary political division of their society. "Disregarding all minor questions of principle or policy, and having solely in view the maintenance of our hereditary civilization and Christianity menaced by a stupid Africanization we appeal to the men of our race, of whatever language or nationality, to unite with us against that supreme danger." They repeated the call to "the men of our race" for "a timely and proclaimed union of the whites as a race." The White League transposed the sectionalism of the Confederacy into the racism of the Southern Democratic Party. The white men who reconnoitered around the Clay statue in 1874 proclaimed the virtual end to New Orleans's era of Radical Reconstruction (fig. 39).

The final cessation of efforts to advance equality in the South would not come until the withdrawal of federal troops in 1877, but the failure of Northern will to reform race relations was evident long before, especially in New York and San Francisco. Neither of these cities had a large

Figure 39. "Rout of the Metropolitains, Defait des Metropolitains, New Orleans, September 14, 1874." Courtesy of the Louisiana State Museum. T101.1970.

African American population, much less the particular demographic complexity and political sagacity that generated color-conscious politics in New Orleans. What the Northern cities did harbor, nonetheless, was a virulent growth of racist political rhetoric. In New York the vicious antagonism to African Americans that erupted during the riot of 1863 simmered beneath the surface years afterwards. The press heard it on the streets and in the crowds at political rallies. One Democratic loyalist was heard to opine, "We don't hate the niggers but we don't want to mix with them." Another espoused a more elaborate racial politics, complete with gender components: "That talk about equal rights for the nigger, the franchise and women's rights and all the kind of blarney and soft sawder wouldn't touch a nigger with a pole as long as a fishing-rod, and if Sambo with all the education in the world popped the question to one of these preacher's daughters he'd be heartily kicked off his pains and ordered to clear out at once."[12] Such vernacular racism was fed by streams of partisan rhetoric. For years after the war both Democrats and Republicans played on racial themes for partisan advantage. Insinuations about race hovered over the mayor's election of 1867, for example, even in a municipality whose citizens were overwhelmingly white. The *Herald* evoked the specter of racial division by clever pairings of bold print titles. Side by side on the same page, one could read of "Negro barbarism" in Southern Reconstruction and of "Fanatical Radicals" at work in New York City to constrict the rights of Roman Catholics. A few days later they paired "Radicals in Congress" with "Negro Barbarism in Haiti."

It would seem that the more distinct racial terminology that had emerged out of the Southern politics of Reconstruction was amplified in the North. While the bloody shirt waved from Republican podiums, the Democrats dwelt on the partisan implications of Negro suffrage. At a rally in November 1867 the Honorable J. B. Thayer plotted out the familiar interpretation of the war and Reconstruction as a scheme to expand the Republican vote. As he put it, "Six hundred thousand blacks have been made voters and nearly a million whites have been disenfranchised." Another speaker added an ethnic dimension to the vote count. Noting that the franchise was a privilege, not a right, he judged the Sons of the Emerald Isle and Germany worthy of that trust because they belong to the "Caucasian race, destined to rule the world." To the rhetorical question whether Negro suffrage "would elevate the standard of Civilization in this country," the audience responded with "cries of 'NO! NO!'" If we are to believe the audience reaction at such rallies as these, Northern voters were as attuned to the language of race, including the terms *Negro* and *Caucasian,* as were the residents of multiracial New Orleans.[13]

The postwar crash course in racial politics was even more intensive in San Francisco, where its key category was neither Caucasian nor Negro but "Mongolian." At a rally on July 10, for example, the *Bulletin* said the Democrats were interested in hearing only about the issues of Chinese suffrage. And they certainly got an earful. Democratic oratory ricocheted through the public sphere, sparking a firestorm of anti-Chinese hysteria. Even the Republicans were pushed into a defensive position from which they repeatedly assured voters that despite their support for the Fifteenth Amendment they opposed suffrage for those of Asian ancestry. This slogan was prominently displayed at a September rally: "The Union Party is Opposed to Chinese Suffrage." Because the Golden Gate had opened up to peoples from all around the globe the questions of citizenship and difference raised by the Civil War provoked an especially intricate assessment of the demographics of suffrage. One Republican speaker felt compelled to comment "upon women voting, Negro voting and Chinese voting and opposed them all except in the case of intellectual property-owning whites." In San Francisco Mongolians and African Americans were linked together in a single standard of exclusion labeled racial.[14]

The escalating racial rhetoric of the campaign rally, North as well as South, proved to be a capacious trope for political exclusions. It even put "white" manhood suffrage in jeopardy. A shocking turn of principle was expressed at a Democratic rally of August 26 when one speaker referred to the "foolishness" of manhood suffrage and the "universal brotherhood of man." Postwar suffrage politics exposed the shallowness of the commitment to equal rights among voters and politicians. The Republicans were put in a particularly uncomfortable position: To rebut the charge that they supported Chinese as well as black suffrage they came up with this short list of those qualified to vote: "native Americans, exclusive of Indian tribes" and "persons of foreign birth who can live up to the requirements of the naturalization law." The underlying logic here would appear to be geographic, confining the franchise to those who traced their descent to Europe. But this Eurocentric principle was never explicit, or inviolate. Another politician would restrict the vote to "a race that can assimilate to us." This standard was perhaps a little irksome to many nativists who would draw the boundaries of civilization around the Anglo-Saxon tribes of Europe, but even they acknowledged that most all European immigrants "would assimilate at least in two or three generations."[15]

The advance of civil rights in the reconstructed South boomeranged up North, where the prospect of multiracial democracy put the expansion of the suffrage to a decisive stop. No Northern state moved independently to enfranchise blacks during or after the Civil War, and the Reconstruction debates only underscored the assumption that active, that is, democratic citizenship would be the privilege of white men. Ironically, the strongest champions of expanding suffrage before the war, the Democratic Party and recent immigrants from Ireland, were among the most vocal supporters of the move to deny the vote on the basis of race. The blunt line between white and colored reduced differences to dualism and made suffrage politics, once the cutting edge of expanding democratic participation, a boundary of exclusion.

The close of Reconstruction was a watershed but not a complete counterrevolution. Not all the advances of the Reconstruction era were lost, certainly not immediately. New Orleans street cars would remain integrated until 1902. Blacks would parade proudly in an 1882 Garfield procession, and Africans Americans even participated in the Democratic

Party of New Orleans. Most of all, the African American's right of suffrage had not yet been eviscerated as seen in another meeting called for October 29, 1874. On a single day's notice, 4000 to 5000 people congregated at Lafayette Square to protest a threatened tightening of the qualifications for naturalization. One contingent among the predominantly Irish and German participants in that rally is worthy of special note: "The third ward colored Democratic Club marched to the meeting, some two hundred strong."[16] At least some African Americans maintained this toehold in the public sphere, where they could practice the democracy of the public meeting and mingle in this case with immigrants and working men. One thing was certain: The fierce struggles in New Orleans had taken the specters of racial differences that might be found in a Mardi Gras tableau, cast them in dualistic terms, and installed them squarely in the center of American political culture.

Hibernian Riot and the Revolt of the Capitalists, New York, 1871

The mottled political identity of New York City was also recast according to the racial script of Reconstruction. The immediate aftermath of the war found Republicans in control of the state government and treating the Democratic majority of Gotham as what one historian has called "surrogate Southerners." The radical agenda for the city included such measures as a professional fire department, public health legislation, tenement house regulation, and Negro suffrage. All but the last reform had been accomplished by 1868. The Republicans retreated from a campaign for the rights of Negroes when they saw enthusiasm for such a radical doctrine wane, nationwide and locally. Indeed, the unpopularity of their civil rights policies was critical to the Republican defeat in the 1868 elections. When the Democrats returned to the majority in both Albany and Gotham, the long season of civil wars seemed finally to be drawing to an end. In 1870 the city obtained a new state charter whereby locally elected officials reclaimed control of the streets, Central Park, and the municipal budget, which had become grossly inflated in the industrial metropolis.[17]

Hence, it was the Democrats who held power in July 1871 when ethnic warfare returned to the streets of New York. Although the fighting along the Orangemen's parade route fed on long-standing ethnic antagonism, its political meaning was far more complex and insidious. The battle of Eighth Avenue was called a "Tammany riot" by the local press and by a Committee of Seventy, which had exposed major fraud at the

Board of Supervisors just days before the fateful parade. Outrage about this Orange riot was quickly converted into the first salvos in a successful campaign to route Tammany from City Hall in the next election. Some even suspected that the bloody episode was engineered for this political purpose. The most critical consequence of the Hibernian riot, at any rate, was the removal from office of supervisor William "Boss" Tweed, whose name would ever after be a synonym for "corruption" and "dirty politics." The civic reformers who came to power in the wake of the Orange riot proudly named their campaign an "insurrection of the capitalists," denoting the refusal of these wealthy citizens to pay taxes until the fiscal extravagance of the Tammany Democrats was put in check. The fact that Tammany Hall gave aid and comfort to riotous Hibernians was but one element of their offensive political practices. Whatever it is called, the confluence of events in New York in the summer of 1871 would exact another revision in the language and method of urban politics and set a standard for the rest of urban American for well into the future. The Redemptionist government of New Orleans, for example, took the name Committee of Seventy and founded its administration not just on the principle of whiteness but also on the mission of routing out "Tweedism."[18]

Some of the conditions for this transformation of public practice had been present in New York for some time. In fact the battle lines against the Democrats had been drawn on ethnic, religious, and class ground since at least the days of Fernando Wood. In the late 1860s the name of William Tweed was occasionally invoked to represent the Tammany functionaries who took profit in public office. After years of parrying his sociability at fire houses and ward meetings into votes and a succession of minor offices Tweed became street commissioner and the chair of the Board of Supervisors, where he enjoyed ready access to the swollen city coffers. The short time of Tweed's tenure, 1865 to 1871, coincided with a major expansion of the city debt, from $20 million in 1860 to $67 million in 1871. William Tweed and his associates cashed in on the lucrative city contracts for such major projects as laying pipe on the aqueduct, developing the Upper West Side, and building a new courthouse. The scale of development had long since removed these decisions from the public forum of the City Council and gave functionaries like Tweed extraordinary power behind the scenes. But if Tweed was a convenient and hardly innocent target for the outrage of reformers and parsimonious taxpayers, he was only one fixed point in a whirlwind of administrative change and political chicanery around the time of the Orange riot.[19]

First of all, there was the continuing prominence of ethnicity in New York politics. That term served as an apt designation of the divisions of the people of New York before the war, based in religion and nationality, rather than the racial division that had reached an ugly zenith in the New York draft riots. As the war receded from political memory (and after hundreds of the African Americans who had been terrorized by the riots fled the city) ethnic and religious antagonism resumed predominance in the public mind. Irish nationalism in particular became more robust after the war, nourished by the Fenian movement and continuing immigration, which made the sons and daughters of Erin over 20 percent of the city's population. Certainly, ethnicity was never far from the surface of public discourse in 1871. In the heat of the political campaign that followed the riots the *Times* intoned: "The ring is entirely in the control of the Romanists . . . even to parading in green garments and forbidding Protestants the use of the streets for processions." There were more material interests at stake here as well. In 1871 the Protestants charged that Irish Catholics were taking over the public schools, occupying teaching posts, refusing to use the Protestant Bible, and securing funds for their parochial institutions. They accused Irish Catholics of regarding "the government as their private property, subject only of course, to the general lien held on all their possessions by the pope and priesthood." The paranoia fed on deeper private animosities as well. Robert Roosevelt, leader of the anti-Tammany Democrats, simply called the Irishman "A low, venal, corrupt, unintelligent brute."[20]

The reformers who vaulted into the public limelight after the Hibernian riot also revealed, if they did not acknowledge, their own ethnic identity. When they won the election, they pointedly refused to appoint Irish Catholics to public office. The call to arms against Tammany that appeared in the *Nation* magazine just after the riot referred quite explicitly to the desire for clean and honest government as an "Anglo-Saxon Trait," thus repeating a theme that often could be found in the fine print of reformer speeches. Another column of the *Times* raised the political lament, "Pity the Poor Protestant." In fact the whole reform discourse was written in a kind of Protestant cultural code. A key document issued in explanation of the campaign against Tammany posed the reform goals in moral terms: as an attempt to "purify" and "redeem" the polity and to restore "religious liberty." Conversely, the opposition was characterized by a litany of vices, often laced with sexual allusions: the machine was "vile," "defiled," of "low nature," and known to "violate the ballot box."[21] Gender was also on the mind of the compiler of the influential reform document, *The Hibernian Riot and the Revolt of the Capitalists,* which posed the issue as nothing less than "whether or not Americans are emasculated." The ploy was used again by Thomas Nast, whose allegoric etching on the cover represented the city as a fair maiden in classic attire about to be ravished by a simian-featured Irishman. Conversely, the reformers pictured Irish Catholic women among the rioters as grotesque viragos. Ethnic prejudice reversed the sexual stereotypes thus: "Soon after the procession had started a ferocious looking woman rushed out from the sidewalks seized the regalia of one of the Orangemen and attempted to pull them from his shoulders. A soldier warned her back with the butt of his musket, but the infuriated Amazon spit in his face and with shrieks of rage, reproached her country men for their cowardice."[22]

The Orange riot seemed to reinscribe the familiar language of ethnic difference on New York politics, merely updating the divisions between Anglo and Irish, Catholic and Protestant, with some filigree of gender iconography. The ethnic contest also retained something of its antebellum flavor, consisting as it did of the direct combat of a varied cast of seasoned voters and experienced politicians. Because the majority of electors in New York were foreign born, the public language of ethnic difference was craftily deployed. The anti-Tweed forces vigorously recruited German immigrants, courting their votes with benign stereotypes: invoking the fabled Teutonic love of outdoor amusements, for instance, as cause to oppose Tweed's misuse of parks funds. The Germans responded by forming a number of ward-level anti-Tweed clubs and conjointly endorsing the reform slate in the municipal election. Finally, the Irish Catholic American citizen, as the Know-Nothings had learned, was so powerful a political adversary that even reformers had to court them at the ballot box. The anti-Tweed faction recruited one Charles O'Connor as their mayoral candidate, describing him as a "warmhearted Irishman." In sum ethnic politics was alive and strong, but multifarious, and not meshed tightly enough to carry the full weight of transforming the public discourse in New York.[23]

It was the genius of the municipal reformers to fine-tune a category of the people capable of transcending the ethnic division: that omnibus identity, already on the scene during the civil wars of the 1850s, was called taxpayer. The full name of the Committee of Seventy was the Executive Committee of Citizens and Taxpayers for the Financial Reform of the City of New York. Invitations to the meetings of the reform coalition were addressed to property owners and taxpayers. The ward-level meetings were frequently called taxpayers and citizens meetings. The first act of insurrection of the capitalists was to secure some 1000 signatures on a pledge not to pay taxes until the books of the machine were opened to the public. The reformers applied the political label *taxpayer* with great latitude, extending it far along the class hierarchy. By suppressing profits and reducing business, they argued, municipal corruption and high taxes inhibited the growth in jobs, raised prices, and hence was costly for everyone. The reform press repeatedly cast the poor working man as Tweed's special prey. Because the majority of citizens were not propertyholders and not subject to municipal assessment, however, the "taxpaying public" was actually a quite restricted fellowship. The reformers would grant them special and unequal citizenship. Both the *Times* and the *Nation* floated the idea that the city should be run like a company in which only stockholders (i.e. taxpayers) would be allowed to vote, at least on fiscal matters. Certainly, disgruntled taxpayers had long held a prominent position in American political discourse, but this apparition in the 1870s had novel implications. It conspired to place a de facto property requirement on the suffrage, reversing fifty years of democratic momentum. The Committee of Seventy placed the taxpayer in the place where the common man once stood and placed a symbolic economic restriction on civic participation.[24]

This was just one way in which the New York reformers of the 1870s subtly subverted public democracy. Although the reformers still honored some traditions of the public meetings—such as forming ward-level clubs among workers, Germans, and even "colored men"—these were not their favored political methods. The founding meetings of the reform coalition convened in offices on Nassau and Wall Streets or in such elite circles as the Union League Club. They were called secret without apology. Reform meetings were often created by "invitation" and described as congregations of the "best men." In fact they were the richest men, almost all of them either bankers, lawyers, or merchants. The Committee of Seventy routinely met secretly at the quarters of the Chamber of Commerce, adjourned the public rally to form a secret vigilance committee, and often delegated tasks to committees of two to five men. In a curious and unprecedented custom for public meetings (and particularly odd, given the wealth of those involved) the Committee of Seventy asked for contributions to finance their work, complaining that politics was too costly a distraction from their businesses. In short the organizational model of this new politics was not the public meeting but the board meeting. The *Nation* put it bluntly: It used a railroad joint stock company as the model for good government.[25]

These innovative political practices were introduced in an eclectic new language whose harping on virtue, economy, tax, and finance seemed more appropriate to either the church or the corporate office than the public podium. The most curious new medium of communicating a political argument was the arithmetic symbol. The front page of the *Times,* for days on end, was given over to nothing but financial records. Columns of figures, recording expenditures for parks, stationery, sewage, the costly Court house became the currency of political discussion. In fact the power of Tweed first began to unravel when the bond holders began to balk at financing the mounting city debt. It was truly a "revolt of the capitalists," and it seemed as if the public sphere had turned overnight into an accounting office.

At other times the venue of politics was changed to even stranger quarters, the drawing room. The reformers recruited the honest prosecutor Charles O'Connor to run for public office in a highly stylized public ritual staged not in a saloon or hall but a parlor. The courtship was described thus: "Mr. Connor meeting the visitors at the door welcomed them cordially and conducted them to the drawing room." The reform press had a peculiar fondness for interior decorating. Of the Tweed club house, said the *Times,* "The house has been entirely redecorated, repaired, papered and furnished. On the first floor is a handsome parlor with rosewood furniture covered with velvet." Indeed, much of the animosity toward Tweed fed off his family pretensions: the opulent furnishings of his mansion and the ostentatious wedding celebration of his daughter. The writer for the *Times* seems to have had quite an interest in domestic matters, for he even described the improvement of the park as being "done over as the ladies say." The *Times* envisioned its readers in the same domestic spaces: *Times* reporters were fond of interviewing the man in the street on his way home to the suburbs in New Jersey and Brooklyn or finding a subscriber ensconced at the breakfast table with his wife and his newspaper. The domestic culture evoked in the *Times* was another indication that politics was taking a privatizing turn in 1871.[26]

The anti-Tweed campaign also found a way to do without public meetings as a means of transmitting information to the citizenry. It went directly to the editors of the big dailies and inverted the old relationship between the press and the party. Where formerly the party made the press its agent and ally, the anti-Tweed campaign was largely the initiative of the *New York Times*. Only after a long publicity campaign in its pages did the reform movement generate a popular organization and public action. The exhaustive reporting of the *Times* created the discourse on corruption, targeted Tweed, exposed official after official, until city government was saturated with images of financial scandal. The reformers acquired this persuasive power through association with a new style of journalism that had developed during and since the war and was increasingly tied to advertising and business connections. The big urban dailies were no longer the fiefdom of crusading editors but million-dollar industries manufacturing news by employing scores of reporters. By 1870 the professional reporter had become a specialist in ferreting out corruption, both in Washington and around City Hall. In covering the Manhattan political scene the muckraking journalist found a brilliant colleague in cartoonist Thomas Nast. Nast's sketches converted scattered charges of municipal malfeasance into a graphic iconography of public vice called the Tweed Ring. In no small part it was Tweed's physiology as sketched by Nast (and his gargantuan belly, to be precise) that made him the perfect personification of corruption. The work of journalists and cartoonists, calculated imagery rather than associated action, were the medium of a politics of publicity (fig. 40).[27]

From the command post at the *Times* the anti-Tweed forces took their cause first to the courts, not the voters. They issued an unrelenting shotgun fire of accusations against Tammany officials, naming names, labeling associations, and crafting ethnic slurs until the city officeholders and contractors, justifiably or not, must have been terrorized. The culmination of the campaign was reached when a judge, whose every word and movement were watched in the *Times*, indicted Tweed and two associates on minor charges provoking their resignation. The "Boss" was convicted but retained his popularity among the majority of voters long after the press and the judiciary had driven him from office and into political exile.[28] This practice, a kind of politics through indictment, was one of several reforming practices that detoured politics away from the electoral arena. In 1871 the *New York Times* was so bold as to question even universal white male suffrage. Its editors proposed that only taxpayers should be entitled to vote for financial offices. The *Nation* went even further, calling manhood suffrage a "foolish anachronism." The brakes were already put on the expansion of democratic participation during the elections of the 1870s, when state law had tightened naturalization and registration regulations. The reformers followed with calls

Figure 40. "Who Stole the People's Money?" Thomas Nast, *New York Times*, 1871.

for a new charter in 1872 designed to reduce government to providing the public infrastructure necessary for private business and administered primarily through a weak board of annually elected aldermen and appointed experts.[29]

In fact, the anti-Tweed forces had accomplished a municipal coup. Operating through private circles, through the channels of the press, and without benefit of a plebiscite, they actually changed both the personnel and structure of municipal government. While never defeated at the ballot box, elected officials associated with the Tweed Ring were hounded from office by persistent press attacks. They were replaced by a new species of public administrators personified by Andrew Green, new czar of the Central Park Commission and the embodiment of the apolitical, businesslike, and efficient style of municipal government. Green became the model professional of the public realm. By judicial injunction, without official accountability to the electorate, he oversaw and signed every municipal payment, holding hostage not just builders, contractors, and bondsmen but desperate workers dependent on the wages from city projects. Under Tweed the Central Park Commission had returned to city control and become a reservoir of such municipal jobs. Municipal reform as practiced by Green undercut both pork-barreling and public works.[30]

But in some ways, Green's operations and that of the ring were not that different. Tammany politics in the 1860s were also operating in a less ideological, more bureaucratic style in which the contract supplanted the vote as the "mother's milk" of politics. Democratic administrations of the Tweed era had rewarded select constituents with lucrative contracts building Central Park, furnishing the Courthouse, and coincidentally employing many poorer citizens. Before and after the Tweed scandal wealthy financiers would continue to exert exorbitant private power among politicians, both Democrats and Republicans.[31] Tweed would be succeeded by a more efficient political manager at Tammany Hall, John Kelly. A crony of such affluent conservative Democrats as August Belmont of the House of Rothschild and iron manufacturer Adam Hewitt, Kelly engineered a more bureaucratic and less representative machinery of urban politics, featuring district clubs rather than ward meetings as the partisan links between the governors and the governed.[32] The exposure of the Tweed Ring may not have dramatically affected how city business was conducted, but it did unleash a contagious suspicion of public spending, a political disease that spread like a virus through American cities. In the aftershock of the New York scandal city officials, "machines" no less than reformers, began to fear the wrath of the taxpayers and adopt conservative financing methods. The Tweed scandal released into the public sphere that familiar political phantom, the balanced budget.[33]

In New York in the 1870s a novitiate of political reformers had devised a new way of exercising citizenship. From just off stage of the public sphere (in places such as the offices of the *New York Times* and the Committee of Seventy), it sent forth such political innovations as a new sobriquet for the people (the taxpayer), a new language of politics (similar to accounting), a new technique of mobilization (initiated by the press), a new kind of accountability (to the courts, not the electors). At no point in this circuit of political action was a public meeting required. The radical revisions of the political process that followed the Orange riot were also manifest in other American cities. The names of taxpayers' and citizens' parties appeared regularly on ballots in San Francisco and New Orleans. In fact San Francisco had moved decisively toward this less democratic mode of urban administration under the vigilance committee, whose political arm, the People's Party, continued to operate in secret nominations of the "best men." The San Francisco franchise was also patrolled by a registration law beginning in 1866. In New Orleans both Reconstruction and Redemptionist governments adopted similar procedures, more bureaucratic than democratic. The city charter of 1871 dramatically reduced the representative legislative branch, made elections citywide and further from constituents, and gave major power to an administration of seven state-appointed officials. The operation of the federal government in New Orleans was also in the business of manipulating the franchise, and not entirely in the progressive direction of the Fifteenth Amendment. The Republicans disenfranchised ex-Confederates as they enfranchised blacks and tightened restriction on immigrants. The federal franchise law of 1870 made the falling away from basic democratic faith a public policy.[34]

This retreat from the public sector and the slackening of the democratic expansion of the franchise were overreactions to official graft and inefficiency in New York and elsewhere. The late nineteenth century saw a multiplication of the tasks before big cities and strained political and administrative structures to the breaking point. The sheer magnitude of organizational problems in the big city created the financial confusion that could breed both the reality and the exaggeration of municipal corruption. Tweed's massive budgets and probable profit taking off projects such as the development of the Upper West Side had been anticipated by the corruption among Republicans during the Civil War and were mirrored by carpetbaggers and scalawags in the South and the Custom Officials and funders of the national debt in New York City. Corruption would surface in the building of City Hall in San Francisco and the New

York Courthouse, and reformers would do little better than machines in keeping down their cost. In fact the Tweed administration did a relatively valiant job of creating new administrative structures for the rapidly growing city—a new state charter that returned power to the city and a spate of new city commissions—and improved and expanded streets. The monumental civic project of the late nineteenth century, the Brooklyn Bridge, was also initiated under Tweed. By the late 1870s even operating the small city of San Francisco required issuing almost 300 franchises to private companies. Moreover, governments everywhere, at the state, national, and local level, were also snared in a larger web of corporate entanglements epitomized by their investments in railroads. Finally, rising debt and the panic of taxpayers in the 1870s were provoked more by financial maneuvers and interest rates set on Wall Street than by chicanery at Tammany Hall.[35]

Andrew Green, like Boss Tweed, could not make much financial sense of the eighty-odd departments expending New York taxpayers' money in the 1870s. Unraveling this skein of public finance is best left to some patient economic historian. The concern for students of public life is how men and women interpreted these public problems and intervened to resolve them. The politics of publicity that orchestrated the Tweed scandal had helped to set in place the new system of urban administration described by Jon Teaford. Teaford offers a lucid picture of the modus operandi of American cities between 1870 and 1900 and argues that cities such as New York, New Orleans, and San Francisco enacted major civic improvements and in fact delivered disproportionate benefits to the most dyspeptic reformers and middle-class professionals and financial elites. The reforms of urban government in the late nineteenth century invested more authority in professional departments, appointed commissioners, and impervious financial officers like Comptroller Andrew Green, leaving the ward the major space of more popular direct democracy. Even as these neighborhood public meetings declined in relative significance, the perception of cities as the vice-ridden fiefdoms of immigrant ward heelers and corrupt politicians continued to rob citizens of opportunities for democratic deliberation and public pride. This diminished faith in democracy itself was in part the legacy of laissez-faire ideology, in part provoked by the chaos of the streets and the public ledgers, in part a tribute to the ingenuity of reformers. But it was also propelled by the changes in the way the people imagined themselves in relation to one another, Orange or Hibernian, black or white. That process of redefining the people took another major turn late in the 1870s and was staged with particular panache and peril in San Francisco.

Labor, Capital, and "Coolie": San Francisco, 1877

In the midst of the Tweed scandal groups of working men calling themselves Eight Hour Leagues assembled on the streets of New York, San Francisco, and other cities. Working men had begun to appear more prominently in urban public life in the late 1860s and would be key actors in American politics as the decade of the 1870s came to a close. The panic of 1873 and years of depression that followed threw as many as two thirds of industrial laborers out of work and brought angry men and women into the streets once again to demand jobs and seek political redress. With the great railroad strikes of 1877 "Labor and Capital," locked in conflict, would capture the headlines across America. This development in urban politics made its most spectacular appearance in San Francisco. The Workingmen's Party of California, which formed there in the fall of 1877, provides a focus for this search for public consciousness of class differences. By capturing the public space in San Francisco and the public stage nationally the WPC exemplified another potent new way of politicizing urban difference.

The remarkable notoriety achieved by the Workingmen's Party of California in 1877 came after long years of relatively quiet mobilization by San Francisco trade unions. The late 1860s found the city's workers gathering in ward-level clubs, parading on the Fourth of July, and even sharing in a symbolic national victory with the Eight Hour Act of 1868. In San Francisco the units of the workingmen's movement were defined by their different occupations, from the relatively common workers such as longshoremen and quarrymen to the more skilled such as builders and shipwrights. But in the fashion of the American parade these different occupational associations were capable of coordinated action. In 1867 the carpenters adopted the surname the Eight Hour League and marched in the Independence Day parade just in front of the brewers and milkmen and behind the butchers, who proclaimed, "We are the bone and sinew of the country." Such groups as this joined together a few days later to form a "working men's convention." Self-identified working men were simultaneously declaring their independence from the Democratic Party. Slates of labor parties, some with names like the Taxpayers and Mechanics Party, stood for local election and gave expression to multiple ways of constructing the people according to class.[36]

The amalgamation of worker consciousness had to cut against the grain of ethnic loyalties as well as craft and industrial divisions. The mobilization of radical working men in New York had a particularly strong ethnic character. The report on a June 9, 1872, labor meeting noted: "The Germans as usual, were in the strongest force at Teutonic Hall." In fact the eight-hour parade started at the German assembly rooms. Irish immigrants, meanwhile, still clustered in unskilled manual jobs, especially around the docks, where close ethnic brotherhoods were maintained by such organizations as the Irish Longshoremen's Society Benevolent Association. This fraternal order of coworkers defined its membership as "white only" and excluded Italians and Poles as well as African Americans.[37] New York workers would at times cross ethnic lines—for example, the cigarworkers' strikes united a variety of immigrants, including newcomers such as the Bohemans. In general, however, worker solidarity grew by weaving neighborhood, ethnic, and occupational loyalties into a rough-textured collectivity.[38]

In the 1870s some descent groups stood out more flagrantly than others within the urban working population. Animosity to African Americans seemed to have moderated somewhat over time, and some genuine workers' alliances were soon forged across the color line. In New York the German labor movement was conciliatory to workers of African American descent, and incidents of interracial strife at the workplace declined. Worker solidarity actually crossed the racial divide in New Orleans. The workingmen's political alliances that had emerged along with Know-Nothingism in the 1850s became a powerful constituency during the Union occupation and exerted some influence among Radical Republicans. After the war workers rallied for higher wages in public works and at the docks. Gatherings of workers along the Levee were remarkable in that they included whites and blacks, in separate but not overtly antagonistic groupings. During the same decade, when white supremacy conquered the political arena, the racial cooperation among dock workers nurtured a kind of interracial solidarity. In the winter of 1880, a crucial stage in the story of interracial unions as told by Eric Arnesen, black and white workers joined in the same labor organization, the Cotton Men's Executive Council. Later, a parade of working men linked "Black and white, male and female, adult and children."[39]

In general working men had secured prominent billing in the urban politics of the 1860s and 1870s. Furthermore, unlike the workingmen's parties of the Jacksonian era—with their artisan, Anglo-Saxon, Protestant homogeneity—the unions of the 1870s showed a capacity to incorporate the divisions of ethnicity, at times even race.[40] The postwar labor movement was also capable of taking a stand directly in opposition to their polar antagonist, the capitalist. Whether they were confronting the railroad tycoons in the North or the planters and cotton merchants in the South, workers excoriated the ruling class with increasing ferocity. The militancy mounted with the prolonged depression and peaked with and national railroad strikes of 1877. In this tense atmosphere San Francisco's police chief acted decisively: He placed an order for hundreds of new pistols and thousands of rounds of extra ammunition. Some small disturbances that followed a meeting of working men in late July led to the reconvening of the vigilance committee; up to 4000 men patroled the streets through the rest of the summer. New York's labor militants were reined in by the standards of law and order, which waxed strong after the Hibernian riot. When workers and the unemployed rallied for jobs and public relief in Tompkins Square in 1874 and again in 1877, the police were armed, mounted, and ready. Citing the law that restricted parades, the police charged a peaceful and immobile rally in 1874. This was just treatment for "communists," said the mainstream press. The New York meetings of the unemployed in 1877 provoked a similar combination of alarm at dissent and complacency with state power; they brought headlines such as "Communists Fizzle" or "Rout of the Reds."[41]

Despite growing working-class consciousness and organization, however, the labor movement rarely became a key player in the civic life of the big cities before the 1880s. San Francisco was unusually precocious. The Workingmen's Party of California managed to circumvent official opposition, which featured vigilante threats, bans on public meetings, and the repeated arrest of its leaders, to win municipal office and rewrite the state constitution. The flamboyantly public history of the WPC usually commences with a small gathering called by a group of socialists to show sympathy for the striking railroad workers in late July 1877. Like similar meetings in New York, this attempted mobilization of the working class took place on the margins of public space, not the tattered workingmen's plaza in the Lower East Side but the disheveled open space around the construction site of San Francisco's new City Hall. This space, a monument to the slow, miserly investment in public projects, became christened the sandlots and served as the site for a remarkable congregation of the people. The assembly on this July evening was rather lackluster: The speech by the California socialists was reputedly dull and frequently interrupted by catcalls. In retrospect this meeting was notable for several intertwined reasons. First, it was the location of a small riot, when a few members of the crowd—young, unemployed men ("hoodlums" in contemporary parlance)—adjourned the meeting by rampaging through the places of Chinese employment. Second, this meeting was the first in a long sequence of rallies at the sandlots, including one in early September that formed the Workingmen's Party of California. Third, the July rallies were the launching pad for the charismatic leader of the WPC, a political wizard named Dennis Kearney.[42]

Kearney attacked the capitalists and mobilized the workers with unparalleled venom and virtuosity. In November he goaded a meeting of workers into a procession to a monument of capitalism with these words: "I tell you with a column of twenty-five thousands marching through Kearny Street to Market Street and down to the Pacific Mail Steamship Companies wharf, you will make the capitalists respect and tremble." The capitalists were identified by name and address and stung by resolutions. Mr. Charles Crocker on Nob Hill was the target of this act of a workers' public meeting: "Whereas the owners of the Union and Pacific Railroad have defrauded the people of millions," their corporate charter granted by the state "should be annulled."[43] With rhetoric like this and incommensurate if unconventional methods of organization, Dennis Kearney would publicize the opposition between labor and capital across the country. He lingered around the sandlots after the July riots, became a central speaker in the "meetings of the unemployed," and was on the podium when the ad hoc public meeting took the name of the Workingmen's Party in September.

He did not create the movement from whole cloth, however, but rather stitched a variety of scattered groups and diffuse discontent into a powerful political force. A look at the units in the Thanksgiving Day parade of 1877 reveals the nature of the coalition. Most of the groups who marched together that day were not coworkers. Organized principally by ward, they were often reincarnations of Democratic Party clubs. Some of these partisan, grassroots institutions were also a permutation of the Eight Hour Leagues that had formed a decade earlier. Both Democrats and workers, moreover, had also been incarnated as "anti-coolie clubs," on the scene long before Dennis Kearney raised his tarnished silver voice over the sandlots. The worker politics of the 1870s drew more selectively on ethnic associations. To some of his contemporaries Kearney himself was the quintessential rowdy Irishman, called in the press "a big red-mouthed Irish Mick." Kearney pointedly eschewed this Irish identity. In 1878 he refused to wear a shamrock on St. Patrick's Day and mounted a workingmen's parade at cross currents to that of the Hibernians. He also adamantly opposed the local Catholic hierarchy. By ranking the identity of workers above that of Irishmen Kearney did not close the issue of ethnicity and politics. He defined the American working man, and woman too, in opposition to another descent group, immigrants from China. The weight of the evidence concurs with Alexander Saxton's argument that the Chinese where the working men's "indispensable enemy," the negative pole around which they constituted themselves in the public sphere.[44]

Opposition to the Chinese was central but hardly unique to the WPC. This brand of xenophobia had been widespread since at least the 1860s. It had been organized late in that decade into the anti-coolie clubs that provided the infrastructure on which the Workingmen's Party built itself into prominence in the late 1870s. By then, opposition to the Chinese had become the unifying local prejudice, shared by Republicans, Democrats, employers, and workers. Both major parties wrote the restriction of Chinese immigration into their platforms the spring before the Workingmen's Party formed.[45] The Chinese represented a stark and uncomplicated other. They were cast as sojourners, not potential citizens, with neither Tammany Hall nor Radical Republicans to court their votes. Religion, custom, language, segregation in Chinatown, not just skin color, set them apart. As early as 1862 this bold difference was given a racial name. A treatise on immigration published in San Francisco that year maintained that "To the Caucasian race, with its varied types, has been assigned the supremacy in elevation of mind and beauty of form over all mankind." From this assertion immigration restriction followed as the "law of nature to preserve the purity of the race."[46]

The genius of Dennis Kearney was to mobilize preexisting opposition to the Chinese and harness it to a political force, the Workingmen's Party. A unique and caustic blend of race and class consciousness was the key ingredient of Kearney's political sorcery. Broadsides billed the meeting of July 25 as an "anti-Coolie Demonstration." One placard put it in the confident but confused language of race: "away with all Chinamen, white or colored." Those who gathered at the sandlots could read the racial caste of the movement off such slogans as "Anti-coolie Club—Self Preservation is the First Law of Nature." The language of race politics was also put in the ugly personal terms that fed two decades of street violence: taunts of "Mongolian leper" or "Take the Chinamen out by the Neck" or simply "hang them." From his sandlot podium Kearney embroidered and amplified the xenophobic cries of the crowd with sadistic skill: "We will take them by the throat, squeeze their breath out, and throw them into the sea."[47]

With galvanizing images such as this Kearney and the WPC converted workers into whites. Neither Irish, nor Democrats, nor longshoremen, the people cheering at the sandlots were a race unto themselves. Their new identity was put in the form of a resolution at a public meeting on November 25: "We admit that the interests of capital and labor are identical, but consider that in as much as wealth cannot be acquired without the assistance of the laboring classes, capitalists have no right to employ 'coolie labor' to the detriment and degradation of the white working class." The working men of California had formed their own white leagues in the fall and winter of 1877. The banners held high in the Thanksgiving parade spelled it out: "This is a country for free white labor, not coolie labor." The resolutions at another sandlot convention enveloped the doctrine of the family wage in racial terms: "Every white man who is willing and able to work is entitled to have employment furnished to him at wages sufficient to provide for himself and family." Another group simply carried aloft the banner of its club, "the Caucasian."[48] In sum the Workingmen's Party of California had opened up a second flank of that dualistic and negative definition of the people that had evolved almost at the same time in New Orleans.

In the last analysis the most unique feature of the Workingmen's Party was neither its class consciousness nor its racism but the way it brought them together to create a powerful new form of political mobilization. The base of Kearney's operation was the dependable foundation of democratic insurgency, urban social space. The sandlots were an open amphitheater where up to 8000 partisans met every Sunday well into the 1880s. From this central place for mass meeting the party fanned out into the city. Nearly every night of the week, working men met as neighborhood congregations, in saloons, small public halls, or on street corners. Kearney sent his virulent message through this circuit of public meetings. Any given night might find him stopping to orate on the corner of Powell and Pine, dropping in at the Irish-American Hall, or lighting a bonfire at Tenth and Howard. Neither frequent arrests nor the limits of the built environment deterred Dennis Kearney. One evening when he was turned away from one public hall after another—Garibaldi, Lafayette, Irish American, and Charles Oak—he rallied the troops on the spacious steps of the United States Mint. For two years the local press followed the itinerary of Dennis Kearney as he moved first through the city, then through the state, and then on to a cross-country tour that commenced with a parade to the train depot and a farewell serenade. This was quite literally a social movement.

In fact motion, not location, was a key to the WPC's success. A typical meeting of the party changed setting at least once and in such a way as to give the audience a sense of effective participation. A rally might culminate in a march to the railroad offices, the ship company, or an opposition meeting. In one dramatic foray Kearney led his followers to the very threshold of the ruling class: Charging up Nob Hill to the citadel of mansions belonging to railroad magnates, he fired a volley of anticapitalist rhetoric directly into the parlors of the ruling class. The mobilization of workers on the streets of San Francisco was also driven by the powerful expressive uses the organizers made of public space. When not in motion, the meetings of the WPC were enlivened with skits, farces, songs, and poems as well as Kearney's fiery oratory. A not atypical meeting of the eighth ward Workingmen's Club featured a burlesque of the Crocker family and a treatise entitled "The Indictment of Capital by the People" set to verse and music by a Mrs. Brustein. The grand finale of this mobile political spectacle was that Thanksgiving Day parade in the fall of 1877. With powerful political theater like this, the Workingmen's Party succeeded in making labor a contender in the high stakes civic battles of the industrial city. This masterful agitation and mobilization overcame the indifference of the daily press to worker concerns and countered journalistic arts of publicity with the workers' talent for protest (fig. 41).[49]

The whirlwind of the WPC propagated the discontent of San Francisco's working people across the country but in the same motion detached their protest from its moorings in city space. First, the stock and trade of this species of politics became not associated actions but powerful symbols, slogans, and spectacles—that is, the stuff of publicity, not public meeting. Second, it turned progressively away from the concrete needs of unemployed workers to symbolic enemies such as the Chinese. Third, and as a consequence, the movement degenerated into a campaign focused on a single issue. Although the WPC raised an extensive series of public concerns and proposed some radical ideas—control of corporations, regulation of public transportation and utilities, compulsory education—it was willing in the end to sacrifice them all for a Chinese Exclusion Act. Finally, and in summation, the WPC wavered from the pursuit of the public good, widely conceived, toward a narrow interpretation of the civic domain.

Figure 41. "The Latest Phase of American Politics—a Sunday Matinee on the Sand-lot," *The Wasp,* 1880. Courtesy of the Bancroft Library.

However brilliant Kearney's tactics, the current of popular opinion he unleashed ran along the already well-rutted privatizing channels of American political development. Kearney's rhetoric pulled politics into the same direction favored by anti-Tweed forces and the taxpayers' parties. As he put it in 1878, "The man that works for Crocker at a dollar a day pays more taxes than Charles Crocker. The Poor man is the taxpayer of the community." In 1880 he said it even more loudly and clearly: "The Poor Man pays the Taxes of the bond holder millionaire." Kearney and his party let their alliances to the taxpaying citizen eat away at the democratic franchise. They supported revisions in the state constitution that imposed a poll tax and property qualifications for voting. Neither did the WPC lend much support to public projects that might, among other things, create jobs for the unemployed who gathered at the sandlots. At the same time that Kearney was mobilizing working men and women at the sandlots another smaller movement was assembling in San Francisco in support of municipal efforts to provide a public water supply. Kearney opposed the controversial project, converting popular distrust of big expensive government into more grist for the populist mill.[50]

The firebrand of the sandlots contributed to the loss of confidence in representative government and elected officials. No one was more merciless toward politicians. When he disrupted a meeting on the water issue, Kearney reportedly "Put his Feet down on all Politicians." He regularly removed experienced party men from his organizations in a process he called "weeding out the politicians." Kearney launched an explosive barrage of charges against no less a politician than President Grant, whom he called in 1879 a "mendacious lobbyist and paid attorney of every grasping, soulless corporation throughout the land, thieving settlers, rascally Indian agents, dishonest army officials, cheating syndicates, floaters of false bonds, bread-and-butter Beechers."[51] Certainly, charges similar (if not quite as colorful) to these can be substantiated in 1877 (and today). Profit taking at public expense, by private citizens and public officials, was especially tempting during and after the Civil War, when the difficulty of administrating cities and solving urban problems was growing faster than organizational skill or bookkeeping capacity could comprehend. Still, the equation of venality with politics and, conversely, good government with reduced spending was not inevitable. To regard the democratically elected urban government as greedy, venal, corrupt— rather than overburdened and disorganized and in need of administrative reform—was to lose trust in the capacity of the people and their representatives to engage in public coordinated action. In this narrow construction of the possibilities of public life the Workingmen's Party concurred with the reforming gentry of New York and the Redeemers in New Orleans.

Within this increasingly demoralized civic ambiance the ugly and negative matter of racism loomed even larger. Racism was the message that the Workingmen's Party of California most successfully transmitted across the country. In the late 1870s a national consensus was forming around racial ideology, and its focus was a tiny, vulnerable group of immigrants from China. Kearney's pronouncements were watched nationwide; his visit to New York in 1878 was so menacing that the Seventh Regiment was placed on alert; and in 1882 the issue about which he had drummed up so much excitement was written into law.[52] The daily press of each city picked up the Chinese question with speed and alacrity, even transmitting rumors that local employers were about to import Chinese laborers to break strikes from coast to coast. The press converted the California politics of Chinese exclusion into an extended national conversation about racial difference more broadly construed. In many ways the Chinese of San Francisco provided more fitting subjects for racial ideology than did the African Americans of the South. Recent émigrés from Asia were unencumbered by the political status and identity that

African Americans had earned in the abolition movement and during Reconstruction. With few political protectors, with almost no experience of American citizenship, an immigrant from China served as a radically other American, a blank slate on which to write the bold, biological categories of racial difference. A lecture in Dashoway Hall in 1877 spoke decisively: "the laws of nature and place of man demand that two distinct races should never be brought in direct contact." The speaker was referring to the Chinese, who unlike blacks had no legal claims on citizenship. Another California writer set the Chinese apart from Europeans, saying, "The China man is not an immigrant in any sense of the word." Others claimed that the Chinese were even more menacing than African Americans. The "system of coolie labor," he warned, is "death to free white labor . . . a system of slavery which is far more degrading and servile than the worst type of African slavery."[53] The political campaign against Chinese immigrants distilled a pure racial concentrate and transmitted a potent racial category it called mongolian across the country. It showed up even in the parade of comic differences at Carnival time in New Orleans.

The California variety of racial categorization became the focus of serious national attention in 1879 and 1880 when the U.S. Congress began to consider a bill to ban immigration from China. The New Orleans press was almost as attentive to the debate as the *San Francisco Chronicle,* whose headlines read "Solid South on the Chinese Bill." By 1880 the New York Democratic Party was as anti-Chinese as its San Francisco and New Orleans counterparts. Protestant ministers lined up with Catholic working men in the anti-Chinese consensus. A Republican rally held in San Francisco on March 12, 1879, attacked the opposition to the Chinese Exclusion Act in a religious language of difference. The Chinese immigrant was not a coolie but a "heathen," and St. Paul rather than Dennis Kearney was the prophet who warned of the threat to "thousands of youth who have been overwhelmed by the pagan tide."[54] It would seem that every class, all ethnicities, both genders, and three cities had come together in opposition to the Chinese, who huddled in San Francisco and were herded outside the public sphere. The Chinese Exclusion Act passed Congress in 1882 with a vote of 202 yeas, 37 nays, and 51 absent. The shadowy signs of racial exclusion, once the fantasies of carnival clubs, had become public, federal law.

The success of the California campaign against the Chinese inspired the *Picayune* to recite this quick lesson in racial theory

These things clearly indicate that the normal status of the Caucasian is now generally recognized by the people of all parties, and we shall hear but little more of the Negro in national legislation. His status is fixed by the law and that law is universally recognized. He has become an American citizen, and has ceased to be a ward of the nation. As such he must work out his own history on the basis of Anglo-Saxon civilization, and withstand the competition of a race that has the highest claims for the most perfect combination of intellect, muscle, energy, and pluck.

This statement translated citizenship into a license to compete without public assistance in the American marketplace. The *Picayune* neither disguised nor apologized for the assumption that such citizenship also spelled failure for those who bore the crushing disadvantages of former slaves. This bone-chilling forecast also tied together the two most critical changes in the public sphere after the Civil War. The same political process that enacted racial exclusion also, and not coincidentally, narrowed the substantive meaning of the public. A single gesture closed the doors on Chinese immigrants, sentenced African Americans to internal exile, and closed down the public sphere to projects that intervened in the free play of the marketplace.

Gender and Reactionary Populism

In 1877 in San Francisco labor history swerved off course, turning class consciousness back into racial antagonism. The conjuncture is an early example of what Nancy MacLean has called reactionary populism.[55] And as so often the case, the construction of racial reaction was shored up by the ideology and structure of gender difference. In the 1870s in San Francisco racial paranoia built up around the anomalies in the gender division of labor. A number of historians have confirmed what some argued at the time, that the "coolie" was rarely a direct competitor for the white working man and the unemployed of San Francisco. He was hardly stealing anyone's family wage. The Chinese tended to congregate in service and unskilled factory jobs where their movements in the labor force were contained by the Six Chinese Companies. They certainly were not the cause of the depressed economy of the 1870s. In some ways the chief economic rival of the Chinese laborer was not a working man but his sister or daughter. Chinese workers were concentrated in the usually female sectors of domestic service and laundry work. The only industry with a serious representation of Chinese was cigar and tobacco manufacturing, where white women also labored in low-skilled jobs for less than a living wage. This in fact was dimly acknowledged in the Workingmen's Party convention. Among the first resolutions passed at the sandlots was one that enjoined local manufacturers to give "employment to white women whenever possible." Even earlier one anti-coolie club proclaimed, "Women's right to No more Chinese Chamber Maids," and, "Our Women are Degraded by Coolie Labor." The graphic imagery that linked coolie labor to white womanhood was even more brazen. One club sketched "the future of California as a white woman at work while Chinese men staggered under bags of gold."[56]

Questions of gender affected the Workingmen's Party in multiple, often contradictory ways. Because women traditionally sought jobs in domestic service and light industry, where the Chinese workers clustered, a significant number of women gathered around the sandlot. The interests of these women were acknowledged when some of their number assumed a certain public stature, appearing as speakers, vice-presidents, and members of the parade committee. This recognition of women workers was checked, however, by a second element of the Workingmen's political culture, the concept of the family wage, which tended to disregard women's labor. The ideal of a male wage sufficient to support a whole family was designed to shelter wives and mothers from the labor market. This more domestic and passive ideal of working-class womanhood was crudely expressed by a banner carried in the November 30 parade: "Don't Cry mother, the China man will soon leave." Mothers, wives, and children served primarily as justification for a white male wage scale that was more remunerative than the paltry sums Chinese bachelors were willing to accept. An anti-Chinese farce put this economic theory in graphic racist and sexist terms: "White man damn fools; keep wifee and children—cost plenty money; Chinaman no wifee, no children, save plenty money. By and by, no more white working men in California all Chinamen—Sabee?" That the white working men of San Francisco, and especially the nefarious hoodlums, were themselves disproportionately unmarried only exacerbated the bitter contradictions that lent rhetorical power to such gender images.[57]

The stockpile of sex stereotypes also supplied rhetoric with which to attack capitalists. Kearney often fired misogynist barbs at the ruling elite of San Francisco. He was fond of casting aspersions on the pretensions of the wives of Nob Hill, insults the rank and file were happy to pick up. On November 25, 1877, the eighth-ward club was treated to a skit called "Working Men's Riot on Nob Hill," which featured characters such as Miss Croaker and Miss Bertie Olmsted covering in their drawing rooms in fear of an assault of the working class. The farce was described as a "broad burlesque" of the bourgeois home and was "received with cheers by the audience." Like the rhetoric of the family wage, this convergence of gender around race politics had real if illusive connections with social behavior. Mrs. Crocker as well as her husband played an active and public role in Chinese American history. He profited from cheap Chinese labor and she was known for her missionary work among Chinese immigrants, including sponsoring Sunday school picnics that were reported in the popular press. The example of such ministrations that most annoyed the Workingmen's Party was the Presbyterian Mission Home, which provided a refuge for Chinese prostitutes. News of this kind of violation of gender, class, and sexual boundaries led some lower-class men to riot outside this institution of female benevolence.[58]

With a final vicious flourish, race politics exploited the sexual tensions of the gender system. The rhetoric of race and misogyny reached new lows in San Francisco in the 1870s. In bitter sardonic tones the working men charged that the well-known champion of the Chinese, Reverend Otis Gibson, "says that the leprous Chinese will make good husbands for our daughters." Another paid a nasty, sarcastic compliment to Chinese men, calling them "cooks of dainty dishes and . . . substitutes for ladies' maids." The familiar scapegoat of racial politics, the prostitute, bore the brunt of these attacks and also provided a critical hinge of immigration politics. The San Francisco ordinance banishing Chinese prostitutes had been ruled unconstitutional under the provisions of the Civil Rights Act of 1866, prompting local opponents of the Chinese to take their racial agenda to Congress. Virulent rhetoric about the contagion of prostitution was a major propellant of the first legislative success of the anti-Chinese movement at the federal level, the Page Act of 1874. The namesake of a California congressman, the act restricted two classes of immigrants from China: laborers and women suspected of entering the United States for "indecent purposes." The effect of the Page Act was felt most deeply by female immigrants, who were subjected to interrogation as to their moral character and whose numbers relative to men diminished even further after 1874. At the same time that the consul general in Hong Kong was enforcing the Page Act, the municipal authorities, especially the police and the medical officers of San Francisco, were evicting and harassing the prostitutes of Chinatown on the grounds of their threat to public health. The increasingly familiar function of gender in race politics, as defining the most contaminating other by invoking a sexual taboo, was practiced with a vengeance in San Francisco in the

1870s.[59] A polemic by Jennette Blakeslee Frost entitled *California's Greatest Curse* condemned "the dusky Mongolians" as "promoters of unheard of vice of the lowest and most disgusting character, that they engender diseases of the most appalling and malignant types, and that the effect of Chinese women in our midst will be known and felt for generations to come."[60]

The place of women in the anti-Chinese campaign was suggestive of a perilous entanglement between gender and racial politics. When race entered public discourse, gender and sexuality commonly served as escorts. Certainly, this relationship had been forged with a vengeance after the American Civil War, especially in New Orleans but in New York and San Francisco as well. The descent into the sexual politics of the lynch mob began quite slowly. In the 1860s the New Orleans press recorded a few sporadic, sexually charged incidents of racial politics: a report of a black man raping a white women in Memphis, for example, and accusations that Republicans were amalgamationists. This sexualized rhetoric of race was largely suppressed in the years of Radical dominance, when gender politics took a less virulent form. It consisted largely of routine insults to African American women such as the allusion to "ponderous African Venuses" in the city park and empathic messages to white women who had to share the streetcars with freedmen. The leaders of the black suffrage movement were known to respond in kind. The *Tribune* of October 29, 1867, took on an uncharacteristically spiteful tone when it condemned the "secessh women" who resisted the integration of streets cars, sardonically calling them "fair daughters of the crescent city" and pointedly enclosing the term "white lady" in quotation marks. By making jokes at the expense of "a fair beauty perfectly intoxicated" and impugning the motherhood of another white woman, the *Tribune* engaged in its own invidious stereotyping on the grounds of sex.[61]

As Reconstruction policies eroded the social and statutory distinctions between former masters and their former slaves, taboos against interracial sexual relations became increasingly vital markers of the racialized boundaries between Southern people. Gender shored up racial boundaries in social as well as sexual relations. After the war, when New Orleans was flooded with migrants from the outlying plantations, the sexes and the races mingled with one another on a routine and seemingly anarchic basis. The segregation between male and female provided a powerful, indirect way of monitoring race relations in urban public space. It will be recalled from an earlier chapter that the first attempts to legitimize the segregation of New Orleans street cars were proposed as a means of providing for the comfort of ladies. White men, after all, should be expected to take care of themselves: but the frailty of white womanhood justified de jure racial separation. The rhetorical insertion of women into Southern politics would continue through the 1870s, when the protection of ladies became a key argument for replacing the Metropolitan Police with white guardians of feminine honor on the city streets. At the same time Confederates experienced their loss of power in gendered terms: The call to battle at the Clay statue in 1874 justified insurrection: "to such extremities are you driven that manhood revolts at further submission."[62] Gender, in sum, supplied the sexual prohibitions, codes of segregation, and rhetorical power with which to mortar the rising wall of racial segregation.

The increasing prominence of gender in the articulation of difference signaled the maturation of race (not slavery) as the overarching divide of the postwar municipality. The assault of the White League in 1874 had been ushered in not just by arms shipments and mass meetings but by a strident "Appeal of the Women to the Men of New Orleans."

Our cheeks tingle with shame, that in broad daylight, upon our most frequented thoroughfares, almost within your sight and hearing we are subjected to assault and insult! Even our homes are insecure. To whom, under high heaven can we look for aid but to you? Unlike our Northern sisters, we are content to leave to you the pulpit, the rostrum, and the ballot box. You are the custodians of our most cherished rights. Will you prove recreant to the trust and resign, without a struggle, to the invader, all for which our countrymen have died?

Having deployed gender in the service of racial politics, the anonymous ladies issued a poignant appeal to family loyalty: "All is at stake! The integrity of your race, the preservation of your free-born heritage, the honor of your wives and daughters." Adding fuel to the flames of racism, the press pointedly noted that just the day before the White League was summoned to the Clay statue a black man had assaulted a white lady in the street.[63]

The insidious gender politics that contributed to the ultimate failure of Reconstruction were not some uncontrollable eruption from the psychosexual depths. This failure was managed politically and dependent on the social structure of gender. The rhetorical use of femininity required that women be excluded from direct participation, in their own right, in the public sphere. Women served repeatedly as the last best excuse for the exclusionary clauses that still marked American democracy.[64] Their name was invoked repeatedly during the suffrage debates of the 1860s and

1870s as the last refuge of political inequality. Opponents of Chinese voting found assurance in the argument that "The ladies do not vote but still none of these classes complain of oppression." Denying the vote to those of Asian descent was no more prejudicial, it was claimed, than disenfranchising "our wives and children." In the debate about who is a citizen of the public sphere, gender served as the final formidable roadblock in the path of democratic expansion before 1880. Few of even the most Radical Republicans would stand with Susan B. Anthony when she claimed the right to vote under the provisions of the Fourteenth Amendment.[65] When Victoria Woodhull not only tried to exercise the franchise in New York City but campaigned for the office of president, it was seen more as a circus performance than an act of citizenship. Denied the franchise and public office, women remained available for the manufacture of provocative political symbolism. The old female allegories were dusted off in the 1870s and used with particular ardor to represent the ravages of municipal corruption (figs. 42–43).

Not even the New Orleans radicals recognized a woman's right to the franchise. The most magnanimous schemes of racial democracy were at best myopic about gender and at worst misogynist. The radicalism of Jean Houzeau reached its outer limits at a sexual divide. "Would we leave [the black man] suspended between liberty and virility, if I dare express myself in this way? Would he be considered a legal minor as women are?" The overwhelming majority of men and women would have no quarrel with the equation of suffrage and virility. The Conservative Democrats simply pointed to the unquestioned disenfranchising of women to dispel the "nonsense" that suffrage should be truly universal. Though the term *women's suffrage* was rumored to have been uttered at the Radical convention of 1867–1868, it was never elevated to a serious issue or major discussion.[66] The only immediate alteration of Southern women's status after the Civil War was to boost white women a little further up the symbolic pedestal. New Orleans ladies of both races were invited to the rallies of Republicans and civil rights advocates. But neither side of the political divide proposed enrolling women in the formal public.[67] The inscription of the word "male" into the guarantees of citizenship in the Fourteenth and Fifteenth Amendments stood as an emphatic mark of gender exclusion in American public life. The expansion of democracy had clearly reached an impasse with the end of Reconstruction, and the bottleneck was a matter of race and gender.

Still, the extraordinary experiment in multiracial democracy was not for naught. It lived on, not just in amendments to the constitution but in the political determination of African Americans. New Orleanians of

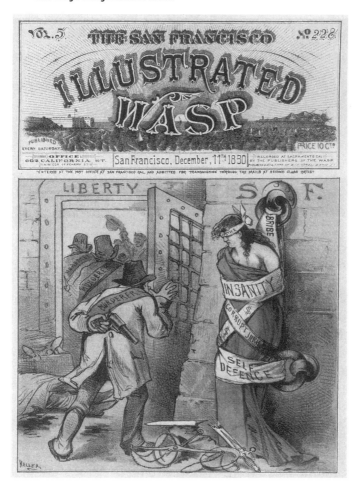

Figure 42. *The San Francisco Illustrated Wasp,* 1880. Courtesy of the Bancroft Library.

African descent waged one particularly heroic offensive in defiance of the White League in the winter of 1874. Fittingly, this last battle was mounted in the social public of the school and involved women as well as men. On December 15, much to the surprise of local newsmen, three students of African American descent appeared at the Girls' High School and announced their intention to take the examination for admission. When these anonymous students and their teacher, identified only as Miss Woods, refused to retreat, a stylized exercise in race and gender politics ensued. The white girls took the next step. Adjourning to the home of one of their number, they wrote a refusal to even receive diplo-

Figure 43. "A Republican Form of Government, and No Domestic Violence." Thomas Nast, 1875. Courtesy The Historic New Orleans Collection, Museum/Research Center

mas from an integrated school. Black men next stepped on stage, attempting to integrate the Boys' High School. These "Negroes—some quite black" (including the son of the lieutenant governor by one report)—were promptly repulsed by white male students who then marched to the girls' school offering the young ladies protection and

Figure 44. "U.S. A Plague upon All Your Goes." *The Wasp,* 1879. Courtesy of the Bancroft Library.

then running riot for three days. It was the action of girls that provided the best copy for conservative journalists. They were heroines in the cause of "Purifying the race," brave young white women who stood up for "the rights of their race." Miss Woods and her students held off segregation for another two years but then quietly disappeared from history. Their stand at the school house door would not recur for eighty years or more.[68]

Despite its erratic pacing, this march through municipal history, from Radical Reconstruction in New Orleans, to machines and reformers in New York, and on to the Workingmen's Party in San Francisco, did arrive at a common historical conclusion late in the 1870s. All plots led to a narrowing of the range of public good and public possibility, an increasingly bureaucratized politics, a reliance on publicity more than public association, and a dualistic definition of the differences among the people—a public divided into white and colored, male and female. The two major tendencies of the postbellum public sphere, the retrenchment of the democratic experiment and the constriction of the public interest, converged in racial ideology. It was in the name of race that American cities pulled out of the social side of the political sphere and left every one, not just those with non-European ancestry, at sea in the rough waters of industrial capitalism. These are the most obvious generalizations to be made about public life in American cities in the years immediately following the Civil War. But this is not the complete picture. It certainly is not the ending. On the streets of America's cities in the 1860s and 1870s some crafty democrats devised ways to challenge the increasingly concentrated powers of industrial capitalism. The members, male and female, of the Workingmen's Party of California, for example, demonstrated not just the ravages of racism but the power to confront the politics of publicity with the protests of a social movement. If the story continued into the next decade we would find that the Workingmen's Party of California was a false start, a pilot project, on the way to the more salubrious and successful labor campaigns of the next decade. And not too many decades after that we find women in the streets parading for votes and picketing for justice.[69] The insurgent politics of African Americans in New Orleans and working people in San Francisco had also staked out the pathways whereby social movements could reinvigorate democracy (Fig. 44).

To pause in 1880 is only to put the promises and the contradictions of heterogeneous democracy front and center in American politics where they still remain despite all the civic wars and civic accomplishments since. Despite the challenges to democracy that were raised at the sandlots of San Francisco, in the press rooms of New York, and around the Clay statue in New Orleans, people still found some public space in the city where they could associate, reinvent themselves, and challenge the powers that be.

EPILOGUE

Picnics were more popular than parades on the 219th anniversary of American independence. The *San Francisco Chronicle* listed the ingredients of the celebration in about the right proportions: "fireworks, parades, picnics, baseball and beer." Neither New York nor San Francisco sponsored official parades on July 4, 1995, and the procession in New Orleans was a small march through a relatively remote quarter of the city. (Its chief advertised attraction was a member of the Neville Brothers Band among the grand marshals.) If the headlines for July 4 are to be believed, public discourse had taken on a bizarre turn in the late twentieth century. The front pages recounted not the words of an oration ringing in a public square but a phantom communication from someone called the Unabomber, who threatened to continue his personal terrorist campaign if his opinions were not published. The space for exercising citizenship and engaging public debate seemed to have shrunk alarmingly. Based on the evidence in the foregoing chapters, one might predict that the extent of government action undertaken in the public name also would have dwindled proportionally. Political commentaries and letters to the editor on July 4, 1995, did indeed anguish about the sorry state of public services. Even the public school system, venerable creation of the era of meeting-place democracy, was crippled by tax cuts and citizens' distrust. A decade into yet another revolt of the taxpayers, city governments were grasping at straws to finance vital public projects. Officials in each city pleaded with the federal government not to close the military bases that had been a critical but covert subsidy to their municipalities during the Cold War.

Yet beyond the headlines in the municipal section of the newspapers, there was some evidence that the terrain of democracy was mapped out in much the same way that Tocqueville had found it more than 150 years before. Some citizens made themselves heard in unofficial, voluntary, and segmented public meetings. Not even the withering heat of July adjourned the public meetings in New Orleans in 1995. An ad hoc meeting called the Black Forum convened in a huge sports stadium in conjunction with something called the Essence Music Festival. The Superdome, site of circuses and superbowls, rang with a high volume of citizen discontent. Philosopher Cornell West vowed in the name of African Americans that "They would never allow misery to have the last word, they would never allow suffering and sorrow to have the last word." New York's controversial spokesman for racial politics, Al Sharpton, took the podium to remind affluent African Americans of their debts to public democracy: "Michael Jackson needs to know that SONY's marketing department didn't cross him over. Martin Luther King and Fannie Lou Hamer crossed him over." The words that broke the public silence in 1995 kept both diversity and civic warfare alive. Maxine Waters, congresswoman of South Central Los Angeles, informed the readers of the Metro News section of the *New Orleans Picayune* of her militant intention to rebuild a ravished urban neighborhood: "go to the banks. Shut them down if they're not investing in the community."

On the editorial page other voices continued America's family quarrel about proper public decorum. The July 4 homily of syndicated columnist Molly Ivins exalted that "The U.S.A. requires a considerable tolerance for diversity and a fondness for dissent. The full-throated roar of a free people exercising their constitutional right to free speech can be a little deafening at times." As if to prove Ivins' point, a contrary opinion was expressed on the editorial pages by columnist Debra Saunders, who objected to the agenda of the New Orleans Black Forum. "Race preferences" and "redistributionist government," she said, foster dependency and undermine self-reliance and individual merit. Saunders aimed her counterattack at the easy target of the liberal city of San Francisco, whose school system ordained the teaching of "interdependence and cultural diversity." This battle of the pundits was not just an artifact of a quiet July 4 newsday. It was part of a small civic war waged around policies of affirmative public action on behalf of race and gender equality and for the rights of immigrants. Coincidentally, perhaps, this updated debate about social differences shared the public spotlight with demands to cut taxes and diminish the cost of maintaining the public domain.

The classic quandary of American democracy has not been resolved. Strenuous airing of civic differences seems to coexist with a thin record of public actions in the name of some common good, be it for schools, social benefits, or parade grounds. It would seem that our citizenry is more diverse and our governments more niggardly than ever. Much as it was over a century ago, democracy remains in tension and public well-being in suspension. There is no resolution to that quandary on the immediate political horizon. But one still worries if the delicate balance of civic warfare and public welfare will last forever and whether it can withstand the radical tests ahead in the twenty-first century. In this context stories of the tattered but tenacious democracy of the past bear retelling.

The history I have told commenced during the infancy of a genuine democracy. In American cities between 1825 and 1850 the long-evolving notion of popular sovereignty was translated into concrete democratic practices. The legitimization of party opposition gave teeth to representative government; the public display of social differences (on both an everyday and ceremonial basis) gave substance to political contention; and public meetings occurred throughout civil society, working out a composite public good. These tales of three cities bespeak a democratic heritage too seldom given its due by historians and political commentators. Democratic institutions were not just an outgrowth of American individualism nor an extension of community but a practice of voluntary and heterogeneous association. Urban democracy would always be a piecemeal, incomplete, and associated project, but before 1850 American citizens took two critical steps in the long progression that keeps democracy alive. First, they eliminated property restrictions on the franchise and, second, they admitted religious and ethnic minorities into the polity. Multiplicity and opposition were not just descriptive characteristics of antebellum democracy: They were its nourishment. Loco-Focos, propertyless craftsmen, and Irish newcomers defined democracy by demanding admission and creating many a donnybrook before they won their place in the public sphere. From the first, urban democracy operated through vigorous confrontations and bloodless civic wars. And between 1825 and 1850 democracy won.

Heterogeneous, public democracy was intrinsically volatile. Because it operated through representation, election, vote counts, and parliamentary opposition, it regularly created almost as many disgruntled losers as cautious winners. The precariousness of democratic urban gov-

ernment in the nineteenth century was easy prey to the abuse of demagogues or venal politicians. Severing the link between socioeconomic
status and political rights—to vote, hold office, and enjoy public access—lent additional instability to the public realm. While democracy
broadened political participation, it also tended to reduce some incentives for public service. This conundrum worked itself out in a particularly vexing way in antebellum America. Democratic insurgents made
their way into municipal politics in opposition to mercantile elites who
had previously exercised patrician influence and public largesse in the
same gesture. Jacksonians often dismissed the public benevolence of
Federalists and Whigs along with their elite prerogatives. Democracy
was linked to laissez-faire economics very early in American history, tip-
ping the balance of politics away from positive, coordinated public action, especially in the vital and expanding market sector.

Built on this delicate equilibrium, and strained by the individualizing
tendencies of the vigorous market economy, urban democracy nearly
toppled in the 1850s and 1860s. Indeed, by any reasonable standard
democracy failed: It led to fifteen years of extreme instability on the municipal front and to a civil war that claimed more than half a million
lives. Headlines in the city newspapers revealed a horrific side of our history: hangings in Portsmouth Square, deadly race wars in New Orleans,
and pogroms against African Americans and armed police assaults on
crowds of civilians in New York. These battles were not just routine political contests. They were violent disputes about the legitimacy of public
authority under representative democracy: They were civil, not civic,
wars. The infant democracy came apart under immense external pressures including voluminous and diverse immigration, geometric population growth, and the dislocations of the early stages of industrial capitalism. But the crisis of the 1850s also evolved from tensions intrinsic to
antebellum democracy.

The structural strains first became visible in a sequence of municipal
civil wars that began with the vigilantes and extended to the kindred political phenomena of Know-Nothingism and nonpartisan parties. All
these municipal insurgencies were due in part to a failure of democratic
trust among large portions of the citizenry who joined or condoned the
retreat from public space, from open electoral contest, and from sharing
the polity with cultural strangers, recent immigrants, Roman Catholics,
or African Americans. The fair-weather democrats claimed their own
ethnicity, religion, and economic interest as the unified and inclusive domain of "Americans" or "Citizens." Under these social conditions and

political pressures city governments (often under state directives) re-sorted increasingly to coercive methods of patrolling urban diversity and disorder: They grew intolerant of civic war. By arming the police and en-listing the aid of the state militia, city officials began to militarize the polity even before the Civil War. That national mobilization was pro-voked by another fatal flaw that lay at the core of American constitu-tional democracy. The democracy was erected on a great exception, based in slavery, entwined with descent from Africa, and written into the ground rules of citizenship with the phrase "white only." The inevitable democratic challenge to the slave system took center stage at midcentury and transformed a distinction that was one of many gradations of urban differences into a political priority and catalyst for conflict. Caught up in a massive military struggle organized from Washington and Richmond, the increasingly racialized divisions in the city picked up velocity and with the draft riots of 1863 erupted into the most uncivilized civil war.

Neither civic warfare nor democratic experiment ended at Appomat-tox. Triumphant Radical Republicans in Washington conferred on African Americans the citizenship that had been denied them in the North as well as the South. That critical step toward multiracial democ-racy was propelled by the action of African Americans who exploited the strategic advantages of local public spaces such as the streets and squares of New Orleans. In the North, meanwhile, partisan opposition was re-stored along a battle line between "machines" and "reformers." After the Civil War democratic contention operated on an altered political field and with new tactics. The exploding population, the volatility of rapid urban transportation, and the overcrowding of local spaces of assembly reduced the possibility for integrative sociability and ceremony at the same time that they justified more surveillance of public life. The con-current expansion of political bureaucracy further widened the gulf be-tween neighborhood sociability and the actions of big city government. The compacted spaces of the modern industrial city were not hospitable to the network of public meetings that once communicated or con-ducted a large portion of civic business. It was hard to find a commodi-ous central public place from which to mount an offense against the eco-nomic power that was amassing at the national offices of railroads and banking houses.

Under these circumstances the communication and opposition so es-sential to democracy were increasingly conducted not through public meetings but through publicity. The most obvious venue of publicity was the city press, now a million-dollar industry that was particularly effective in propagating the reformers' political agenda. The reformers, who often called themselves taxpayers, were, however, shy of open public meetings and stingy about extending democratic rights. Civic ceremonies of the period were also becoming more reticent about displaying and honoring the separate and distinctive social elements of the postwar democracy. In general civic culture was more flimsy and evanescent in the 1870s than in the 1840s: Fireworks provided an electric charge for patriotic unity, not the didactic displays of social and political differences. Still, the city harbored spaces where distinctive and discontented segments of the population could find and express themselves. Disheveled public spaces such as the sandlots of San Francisco, Thompkins Square in New York, or Congo Square in New Orleans became staging grounds for a powerful articulation of class differences. The example of the Workingmen's Party of California showed the ingenuity and tenacity of the democracy of difference. Exploiting the potential for mounting polemic and publicity in the streets, Dennis Kearney mobilized a new political identity called workers and just as defiantly named and confronted the capitalist. This successful publication and mobilization of discontent, conducted from a space outside established political institutions, was a harbinger of modern American social movements. The WPC was the advanced force of what would be a "Great Upheaval" of labor that would in the 1880s challenge the economic concentrations of the industrial era. Simply put, the politics of publicity coexisted with, and was sometimes countered by, the politics of protest. But as of 1880 the labor movement fell far short of its potential. The major contribution of the Workingmen's Party, allied with Southern Redemptionists, was to reinstall one of the most tenacious exclusionary clauses of American democracy—"white only." When what Pierre Van den Berghe has termed Herrenvolk democracy came of age during Reconstruction, it was grounded in a scheme of racial classification that consigned Chinese immigrants as well as those of African descent to internal civic exile. The racists of the 1870s cunningly plumbed the depths of gender symbolism to reinforce the united political stance of the white man. The battle continues.

This schematic history of civil wars was pieced together from the public records of three unique and scattered cities. While the story of each city was unique in timing, detail, principle characters, and minor incidents, the plots of all three moved in the same direction. Loco-Foco meeting-place democracy triumphed everywhere before 1850. The retreat from public democracy soon thereafter was most swift and virulent among the vigilantes of the West (where shallow roots in public culture gave it particular force), but more secretive, "nonpartisan" politics disrupted the course of democracy in all three cities. Racism grew up around San Francisco's Chinatown as well as among Redemptionists of New Orleans in the late 1870s; indeed, these regional racisms reinforced and fed off one another. New York City also played host to racial stereotyping—of the Irish, the African, the Anglo-Saxon. The political process in each city had become more brittle in the 1870s as it became constrained in narrower public spaces, more bureaucratic procedures, and under closer police surveillance, but citizens of each city still found ways to construct new political identities and mount public protests: mass meetings of the unemployed in Thompkins Square, multiracial unions on the docks of New Orleans, gatherings of thousands of San Franciscans at the sandlots.

That heterogeneous democracy staid its serpentine course through these civil wars is testimony to the unique historical possibilities of American cities early in the nineteenth century. Civic life was thrown open to democratic discussion in close and commodious public spaces, city streets, and squares that teemed with newcomers, immigrants, and strangers. Because those antebellum conditions were unique and cannot be reproduced, it is unclear whether the public democracy of difference could have been created at another time and place: It found a hostile climate in the 1850s or the 1860s. To this day America's peculiarly heterogeneous democratic practices are carried forward on the momentum of the meeting-place democracy of the antebellum city. To those who continue to count on that commitment to democracy and diversity, this bit of history is worthy of respectful but critical consideration. These city stories provide few simple lessons or guarantees, but they contain possibilities, warnings, and glimmers of illumination. On the simplest level this history warns against looking to the past for some harmonious, decorous, unified public sphere that will serve as the singular model of democratic politics. Conversely, it begs attention and appreciation for the shrill-voiced, loud-mouthed, rowdy, demanding, contentious citizenry. Democracy is a politics not of unity but of opposition. It is energized and activated not by individual virtue or the private market but by demands for participation and a share of power enacted at specific points of difference and discontent. In complex, democratic societies civic wars are the pragmatic and historical platforms of citizenship. If democracy thrives on the public airing of differences, even to the point of disorder, it wilts in an atmosphere of coercion and withdrawal from conflict. While attempts to make cities comfortable and safe for a wide range of citizens—the work of reformers such as Olmsted and Greeley—deserve commendation, too exacting standards of orderliness in the streets can incur devastating human costs. The forces of order—armed vigilantes, militias, policemen, and a war machine organized in the name of Union and Confederacy—created the greatest carnage in the last century. A refined and careful tolerance of civic warfare, on the other hand, is essential to a heterogeneous democracy. Public contests fed by social differences remain the kinesthetic force that keeps democracy alive and power in check. At its blemished best these civic battles can produce such public goods as Jackson Square, the American parade, and thousands of honest jobs building the Croton Aqueduct and Central Park.

The headlines of 1995 suggest, however, that the pragmatics of making public policy through civil war may be reaching a point of diminishing returns. Americans are still fighting ferociously along lines of difference that were set in place more than a century ago. As the battle storms the general public welfare has dwindled into the national stinginess as tallied by one of the most niggardly national budgets in the industrialized world. This paltry sense of public responsibility is also part of the heritage of America's heterogeneous urban polity, and it does prompt skepticism about the cost of democratic civic warfare. Rather than lamenting this intrinsic contentiousness, however, democratic citizens might better improve the practice of disagreement, perfect, that is, the process whereby the inevitable social differences, and wonderful cultural variations among us, are converted into political positions. The foregoing record indicates first of all the importance of distinguishing among the myriad axes of difference that have animated public democracy in America. Most major streets in an American city, in the nineteenth century and today, will expose a multitude of social differences, each of them immediate and vivid but too diverse and fluid to be rigidly classified. From a certain angle of vision these variations still appear like a kaleidoscope in their bright and pleasing impact. Energetic citizens are still shaping these differences into voluntary associations that can do public business in a decentralized, participatory fashion. These are differences that make for excitement and pleasure and can easily blend into the civic good feeling of the parade.

But a second kind of division is all too visible on our city streets: this is the mark of unequal distribution of rights, powers, and resources. So often arbitrary, unjust, and inhumane, these differences breed democratic disorder. It is when social differences become entwined with economic inequity, and when both become polarized, that civic contentions can escalate to civil war. Yet democracy, particularly in the city, also makes injustices vivid and provides for the possibility of political redress. When inequities are fashioned into civic identities, they can also become the political standpoints from which demands for political representation and equity are mounted. They translate the social citizenship of the streets and the cultural citizenship of parades into renewed public energy and release immense political creativity. Such expressions of difference often take belligerent forms, but they can also work to expand rights, erase inequities, and vivify democracy. Such aggressive democratic initiatives also provoke counteridentities. These reactive constructions of difference, like the nativists of the 1850s and the white leagues of the 1870s, tend to operate by distinctive political tactics. They invoke symbols of unity and singularity, "white" and "American" among them, rather than display themselves in their specificity, their particular, or shared, wants and needs. Pretenders to such universalizing identities—whites, Americans, taxpayers, citizens—often construe differences in categorical and polarized ways. Some have a pronounced taste for blunt oppositions such as black and white, male and female, native and foreigner, honest and corrupt, while others have a special affinity for the emotion-laden language of gender and sexuality. The rhetoric of gender was a particularly versatile tool for manipulating political differences in the nineteenth century, for references to women could be invoked both to symbolize the borders between groups and to justify the exclusion of some members of the city from participation in democratic civic life. Gender differences seldom provoked direct and forceful civic wars in the nineteenth century. But this war, which was *not* fought, haunted the public sphere in sinister ways such as its use in the contaminated language of racism.

These various expressions of differences—some pluralistic, some dualistic, some suppressed—operated in antithetical ways, and only the first had entirely sanguine consequences for democracy. But none of them can be reduced to anthropomorphic terms. They do not designate simple tribes. Each is a specific historical position on the democratic battlefield and a mutable and incomplete reading of the society at large. The general pattern of perceiving difference has, however, evolved over time: The eclectic varieties of the antebellum kaleidoscope tended to become dwarfed by the polarizations of the late nineteenth century. The later differences, while more rigid and one dimensional, could be powerful forces for good as well as ill. The workingmen's parties of the 1870s formed directly on the axis of inequality that cut through the social order along a line of relative power and wealth. They make questions of justice and equity explicit and vocal. Yet the Workingmen's Party of California also offers the most egregious example of how the pursuit of equality could be waylaid by racial scapegoating. There is no escaping the need to examine the specific and unpredictable ways differences are positioned historically and in relation to one another. In fact a democratic society may need to studiously create more differences, not fewer. Some of the most important battles that democracy could wage were only dimly apparent as of 1880. The Workingmen's Party of California was in some respects an off-key overture to the powerful labor movement of the next decade. In the 1880s national trade unions and groups such as the Knights of Labor would formulate a full agenda of public projects as part of their demands for social justice.

Yet further off in the wings of American political development was the project of mobilizing women as full participants in public democracy. The mobilization of middle-class women in public space would not reach a critical mass until late in the nineteenth century, at a time when democratic allegiances had weakened among many of their class and kinsmen. The lack of synchrony in the course of women's rights and that of democratic urban politics was full of consequence. It left sexual differences below the surface of public debate, where they could be mined for treacherous, often racist, rhetorical purposes. This timing also fed into the now well-documented gender politics of the Progressive era, making women better schooled for state building than for democratic electioneering. Still, the delayed prospect of degendering democracy held immense promise. It could double citizen participation, erode a major symbolic grounds for political scapegoating, and introduce a whole bevy of formerly privatized iniquities into public discussion. The promise and possibilities of the democratic experiment have not been exhausted; they continue to expand through the elaboration of differences.

The full scope of the democracy of difference extended not just across time but through several planes of citizenship. It panned far out from the halls of government and defied the rational-critical standards attributed to the classic public sphere. Citizens could participate in the collective life of the polity when they attended civic ceremony and even when they informally associated with one another. City living maximized the opportunities for practicing spatial and cultural citizenship. To judge a polity by just the outcomes of elections—the aridity of highly literate political discourse and the often ugly slogans of reaction—is to cut off access to a vital school of democracy. The rugged reciprocities and often begrudging respect that can be found at busy city intersections, along parade routes, at amusements parks and baseball games, and during carnival time build reservoirs of public trust and warmly evoke the interdependency of citizenship. These reserves of everyday and festive citizenship are too seldom tapped by parties, politicians, and protesters. These pleasures of the city, no less than the virtue of citizens and the sagacity of statesmen, are vital nutrients of civic health. They are positive incentives to invest in public goods, even to pay more taxes. If this quotidian heterogeneity of public life was nurtured and brought more directly into formal politics, we might better imagine the possibilities and recognize the necessity of positive action in the name of all of us.

These pragmatic observations are for naught if the space for practicing all forms of citizenship—the quotidian, ceremonial, and political—is not kept intact and held open. All the above is to stake a special claim for the city, for local, urban places, as a precious resource of democracy. These stories may have been set in three localities, but the plots were quickly diverted to, by, and through a federal system. The local, the state, the sectional, and the national levels compounded and complicated civic warfare. Given the potential distortions of such a far-flung national polity and the remoteness of federal government, it is imperative to return repeatedly to the local, urban base of democratic practice. The antebellum city's contribution to democracy can, without too much distortion, be condensed into a crude formula. It provided the mix of social difference, the commodious public spaces, and a leaven of republican and equal rights ideology in just the combination and quantity that dissolved old habits of deference and made it possible to pursue the public welfare through a democratic process of association and opposition. But already by the 1870s the formal political sphere was receding from these local, urban spaces of heterogeneous public sociability. The pace of both the privatization of social life and the centralization of both government and economics has been accelerating ever since. Yet the American city remains a particularly hospitable environment for practicing the democracy of difference, and in 1995 it is in trouble, all too often beleaguered, maligned, publicly shunned, and said to be technologically obsolete. It is not wildly apocalyptic to wonder if this precious spawning ground of heterogeneous democracy will survive through the twenty-first century. The history of vigorous public democracy in the last century warns of the magnitude of such a loss but also registers the civic resilience that has survived such hard times in the past and garners hope from the stubbornness of those who made and continue to use the democracy of the city.

Just a few months after the tepid Fourth of July celebration of 1995, a far more exuberant celebration occurred in my city of San Francisco. The inauguration of the city's fifty-first mayor, Willie Lewis Brown, Jr., was the occasion for one of the best-ever public frolics. The mayor entertained a crowd estimated at between 50,000 to 100,000 San Franciscans that evening. The people, the mayor, and their music, dance, theater, and food filled a cavernous old pier inside the Golden Gate with a flamboyant display of civic spirit. Above it all wafted what seemed like hundreds of colorful paper banners. Each one proclaimed San Francisco "Unity," but in the name of a different association—a neighborhood, trade union, child care center, anything from the Samoan National Association to the Harvey Milk Institute of Gay and Lesbian Studies. Such voluntary, politicized, and diverse associations found a place at the festive table and before that in the electoral arena. That jubilee renewed civic vows to invest in the city and inspired confidence that the great experiment in democracy is hardly over. The election of Willie Brown, who grew up on the African American side of a segregated Southern town, recalled the victories of civic wars in the past. The city is still a place where men and women like Miss Woods of New Orleans could stand, claim her public share, and vow "That she would stay there if every body left 'ceptin' her."

NOTES

Introduction

1. Edward Countryman, *Americans: A Collision of Histories* (New York: Hill and Wang, 1996), Eric Foner, *Reconstruction: America's Unfinished Revolution, 1863–1877* (New York: Harper and Row, 1988), introduction, and Alan Dawley, *Struggles for Justice: Social Responsibility and the Liberal State* (Cambridge: Harvard University Press, 1991), are among the most successful recent syntheses. Jürgen Habermas, "The Public Sphere: An Encyclopedia Article," *New German Critique* 5, no. 2 (1974): 49–55.

2. Thomas Bender, "Wholes and Parts: The Need for Synthesis in American History," *Journal of American History* 73 (1986): 113, and idem, *Intellect and Public Life: Essays on the Social History of Academic Intellectuals in the United States* (Baltimore: Johns Hopkins University Press, 1993); Craig Calhoun, ed., *Habermas and the Public Sphere* (Cambridge: MIT Press, 1992), 49–55.

3. Hannah Arendt, *The Human Condition* (Chicago: University of Chicago Press, 1958); Arlene Saxonhouse, "Classical Greek Conceptions of Public and Private," in *Public and Private in Social Life*, ed. S. I. Benn and G. F. Gaus (London: Croom Helm, 1983); Hanna Fenichel Pitkin, "Justice: On Relating Public and Private," *Political Theory* 9 (1981): 327–52; Claude Lefort, *Democracy and Political Theory*, trans. David Macey (Minneapolis: University of Minnesota Press, 1988).

4. Jürgen Habermas, *The Structural Transformation of the Public Sphere*, trans. Thomas Berger (Cambridge: MIT Press, 1989).

5. John Dewey, *The Public and Its Problems* (Chicago: Swallow Press, 1954), 12.

6. Dewey, *Public and Its Problems*, 33; Robert B. Westbrook, *John Dewey and American Democracy* (Ithaca: Cornell University Press, 1991), chap. 9; Andrew Arato and Jean Cohen, "Civil Society and Social Theory," *Thesis Eleven*, no. 21 (1988): 40–60; John Keane, *Democracy and Civil Society* (New York: Verso,

317

1988); Iris Young, *Justice and the Politics of Difference* (Princeton: Princeton University Press, 1990); Mary Dietz, "Context Is All: Feminism and Theories of Citizenship," *Daedalus* 116, no. 4 (Fall 1987): 1–24; Nancy Fraser, "Rethinking the Public Sphere," in *The Phantom Public Sphere,* ed. Bruce Robbins (Minneapolis: University of Minnesota Press, 1993); Seyla Benhabib, *Situating the Self* (New York: Routledge, 1992), 93, 102; Michael Warner, *The Letters of the Republic: Publication and the Public Sphere in Eighteenth-Century America* (Cambridge: Harvard University Press, 1990).

7. Lefort, *Democracy and Political Theory,* 230; Chantal Mouffe, *The Return of the Political* (New York: Verso, 1993).

8. Habermas, *Structural Transformation,* 211; Arendt, *Human Condition,* 50–58.

9. Lefort, *Democracy and Political Theory,* 168–69; Alexis de Tocqueville, *Democracy in America,* ed. Richard D. Heffner (New York: Mentor, 1956), 108, 198–199.

10. Russell L. Hanson, *The Democratic Imagination in America* (Princeton: Princeton University Press, 1985), chaps. 1–4; Robert Dahl, *Democracy and Its Critics* (New Haven: Yale University Press, 1989); Donald W. Rogers, ed., *Voting and the Spirit of American Democracy* (Urbana: University of Illinois Press, 1990); Andrew W. Robertson, *The Language of Democracy: Political Rhetoric in the United States and Britain, 1790–1900* (Ithaca: Cornell University Press, 1995); Gordon Wood, "The Democratization of Mind in the American Revolution," in *Leadership in the American Revolution* (Washington, D.C.: Library of Congress, 1974); idem, *The Radicalism of the American Revolution* (New York: Vintage Books, 1991); Robert Weibe, *Self-Rule: A Cultural History of American Democracy* (Chicago: University of Chicago Press, 1995).

11. Thomas Bender, "Metropolitan Life and the Making of Public Culture," in *Power, Culture, and Place,* ed. John Hull Mollenkopf (New York: Russell Sage, 1988); Stephen Skowronek, *Building a New American State: The Expansion of National Administrative Capacities, 1877–1920* (Cambridge: Harvard University Press, 1982); Richard Hofstader, *The Idea of a Party System* (Berkeley: University of California Press, 1969); Richard L. McCormick, *The Party Period and Public Policy: American Politics from the Age of Jackson* (New York: Oxford University Press, 1986); Michael McGerr, *The Decline of Popular Politics, 1865–1928* (New York: Oxford University Press, 1986); Alfred Young, *The Democratic Republicans of New York* (Chapel Hill: University of North Carolina Press, 1967).

12. Warner, *Letters of the Republic,* chaps. 1 and 2.

13. Michael Schudson, *Discovering the News: A Social History of American Newspapers* (New York: Basic Books, 1978); Donald Schiller, *Objectivity and the News: The Public and the Rise of Commercial Journalism* (Philadelphia: University of Pennsylvania Press, 1981).

14. Tocqueville, *Democracy in America,* 202.

15. Lynn Lofland, *World of Strangers* (New York: Basic Books, 1973); Jane Jacobs, *The Death and Life of Great American Cities* (New York: Vintage Books, 1961), 56; Richard Sennett, *The Conscience of the Eye: The Design and Social Life of Cities* (New York: Knopf, 1990).

16. Clifford Geertz, *The Interpretation of Culture* (New York: Basic Books, 1973); Frank Manning, ed., *The Celebration of Society: Perspectives on Contemporary Cultural Performance* (Bowling Green, Ohio: Bowling Green University Popular Press, 1983); Victor Turner, *Celebration* (Washington, D.C.: Smithsonian Institution Press, 1982); Richard Sennett, *The Uses of Disorder: Personal Identity and City Life* (New York: Knopf, 1970).

Chapter 1

1. Lady Emmeline Stuart Wortley, *Travels in the United States in 1849 and 1850* (London: Richard Bentley, 1851), 2.

2. For the most sophisticated rendering of this bleaker side of the antebellum culture, see Amy Gilman Siebnick's *The Mysterious Death of Mary Rogers: Sex and Culture in Nineteenth-Century New York* (New York: Oxford University Press, 1995).

3. U.S. Census Bureau, *The Census of 1850* (Washington, D.C.: U.S. Government Printing Office, 1852), 249, 474, 558–59, 614–15.

4. Amy Bridges, *A City in the Republic: Antebellum New York and the Origins of Machine Politics* (Cambridge: Harvard University Press, 1984); Sean Wilentz, "The Rise of the American Working Class, 1776–1877," in *Survey in Perspectives on American Labor History: The Problem of Synthesis*, ed. J. Carroll Moody and Alice Kessler-Harris (De Kalb: Northern Illinois University Press, 1989); Richard B. Stott, *Workers in the Metropolis: Class, Ethnicity, and Youth in Antebellum New York* (Ithaca: Cornell University Press, 1990); Christopher L. Tomlins, *Law, Labor, and Ideology in the Early American Republic* (Cambridge: Harvard University Press, 1993); Robert J. Seinfeld, *The Invention of Free Labor: The Employment Relation in English and American Law and Culture, 1350–1870* (Chapel Hill: University of North Carolina Press, 1991); Neil Larry Shumsky, *The Evolution of Political Protest and the Workingmen's Party of California* (Columbus: Ohio State University Press, 1991).

5. Kevin Lynch, *The Image of the City* (Cambridge: MIT Press, 1970), and idem, *City Sense and City Design: Writings and the Projects of Kevin Lynch* (Cambridge: MIT Press, 1990).

6. See Charles Lockwood, *Manhattan Moves Uptown: An Illustrated History* (Boston: Houghton Mifflin, 1976); Elizabeth Blackmar, *Manhattan for Rent, 1785–1850* (Ithaca: Cornell University Press, 1989); Pierce F. Lewis, *New Orleans: The Making of an Urban Landscape* (Cambridge: Harvard University Press, 1976); John P. Young, *San Francisco: A History of the Pacific Coast Metropolis* (San Francisco: Clarke, 1912); Helen Troap Purdy, "Portsmouth Square," *California Historical Society Quarterly* 3 (1924): 30–44.

7. Lydia Marie Child, *Letters from New York* (New York: C. S. Fanes, 1845), 96–99; Wortley, *Travels in the United States*; Thomas Richard, Diary, Mar. 15, 1839 (New Orleans Collection, Tulane University Library); Martha Lamb, "Life in New York Fifty Years Ago," *Magazine of American History* (Mar. 1890); M. B. Buckley, *Diary of a Tour in America*, ed. Kate Buckley (Dublin: Sealy, Bryers, and Walker, 1886).

8. Jessie J. Poesch, *The Art of the Old South: Painting, Sculpture, Architecture, and the Products of Craftsmen, 1560–1860* (New York: Knopf, 1983), 37; Leonard V. Huber, *New Orleans: A Pictorial History* (New York: American Legacy Press, 1981), 2–5; John W. Reps, *The Making of Urban America: A History of City Planning in the United States* (Princeton: Princeton University Press, 1992).

9. Huber, *New Orleans*, 88; Lewis, *New Orleans*; Hodding Carter, ed., *The Past as a Prelude: New Orleans, 1718–1968* (New Orleans: Tulane University Press, 1968).

10. George Tays, "Portsmouth Plaza," 1938 (typescript, Bancroft Library, University of California, Berkeley); Purdy, "Portsmouth Square," 3.

11. Reps, *Making of Urban America*, 298.

12. Blackmar, *Manhattan for Rent*, 94; Hendrik Hartog, *Public Property and Private Power* (Chapel Hill: University of North Carolina Press, 1983); M. Christine Boyer, *Manhattan Manners: Architecture and Style, 1850–1900* (New York: Rizzoli, 1985); Reps, *Making of Urban America*, 298.

13. See Minutes of the Common Council of the City of New York, Jan. 17, 1825, 288–89; Mary J. Flannelly, "City Hall" (typescript, fall 1975, Municipal Archives, New York City), 7; Isaac Newton Phelps Stokes, *The Iconography of Manhattan Island, 1498–1909,* 6 vols. (New York: R. H. Dodd, 1915–25), 3:429, 463–65, 584–85.

14. Eric Sandweiss, "Claiming the Urban Landscape: The Improbable Rise of an Inevitable City," in *Eadweard Muybridge and the Photographic Panorama of San Francisco, 1850–1880,* ed. David Harris (Montreal: Centre Canadien d'Architecture, 1993).

15. New Orleans Mayors Messages, Dec. 1, 1827 (Transcripts and Translations from the French, 1825–1852, New Orleans Public Library).

16. Marta Gutman, "New York City's Broadway: Heterogeneity, History, and Public Space" (unpublished manuscript, 1991, courtesy of the author).

17. Thomas F. DeVoe, *The Market Book* (New York: De Voe, 1862); Blackmar, *Manhattan for Rent*, 96; Huber, *Pictorial History*, 195–98.

18. James E. Vance, *Geography and Urban Evolution in the San Francisco Bay Area* (Berkeley: Institute for Governmental Studies, University of California, Berkeley, 1964).

19. Tyrone Power, *Impressions of America during the Years 1833–1835* (London: Bentley, 1836); Henry A. Kmen, *Music in New Orleans: The Formative Years, 1791–1841* (Baton Rouge: Louisiana State University Press, 1966); Alvin F. Harlow, *Old Bowery Days: The Chronicle for a Famous Street* (New York: D. Appleton, 1931); Theodore Junior Shank, "The Bowery Theater, 1826–1836," Ph.D. diss., Stanford University, 1956; Lawrence Levine, *Highbrow/Lowbrow* (Cambridge: Harvard University Press, 1988); Lula May Garett, "San Francisco in 1851," as described by eyewitnesses, *California Historical Society Quarterly* 11, no. 22 (1943): 253–280.

20. Wortley, *Travels in the United States*, 2; Child, *Letters from New York*, 96–99; Richard Butsch, "Bowery B'hoys and Matinee Ladies: The Re-Gendering of Nineteenth-Century American Theater Audiences," *American Quarterly* 46 (Sept. 1994): 374–405.

21. Rodman Gilder, *The Battery* (Boston: Houghton Mifflin, 1936); Harlow, *Old Bowery Days;* Stephen Jenkens, *The Greatest Street in the World: Broadway* (New York: Putnam, 1911).

22. Dell Upton, "The Master Street of the World: The Levee," in *Streets: Critical Perspectives on Public Space,* ed. Zeynep Celik, Diane Favro, and Richard Ingersoll (Berkeley: University of California Press, 1994).

23. Lewis William Newton, *The Americanization of French Louisiana: A Study of the Process of Adjustment between the French and Anglo-American Population of Louisiana, 1803–1860* (New York: Arno Press, 1980), 157; James F. Richardson, *The New York Police: Colonial Times to 1901* (New York: Oxford University Press, 1970); Roger Lane, *Policing the City: Boston, 1822–1885* (Cambridge: Harvard University Press, 1967); James F. Richardson, *Urban Police in the United States* (Port Washington, N.Y.: Kennikat Press, 1974); Dennis Charles Rousey, "The New Orleans Police, 1805–1889: A Social History," Ph.D. diss., Cornell University, 1978; Wilbur R. Miller, *Cops and Bobbies: Police Authority in New York and London, 1830–1870* (Chicago: University of Chicago Press, 1977); Polly Welts Kaufman, ed., *Apron Full of Gold: The Letters of Mary Jane Megguier from San Francisco, 1849–1856* (San Marino, Calif.: Huntington Library, 1947), 46.

24. New Orleans Mayors Messages, Sept. 4, 1830; Christine Stansell, "Children and Uses of the Streets," in *Unequal Sisters: A Multicultural Reader in U.S. Women's History,* ed. Ellen Carol Dubois and Vicki L. Ruiz (New York: Routledge, 1990); William Whyte, *City: Rediscovering the Center* (New York: Doubleday, 1988).

25. New Orleans Mayors Messages, Oct. 5, 1840.

26. Grace King, *New Orleans: The Place and the People* (New York: Macmillan, 1907); Charles Hanswell, *Reminiscence of an Octogenarian in the City of New York, 1816–1860* (New York: Harper, 1896), 27; Gilder, *The Battery;* E. O. Crosby, Diary (Bancroft Library, University of California, Berkeley). See Levine, *Highbrow/Lowbrow,* and David Grimsted, *Melodrama Unveiled. American Theater and Culture, 1800–1850* (Chicago: University of Chicago Press, 1968).

27. *New Orleans Daily Picayune,* Feb. 14, 1837, quoted in Kmen, *Music in New Orleans,* 202; *Daily Alta California,* Feb. 23, 1849.

28. Kmen, *Music in New Orleans; New Orleans Daily Picayune,* Dec. 16, 1837.

29. *New Orleans Daily Picayune,* Feb. 8, 1837; Power, *Impressions of America.*

30. *New York Herald,* Jan. 2, 1843; Edward Durrell, *New Orleans as I Found It* (New York: Harper, 1848), 26.

31. Hanswell, *Reminiscences of an Octogenarian,* 35; Liliane Crété, *Daily Life in Louisiana, 1815–1830* (Baton Rouge: Louisiana State University Press, 1981), 63–64.

32. E. Merton Coulter, *The Other Half of New Orleans* (Baton Rouge: Louisiana State University Press, 1939), 41–48.

33. Crété, *Daily Life in Louisiana,* 52; Power, *Impressions of America,* 48; see Benjamin Albert Botkin, ed., *New York City Folklore* (New York: Random House, 1956); Statement of Events in California as Related by Judge E. O. Crosby for the Bancroft Library, 1878 (Hubert Howe Bancroft Collection, Bancroft Library, University of California, Berkeley), 121–23.

34. Durrell, *New Orleans as I Found It*, 29–30; Harris, ed., *Eadweard Muybridge and the Photographic Panorama*, Plate 10 (p. 75), reveals "varied occupational and national types: trappers, miners, Chinese, and Mexicans." A total of only three women appear.

35. Durrell, *New Orleans as I Found It*, 26; *New Orleans Daily Picayune* 1837, quoted in Carter, *Past as Prelude*, 358.

36. Child, *Letters from New York*, 167; *New Orleans Daily Picayune*, Sept. 13, 1837.

37. Etienne Mazureau Deposition, Dec. 18, 1813 (Heartman Collection of Manuscripts of Slavery, University Archives, Xavier University Library, New Orleans, Box VIII). Dell Upton has generously shared this archival treasure with me.

38. Durrell, *New Orleans as I Found It*, 42.

39. *New Orleans Daily Picayune*, Gilder, *Battery*, 147.

40. Child, *Letters from New York*, 193–95; Durrell, *New Orleans as I Found It*, 35.

41. Arthur Quinn, *The Rivals: William Gwin, David Broderick, and the Birth of California* (New York: Crown, 1994), 17.

42. Crété, *Daily Life in Louisiana*, 30–55; Fredrika Bremer, *America of the Fifties: Letters of Fredrika Bremer*, ed. Adolf Benson (New York: American-Scandinavian Foundation, 1924); Durrell, *New Orleans as I Found It*.

43. Blackmar, *Manhattan for Rent*.

44. George W. Putnam, "The Physiognomy of Cities," *American Review* (Sept. 1847): 233.

Chapter 2

1. *New York Herald*, July 23, 1850.

2. Ibid.

3. Proceedings of the City Council, First Municipality (manuscript, Louisiana Division, New Orleans Public Library, Apr. 10, 1824, Apr. 18, 1825, May 14, 1825); Edgar Ewing Brandon, ed., *A Pilgrimage of Liberty: A Contemporary Account of the Triumphal Tour of General Lafayette* (Athens, Ohio: Lawhead Press, 1944); *The Visit of General Lafayette to Louisiana* (New Orleans: Cruzat, 1825).

4. Peter Burke, *Popular Culture in Early Modern Europe* (London: T. Smith, 1978); Richard Trexler, *Public Life in Renaissance Florence* (New York: Academic Press, 1980); Robert Darnton, *The Great Cat Massacre and Other Episodes in French Cultural History* (New York: Basic Books, 1984).

5. Brandon, ed., *Pilgrimage*; *Visit of General Lafayette*.

6. Cadwallader D. Colden, *Memoir at the Celebration of the Completion of the New York Canals* (New York: Corporation of New York, 1825); *Evening Post*, Nov. 3–7, 1825.

7. Colden, *Memoir*, 155.

8. Brandon, ed., *Pilgrimage*, 173, 179.

9. Colden, *Memoir*, 119; *New York Post*, Nov. 5, 1825.

10. Colden, *Memoir*.

11. Mary P. Ryan, *Women in Public: Between Banners and Ballots, 1825–1880* (Baltimore: Johns Hopkins University Press, 1990), chap. 1; Lynn Hunt, *The Family Romance of the French Revolution* (Berkeley: University of California Press, 1992), 61–66.

12. Proceedings of the City Council of New Orleans (manuscript, Louisiana Division, New Orleans Public Library, Aug. 10, 1826, Jan. 7, 1840); Minutes of the New York City Council, June 4, 1827, Jan. 11, 1828.

13. *New Orleans Daily Picayune*, July 4, 1837; *New York Herald*, July 2–4, 1850.

14. *New York Tribune*, July 5, 1849; *New York Herald*, July 5, 1849.

15. Colden, *Memoir*, 129.

16. Benson J. Lossing, *History of New York City* (New York: A. S. Barnes, 1884), 60.

17. See Thomas Bender, *New York Intellect: A History of Intellectual Life in New York City, from 1750 to the Beginnings of Our Own Time* (New York: Knopf, 1987), Part 1.

18. Edward Pessen, *Jacksonian America: Society, Personality, and Politics* (Homewood, Ill.: Dorsey Press, 1978); Thomas Bender, *New York Intellect* (Baltimore: Johns Hopkins University Press, 1987), and idem, *Intellect and Public Life*, 16–29; Sean Wilentz, *Chants Democratic: New York City and the Rise of the American Working Class, 1788–1850* (New York: Oxford University Press, 1985), 372, 414; Howard Rock, *Artisans of the New Republic: The Tradesmen of New York City in the Age of Jefferson* (New York: New York University Press, 1979).

19. Werner Sollors, *Beyond Ethnicity: Consent and Descent in American Culture* (New York: Oxford University Press, 1986).

20. *California Alta*, Mar. 17, 1851.

21. R. A. Burchell, *The San Francisco Irish, 1848–1880* (Berkeley: University of California Press, 1980).

22. *Irish American*, Dec. 23, 1849, and Mar. 17, 1850.

23. *Irish American*, May 12, 1850.

24. *Irish American*, Feb. 1, Jan. 13, 1850; Benedict Anderson, *Imagined Communities: Reflections on the Origins and Spread of Nationalism* (New York: Verso, 1985).

25. *Irish American*, Aug. 12, 1849, May 19, 1850; Eric Arnesen, *Waterfront Workers of New Orleans: Race, Class, and Politics, 1863–1923* (New York: Oxford University Press, 1991), 21.

26. *Irish American*, Jan. 6, 1850; Iver Bernstein, *The New York City Draft Riots: The Significance for American Society and Politics in the Age of the Civil War* (New York: Oxford University Press, 1990); Roger Shugg, *Origins of Class Struggle in Louisiana* (Baton Rouge: Louisiana State University Press, 1939).

27. *New York Herald*, Mar. 18, 1850, and *New York Tribune*, Mar. 18, 1850.

28. Buckley, *Diary of a Tour in America*, 256–62; Brandon, ed., *Pilgrimage*.

29. Roger Lotchin, *San Francisco, 1846–1856: From Hamlet to City* (Lincoln: University of Nebraska Press, 1974).

30. Shane White, "It Was a Proud Day": African-American Festivals and Parades in the North, 1741–1834," *Journal of American History* 81 (1994): 13–50; Richard Roediger, *Wages of Whiteness: Race and the Making of the American Working Class* (New York: Verso, 1991).

31. Purdy, "Portsmouth Square," 270.

32. Bremer, *America of the Fifties,* 279.

33. See Reid Mitchell, *All on a Mardi Gras Day: Episodes in the History of New Orleans Carnival* (Cambridge: Harvard University Press, 1995), chap. 2.

34. Shugg, *Origins of Class Struggle in Louisiana;* Richard Wade, *Slavery in the Cities: The South, 1820–1860* (New York: Oxford University Press, 1964); *New Orleans Daily Picayune,* Feb. 5, 1845; John Blassingame, *Black New Orleans, 1860–1880* (Chicago: University of Chicago Press, 1973).

35. White, "It Was a Proud Day," 13–15.

36. *New Orleans Daily Picayune* Dec. 4, 1847.

37. Charles Burr Todd, *A Brief History of New York* (New York: American Book, 1899); *Daily Alta California,* Feb. 24, 1852, July 6, 1850.

Chapter 3

1. J. T. Headley, *The Great Riots of New York, 1712–1871* (New York: E. B. Treat, 1873), 69–80; *New York Evening Post,* Apr. 6–18, June 23, 1835; Paul O. Weinbaum, *Mobs and Demagogues: The New York Response to Collective Violence in the Early Nineteenth Century* (Ann Arbor: UMI Research Press, 1979).

2. *New Orleans Daily Picayune,* Nov. 23, 1837; Nov. 1, 1849; *New York Evening Post,* Oct. 30, 1835.

3. Edmund Morgan, *Inventing the People: The Rise of Popular Sovereignty in England and America* (New York: W. W. Norton, 1988); James Kettner, *The Development of American Citizenship, 1608–1870* (Chapel Hill: University of North Carolina Press, 1978).

4. F. Byrdsall, *The History of the Loco-Foco or Equal Rights Party* (New York: Clement and Packard, 1842), 25.

5. Alexis de Tocqueville, *Democracy in America,* ed. Richard D. Heffner (New York: Mentor Books, 1956), 205

6. *New York Evening Post,* Jan. 1, 5–7, 20, Feb. 3, 19, 24, Mar. 2, 7, 1835.

7. Arthur Charles Cole, *The Whig Party in the South* (1914; reprint, Gloucester, Mass.: P. Smith, 1962).

8. *New Orleans Daily Picayune,* Feb. 6, 16, Mar. 30, Apr. 24, May 5, 14, June 15, Aug. 19, Oct. 1, 15, Dec. 3, 1847.

9. *Daily Alta California,* Feb. 1, 12, 22, June 14, 1849.

10. Noah Webster, quoted in Tomlins, *Law, Labor, and Ideology in the Early American Republic,* 38.

11. Reps, *Making of Urban America,* 81–85. Upton, "Master Street of the World."

12. *The Laws and Ordinances of the City of New Orleans from the Consolidation of Municipalities, 1852, to November 1, 1887* (Manuscript Division, New Orleans Public Library), 1852, 31–32.

13. Robin Einhorn, *Property Rules: Political Economy in Chicago, 1833–1872* (Chicago: University of Chicago Press, 1991); Blackmar, *Manhattan for Rent,* 159.

14. *Manual of the Corporation of the City of San Francisco . . .* (San Francisco: G. K. Fitch, 1852); George F. Comstock, ed., *Reports of Cases Argued and Deter-*

mined in the Court of Appeals of the State of New York, 4 vols. (Syracuse, 1851), 4:419–43.

15. Report of City Engineer Joseph Pelie, New Orleans, Sept. 30, 1831 (Rosemunde E. and Emile Kuntz Collection, 1655–1910, Tulane University Library).

16. *New York Evening Post,* Dec. 19, 1847. *A General Digest of the Ordinances and Resolutions of the Corporation of New Orleans* (New Orleans: n.p., 1831), 89–91.

17. *New York Evening Post,* Dec. 21, 1835. *Digest of Ordinances, Resolutions, and By-Laws* (New Orleans: Gaston Brusle, 1836), 99–109.

18. *New Orleans Digest of Ordinances,* 1840, 3–5

19. Stephen F. Ginsberg, "Above the Law: Volunteer Firemen in New York City, 1836–1837," *New York History* 50, no. 2 (Apr. 1969): 165–86.

20. Minutes of the Common Council of New York, Apr. 5, 1824.

21. Bridges, *City in the Republic,* 72.

22. *New Orleans Daily Picayune,* Aug. 11, 1947.

23. Society for the Reformation of Juvenile Delinquents in the City of New York, *Documents Relative to the House of Refuge* (New York: Mahlon Day, 1832).

24. Minutes of the Common Council of New York, Jan. 11, 1830; George Ashton Black, "The History of Municipal Ownership of Land or Manhattan Island," in *Studies in History, Economics, and Public Law* 1 (1897): 165–249; L. Ray Gunn, *The Decline of Authority, Public Economic Policy, and Political Development in New York State, 1800–1860* (Ithaca: Cornell University Press, 1988), chap. 1.

25. Minutes of the Common Council of New York, June 21, 1830; *New Orleans Daily Picayune,* Aug. 12, 19, Oct. 14, 1847; Proceedings of the City Council, First Municipality, Jan. 7, 1840; Carl F. Kaestle, *The Evolution of an Urban School System: New York City, 1750–1850* (Cambridge: Harvard University Press, 1973).

26. See the charters of New Orleans, New York, and San Francisco; *New Orleans Digest of Ordinances,* 1835, 1846.

27. *New Orleans Bee,* Feb. 25, 1834; *New Orleans Daily Picayune,* Mar. 28, 1834; *New York Evening Post,* Nov. 8, 1827.

28. *New York Evening Post,* Mar. 12, 1835.

29. *New York Evening Post,* Oct. 30, 1895; Arthur Schlesinger, Jr., reported this event with the flair it deserved in *The Age of Jackson* (Boston: Little, Brown, 1946), 191.

30. *New York Evening Post,* Oct. 30 and Nov. 12, 1835.

31. Byrdsall, *History of the Loco-Foco,* 24, 45.

32. *New York Evening Post,* July 2, 1827; *New Orleans Bee,* Feb. 20, 1834, Nov. 16, 1837.

33. John Ashworth, *"Agrarians and Aristocrats": Party Political Ideology in the United States, 1837–1846* (London: Royal Historical Society, 1983).

34. *New York Evening Post,* Apr. 17, 1835; *New Orleans Daily Picayune,* Apr. 5, 1846.

35. Thomas Brown, *Politics and Statesmanship: Essays on the American Whig Party* (New York: Columbia University Press, 1985), 29; Cole, *Whig Party in the South,* 311–13; Ashworth, *"Agrarians and Aristocrats,"* 20–126.

36. Ashworth, *"Agrarians and Aristocrats,"* chap. 2; see the *New Orleans Daily Picayune,* Apr. 5, 1846; *Daily Alta California,* Mar. 22, 1849; *New York Tribune,* Mar. 24, 29, 31, 1848.

37. *Daily Alta California,* Apr. 25, 1850; *New York Evening Post; New Orleans Daily Picayune.*

38. Jean Baker, *Affairs of Party: The Political Culture of Northern Democrats in the Mid-Nineteenth Century* (Ithaca: Cornell University Press, 1983); McGerr, *Decline of Popular Politics; New York Evening Post,* Apr. 3, 1835.

39. Byrdsall, *History of the Loco-Foco,* 168; *New York Tribune,* Apr. 29, May 4, May 24, 1848.

40. Byrdsall, *History of the Loco-Foco,* 27

41. Cole, *Whig Party in the South,* 332–34; Joseph Blau, ed., *Social Theories of Jacksonian Democracy: Representative Writing of the Period, 1825–1850* (New York: Hafner, 1947).

42. *New York Evening Post,* Apr. 17, 15, 1835; M. J. Heale, "From City Fathers to Social Critics: Humanitarianism and Government in New York, 1790–1860," *Journal of American History* 63 (1976).

43. *New York Evening Post,* Nov. 4, 1835; *New Orleans Daily Picayune,* Apr. 5, 1846.

44. *New York Evening Post,* Apr. 2, 1835.

45. Lee Benson, *The Concept of Jacksonian Democracy: New York as a Test Case* (Princeton: Princeton University Press, 1984).

46. See Ryan, *Women in Public,* chap. 2.

47. Phyllis F. Field, *The Politics of Race in New York: The Struggle for Black Suffrage in the Civil War Era* (Ithaca: Cornell University Press, 1982); Noel Ignatiev, *How the Irish Became White* (New York: Routledge, 1995).

48. Headley, *Great Riots of New York,* chap. 6; *New York Evening Post,* July 5, 8, 18, 1834, Oct. 2, 1833; Weinbaum, *Mobs and Demagogues;* Linda Kerber, "Abolitionists and Amalgamators: The New York City Race Riots of 1834," *New York History* 48 (1967): 28–39.

49. Field, *Politics of Race,* chap. 2.

50. J. Ross Browne, *California Constitutional Convention, 1849: Report of the Debate on the Convention of California* (Washington, D.C.: J. T. Towers, 1850), 341; Robert F. Heizer and Alan F. Almquist, *The Other Californians* (Berkeley: University of California Press, 1971), chap. 4; Tomás Almaguer, *Racial Fault Lines: The Historical Origins of White Supremacy in California* (Berkeley: University of California Press, 1994).

51. Browne, *California Constitutional Convention,* 72, 49, 69, 143, 64.

52. Ibid., 73.

53. Heizer and Almquist, *Other Californians,* 99.

54. *Daily Alta California,* Aug. 4, 1849; *New York Evening Post,* Apr. 12, 1835; Black, "History of Municipal Ownership of Land on Manhattan Island," 165–249; Blackmar, *Manhattan for Rent.*

55. *New York Evening Post,* Oct. 30, 1835; Gunn, *Decline of Authority;* Blackmar, *Manhattan for Rent.*

56. Gunn, *Decline of Authority,* 257.

57. McCormick, *Party Period and Public Policy*; Skowronek, *Building a New American State*; Sam Bass Warner, *The Private City: Philadelphia in Three Periods of Its Growth* (Philadelphia: University of Pennsylvania Press, 1987); Einhorn, *Property Rules*; Gary Lawson Browne, *Baltimore in the Nation, 1789–1861* (Chapel Hill: University of North Carolina Press, 1980).

58. Jon C. Teaford, *The Municipal Revolution in America: Origins of Modern Urban Government* (Chicago: University of Chicago Press, 1975), 104–5.

59. Headley, *Great Riots of New York*, 74.

60. *New Orleans Daily Picayune*, Mar. 31, 1848; *Daily Alta California*, Aug. 4, 1849; *New York Evening Post*, Apr. 12, 1835.

61. Weinbaum, *Mobs and Demagogues*, 34, 36. Byrdsall, *History of the Loco-Foco*, 109–25. Weinbaum along with Paul Gilje and Michael Feldberg have conducted meticulous studies of the antebellum riots that confirm their high frequency but relative low cost in life, limb, and property and the general tolerance of disorder before 1845. Michael Feldberg, *The Turbulent Era: Riot and Disorder in Jacksonian America* (New York: Oxford University Press, 1980); Paul Gilje, *The Road to Mobocracy: Popular Disorder in New York City, 1763–1834* (Chapel Hill: University of North Carolina Press, 1987).

Chapter 4

1. *Daily Alta California*, Nov. 6, 14, 27, 1855.

2. *Daily Alta California*, Nov. 27, 1855.

3. Peter George Buckley, "To the Opera House: Culture and Society in New York City, 1820–1860," and idem, "Culture, Class, and Place in Antebellum New York," in *Power, Culture, and Place: Essays on New York City*, ed. John Hull Mollenkopf (New York: Russell Sage, 1988).

4. This account is drawn from the *New York Times*, May 10, Nov. 7–14, 1857; Jan. 3, July 14, 1863; *New York Tribune*, May 11, 1849; Jan. 1–3, July 11–21, 1863; see also Emmons Clark, *History of the Seventh Regiment of New York, 1806–1889* (New York: [Seventh Regiment], 1890); Bernstein, *New York City Draft Riots*, 84, 113, 138; Adrian Cook, *The Armies of the Streets: The New York City Draft Riots of 1863* (Lexington: University of Kentucky Press, 1974), 54; Headley, *Great Riots of New York*, 172, 196.

5. Mary Floyd Williams, *History of the San Francisco Committee of Vigilance of 1851: A Study of Social Control on the California Frontier in the Days of the Gold Rush* (1921; reprint, New York: Da Capo Press, 1962), 205.

6. Robert M. Senkewicz, *Vigilantes in Gold Rush San Francisco* (Stanford: Stanford University Press, 1985), 107–22; *Daily Alta California*, Jan. 11, 1850; Aug. 19, 1854.

7. *Daily Alta California*, Aug. 4–Sept. 7, 1854.

8. Ibid., May 23, 26, 30, 1855.

9. Ibid., May 13, 20, 1855.

10. Philip J. Ethington, *The Public City: The Political Construction of Urban Life in San Francisco, 1850–1900* (New York: Cambridge University Press, 1994), 94. While Ethington argues strenuously that the nativism was not the primary, sufficient, or expressed intention of the Vigilance Committee he also demon-

strates that its composition was extraordinarily biased; while merchants were overrepresented by a factor of two, Irish Americans were only one fifth as likely to join than other ethnic groups.

11. *Daily Alta California,* May 16, 1856.

12. *Daily Alta California,* May 15, 1856.

13. Ibid., Aug. 12, 13, 24, 1856; Sept. 13, 1856; for further detail, see Ethington, *Public City,* as well as Senkewicz, *Vigilantes in Gold Rush San Francisco,* 27–29, 45; and Burchell, *San Francisco Irish,* 110, 113, 121.

14. *New Orleans Delta,* June 3, 1858; *New Orleans Daily Picayune,* June 3, 1858.

15. Just who was responsible for these deaths, ethnic opponents, or friendly fire is an unresolved question. See Alcee Fortier, *A History of Louisiana,* 4 vols. (Baton Rouge: Cloiter's Publishing Division, 1972).

16. See Robert C. Reinders, *End of an Era: New Orleans, 1850–1860* (New Orleans: Pelican Pub. Co., 1964); also consult Richard R. Tansey, "Social Democracy and the New Orleans Police, 1850–1860," M.A. thesis, Florida State University, 1971; John S. Kendall, "The Municipal Election of 1858," *Louisiana Historical Quarterly* 5 (1922).

17. Darrel Overdyke, "History of the American Party in Louisiana," Part 1, *Louisiana Historical Quarterly* 15 (1932): 581–88.

18. *New Orleans Bee,* Mar. 24, Sept. 13, 19, 1854.

19. Ibid., Sept. 1, 10, 13, 1854.

20. *New Orleans Delta,* Mar. 15, 1856.

21. *New Orleans Daily Picayune,* June 3, 1856.

22. *New Orleans Bee,* Sept. 13, 19, 1854; *New Orleans Delta,* June 3, 1856.

23. Kendall, "Municipal Election of 1858."

24. *New Orleans Daily Picayune,* May 23, 27, 28, 1858; *New Orleans Bee,* May 21, 1858; *New Orleans Delta,* May 19, 22, 1858; Fortier, *History of Louisiana,* 3:256; Tansey, "Social Democracy and the New Orleans Police," 38–39.

25. *New Orleans Daily Picayune,* June 3, 1858.

26. Samuel Augustus Pleasant, *Fernando Wood of New York* (New York: AMS Press Inc., 1960), 44–48; *New York Tribune,* Oct. 31, 1854; Louis Dow Scisco, *Political Nativism in New York State* (New York: Columbia University Press, 1901), 203–25; William Gienapp, *The Origins of the Republican Party, 1852–1856* (New York: Oxford University Press, 1987), 226–27.

27. Scisco, *Political Nativism in New York State,* 203–10; *New York Tribune,* Oct. 4, 6, 7, 10–11, 13, 17, 28, 31, 1854; *New York Tribune,* Nov. 3, 4, 7, 10, 1854.

28. David Montgomery, *Citizen Worker: The Experience of Workers in the United States with Democracy and the Free Market during the Nineteenth Century* (New York: Cambridge University Press, 1993), 68–70. For a full account see Paul Weinbaum, "Temperance, Politics, and the New York City Riots of 1857," *New York Historical Society Quarterly* 59 (1975): 246–70, and Joshua Brown, "The Dead Rabbit–Bowery Boy Riot: An Analysis of the Antebellum New York Gang," M.A. thesis, Columbia University, 1976.

29. Pleasant, *Fernando Wood of New York,* 48, 79–81.

30. *New York Times* and *New York Tribune,* July 4–15, 1857.

31. *New York Tribune,* July 6, 1857; Headley, *Great Riots of New York,* 129–35.

32. *New York Tribune,* Aug. 28, 1857.

33. Headley, *Great Riots of New York*, 133.

34. Stott, *Workers in the Metropolis*; Montgomery, *Citizen Worker*; Elliott J. Gorn, "'Good-Bye Boys, I Died a True American': Homicide, Nativism, and Working-Class Culture in New York City," *Journal of American History* 74 (1987): 388–410.

35. Phillip J. Ethington, "Vigilantes and the Police: The Creation of a Professional Police Bureaucracy in San Francisco, 1847–1900," *Journal of Social History* 21, no. 2 (Winter 1987): 197–227; Lane, *Policing the City*; Richardson, *New York Police*, and idem, *Urban Police in the United States*; Eric Monkkonen, *Police in Urban America, 1860–1920* (New York: Cambridge University Press, 1981); Michael Katz, "Origins of the Institutional State," *Marxist Perspectives* 1 (1978); Rousey, "New Orleans Police"; Miller, *Cops and Bobbies*; John C. Schneider, "Public Order and the Geography of the City: Crime, Violence, and the Police in Detroit, 1845–1875," *Journal of Urban History* 4 (1978): 183–208; Sidney L. Harring, *Policing a Class Society: The Experience of American Cities, 1865–1915* (New Brunswick, N.J.: Rutgers University Press, 1983); Charles Royster, *The Destructive War* (New York: Knopf, 1991), 131–39.

36. Quinn, *Rivals*.

37. Joseph Logsdon and Caryn Cossé Bell, "The Americanization of Black New Orleans, 1850–1900," in *Creole New Orleans: Race and Americanization*, ed. Arnold R. Hirsch and Joseph Logsdon (Baton Rouge: Louisiana State University Press, 1992), 201–61.

38. Gienapp, *Origins of the Republican Party*; Michael F. Holt, *Political Parties and American Political Development from the Age of Jackson to the Age of Lincoln* (Baton Rouge: Louisiana State University Press, 1992); and idem, *The Political Crisis of the 1850s* (New York: Wiley, 1978). Also William W. Freehling, *The Reintegration of American History: Slavery and the Civil War* (New York: Oxford University Press, 1994); Eric Foner, *Free Soil, Free Labor, Free Men: The Ideology of the Republican Party before the Civil War* (New York: Oxford University Press, 1995), introduction.

39. Dale Baum, *The Civil War Party System: The Case of Massachusetts, 1849–1876* (Chapel Hill: University of North Carolina Press, 1984).

40. Paul Kleppner, *The Third Electoral System, 1853–1892* (Chapel Hill: University of North Carolina Press, 1979), 97–142.

41. *Daily Alta California*, May 12, 1863; *New York Times*, Nov. 2, 1861.

42. *New York Times*, Oct. 26, 1861.

43. Ibid., Nov. 2, 1861.

44. Pleasant, *Fernando Wood of New York*.

45. *New Orleans Delta*, May 25, 1858.

46. *Daily Alta California*, May 7, 1855; *New York Herald*, Oct. 26, Nov. 4, 1861.

47. *San Francisco Bulletin*, Sept. 22, 1856; *Daily Alta California*, May 7, 1855.

48. *New York Herald*, Nov. 28, 1861; *New York Times*, Nov. 2, 28, 1861.

49. Ethington, *Public City*, 112–17; Tansey, "Social Democracy and the New Orleans Police."

50. *New York Times*, Nov. 4, 1861.

51. *New York Herald*, Nov. 28, 1861.

52. Winfield J. Davis, *A History of Political Conventions in California, 1849–1892* (Sacramento: California State Library, 1893).

53. *Daily Alta California,* May 14, 1863.

54. Davis, *History of Political Conventions in California;* Pleasant, *Fernando Wood of New York;* Tyler G. Anbinder, "Fernando Wood and New York's Secession from the Union: A Political Reappraisal," *New York History* 68 (1987): 66–92; *New York Times,* July 11, 1856; *New York Tribune,* Nov. 3–14, 1857; Herbert S. Gutman, "The Tompkins Square Riot in New York City on January 13, 1874: A Re-examination of Its Causes and Its Aftermath," *Labor History* 6 (1965): 49–67.

55. The works to which I am in particular debt include Baum, *Civil War Party System;* Ernest A. McKay, *The Civil War and New York City* (Syracuse: Syracuse University Press, 1990); Foner, *Reconstruction;* Gienapp, *Origins of the Republican Party;* Michael Holt, *The Political Crisis of the 1850s* (New York: Wiley, 1978); Kleppner, *Third Electoral System;* Joel H. Sibley, *The American Political Nation, 1838–1893* (Stanford: Stanford University Press, 1991).

56. Ethington, "Vigilantes and the Police"; John S. Hittell, *A History of the City of San Francisco* (San Francisco: A. L. Bancroft, 1878), 349–50.

57. *New Orleans Daily Picayune,* Apr. 26–May 1, 1861; see also Ted Tunnell, *Crucible of Reconstruction: War, Radicalism, and Race in Louisiana, 1862–1877* (Baton Rouge: Louisiana State University Press, 1984); and Gerald Mortimer Capers, *Occupied City: New Orleans under the Federals, 1862–1865* (Lexington: University of Kentucky Press, 1965), 48–70.

58. Ryan, *Women in Public,* introduction.

59. Pleasant, *Fernando Wood of New York,* 100–131.

60. *New York Herald, New York Times, New York Tribune,* July 14–20, 1863.

61. This sequence has been traced through the *New York Tribune,* the *New York Times,* and the *New York Herald.*

62. *New York Tribune, New York Times, New York Herald,* July 14–20, 1863.

63. George Fredrickson, *The Black Image in the White Mind: The Debate on Afro-American Character and Destiny, 1817–1914* (New York: Harper and Row, 1971).

64. Baker, *Affairs of Party,* chap. 6; Roediger, *Wages of Whiteness;* Eric Lott, *Love and Theft: Blackface Minstrelsy and the American Working Class* (New York: Oxford University Press, 1993); Ignatiev, *How the Irish Became White;* Richard Slotkin, *The Fatal Environment: The Myth of the Frontier in the Age of Industrialization, 1800–1890* (New York: Atheneum, 1985).

65. *New York Times,* Nov. 6, 1861.

66. *New York Times,* May 10, 1857; *New Orleans Delta,* Apr. 14, 1856; *New Orleans Bee,* Apr. 10, 1858.

67. Field, *Politics of Race; New York Times,* Nov. 3, 1860; Nov. 6, 1861.

68. Ethington, *Public City,* chap. 4.

69. Charles Graham Halpine, *The Life and Adventures, Songs, Services, and Speeches of Private Miles O'Reilly* (New York: Carleton Publisher, 1864), 55; *New York Tribune,* Apr. 8, 1863.

70. See *New York Tribune, New York Times,* and *New York Herald* throughout the fall of 1863; McKay, *Civil War in New York City,* chap. 11.

71. Pleasant, *Fernando Wood of New York;* see also *New York Herald,* Mar. 7, 1863.

72. *New York Herald,* June 4, 1863: Nov. 28, 1861; Mar. 7, 1863; Pleasant, *Fernando Wood of New York,* 162.

73. *New York Tribune,* July 15, 1863; Nathaniel Willis, quoted in the *New York Tribune,* July 20, 1863.

74. Holt, *Political Parties and American Political Development,* 283–90.

75. Montgomery, *Citizen Worker,* and idem., *Beyond Equality: Labor and the Radical Republicans, 1862–1872* (New York: Knopf, 1967); *New York Tribune,* May 19, July 16, 1863; *New York Herald,* Mar. 24, 1863.

76. *New York Herald,* Nov. 28, Mar. 24, 1863; *New York Tribune,* Apr. 14, 1863.

77. See Bernstein, *New York City Draft Riots,* 114–24; Cook, *Armies of the Streets;* Field, *Politics of Race.*

78. Tunnell, *Crucible of Reconstruction,* 81–83.

79. Ibid.; Jean-Charles Houzeau, *My Passage at the New Orleans Tribune, A Memoir of the Civil War Era,* ed. David Rankin, trans. Gerard F. Denault (Baton Rouge: Louisiana State University Press, 1984): *San Francisco Pacific Appeal,* Apr. 11, 1863.

80. See also Arnesen, *Waterfront Workers of New Orleans,* 4–8; Bernstein, *New York City Draft Riots,* 117–24.

81. See the *New York Times, New York Tribune,* and *New York Herald* through the spring and summer of 1863; also see Ryan, *Women in Public,* and the *New York Tribune,* Mar. 16, 1863.

Chapter 5

1. Harris, ed., *Eadweard Muybridge and the Photographic Panorama,* 122–23; Peter Hales, *Silver Cities: The Photography of American Urbanization, 1839–1915* (Philadelphia: Temple University Press, 1984), 67–131.

2. *New York Tribune,* May 24, 1883.

3. Thomas Bender, "Metropolitan Culture: Brooklyn Bridge and the Transformation of New York," *Annals of the New York Academy of Sciences* 424 (1984): 325–32.

4. U.S. Census Bureau, *Census of 1870* (Washington, D.C.: U.S. Government Printing Office, 1872), 15–17, 212–13, 792–99.

5. U.S. Census Bureau, *Census of 1880* (Washington. D.C.: U.S. Government Printing Office, 1882), xxxiv–xxxvi, 255, 558–59; see also Stott, *Workers in the Metropolis,* 28–31.

6. U.S. Census Bureau, *Census of 1880,* 891–92, 902.

7. Ibid., 586–87; Arnesen, *Waterfront Workers of New Orleans,* 13–14.

8. Hales, *Silver Cities,* 127.

9. U.S. Census Bureau, *Census of 1870,* 337; U.S. Census Bureau, *Census of 1880,* 558; Benjamin E. Lloyd, *Lights and Shades in San Francisco* (San Francisco: A. L. Bancroft, 1876), 209–25.

10. Lloyd, *Lights and Shades in San Francisco,* 225, 237; James W. Buel, *Mysteries and Miseries of America's Great Cities* (San Francisco: A. L. Bancroft, 1883), 270.

11. B. S. Brooks, *Appendix to the Opening Statement and Brief of B. S. Brooks on the Chinese Question, Referred to the Joint Committee of the Senate and House of Representatives* (San Francisco: Women's Cooperative Printing Union, 1877), 137–41.

12. Carol Roland, "The California Kindergarten Movement: A Study in Class and Social Feminism," Ph.D. diss., University of California, Riverside, 1980, 27–30; Kenneth A. Scherzer, *The Unbounded Community: Neighborhood Life and Social Structure in New York City, 1830–1875* (Durham: Duke University Press, 1992), chap. 5; Alvin Averbach, "San Francisco's South of Market District, 1850–1950: The Emergence of a Skid Row," *California Historical Quarterly* 52, no. 3 (1973): 197–220; U.S. Census Bureau, *Census of 1870*.

13. *A History of Real Estate, Building, and Architecture in New York City* (1898; reprint, New York: Arno, 1967), 61; Neil Larry Shumsky, *The Evolution of Political Protest and the Workingmen's Party of California* (Columbus: Ohio State University Press, 1991), 96–97; see also Lockwood, *Manhattan Moves Uptown,* xviii; and Boyer, *Manhattan Manners,* 31, 32, 141.

14. Scherzer, *Unbounded Community.*

15. *History of Real Estate, Building, and Architecture in New York City,* 61; Lockwood, *Manhattan Moves Uptown;* James Blaine Walker, *Fifty Years of Rapid Transit, 1864–1917* (New York: Law Print. Co., 1918), 6–8.

16. Elizabeth Colins Cromley, *Alone Together: A History of New York's Early Apartments* (Ithaca: Cornell University Press, 1990), 62–128; Elizabeth Hawes, *New York, New York: How the Apartment House Transformed the Life of the City* (New York: Knopf, 1993); U.S. Census Bureau, *Social Statistics of Cities and Parks* (Washington, D.C.: U.S. Government Printing Office, 1881), 273, 805.

17. Richard Plunz, *A History of Housing in New York City* (New York: Columbia University Press, 1990), chaps. 2 and 3.

18. Boyer, *Manhattan Manners,* 154–65; Cromley, *Alone Together;* Walker, *Fifty Years of Rapid Transit.*

19. Michael Corbett and Charles Hall Page, *Splendid Survivors: San Francisco's Downtown Architectural Heritage* (San Francisco: S. F. Foundation for Architectural Heritage, 1979), 24–26; Huber, *New Orleans,* 94–98.

20. Anne Bloomfield, "The Real Estate Associates: A Land and Housing Developer of the 1870's in San Francisco," *Journal of the Society of Architectural Historians* 37 (1978); and Richard Walker, "Landscape and City Life: Four Ecologies of Residence in the San Francisco Bay Area," *Ecumene* 2 (1995): 33–64.

21. Walker, *Fifty Years of Rapid Transit;* Paul Groth, *Living Downtown: The History of Residential Hotels in the United States* (Berkeley: University of California Press, 1994).

22. Thomas Bender and William R. Taylor, "Culture and Architecture: Some Aesthetic Tensions in the Shaping of Modern New York City," in *Visions of the Modern City,* ed. William Sharpe and Leonard Wallock (Baltimore: Johns Hopkins University Press, 1987); William Taylor, *In Pursuit of Gotham: Culture, and Commerce in New York* (New York: Oxford University Press, 1992).

23. Junius Browne, *Great Metropolis: A Mirror of New York* (Hartford, N.J.: American Publishing, 1869), 130, 341; George Ellington, *The Women of New York, or, Social Life in the Great City* (New York: New York Book Co., 1870), 18–19;

Matthew Hale Smith, *Sunshine and Shadow in New York* (Hartford: n.p., 1869), 27–28.

24. Hales, *Silver Cities*, 88–96.

25. John Disturness, comp., *New York as It Was and as It Is* (New York: D. Van Nostrand, 1876); Susan S. Arpad, *The Diary of a True Woman* (Athens: Ohio University Press, 1984), 44–45; Frederick W. Nolan, *The Life and Death of John Henry Tunstall: The Letters, Diaries, and Adventures of an Itinerant Englishman* (Albuquerque: University of New Mexico Press, 1965); Horatio Alger, Jr., *Ragged Dick or, Street Life in New York with the Boot Blacks* (New York: Signet, 1990), 57–58.

26. Boyer, *Manhattan Manners*, 42–46; Robert Hendrickson, *The Grand Emporiums: The Illustrated History of America's Great Department Stores* (New York: Stein and Day, 1979), 16, 36; Ralph M. Hower, *A History of Macy's of New York* (Cambridge: Harvard University Press, 1943), 60–69, 160–66, 196.

27. Neil Shumsky, "Frank Rooney's San Francisco—His Diary, April, 1875–March, 1876," *Labor History* 17 (1976): 245–65; Lewis C. Gunn and Elizabeth LeBreton Gunn, *Records of a California Family* (San Diego: n.p., 1928), 259–66; Lucy Jones, Diary (Bancroft Library, University of California, Berkeley), 1874; Sherzer, *Unbounded Community;* David Scobey, "Anatomy of the Promenade: The Politics of Bourgeois Sociability in Nineteenth-Century New York," *Social History* 17, no. 2 (May 1992); *Daily Alta California,* Feb. 23, 1872.

28. A. T. Spotts, *A History and Report of the Construction of the New City Hall from April 4, 1870, to November 18, 1879* (San Francisco: W. Nittinton, 1886); Harold Kirker, *California Architectural Frontier: Style and Tradition in the Nineteenth Century* (San Marino, Calif.: Huntington Library, 1960), 97–99.

29. The Valedictory of Honorable Thomas H. Selby, San Francisco Board of Supervisors, 1871 (Bancroft Library, University of California at Berkeley); see also Mary P. Ryan, "American City Halls as Sites of Nineteenth-Century Public Life" (typescript, Department of History, University of California, Berkeley).

30. Eugene P. Moehring, *Public Works and Urban History: Recent Trends and New Directions* (Chicago: Public Works Historical Society, 1982); Jon C. Teaford, *The Unheralded Triumph: City Government in America, 1870–1900* (Baltimore: Johns Hopkins University Press, 1984).

31. Ronald L. Forman and Joseph Logsdon, *Audubon Park: An Urban Eden* (New Orleans: Audubon Park Zoological Garden, 1985).

32. Ann L. Buttenwieser, *Manhattan Water Bound: Planning and Development of Manhattan's Waterfront from the Seventeenth Century to the Present* (New York: New York University Press, 1987), 69; *Report of the Special Committee on Pavements of the Board of Supervisors of the City and County of San Francisco* (San Francisco, 1870), 3–4; see also U.S. Census Bureau, *Social Statistics of Cities and Parks,* and idem, *Census of 1880.*

33. San Francisco Park Commissioners, *The First Biennial Report, 1870–1871* (San Francisco: n.p., 1874), 72; Guy Griffen and Helen Griffen, *The Story of Golden Gate Park* (San Francisco: Phillips and Van Orden Co., 1949), 13–14; see also Galen Cranz, *Changing Roles of Urban Parks: From Pleasure Garden to Open Space* (Berkeley: Institute of Urban and Regional Development, 1978).

34. *Daily Alta California,* Jan. 20, Feb. 23, 1878; Griffen and Griffen, *Story of Golden Gate Park,* 15; "Parks of San Francisco," *Overland Monthly* (Mar. 1891).

35. *To His Excellency William Irwin, Governor of California, from the Park Commissioners of San Francisco* (San Francisco: B. F. Sterett, 1876), 31; Griffen and Griffen, *Story of Golden Gate Park,* 16; see also Barry Kaplan, "Andrew H. Green and the Creation of a Planning Rationale: The Formation of a Greater New York City, 1865–1890," *Urbanism Past and Present* 8, no. 8 (1979): 33–34.

36. See David Schuyler, *The New Urban Landscape: The Redefinition of City Form in Nineteenth-Century America* (Baltimore: Johns Hopkins University Press, 1986), for a sympathetic and thorough account of Olmsted's position.

37. San Francisco Park Commissioners, *Second Biennial Report, 1872–1873* (San Francisco: n.p., 1874), 63.

38. Ibid., 74.

39. Harold Wheeler, comp., *Statutes, Ordinances, and Laws Relating to the Park Commissioners of the City and County of San Francisco, 1891* (San Francisco: H. S. Crocker Co., 1894), 79; Lloyd, *Lights and Shades in San Francisco,* 121–25; William Laird MacGregor, *San Francisco, California, in 1876* (Edinburgh: Thomas Laurie, 1876), 15, 41.

40. San Francisco Park Commissioners, *Second Biennial Report,* 58.

41. Lloyd, *Lights and Shades in San Francisco,* 121–25; MacGregor, *San Francisco, California, in 1876,* 15, 41.

42. Rowena Beans, "Inasmuch...," *The One Hundred-Year History of the San Francisco Ladies' Protestant Relief Society, 1853–1953* (San Francisco: n.p., 1953), 13–31; U.S. Census Bureau, *Census of 1880.*

43. Charles Loring Brace, *The Dangerous Classes of New York and Twenty Years Work among Them* (New York: Wynkoop and Hallenbeck, 1872) 14, 80; Ellington, *Women of New York,* 116.

44. Mary Duffy Hardy, as quoted in Bayrd Still, *Mirror for Gotham: New York as Seen by Contemporaries from Dutch Days to the Present* (New York: New York University Press, 1956), 196–202; Joy J. Jackson, *New Orleans in the Gilded Age, 1880–1896* (Baton Rouge: Louisiana State University Press, 1969).

45. William Taylor, *Seven Years Street Preaching in San Francisco, California* (New York: London Press, 1875), 345–46; William Dean Howells, "Their Wedding Journey," *Atlantic Monthly* (July 1871): 29–40.

46. Henry James, *Washington Square* (New York: Vintage Books, 1990).

47. Frederick Law Olmsted, *Public Parks and the Enlargement of Towns* (1870; reprint, New York: Arno Press, 1970), 17–18; S. B. Sutton, ed., *Civilizing American Cities* (New York: Oxford University Press, 1979), 57.

48. Sutton, ed., *Civilizing American Cities,* 57–79.

49. Stuart M. Blumin, introduction to *New York by Gaslight and Other Urban Sketches,* by George G. Foster (Berkeley: University of California Press, 1990); Christine Stansell, *City of Women: Sex and Class in New York, 1789–1860* (New York: Knopf, 1986); John F. Kasson, *Rudeness and Civility: Manners in Nineteenth-Century Urban America* (New York: Hill and Wang, 1990).

50. Browne, *Great Metropolis,* 28.

51. Ibid., 525; Smith, *Sunshine and Shadow in New York,* 209; "The Street Arabs of New York," *Appleton's Journal* (Jan. 1, 1873): 47–48.

52. Browne, *Great Metropolis,* 276; Ellington, *Women of New York,* 173; Marie Louise Hankins, *Women of New York* (New York: Hankins, 1861), 99.

53. Edward Crapsey, *The Nether Side of New York; or, the Vice, Crime, and Poverty at the Great Metropolis* (New York: Sheldon, 1872), 163; Buel, *Mysteries and Miseries,* 280; Ernest Duvergier de Hauranne, *A French Man in Lincoln's America* (Chicago: Lakeside Press, 1975), 253–58, 287.

54. Crapsey, *Nether Side of New York,* 145, 158; Browne, *Great Metropolis,* 458.

55. Browne, *Great Metropolis,* 67; Ellington, *Women of New York,* 320; Lloyd, *Lights and Shades in San Francisco,* 298; *New Orleans Daily Picayune,* Jan. 23, 27, 1877.

56. Timothy Gilfoyle, *City of Eros: New York City, Prostitution, and the Commercialization of Sex, 1790–1920* (New York: W. W. Norton, 1992).

57. Browne, *Great Metropolis,* 29, 94; Ellington, *Women of New York,* 19; Still, *Mirror for Gotham,* 202.

58. U.S. Census Bureau, *Census of 1880,* 566; Smith, *Sunshine and Shadow in New York,* 4–5.

59. Brown, "The 'Dead Rabbit'–Bowery Boy Riot," 7–9.

60. Municipal Archives Manuscript Report of the Board of Health, Aug. 20, 1873 (New York Municipal Archives, Havermeyer Papers), 15–16; *San Francisco Municipal Reports* (San Francisco: Cosmopolitan Printing Co., 1869–), *1868–1869,* 30, 461–63; *San Francisco Municipal Reports, 1877–1878,* 903.

61. Robert M. Fogelsen, *America's Armories: Architecture, Society, and Public Order* (Cambridge: Harvard University Press, 1989), 156; Henry J. Leovy, ed., *The Laws and General Ordinances of the City of New Orleans* (New Orleans: E. C. Wharton, 1857).

62. B. S. Brooks, *Appendix to the Opening Statement and Brief of B. S. Brooks on the Chinese Question, Referred to the Joint Committee of the Senate and House of Representatives* (San Francisco: Women's Cooperative Printing Union, 1877).

63. See Gunther Barth, *Bitter Strength: A History of the Chinese in the United States, 1850–1870* (Cambridge: Harvard University Press, 1964); Stuart Creighton Miller, *The Unwelcome Immigrant: The American Image of the Chinese, 1785–1882* (Berkeley: University of California Press, 1969).

64. See *San Francisco Municipal Reports, 1865,* and *San Francisco Municipal Reports, 1866.*

65. Brooks, *Appendix to the Supplement and Brief of B. S. Brooks on the Chinese Question,* 54.

66. Roger Fisher, "A Pioneer Protest: The New Orleans Street Car Controversy of 1867," *Journal of Negro History* (1968): 219; James M. McPherson, *The Struggle for Equality: Abolitionists and the Negro in the Civil War* (Princeton: Princeton University Press, 1964); Roger Fisher, *The Segregation Struggle in Louisiana* (Urbana: University of Illinois Press, 1974).

67. *New Orleans Daily Picayune,* May 16, 23, 1867.

68. *Louisiana Tribune,* Oct. 29, 1867.

69. "Table Talk," *Appleton's Journal* (Dec. 2, 1871): 638, quoted in Plunz, *History of Housing in New York City,* xxxi.

70. Ibid.

Chapter 6

1. *New York Herald,* Apr. 26, 1865.

2. *San Francisco Examiner,* June 24, 1876.

3. WPA Northern California Writer's Project, *Festivals in San Francisco* (San Francisco: Grabhorn Press, 1939), 1, 53.

4. *Daily Alta California,* Jan. 25, 1877.

5. *San Francisco Elevator,* June 30, 1865; Jan. 3, 1866; *New Orleans Daily Picayune,* Jan. 15, Aug. 5, Nov. 20, 1877; Blassingame, *Black New Orleans,* 143–45; *New York Tribune,* Feb. 21, 1869; *San Francisco Elevator,* June 30, 1865.

6. See Michael Gordon's detailed and thoughtful reconstruction of these events, *The Orange Riots: Irish Political Violence in New York City, 1870 and 1871* (Ithaca: Cornell University Press, 1993).

7. All references are drawn from the *New York Times, New York Herald,* and *New York Tribune* for July 11–15, 1870–1871; see also Gordon, *Orange Riots,* and Bernstein, *New York City Draft Riots,* for further detail.

8. *New York Tribune,* July 10, 1871; Gordon, *Orange Riots,* 33.

9. *New York Herald,* Mar. 17, 1867.

10. Ibid., July 10, 11, 12, 1871.

11. *New York Tribune,* July 11, 1871.

12. Headley, *Great Riots of New York,* 302; *New York Times,* July 13, 1871.

13. *New York Times,* July 13, 1871.

14. Headley, *Great Riots of New York,* 302–5; *New York Tribune,* July 13, 1871; *New York Times,* July 14, 1871; *New York Herald,* July 13, 1871.

15. *Civil Rights, the Hibernian Riot, and the "Insurrection of the Capitalists": A History of Important Events in New York in the Midsummer of 1871* (New York: Baker and Godwin, 1871), 29; see also the *New York Tribune,* July 13, 1871; *New York Herald,* July 13, 1871.

16. *New York Tribune,* Mar. 18, 1873; *San Francisco Alta,* Feb. 23, 1875.

17. *San Francisco Chronicle,* Dec. 25, 1875; *New York Tribune,* Dec. 25, 1872.

18. *New York Tribune,* July 5, 1880; July 4, 1878; Mar. 18, 1880.

19. *New Orleans Bee,* July 4, 1865.

20. *New Orleans Daily Picayune,* July 6, May 18, 1865; see also *New Orleans Bee,* July 6, 1865.

21. *New Orleans Bee,* July 6, 1866.

22. *New Orleans Daily Picayune,* Mar. 4, 1866; Mar. 5, 1868; *New Orleans Bee,* July 6, 1866.

23. *New Orleans Daily Picayune,* Mar. 4–5, 1874; *New Orleans Bee,* July 4, 1866.

24. *New Orleans Daily Picayune,* Apr. 11, 1874; Ladies Benevolent Association, "Memorial Day Apr. 6, 1875" (typescript, Louisiana Historical Association Library, Tulane University).

25. *New Orleans Daily Picayune,* Jan. 7, Apr. 7, 1877; see also Foner, *Reconstruction,* 569–70, 580–82.

26. *New Orleans Daily Picayune,* Apr. 17, May 11, Sept. 15, 1877.

27. Ibid., Mar. 6, 1878.

28. Ibid., Feb. 24, 1879; Feb. 13, 1877.

29. See Samuel Kinser, *Carnival American Style: Mardi Gras at New Orleans and Mobile* (Chicago: University of Chicago Press, 1990), 100–101, 111–13.

30. *New York Herald,* July 13, 1871.

31. *New York Herald,* July 4, 1876; *Daily Alta California,* July 4, 1871.

32. *New Orleans Daily Picayune,* June 15, 16, 1877

33. Ibid.; *Daily Alta California,* Mar. 17, 1879; May 5, 1877; July 4, 1879.

34. *New Orleans Daily Picayune,* Nov. 1, 1877.

35. Ibid., Mar. 6, 1871.

36. *San Francisco Call,* July 4, 1878; *New Orleans Daily Picayune,* Feb. 18, 1874.

37. *Daily Alta California,* Aug. 11, 13, 18, 19, 22, 1856.

38. *New York Tribune,* Mar. 13, 1866; *San Francisco Call,* July 4, 1868; Mar. 18, 1871; Mar. 19, 1878; Mar. 17, 1879.

39. *San Francisco Call,* July 6, 1875.

40. *New Orleans Daily Picayune,* Nov. 26, 1877; *San Francisco Call,* Mar. 18, 1873.

41. *New York Tribune,* Mar. 17, 1854.

42. *New Orleans Daily Picayune,* Apr. 29, 1877; *Daily Alta California,* Dec. 25, 1866; Dec. 24, 1869; Jan. 1, 1867.

43. *New York Tribune,* Nov. 26, 1875.

44. *New York Herald,* Dec. 1, 1871; Nov. 30, 1877; *New York Tribune,* Nov. 27, 28, 1877; Nov. 26, 1875; Nov. 26, 1880.

45. *Daily Alta California,* Sept. 14, 1877.

46. *San Francisco Examiner,* July 4, 1876.

47. Kinser, *Carnival American Style,* 125.

48. *New Orleans Daily Picayune,* Feb. 9, 11, 14, 1877; Gordon, *Orange Riots,* 183–85.

49. Kinser, *Carnival American Style,* 112; Huber, *New Orleans; New Orleans Daily Picayune,* Feb. 9, 11, 1877.

50. McKay, *Civil War in New York,* 240; *San Francisco Pacific Appeal,* Jan. 1, 1866; *San Francisco Elevator,* June 30, 1865; Jan. 5, 1866; *San Francisco Call,* July 5, 1871.

51. *New Orleans Daily Picayune,* Oct. 6, 1877; *Daily Alta California,* Jan. 3, 1865; Garfield Procession Program, "A History of the Proceeding of the City of New Orleans on the Occasion of the Funeral Procession of James A. Garfield" (MSS., Tulane University Library), 68–117.

52. Marcus Christian, "A Black History of Louisiana" (MSS., University of New Orleans Library).

53. Ibid.; *San Francisco Chronicle,* July 4, 6, 1869; July 5, 1870; July 4, 1875.

54. *New York Tribune* and *New Orleans Daily Picayune,* Oct. and Nov. 1877. See also Eileen Boris, "'A Man's Dwelling House Is His Castle': Tenement House Cigarmaking and the Judicial Imperative," in *Work Engendered: Toward a New History of American Labor* ed. Ava Baron (Ithaca: Cornell University Press, 1991), on the cigarmakers' strike.

55. *San Francisco Call, Daily Alta California,* and *San Francisco Chronicle,* Nov. 30, 1877.

56. *San Francisco Examiner,* June 20, 1876; *San Francisco Chronicle,* July 4, 1876.

Chapter 7

1. See Giles Vandal, *The New Orleans Race Riot of 1866: Anatomy of a Tragedy* (Lafayette: University of Southwestern Louisiana Press, 1983), chap. 7.

2. *New Orleans Bee,* May 18, 1865.

3. *New Orleans Daily Picayune,* Mar. 14, Apr. 5–13, May 16, 1866.

4. Ibid., Apr. 5, 13, 29, 1866; May 16, 1866; July 5, 1866.

5. Charles Vincent, *Black Legislators in Louisiana during Reconstruction* (Baton Rouge: Louisiana State University Press, 1976), 62, 185; Houzeau, *My Passage at the "New Orleans Tribune";* see also Charles Vincent, "Black Louisianians during the Civil War and Reconstruction," in *Louisiana's Black Heritage,* ed. Robert Macdonald, John R. Kemp, Edward F. Haas (New Orleans: Louisiana State Museum, 1979); David C. Rankin, "The Politics of Caste: Free Colored Leadership in New Orleans during the Civil War," in *Louisiana's Black Heritage.*

6. *Louisiana Tribune,* Dec. 27, 1864; Jan. 7, 1864.

7. Houzeau, *My Passage at the "New Orleans Tribune",* 96.

8. Vincent, *Black Legislators in Louisiana during Reconstruction,* 66; Houzeau, *My Passage at the "New Orleans Tribune",* 96–97; Foner, *Reconstruction,* 262–80.

9. See Vincent, *Black Legislators in Louisiana during Reconstruction;* Houzeau, *My Passage at the "New Orleans Tribune";* Vandal, *New Orleans Race Riot of 1866.*

10. *New Orleans Daily Picayune,* May 16–17, 1867; *New Orleans Bee,* May 8, 1866; Fischer, *Segregation Struggle in New Orleans,* 36.

11. Annual Report of the Metropolitan Police, 1871 (J. M. Wilson Papers, Tulane University Library); Thomas M. Fiehrer, "The African Presence in Colonial Louisiana: An Essay on the Continuity of Caribbean Culture," in *Louisiana's Black Heritage.*

12. *New York Herald,* Oct. 10, 1867.

13. *New York Tribune,* Oct. 30, Nov. 1, 1867.

14. *San Francisco Alta,* July 10, Aug. 22, 1867.

15. Ibid., Aug. 26, 1867.

16. *New Orleans Daily Picayune,* Oct. 2, 1874.

17. James Mohr, *Radical Republicans and Reform in New York* (Ithaca: Cornell University Press, 1973); Bernstein, *New York Draft Riots.*

18. *Civil Rights, the Hibernian Riot, and the "Insurrection of the Capitalists."*

19. Seymour Mandelbaum, *Boss Tweed's New York* (New York: Wiley, 1965), 136; *New York Times,* Sept. 24, 1871.

20. *New York Times,* Sept. 24, 1871; Gordon, *Orange Riots,* 46.

21. *Nation* (Sept. 7, 1871); *New York Herald,* Mar. 7, 1873; *New York Times,* Sept. 24, 1871.

22. *New York Times,* Sept. 19, 1871; *New York Tribune,* July 13, 1877; *Civil Rights, the Hibernian Riot, and the "Insurrection of the Capitalists."*

23. *New York Times,* Sept. 18, 22, 27, 1871; Oct. 2, 24, 1871.

24. *New York Times,* Sept. 14, 16, 17, 1871.

25. Eric Homberger, *Scenes from the Life of a City* (New Haven: Yale University Press, 1994).

26. *New York Times,* Sept. 29, 1871; Oct. 24, 1871.

27. Mark W. Summers, *The Press Gang: Newspapers and Politics, 1865–1878* (Chapel Hill: University of North Carolina Press, 1994).

28. *New York Times,* Oct. 3, 19, 26, 27, 29, 1871.

29. Bernstein, *New York City Draft Riots,* 231; Andrew H. Green, *A Three Years' Struggle with Municipal Misrule* (New York: Department of Finance, 1874).

30. Steven Erie, *Rainbow's End: Irish Americans and the Dilemmas of Urban Machine Politics, 1840–1985* (Berkeley: University of California Press, 1988), 47.

31. Bernstein, *New York Draft Riots,* chap. 6. provides a detailed account of these political alliances.

32. Martin Shefter, *Political Parties and the State: The American Historical Experiences* (Princeton: Princeton University Press, 1994), 160–64.

33. Kaplan, "Andrew H. Green and the Creation of a Planning Rationale," 33–34, 36; Steven P. Erie, "The Development of Class and Ethnic Politics in San Francisco, 1870–1910" (Ph.D. diss., University of California, Los Angeles, 1975); *New York Times,* Oct. 3, 5, 13, 1871; Terence McDonald, *The Parameters of Urban Fiscal Policy* (Berkeley: University of California Press, 1986).

34. See Bernstein, *New York City Draft Riots;* Erie, *Rainbow's End;* Ethington, *Public City.*

35. Ethington, *Public City;* Teaford, *Unheralded Triumph,* 285–86.

36. *Daily Alta California,* Feb. 21, June 5, July 6–12, 1867.

37. Bernstein, *New York City Draft Riots,* 180.

38. *New York Tribune,* June 9, 1872.

39. Arnesen, *Waterfront Workers of New Orleans,* 25–35.

40. Montgomery, *Beyond Equality.*

41. *New York Times,* Jan. 14, 1874; *New York Tribune,* July 26, 1877; Henry Hiram Ellis to Commanding Officer, Benecia Arsenal, June 25, 1877, Henry Hiram Ellis Papers, California Historical Society.

42. *Daily Alta California, San Francisco Chronicle,* July 25, 1877; see also Alexander Saxton, *The Indispensable Enemy: Labor and the Anti-Chinese Movement in California* (Berkeley: University of California Press, 1971); and Shumsky, *Evolution of Political Protest.*

43. *San Francisco Call,* Nov. 30, 1877; *Daily Alta California,* Nov. 7, 1877.

44. *San Francisco Post,* Aug. 24, 1877; See *Daily Alta California, San Francisco Examiner, San Francisco Call,* and Saxton, *Indispensable Enemy.*

45. Winfield J. Davis, *History of Political Conventions in California, 1849–1892* (Sacramento: California State Library, 1893).

46. Arthur B. Stout, *Chinese Immigration and the Physiological Cause of the Decay of the Nation* (San Francisco: Agnew and Deffebach, 1862), 7.

47. *San Francisco Call,* July 25, 1877; *San Francisco Alta,* Nov. 2, 10, 30, 1877.

48. *San Francisco Alta,* Nov. 15, 25, 1877; see also Ronald Takaki, *Strangers from a Different Shore* (Boston: Little, Brown, 1989).

49. Summers, *Press Gang.*

50. *San Francisco Alta,* Mar. 18, 1878; Oct. 20, 1879: see also William Issel and Robert W. Cherny, *San Francisco, 1865–1932: Politics, Power, and Urban Development* (Berkeley: University of California Press, 1986); and John Young, *San Francisco,* for details on the Spring Valley Water controversy.

51. *San Francisco Alta,* Sept. 10, 1879; Mar. 17, 1878; John Young, *San Francisco,* 537.

52. Takaki, *Strangers from a Different Shore,* 111.

53. *San Francisco Call,* May 7, 8, Oct. 23, 25, 1877; *New York Tribune,* Nov. 11, 1877.

54. *New Orleans Daily Picayune,* Feb. 14, 1879; *Daily Alta California,* Oct. 30, 1879; Mar. 12, 1879.

55. Nancy MacLean, "The Leo Frank Case Reconsidered: Gender and Sexual Politics in the Making of Reactionary Populism," *Journal of American History* 78 (1991): 917–48.

56. *San Francisco Call,* July 9, 16, 1878; *Daily Alta California,* Sept. 22, 1877.

57. *Daily Alta California,* Nov. 30, 1877, and *San Francisco Call,* Nov. 30, 1877; Takaki, *Strangers from a Different Shore,* 104.

58. Peggy Pascoe, *Relations of Rescue: The Search for Female Moral Authority in the American West, 1874–1939* (New York: Oxford University Press, 1990); *San Francisco Call,* Nov. 30, 1877; *San Francisco Chronicle,* Nov. 25, 1877.

59. Sucheng Chan, *Asian Americans: An Interpretive History* (Boston: Twayne, 1991), 54; *San Francisco Call,* Nov. 30, Dec. 8, 1877.

60. Frost, *California's Greatest Curse,* 65, 77, 83.

61. *New Orleans Daily Picayune,* May 16, 1867; *New Orleans Tribune,* Oct. 29, 1867.

62. Fortier, *History of Louisiana,* 3:146.

63. Ibid., 3:139–40.

64. Fredrickson, *Black Image in the White Mind.*

65. Ellen Carol Du Bois, *Feminism and Suffrage: The Emergence of an Independent Women's Movement in America* (Ithaca: Cornell University Press, 1978), chap. 6; idem, "Outgrowing the Compact of the 'Fathers': Equal Rights, Woman Suffrage, and the United States Constitution," *Journal of American History* 74 (1987): 836–56.

66. Rankin, "Politics of Caste."

67. Edmonia Highgate, clippings, 1867 (American Missionary Association Collection, Amisted Archives, New Orleans).

68. *New Orleans Daily Picayune,* and the *New Orleans Weekly Louisianan,* Dec. 15–18, 1871.

69. Ethington, *Public City;* Michael Kazin, *Barons of Labor: The San Francisco Building Trades and Union Power in the Progressive Era* (Urbana: University of Illinois Press, 1987).

SELECTED
BIBLIOGRAPHY

Newspapers

The newspapers listed below were the basis for a systematic survey of the city press for the entire period between 1825 and 1880. More erratic newspaper sources are cited in the footnotes.

The Irish American
New Orleans Bee
New Orleans Daily Picayune
New Orleans Tribune
New York Evening Post
New York Herald
New York Times
New York Tribune
San Francisco Call
San Francisco Daily Alta California
San Francisco Examiner

Public Records

Censuses

U.S. Census Bureau. *The Census of 1820*. Washington, D.C.: U.S. Government Printing Office, 1822.
——. *The Census of 1830*. Washington, D.C.: U.S. Government Printing Office, 1832.
——. *The Census of 1840*. Washington, D.C.: U.S. Government Printing Office, 1842.

——. *The Census of 1850.* Washington, D.C.: U.S. Government Printing Office, 1852.

——. *The Census of 1860.* Washington, D.C.: U.S. Government Printing Office, 1862.

——. *The Census of 1870.* Washington, D.C.: U.S. Government Printing Office, 1872.

——. *The Census of 1880.* Washington, D.C.: U.S. Government Printing Office, 1882.

——. *Social Statistics of Cities and Parks.* Washington, D.C.: U.S. Government Printing Office, 1881.

Mayors' Papers

New Orleans Public Library. Transcripts and Translations from the French, 1825–1852.

New York Municipal Archives. Havermeyer Papers.

Minutes of the City Council

Minutes of the Common Council of the City of New York, 1784–1831, vols. 14–18. New York: City of New York, 1831.

Proceedings of the City Council, First Municipality, Louisiana Division, New Orleans Public Library, 1824–.

Ordinances and Manuals

An Act Concerning the City of San Francisco and to Ratify and Confirm Certain Ordinances. March 11, 1858. Bancroft Library, University of California, Berkeley.

The Amended Charter of the City of New Orleans. New Orleans: Weed and Kelly, 1871.

Digest of Ordinances, Resolutions, and By-Laws. New Orleans: Gaston Brusle, 1836.

A General Digest of the Ordinances and Resolutions of the Corporation of New Orleans. New Orleans: City Council, 1831.

General Orders of the Board of Supervisors and Ordinances of the Park Commissioner. San Francisco: W. M. Hinton, 1878.

Henderson, Violet L., ed. *Synopsis of Ordinances.* New Orleans: City of New Orleans Archives Department, 1839.

The Laws and Ordinances of the City of New Orleans from the Consolidation of Municipalities, 1852, to November 1, 1887. Louisiana Division, New Orleans Public Library.

The Laws of the Town of San Francisco, 1847. San Marino: Hunleigh, 1947.

Leovy, Henry J., ed. *The Laws and General Ordinances of the City of New Orleans.* New Orleans: E. C. Wharton, 1857.

Manual of the Corporation of the City of San Francisco, Containing a Map of the City. San Francisco: G. K. Fitch, 1852.

The New City Charter. San Francisco: San Francisco Commercial Advertiser, 1853.

Ordinances and Joint Resolutions of the City of San Francisco. San Francisco: Monson and Valentine, 1854.

Ordinances and Resolutions of the City of San Francisco, Park Ordinances, 1872. San Francisco: n.p., 1872.

Valentine, D. T., ed. *Ordinances of the Mayor, Aldermen, and Commonalty of the City of New York.* New York: C. W. Baker, 1859.

Wheeler, Harold, comp. *Statutes, Ordinances, and Laws Relating to the Park Commissioners of the City and County of San Francisco.* San Francisco: H. S. Crocker Co., 1894.

Miscellaneous Reports

Brooks, B. S. *Appendix to the Opening Statement and Brief of B. S. Brooks on the Chinese Question, Referred to the Joint Committee of the Senate and House of Representatives.* San Francisco: Women's Cooperative Printing Union, 1877.

Browne, J. Ross. *California Constitutional Convention, 1849: Report of the Debate on the Convention of California.* Washington, D.C.: J. T. Towers, 1850.

City Celebration of the Anniversary of the National Independence, at Lafayette Square. New Orleans: Eva Steam Book and Job Office, 1864. New Orleans Collection, Tulane University Library.

City of New Orleans Controller's Reports, 1854–57. New Orleans: 1856. Louisiana Division, New Orleans Public Library.

Colden, Cadwallader D. *Memoir at the Celebration of the Completion of the New York Canals.* New York: Corporation of New York, 1825.

Comstock, George F., ed. *Reports of Cases Argued and Determined in the Court of Appeals of the State of New York.* Vol. 4. Albany: Gould, Banks, and Gould, 1851.

Davis, Winfield J. *History of Political Conventions in California, 1849–1892.* Sacramento: California State Library, 1893.

Gerard, James Watson, Jr. *A Treatise on the Title of Corporation and Others to the Streets, Wharves, Piers, Parks, and Other Land and Franchises of the City of New York.* New York: Poole and MacLauchen, 1872.

A History of the Proceedings in the City of New Orleans on the Occasion of the Funeral Ceremonies in Honor of Calhoun, Clay, and Webster, Which Took Place on Thursday, December 9, 1852. New Orleans: Office of the Picayune, 1853. New Orleans Collection, Tulane University Library.

Monthly Record of the Five Points House of Industry. New York: The Institution, 1857.

Report of the Select Committee on the New Orleans Riots. Washington, D.C.: U.S. Government Printing Office, 1867. Historic New Orleans Collection, New Orleans.

Report of the Special Committee on Pavements of the Board of Supervisors of the City and County of San Francisco. San Francisco: Steam Printing House of A. L. Bancroft, 1870.

San Francisco Municipal Reports, 1865–1880. San Francisco: Cosmopolitan Printing Co., 1869–. San Francisco Room, San Francisco Public Library.

San Francisco Park Commissioners. *Biennial Reports, 1870–1875.* San Francisco: n.p., 1874–. San Francisco Room, San Francisco Library.

Society for the Reformation of Juvenile Delinquents in the City of New York. *Documents Relative to the House of Refuge.* New York: Mahlon Day, 1832.

Spotts, A. T. *A History and Report of the Construction of the New City Hall from April 4, 1870, to November 18, 1879.* San Francisco: W. M. Hinton, 1889.

To His Excellency William Irwin, Governor of California, from the Park Commissioners of San Francisco. San Francisco: B. F. Sterett, 1876. Bancroft Library, University of California, Berkeley.

Manuscript Collections

The miscellaneous diaries, letters, and records of associations cited in the footnotes were found diffused through collections in the three cities. For New Orleans the principal repositories were the Historic New Orleans Collection, the Louisiana Division of the New Orleans Public Library, and the Municipal New Orleans Collection of Tulane University. For San Francisco the chief collections were at the Bancroft Library, California Historical Society, and San Francisco Public Library. In New York the Municipal Archives were the richest sources of documentation, supplemented by the New York Public Library and the New York Historical Society.

Published Primary Sources

Alger, Horatio, Jr. *Ragged Dick or, Street Life in New York with the Boot Blacks.* New York: Signet, 1990.

Arpad, Susan S. *The Diary of a True Woman.* Athens: Ohio University Press, 1984.

Bodichon, Barbara Leigh Smith. *An American Diary, 1857–8.* Ed. Joseph W. Reed, Jr. New York: Routledge and Kegan Paul, 1972.

Brace, Charles Loring. *The Dangerous Classes of New York and Twenty Years Work among Them.* New York: Wynkoop and Hallenbeck, 1872.

Brandon, Edgar Ewing, ed. *A Pilgrimage of Liberty: A Contemporary Account of the Triumphal Tour of General Lafayette.* Athens, Ohio: Lawhead Press, 1944.

Bremer, Fredrika. *America of the Fifties: Letters of Fredrika Bremer.* Ed. Adolf Benson. New York: American-Scandinavian Foundation, 1924.

———. *The Homes of the New World.* Trans. Mary Howitt. New York: Harper and Brothers, 1853.

Browne, Junius. *Great Metropolis: A Mirror of New York.* Hartford, N.J.: American, 1869.

Buckley, M. B. *Diary of a Tour in America.* Ed. Kate Buckley. Dublin: Sealy, Bryers, and Walker, 1886.

Buel, James W. *Mysteries and Miseries of America's Great Cities.* San Francisco: A. L. Bancroft, 1883.

Castellanas, Henry C. *New Orleans as It Was: Episodes of Louisiana Life*. New Orleans: L. Graham and Son, 1895.

Chapin, Reverend E. H. *Humanity in the City*. New York: De Witt and Davenport, 1854.

Child, Lydia Marie. *Letters from New York*. New York: C. S. Fanes, 1845.

Civil Rights, the Hibernian Riot, and the "Insurrection of the Capitalists": A History of Important Events in New York in the Midsummer of 1871. New York: Baker and Godwin, 1871.

Clark, Emmons. *History of the Seventh Regiment of New York, 1806–1889*. New York: [Seventh Regiment], 1890.

Costello, Augustine. *Our Police Protectors: A History of the New York Police*. 1885. Reprint, Montclair, N.J.: Patterson Smith, 1972.

Crapsey, Edward. *The Nether Side of New York; or, the Vice, Crime, and Poverty at the Great Metropolis*. New York: Sheldon, 1872.

DeVoe, Thomas F. *The Market Book*. New York: De Voe, 1862.

Diamond, Sigmund, ed. and trans. *A Casual View of America: The Home Letters of Salomon de Rothschild, 1859–1861*. Stanford: Stanford University Press, 1961.

Disturness, John, comp., *New York as It Was and as It Is*. New York: D. Van Nostrand, 1876.

Durrell, Edward. *New York as I Found It*. New York: Harper Books, 1848.

Ellington, George. *The Women of New York, or, Social Life in the Great City*. New York: New York Book Company, 1870.

Foster, George G. *New York by Gaslight: With Here and There a Streak of Sunshine*. New York: Dewitt and Davenport, 1850.

———. *New York in Slices by an Experienced Carver*. New York: William H. Grabe, 1849.

———. *New York Naked*. New York: DeWitt, n.d.

Frost, Jennette Blakeslee. *California's Greatest Curse*. San Francisco: J. Winterburn, 1879.

Green, Andrew H. *A Three Years' Struggle with Municipal Misrule*. New York: Department of Finance, 1874.

Gunn, Lewis C., and Elizabeth LeBreton Gunn. *Records of a California Family*. Ed. Anna Lee Marston. San Diego: n.p., 1928.

Gunn, Thomas Butler. *The Physiology of New York Boarding-Houses*. New York: Mason Brothers, 1857.

Hall, A. Oakey. *The Manhattaner in New Orleans: Or, Phases of "Crescent City" Life*. Ed. Henry A. Kmen. Baton Rouge: Louisiana State University Press, 1976.

Halliday, Samuel B. *The Lost and Found, or Life among the Poor*. New York: Blakeman and Mason, 1859.

Halpine, Charles Graham. *The Life and Adventures, Songs, Services, and Speeches of Private Miles O'Reilly*. New York: Carleton Publisher, 1864.

Hankins, Marie Louise. *Women of New York*. New York: Hankins, 1861.

Hanswell, Charles. *Reminiscence of an Octogenarian in the City of New York, 1816–1860*. New York: Harper, 1896.

Hauranne, Ernest Duvergier de. *A French Man in Lincoln's America*. Chicago: Lakeside Press, 1975.

Headley, J. T. *The Great Riots of New York, 1712–1871.* New York: E. B. Treat, 1873.

Houzeau, Jean-Charles. *My Passage at the "New Orleans Tribune": A Memoir of the Civil War Era.* Ed. David C. Rankin, trans. Gerard F. Denault. Baton Rouge: Louisiana State University Press, 1984.

Howells, William Dean. "Their Wedding Journey." *Atlantic Monthly,* July 1871.

Hudson, Fredrick. *Journalism in the United States from 1690 to 1872.* New York: Harper and Brothers, 1873.

James, Henry. *The Speech and Manners of American Women.* Ed. E. S. Riggs. Lancaster, Pa.: Lancaster House Press, 1973.

———. *Washington Square.* New York: Vintage Books, 1990.

Kaufman, Polly Wetts, ed. *Apron Full of Gold: The Letters of Mary Jane Megguier from San Francisco, 1849–1856.* San Marino, Calif.: Huntington Library, 1947.

King, Grace. *New Orleans: The Place and the People.* New York: Macmillan, 1907.

Lamb, Martha. *A Brief History of the City of New York: Its Origin, Rise, and Progress.* New York: A. S. Baines, 1880.

———. "Life in New York Fifty Years Ago." *Magazine of American History,* March 1890.

Lloyd, Benjamin E. *Lights and Shades in San Francisco.* San Francisco: A. L. Bancroft, 1876.

Lossing, Benson J. *History of New York City.* New York: A. S. Barnes, 1884.

Lowell, Josephine Shaw. *Public Relief and Private Charity.* G. P. Putnam and Sons, 1884.

Lyon, Isaac S. *Recollections of an Old Cartman: Old New York Street Life.* New York: Bound, 1984.

MacGregor, William Laird. *San Francisco, California, in 1876.* Edinburgh: Thomas Laurie, 1876.

Nolan, Frederick W. *The Life and Death of John Henry Tunstall: The Letters, Diaries, and Adventures of an Itinerant Englishman.* Albuquerque: University of New Mexico Press, 1965.

The Old Brewery, and the New Mission House at Five Points, by the Ladies of the Mission. New York: Stringer and Townsend, 1854.

Olmsted, Fredrick Law. *Public Parks and the Enlargement of Towns.* 1870. Reprint, New York: Arno Press, 1970.

"Parks of San Francisco." *Overland Monthly,* March 1891.

Power, Tyrone. *Impressions of America during the Years 1833–1835.* London: Bentley, 1836.

Pussailk, Bernard de. *The Last Adventure: San Francisco in 1851.* Trans. C. Crane. San Francisco: Weitgate Press, 1931.

Putnam, George W. "The Physiognomy of Cities." *American Review,* September 1847.

Rowland, Kate Mason, and Mrs. Moris L. Croxall, eds. *The Journal of Julia Le Grand, New Orleans, 1862–1863.* Richmond: Everett Waddey, 1911.

Russell, William Howard. *My Diary North and South.* Ed. Fletcher Pratt. New York: Harper and Brothers, 1954.

Smith, Helen Ainslie. *Great Cities of the Modern World.* New York: Routledge, 1885.

Smith, Matthew Hale. *Sunshine and Shadow in New York.* Hartford: J. B. Burr, 1869.

Stedman, J. C., and R. A. Leonard. *The Workingmen's Party of California: An Epitome of Its Rise and Progress.* San Francisco: Bacon, 1878.

Still, Bayrd. *Mirror for Gotham: New York as Seen by Contemporaries from Dutch Days to the Present.* New York: New York University Press, 1956.

Stone, William L. *A History of New York City from Discovery to the Present Day.* New York: Virtue and Yorston, 1872.

"The Street Arabs of New York." *Appleton's Journal,* January 1, 1873.

Sutton, Charles. *The New York Tombs: Its Secrets and Its Mysteries.* Ed. James B. Mix and Samuel A. MacKeever. New York: United States Publishing, 1874.

"Table Talk." *Appleton's Journal,* December 2, 1871.

Taylor, William. *Seven Years Street Preaching in San Francisco, California.* New York: London Press, 1875.

Todd, Charles Burr. *The Story of the City of New York.* New York: Putnam, 1880.

The Visit of General Lafayette to Louisiana. New Orleans: Cruzat, 1825.

Whitman, Walt. *New York Dissected.* 1855. Reprint, New York: Rufus Rockwell, 1936.

Wortley, Lady Emmeline Stuart. *Travels in the United States in 1849 and 1850.* London: Bentley, 1851.

Secondary Sources

Almaguer, Tomás. *Racial Fault Lines: The Historical Origins of White Supremacy in California.* Berkeley: University of California Press, 1994.

Anbinder, Tyler G. "Fernando Wood and New York's Secession from the Union: A Political Reappraisal." *New York History* 63 (1987): 66–92.

Anderson, Benedict. *Imagined Communities: Reflections on the Origins and Spread of Nationalism.* New York: Verso, 1985.

Arato, Andrew, and Jean Cohen. "Civil Society and Social Theory." *Thesis Eleven,* no. 21 (1988): 40–64.

Arendt, Hannah. *The Human Condition.* Chicago: University of Chicago Press, 1958.

Arnesen, Eric. *Waterfront Workers of New Orleans: Race, Class, and Politics, 1863–1923.* New York: Oxford University Press, 1991.

Ashworth, John. *"Agrarians and Aristocrats": Party Political Ideology in the United States, 1837–1846.* New York: Cambridge University Press, 1987.

Averbach, Alvin. "San Francisco's South of Market District, 1850–1950: The Emergence of a Skid Row." *California Historical Quarterly* 57 (Fall 1973): 197–220.

Baker, Jean. *Affairs of Party: The Political Culture of Northern Democrats in the Mid-Nineteenth Century.* Ithaca: Cornell University Press, 1983.

Baker, Paula. *The Moral Framework of Public Life: Gender, Politics, and the State in Rural New York, 1870–1930.* New York: Oxford University Press, 1991.

Bancroft, Hubert Howe. *History of California.* 24 vols. San Francisco: History Company, 1886–1890.

Barth, Gunther. *Bitter Strength: A History of the Chinese in the United States, 1850–1870.* Cambridge: Harvard University Press, 1964.

———. *City People: The Rise of Modern City Culture in Nineteenth-Century America.* New York: Oxford University Press, 1980.

Baum, Dale. *The Civil War Party System: The Case of Massachusetts, 1849–1876.* Chapel Hill: University of North Carolina Press, 1984.

Beans, Rowena. "Inasmuch . . ." *The One Hundred-Year History of the San Francisco Ladies' Protestant Relief Society, 1853–1953.* San Francisco: n.p., 1953.

Bedarida, François, and Anthony Sutcliffe. "The Street in the Structure and Life of the City: Reflections on Nineteenth-Century London and Paris." *Journal of Urban History* 6 (1980): 379–96.

Bell, Caryn Cossé. "Revolution, Romanticism, and Reform: The Afro-Creole Protest Tradition in the Origins of Radical Republican Leadership, 1718–1868." Ph.D. diss., Tulane University, 1993.

Bender, Thomas. *Intellect and Public Life: Essays on the Social History of Academic Intellectuals in the United States.* Baltimore: Johns Hopkins University Press, 1993.

———. "Metropolitan Culture: Brooklyn Bridge and the Transformation of New York." *Annals of the New York Academy of Sciences* 424 (1984): 325–32.

———. *New York Intellect: A History of Intellectual Life in New York City, from 1750 to the Beginnings of Our Own Time.* New York: Knopf, 1987.

———. "Wholes and Parts: The Need for Synthesis in American History." *Journal of American History* 73 (1986): 120–36.

Benhabib, Seyla. *Situating the Self.* New York: Routledge, 1992.

Benn, S. I., and G. F. Gaus, eds. *Public and Private in Social Life.* London: Croom Helm, 1983.

Benson, Lee. *The Concept of Jacksonian Democracy: New York as a Test Case.* Princeton: Princeton University Press, 1984.

Bergmann, Hans. "Panoramas of New York, 1845–1860." *Prospects: An Annal of American Cultural Studies* 10 (1985): 119–39.

Bernstein, Iver. *The New York City Draft Riots: The Significance for American Society and Politics in the Age of the Civil War.* New York: Oxford University Press, 1990.

Black, George Ashton. "The History of Municipal Ownership of Land on Manhattan Island." In *Studies in History, Economics, and Public Law.* Vol. 1. New York: Columbia University Press, 1897.

Blackmar, Elizabeth. *Manhattan for Rent, 1785–1850.* Ithaca: Cornell University Press, 1989.

———. "Re-Walking the 'Walking City': Housing and Property Relations in New York City, 1780–1840." *Radical History Review* 21 (1979): 131–48.

Blassingame, John W. *Black New Orleans, 1860–1880.* Chicago: University of Chicago Press, 1973.

Blau, Joseph, ed. *Social Theories of Jacksonian Democracy: Representative Writing of the Period, 1825–1850.* New York: Hafner, 1947.

Bloomfield, Anne. "The Real Estate Associates: A Land and Housing Developer of the 1870's in San Francisco." *Journal of the Society of Architectural Historians* 37 (1978): 13–33.

Bodnar, John. *Remaking America: Public Memory, Commemoration, and Patriotism in the Twentieth Century.* Princeton: Princeton University Press, 1992.

Boris, Eileen. "'A Man's Dwelling House Is His Castle': Tenement House Cigarmaking and the Judicial Imperative." In *Work Engendered: Toward a New History of American Labor,* ed. Ava Baron. Ithaca: Cornell University Press, 1991.

Botkin, Benjamin Albert, ed. *New York City Folklore.* New York: Random House, 1956.

Boyer, M. Christine. *Manhattan Manners: Architecture and Style, 1850–1900.* New York: Rizzoli, 1985.

Bridges, Amy. *A City in the Republic: Antebellum New York and the Origins of Machine Politics.* Cambridge: Harvard University Press, 1984.

Brown, Joshua. "The 'Dead Rabbit'–Bowery Boy Riot: An Analysis of the Antebellum New York Gang." M.A. thesis, Columbia University, 1976.

Brown, Thomas. *Politics and Statesmanship: Essays on the American Whig Party.* New York: Columbia University Press, 1985.

Browne, Gary Lawson. *Baltimore in the Nation, 1789–1861.* Chapel Hill: University of North Carolina Press, 1980.

Bullough, William A. *The Blind Boss and His City: Christopher Augustine Buckley and Nineteenth-Century San Francisco.* Berkeley: University of California Press, 1979.

Burchell, R. A. *The San Francisco Irish, 1848–1880.* Chicago: University of Chicago Press, 1980.

Burke, Peter. *Popular Culture in Early Modern Europe.* London: T. Smith, 1978.

Butsch, Richard. "Bowery B'hoys and Matinee Ladies: The Re-Gendering of Nineteenth-Century American Theater Audiences." *American Quarterly* 46 (1994): 374–405.

Buttenwieser, Ann L. *Manhattan Water Bound: Planning and Development of Manhattan's Waterfront from the Seventeenth Century to the Present.* New York: New York University Press, 1987.

Byrdsall, F. *The History of the Loco-Foco or Equal Rights Party.* New York: Clement and Packard, 1842.

Calhoun, Craig, ed., *Habermas and the Public Sphere.* Cambridge: MIT Press, 1992.

Callow, Alexander B., Jr. *The Tweed Ring.* New York: Oxford University Press, 1966.

Capers, Gerald Mortimer. *Occupied City: New Orleans under the Federals, 1862–1865.* Lexington: University of Kentucky Press, 1965.

Carter, Hodding, ed. *The Past as a Prelude: New Orleans, 1718–1968.* New Orleans: Tulane University Press, 1968.

Certeau, Michel de. *The Practice of Everyday Life.* Berkeley: University of California Press, 1984.

Chan, Sucheng. *Asian Americans: An Interpretive History.* Boston: Twayne, 1991.

Christovich, Mary Louise, et al., eds. *New Orleans Architecture.* 3 vols. Gretna, La.: Pelican Publishing Co., 1971–89.

Cole, Arthur Charles. *The Whig Party in the South.* 1914. Reprint, Gloucester, Mass.: P. Smith, 1962.

Cook, Adrian. *The Armies of the Streets: The New York City Draft Riots of 1863*. Lexington: University of Kentucky Press, 1974.

Corbett, Michael, and Charles Hall Page. *Splendid Survivors: San Francisco's Downtown Architectural Heritage*. San Francisco: S. F. Foundation for Architectural Heritage, 1979.

Coulter, E. Merton. *The Other Half of New Orleans*. Baton Rouge: Louisiana State University Press, 1939.

Cranz, Galen. *Changing Roles of Urban Parks: From Pleasure Garden to Open Space*. Berkeley: Institute of Urban and Regional Development, 1978.

Crété, Liliane. *Daily Life in Louisiana, 1815–1830*. Baton Rouge: Louisiana State University Press, 1981.

Cromley, Elizabeth Colins. *Alone Together: A History of New York's Early Apartments*. Ithaca: Cornell University Press, 1990.

Cross, Ira B. *A History of the Labor Movement in California*. Berkeley: University of California Press, 1935.

Dahl, Robert. *Democracy and Its Critics*. New Haven: Yale University Press, 1989.

Daniels, Douglas Henry. *Pioneer Urbanites: A Social and Cultural History of Black San Francisco*. Philadelphia: Temple University Press, 1980.

Darnton, Robert. *The Great Cat Massacre and Other Episodes in French Cultural History*. New York: Basic Books, 1984.

Davies, Susan Gray. "Theatre of the Streets: Parades and Ceremonies of Philadelphia, 1800–1850." Ph.D. diss., University of Pennsylvania, 1983.

Dawley, Alan. *Struggles for Justice: Social Responsibility and the Liberal State*. Cambridge: Harvard University Press, 1990.

De Vore, Donald E., and Joseph Logsdon. *Crescent City Schools: Public Education in New Orleans, 1841–1991*. Lafayette: University of Southwestern Louisiana Press, 1991.

Dewey, John. *The Public and Its Problems*. Chicago: Swallow Press, 1954.

Dietz, Mary S. "Context Is All: Feminism and Theories of Citizenship." *Daedalus* 116, no. 4 (Fall 1987): 1–24.

Doyle, Elizabeth Joan. *Civilian Life in Occupied New Orleans*. Baton Rouge: Louisiana State University Press, 1955.

Du Bois, Ellen Carol. *Feminism and Suffrage: The Emergence of an Independent Women's Movement in America*. Ithaca: Cornell University Press, 1978.

Einhorn, Robin. *Property Rules: Political Economy in Chicago, 1833–1872*. Chicago: University of Chicago Press, 1991.

Erie, Steven P. "The Development of Class and Ethnic Politics in San Francisco, 1870–1910." Ph.D. diss., University of California, Los Angeles, 1975.

———. *Rainbow's End: Irish Americans and the Dilemmas of Urban Machine Politics, 1840–1985*. Berkeley: University of California Press, 1988.

Ernst, Robert. *Immigrant Life in New York City, 1825–1863*. New York: King's Crown Press, 1949.

Ethington, Philip J. *The Public City: The Political Construction of Urban Life in San Francisco, 1859–1900*. New York: Cambridge University Press, 1994.

——. "Recasting Urban Political History: Gender, the Public, the Household, and Political Participation in Boston and San Francisco during the Progressive Era." *Social Science History* 16 (1992): 301–33.

——. "Vigilantes and the Police: The Creation of a Professional Police Bureaucracy in San Francisco, 1847–1900." *Journal of Social History* 21 (1987): 197–227.

Ewers, H. J., ed. *The Future of the Metropolis.* New York: Walter de Gruyter, 1986.

Feldberg, Michael. *The Turbulent Era: Riot and Disorder in Jacksonian America.* New York: Oxford University Press, 1980.

Fiehrer, Thomas M. "The African Presence in Colonial Louisiana: An Essay on the Continuity of Caribbean Culture." In *Louisiana's Black Heritage,* ed. Robert Macdonald, John R. Kemp, and Edward F. Haas. New Orleans: Louisiana State Museum, 1979.

Field, Phyllis F. *The Politics of Race in New York: The Struggle for Black Suffrage in the Civil War Era.* Ithaca: Cornell University Press, 1982.

Fink, Leon. *Workingmen's Democracy: The Knights of Labor and American Politics.* Urbana: University of Illinois Press, 1985.

Fischer, Roger. "A Pioneer Protest: The New Orleans Street Car Controversy of 1867." *Journal of Negro History* 53, no. 3 (July 1968): 219–33.

Flannelly, Mary J. "City Hall." Typescript, Municipal Archives, New York City.

Fogelsen, Robert M. *America's Armories: Architecture, Society, and Public Order.* Cambridge: Harvard University Press, 1989.

Foner, Eric. *Free Soil, Free Labor, Free Men: The Ideology of the Republican Party before the Civil War.* New York: Oxford University Press, 1995.

——. *Reconstruction: America's Unfinished Revolution, 1863–1877.* New York: Harper and Row, 1988.

Forman, Ronald L., and Joseph Logsdon. *Audubon Park: An Urban Eden.* New Orleans: Audubon Park Zoological Garden, 1985.

Formisano, Ronald P. *The Transformation of Political Culture: Massachusetts Parties, 1790s–1840s.* New York: Oxford University Press, 1983.

Fortier, Alcée. *A History of Louisiana.* Baton Rouge: Cloiter's Publishing Division, 1972.

Fraser, Nancy. "Rethinking the Public Sphere." In *The Phantom Public Sphere,* ed. Bruce Robbins. Minneapolis: University of Minnesota Press, 1993.

Fredrickson, George. *The Black Image in the White Mind: The Debate on Afro-American Character and Destiny, 1817–1914.* New York: Harper and Row, 1971.

Freehling, William W. *The Reintegration of American History: Slavery and the Civil War.* New York: Oxford University Press, 1994.

Garrett, Lula May. "San Francisco in 1851 as Described by Eyewitnesses." *California Historical Society Quarterly* 22 (1943): 253–80.

Geertz, Clifford. *The Interpretation of Culture.* New York: Basic Books, 1973.

Gehman, Mary. *The Free People of Color of New Orleans: An Introduction.* New Orleans: Margaret Media, 1994.

Gienapp, William. *The Origins of the Republican Party, 1852–1856.* New York: Oxford University Press, 1987.

Gilder, Rodman. *The Battery.* Boston: Houghton Mifflin, 1936.

Gilfoyle, Timothy. *City of Eros: New York City, Prostitution, and the Commercialization of Sex, 1790–1920.* New York: W. W. Norton, 1992.

Gilje, Paul. *The Road to Mobocracy: Popular Disorder in New York City, 1763–1834.* Chapel Hill: University of North Carolina Press, 1987.

Ginsberg, Stephen F. "Above the Law: Volunteer Firemen in New York City, 1836–1837." *New York History* 50, no. 2 (April 1969): 165–86.

Goodman, Dena. "Public Sphere and Private Life: Toward a Synthesis of Current Historiographical Approaches to the Old Regime." *History and Theory* 31, no. 1 (1992), 1–20.

Gordon, Michael Allen. *The Orange Riots: Irish Political Violence in New York City, 1870 and 1871.* Ithaca: Cornell University Press, 1993.

———. "Studies in Irish American Thought and Behavior in Gilded Age New York City." Ph.D. diss., University of Rochester, 1977.

Gorn, Elliot J. "'Good-Bye Boys, I Died a True American': Homicide, Nativism, and Working-Class Culture in New York City." *Journal of American History* 74 (1987): 388–410.

Griffen, Guy, and Helen Griffen. *The Story of Golden Gate Park.* San Francisco: Phillips and Van Orden Co., 1949.

Grimsted, David. *Melodrama Unveiled: American Theater and Culture, 1800–1850.* Chicago: University of Chicago Press, 1968.

Groth, Paul. *Living Downtown: The History of Residential Hotels in the United States.* Berkeley: University of California Press, 1994.

Gunn, L. Ray. *The Decline of Authority, Public Economic Policy, and Political Development in New York State, 1800–1860.* Ithaca: Cornell University Press, 1988.

Gutman, Herbert S. "The Tompkins Square Riot in New York City on January 13, 1874: A Re-examination of Its Causes and Its Aftermath." *Labor History* 6 (1965): 49–67.

Gutman, Marta. "New York City's Broadway: Heterogeneity, History, and Public Space." Unpublished manuscript, courtesy of the author.

Habermas, Jürgen. "The Public Sphere: An Encyclopedia Article." *New German Critique* 1, no. 3 (Fall 1974): 49–55.

———. *The Structural Transformation of the Public Sphere.* Trans. Thomas Berger. Cambridge: MIT Press, 1989.

Hales, Peter. *Silver Cities: The Photography of American Urbanization, 1839–1915.* Philadelphia: Temple University Press, 1984.

Hamer, David. *New Towns in the New World: Images and Perceptions of the Nineteenth-Century Urban Frontier.* New York: Columbia University Press, 1990.

Hanson, Russell L. *The Democratic Imagination in America.* Princeton: Princeton University Press, 1985.

Harlow, Alvin F. *Old Bowery Days: The Chronicle for a Famous Street.* New York: D. Appleton, 1931.

Harring, Sidney L. *Policing a Class Society: The Experience of American Cities, 1865–1915.* New Brunswick, N.J.: Rutgers University Press, 1983.

Harris, David, ed. *Eadweard Muybridge and the Photographic Panorama of San Francisco, 1850–1880.* Montreal: Centre Canadien d'Architecture, 1993.

Hartog, Hendrik. *Public Property and Private Power.* Chapel Hill: University of North Carolina Press, 1983.

Heale, M. J. "From City Fathers to Social Critics: Humanitarianism and Government in New York, 1790–1860." *Journal of American History* 63 (1976): 21–41.

Heizer, Robert F., and Alan F. Almquist. *The Other Californians.* Berkeley: University of California Press, 1971.

Hendrickson, Robert. *The Grand Emporiums: The Illustrated History of America's Great Department Stores.* New York: Stein and Day, 1979.

Hershowitz, Leo. *Tweed's New York: Another Look.* New York: Anchor Press, 1977.

Hirsch, Arnold R., and Joseph Logsdon, eds. *Creole New Orleans: Race and Americanization.* Baton Rouge: Louisiana State University Press, 1992.

A History of Real Estate, Building, and Architecture in New York City. 1898. Reprint, New York: Arno, 1967.

Hittell, John S. *A History of the City of San Francisco.* San Francisco: A. L. Bancroft, 1878.

Hofstader, Richard. *The Idea of a Party System.* Berkeley: University of California Press, 1969.

Holditch, W. Kenneth. *In Old New Orleans.* Jackson: University Press of Mississippi, 1983.

Holt, Michael F. *The Political Crisis of the 1850s.* New York: Wiley, 1978.

———. *Political Parties and American Political Development from the Age of Jackson to the Age of Lincoln.* Baton Rouge: Louisiana State University Press, 1992.

Homberger, Eric. *Scenes from the Life of a City.* New Haven: Yale University Press, 1994.

Horsman, Reginald. *Race and Manifest Destiny: The Origin of American Racialist Ideology.* Cambridge: Harvard University Press, 1981.

Howe, Daniel Walker. *The Political Culture of the American Whigs.* Chicago: University of Chicago Press, 1979.

Hower, Ralph M. *A History of Macy's of New York.* Cambridge: Harvard University Press, 1943.

Huber, Leonard V. *Mardi Gras: A Pictorial History of Carnival in New Orleans.* Gretna, La.: Pelican, 1977.

———. *New Orleans: A Pictorial History.* New York: American Legacy Press, 1981.

Hunt, Lynn. *The Family Romance of the French Revolution.* Berkeley: University of California Press, 1992.

Hurston, Zora. "Voodoo in America." *Journal of American Folklore* 44 (1931): 316–417.

Ignatiev, Noel. *How the Irish Became White.* New York: Routledge, 1995.

Issel, William, and Robert W. Cherny. *San Francisco: Presidio, Port, and Pacific Metropolis.* San Francisco: Boyd and Fraser, 1981.

———. *San Francisco, 1865–1932: Politics, Power, and Urban Development.* Berkeley: University of California Press, 1986.

Jackson, Joy J. *New Orleans in the Gilded Age: Politics and Urban Progress, 1880–1896.* Baton Rouge: Louisiana State University Press, 1969.

Jacobs, Jane. *The Death and Life of Great American Cities.* New York: Vintage Books, 1961.

Jenkens, Stephen. *The Greatest Street in the World: Broadway.* New York: Putnam, 1911.

Johnson, David R. *Policing the Urban Underworld: The Impact of Crime on the Development of the American Police, 1800–1887.* Philadelphia: Temple University Press, 1979.

Kaestle, Carl F. *The Evolution of an Urban School System: New York City, 1750–1850.* Cambridge: Harvard University Press, 1973.

Kaplan, Barry. "Andrew H. Green and the Creation of a Planning Rationale: The Formation of a Greater New York City, 1865–1890." *Urbanism Past and Present* 8, no. 8 (1979): 32–41.

Kasson, John F. *Rudeness and Civility: Manners in Nineteenth-Century Urban America.* New York: Hill and Wang, 1990.

Katz, Michael. "Origins of the Institutional State." *Marxist Perspectives* 1 (1978): 6–22.

Katznelson, Ira, and Aristide R. Zolberg. *Working-Class Formation: Nineteenth-Century Patterns in Western Europe and the United States.* Princeton: Princeton University Press, 1986.

Kazin, Michael. *Barons of Labor: The San Francisco Building Trades and Union Power in the Progressive Era.* Urbana: University of Illinois Press, 1987.

———. *The Populist Persuasion: An American History.* New York: Basic Books, 1995.

———. "Prelude to Kearneyism: The 'July Days' in San Francisco, 1877." *New Labor Review* 3 (1980): 5–47.

Keane, John. *Democracy and Civil Society.* New York: Verso, 1988.

———. *Public Life and Late Capitalism: Toward a Socialist Theory of Democracy.* New York: Cambridge University Press, 1984.

Keller, Morton. *Affairs of State: Public Life in Late Nineteenth-Century America.* Cambridge: Harvard University Press, 1977.

Kelley, Robert. *The Cultural Pattern in American Politics: The First Century.* New York: Knopf, 1979.

Kelton, Jane Gladden. "New York City St. Patrick's Day Parade: Invention of Contention and Consensus." *Drama Review* 29, no. 3 (Fall 1985): 95–105.

Kendall, John S. *The Golden Age of New Orleans Theatre.* Baton Rouge: Louisiana State University Press, 1952.

———. *History of New Orleans.* New York: Lewis Publishing, 1922.

———. "The Municipal Election of 1858." *Louisiana Historical Quarterly* 5 (1922): 357–76.

Kerber, Linda. "Abolitionists and Amalgamators: The New York City Race Riots of 1834." *New York History* 48 (1967): 27–39.

Kettner, James. *The Development of American Citizenship, 1608–1870.* Chapel Hill: University of North Carolina Press, 1978.

Kinser, Samuel. *Carnival American Style: Mardi Gras at New Orleans and Mobile.* Chicago: University of Chicago Press, 1990.

Kirker, Harold. *California Architectural Frontier: Style and Tradition in the Nineteenth Century.* San Marino, Calif.: Huntington Library, 1960.

Kleppner, Paul. *The Third Electoral System, 1853–1892.* Chapel Hill: University of North Carolina Press, 1979.

Kmen, Henry. *Music in New Orleans: The Formative Years, 1791–1841.* Baton Rouge: Louisiana State University Press, 1966.

Knobel, Dale T. *Paddy and the Republic: Ethnicity and Nationality in Antebellum America.* Middletown, Conn.: Wesleyan University Press, 1986.

Kohl, Lawrence Fredrick. *The Politics of Individualism: Parties and the American Character in the Jacksonian Era.* New York: Oxford University Press, 1989.

Lane, Roger. *Policing the City: Boston, 1822–1885.* Cambridge: Harvard University Press, 1967.

Lawrence, John Alan. "Behind the Palaces: The Working Class and the Labor Movement in San Francisco, 1877–1901." Ph.D. diss., University of California, Berkeley, 1979.

Lefebvre, Henri. *Everyday Life in the Modern World.* Trans. Sacha Rabinovitch. New Brunswick, N.J.: Transaction Books, 1984.

Lefort, Claude. *Democracy and Political Theory.* Trans. David Macey. Minneapolis: University of Minnesota Press, 1988.

Leonard, Thomas C. *The Power of the Press: The Birth of American Political Reporting.* New York: Oxford University Press, 1986.

Levine, Lawrence. *Highbrow/Lowbrow.* Cambridge: Harvard University Press, 1988.

Lewis, Pierce F. *New Orleans: The Making of an Urban Landscape.* Cambridge: Harvard University Press, 1976.

Lockwood, Charles. *Manhattan Moves Uptown: An Illustrated History.* Boston: Houghton Mifflin, 1976.

Lofland, Lynn. *World of Strangers.* New York: Basic Books, 1973.

Lotchin, Roger. *San Francisco, 1846–1856: From Hamlet to City.* Lincoln: University of Nebraska Press, 1974.

Lott, Eric. *Love and Theft: Blackface Minstrelsy and the American Working Class.* New York: Oxford University Press, 1993.

Lynch, Kevin. *City Sense and City Design: Writings and the Projects of Kevin Lynch.* Cambridge: MIT Press, 1990.

——. *The Image of the City.* Cambridge: MIT Press, 1970.

MacLean, Nancy. "The Leo Frank Case Reconsidered: Gender and Sexual Politics in the Making of Reactionary Populism." *Journal of American History* 78 (1991): 917–48.

Mandelbaum, Seymour. *Boss Tweed's New York.* New York: Wiley, 1965.

Manning, Frank, ed., *The Celebration of Society: Perspectives on Contemporary Cultural Performance.* Bowling Green, Ohio: Bowling Green University Popular Press, 1983.

McCormick, Richard L. *The Party Period and Public Policy: American Politics from the Age of Jackson.* New York: Oxford University Press, 1986.

McDonald, Terrence. *The Parameters of Urban Fiscal Policy: Socioeconomic Change and Political Culture in San Francisco, 1860–1910.* Berkeley: University of California Press, 1986.

McGerr, Michael. *The Decline of Popular Politics, 1865–1928.* New York: Oxford University Press, 1986.

McKay, Ernest A. *The Civil War in New York.* Syracuse: Syracuse University Press, 1991.

McPherson, James M. *The Struggle for Equality: Abolitionists and the Negro in the Civil War.* Princeton: Princeton University Press, 1964.

Meyrowitz, Joshua. *No Sense of Place.* New York: Oxford University Press, 1985.

Miller, Stuart Creighton. *The Unwelcome Immigrant: The American Image of the Chinese, 1785–1882.* Berkeley: University of California Press, 1969.

Miller, Wilbur R. *Cops and Bobbies: Police Authority in New York and London, 1830–1870.* Chicago: University of Chicago Press, 1977.

Mitchell, Reid. *All on a Mardi Gras Day: Episodes in the History of New Orleans Carnival.* Cambridge: Harvard University Press, 1995.

Moehring, Eugene. *Public Works and the Patterns of Urban Real Estate Growth in Manhattan, 1835–1894.* New York: Arno Press, 1981.

———. *Public Works and Urban History: Recent Trends and New Directions.* Chicago: Public Works Historical Society, 1982.

Mohr, James. *Radical Republicans and Reform in New York.* Ithaca: Cornell University Press, 1973.

Mollenkopf, John Hull, ed. *Power, Culture, and Place.* New York: Russell Sage, 1988.

Monkkonen, Eric H. *Police in Urban America, 1860–1920.* New York: Cambridge University Press, 1981.

Monkkonen, Eric H., ed. *Walking to Work: Tramps in America, 1790–1935.* Lincoln: University of Nebraska Press, 1984.

Montgomery, David. *Beyond Equality: Labor and the Radical Republicans, 1862–1872.* New York: Knopf, 1967.

———. *Citizen Worker: The Experience of Workers in the United States with Democracy and the Free Market during the Nineteenth Century.* New York: Cambridge University Press, 1993.

Morgan, Edmund. *Inventing the People: The Rise of Popular Sovereignty in England and America.* New York: W. W. Norton, 1988.

Mouffe, Chantal. *The Return of the Political.* New York: Verso, 1993.

Myers, Gustavus. *The History of Tammany Hall.* New York: Gustavus Myers, 1901.

Nau, John Frederick. *The German People of New Orleans, 1850–1900.* Leider: E. J. Brill, 1958.

Nelson, William E. *The Roots of American Bureaucracy, 1830–1900.* Cambridge: Harvard University Press, 1982.

Newton, Lewis William. *The Americanization of French Louisiana: A Study of the Process of Adjustment between the French and Anglo-American Population of Louisiana, 1803–1860.* New York: Arno Press, 1980.

Nichaus, Earl F. *The Irish in New Orleans, 1800–1860.* Baton Rouge: Louisiana State University Press, 1965.

Nye, Russel Blane. *Society and Culture in America.* New York: Harper and Row, 1974.

Oestreicher, Richard. "Urban Working-Class Political Behavior and Theories of American Electoral Politics, 1870–1940." *Journal of American History* 74 (1988): 1257–86.

Overdyke, W. Darrell. "History of the American Party in Louisiana." Parts 1–5. *Louisiana Historical Quarterly* 15 (1932): 581–88; 16 (1933): 84–91, 256–77, 409–26, 608–27.

Pascoe, Peggy. *Relations of Rescue: The Search for Female Moral Authority in the American West, 1874–1939.* New York: Oxford University Press, 1990.

Pessen, Edward. *Jacksonian America: Society, Personality, and Politics.* Homewood, Ill.: Dorsey Press, 1978.

Phillips, Anne. *Engendering Democracy.* University Park: Pennsylvania State University Press, 1991.

Phillips, Catherine Coffin. *Portsmouth Plaza: The Cradle of San Francisco.* San Francisco: John Henry Nast, 1932.

Pitkin, Hanna Fenichel. *The Concept of Representation.* Berkeley: University of California Press, 1967.

———. "Justice: On Relating Public and Private." *Political Theory* 9 (1981): 327–52.

Pitt, Leonard. "The Beginnings of Nativism in California." *Pacific Historical Review* 30 (1961): 23–38.

Pleasant, Samuel Augustus. *Fernando Wood of New York.* New York: AMS Press, 1960.

Plunz, Richard. *A History of Housing in New York City.* New York: Columbia University Press, 1990.

Poesch, Jessie J. *The Art of the Old South: Painting, Sculpture, Architecture, and the Products of Craftsmen, 1560–1860.* New York: Knopf, 1983.

Purdy, Helen Throop. "Portsmouth Square." *California Historical Society Quarterly* 3 (1924): 30–44.

Putnam, Robert D. "What Makes Democracy Work?" *National Civic Review* 82, no. 2 (Spring 1993): 101–7.

Quinn, Arthur. *The Rivals: William Gwin, David Broderick, and the Birth of California.* New York: Crown, 1994.

Rankin, David C. "The Impact of the Civil War on the Free Colored Community of New Orleans." *Perspectives in American History* 11 (1977–78): 379–416.

———. "The Politics of Caste: Free Colored Leadership in New Orleans during the Civil War." In *Louisiana's Black Heritage,* ed. Robert Macdonald, John R. Kemp, and Edward F. Haas. New Orleans: Louisiana State Museum, 1979.

Reeves, Sally K. Evans, and William P. Reeves, with Ellis P. Laborde and James S. Janssen. *Historic City Park New Orleans.* New Orleans: Friends of the City Park, 1982.

Reinders, Robert C. *End of an Era: New Orleans, 1850–1860.* New Orleans: Pelican, 1964.

Reps, John W. *The Making of Urban America: A History of City Planning in the United States.* Princeton: Princeton University Press, 1992.

Reynolds, Donald Martin. *The Architecture of New York City: Histories and Views of Important Structures, Sites, and Symbols.* New York: Collier Books, 1984.

Richardson, James F. *The New York Police: Colonial Times to 1901.* New York: Oxford University Press, 1970.

———. *Urban Police in the United States.* Port Washington, N.Y.: Kennikat Press, 1974.

Ringenbach, Paul T. *Tramps and Reformers, 1873–1916: The Discovery of Unemployment in New York.* Westport, Conn.: Greenwood, 1973.

Robbins, Bruce, ed. *The Phantom Public Sphere.* Minneapolis: University of Minnesota Press, 1993.

Robertson, Andrew W. *The Language of Democracy: Political Rhetoric in the United States and Britain, 1790–1900.* Ithaca: Cornell University Press, 1995.

Rock, Howard. *Artisans of the New Republic: The Tradesmen of New York City in the Age of Jefferson.* New York: New York University Press, 1979.

Roediger, Richard. *Wages of Whiteness: Race and the Making of the American Working Class.* New York: Verso, 1991.

Rogers, Donald W., ed. *Voting and the Spirit of American Democracy.* Urbana: University of Illinois Press, 1992.

Rogin, Michael Paul. *Subversive Genealogy: The Politics and Art of Herman Melville.* New York: Knopf, 1983.

Roland, Carol. "The California Kindergarten Movement: A Study in Class and Social Feminism." Ph.D. diss., University of California, Riverside, 1980.

Rosenzweig, Roy, and Elizabeth Blackmar. *The Park and the People: A History of Central Park.* Ithaca: Cornell University Press, 1992.

Rousey, Dennis Charles. "The New Orleans Police, 1805–1889: A Social History." Ph.D. diss., Cornell University, 1978.

Ryan, Mary P. "American City Halls as Sites of Nineteenth-Century Public Life." Typescript. Department of History, University of California, Berkeley.

———. *Women in Public: Between Banners and Ballots, 1825–1880.* Baltimore: Johns Hopkins University Press, 1990.

Sandmeyer, Elmer Clarence. *The Anti-Chinese Movement in California.* Urbana: University of Illinois Press, 1991.

Sandweiss, Eric. "Claiming the Urban Landscape: The Improbable Rise of an Inevitable City." In *Eadweard Muybridge and the Photographic Panorama of San Francisco, 1850–1880,* ed. David Harris. Montreal: Centre Canadien d'Architecture, 1993.

Saxton, Alexander. *The Indispensable Enemy: Labor and the Anti-Chinese Movement in California.* Berkeley: University of California Press, 1971.

———. *The Rise and Fall of the White Republic: Class Politics and Mass Culture in Nineteenth-Century America.* New York: Verso, 1990.

Scherzer, Kenneth A. *The Unbounded Community: Neighborhood Life and Social Structure in New York City, 1830–1875.* Durham: Duke University Press, 1992.

Schiller, Donald. *Objectivity and the News: The Public and the Rise of Commercial Journalism.* Philadelphia: University of Pennsylvania Press, 1981.

Schlesinger, Arthur, Jr. *The Age of Jackson.* Boston: Little, Brown, 1946.

Schneider, John Charles. *Mob Violence and Public Order in the American City, 1830–1865.* Minneapolis: University of Minnesota Press, 1971.

———. "Public Order and the Geography of the City: Crime, Violence, and the Police in Detroit, 1845–1875." *Journal of Urban History* 4 (1978): 183–208.

Schudson, Michael. *Discovering the News: A Social History of American Newspapers.* New York: Basic Books, 1978.

Schuler, Kathryn Reinhart. "Women in Public Affairs in Louisiana during Reconstruction." *Louisiana Historical Review* 19 (1936): 668–750.

Schuyler, David. *The New Urban Landscape: The Redefinition of City Form in Nineteenth-Century America.* Baltimore: Johns Hopkins University Press, 1986.

Scisco, Louis Dow. *Political Nativism in New York State.* New York: Columbia University Press, 1901.

Scobey, David. "Anatomy of the Promenade: The Politics of Bourgeois Sociability in Nineteenth-Century New York." *Social History* 17, no. 2 (May 1992): 203–27.

Scott, Donald. "The Popular Lecture and the Creation of a Public in Mid-Nineteenth-Century America." *Journal of American History* 66 (1980): 791–809.

Seinfeld, Robert J. *The Invention of Free Labor: The Employment Relation in English and American Law and Culture, 1350–1870.* Chapel Hill: University of North Carolina Press, 1991.

Sellers, Charles. *The Market Revolution: Jacksonian America, 1815–1846.* New York: Oxford University Press, 1991.

Senkewicz, Robert M. *Vigilantes in Gold Rush San Francisco.* Stanford: Stanford University Press, 1985.

Sennett, Richard. *The Conscience of the Eye: The Design and Social Life of Cities.* New York: Knopf, 1990.

———. *The Fall of Public Man.* New York: Knopf, 1977.

———. *The Uses of Disorder: Personal Identity and City Life.* New York: Knopf, 1970.

Shank, Theodore Junior. "The Bowery Theater, 1826–1836." Ph.D. diss., Stanford University, 1956.

Sharpe, William, and Leonard Wallock, eds. *Visions of the Modern City.* Baltimore: Johns Hopkins University Press, 1987.

Shefter, Martin. *Political Parties and the State: The American Historical Experiences.* Princeton: Princeton University Press, 1994.

Shugg, Roger. *Origins of Class Struggle in Louisiana.* Baton Rouge: Louisiana State University Press, 1939.

Shumsky, Neil Larry. *The Evolution of Political Protest and the Workingmen's Party of California.* Columbus: Ohio State University Press, 1991.

———. "Frank Rooney's San Francisco—His Diary, April, 1875–March, 1876." *Labor History* 17 (1976): 245–64.

Sibley, Joel H. *The American Political Nation, 1838–1893.* Stanford: Stanford University Press, 1991.

Skowronek, Stephen. *Building a New American State: The Expansion of National Administrative Capacities, 1877–1920.* Cambridge: Harvard University Press, 1982.

Slotkin, Richard. *The Fatal Environment: The Myth of the Frontier in the Age of Industrialization, 1800–1890.* New York: Atheneum, 1985.

Smith, Rogers. "The 'American Creed' and American Identity: The Limits of Liberal Citizenship in the United States." *Western Political Quarterly* 41, no. 2 (June 1988): 225–51.

Sollors, Werner. *Beyond Ethnicity: Consent and Descent in American Culture.* New York: Oxford University Press, 1986.

Somers, Dale A. *The Rise of Sports in New Orleans, 1850–1900.* Baton Rouge: Louisiana State University Press, 1972.

Spann, Edward K. *The New Metropolis: New York City, 1840–1857.* New York: Columbia University Press, 1981.

Spoehr, Luther. "Sambo and the Heathen Chinese: Californians' Racial Stereotypes in the Late 1870s." *Pacific Historical Review* 2 (1973): 185–204.

Stansell, Christine. "Children and Uses of the Streets." In *Unequal Sisters: A Multicultural Reader in U.S. Women's History,* ed. Ellen Carol Dubois and Vicki L. Ruiz. New York: Routledge, 1990.

———. *City of Women: Sex and Class in New York, 1789–1860.* New York: Knopf, 1986.

Stokes, Isaac Newton Phelps. *The Iconography of Manhattan Island, 1498–1909.* 6 vols. New York: R. H. Dodd, 1915–25.

Stott, Richard B. *Workers in the Metropolis: Class, Ethnicity, and Youth in Antebellum New York City.* Ithaca: Cornell University Press, 1990.

Summers, Mark W. *The Press Gang: Newspapers and Politics, 1865–1878.* Chapel Hill: University of North Carolina Press, 1994.

Sutton, S. B., ed. *Civilizing American Cities.* New York: Oxford University Press, 1979.

Takaki, Ronald. *Strangers from a Different Shore.* Boston: Little, Brown, 1989.

Tallant, Robert. *The Romantic New Orleanians.* New York: E. P. Dutton, 1950.

Tansey, Richard Randall. "Economic Expansion and Urban Disorder in Antebellum New Orleans." Ph.D. diss., University of Texas, Austin, 1981.

———. "Social Democracy and the New Orleans Police, 1850–1860" M.A. thesis, Florida State University, 1971.

Taylor, William. *In Pursuit of Gotham: Culture, and Commerce in New York.* New York: Oxford University Press, 1992.

Tays, George. "Portsmouth Plaza." Typescript, 1938, Bancroft Library, University of California, Berkeley.

Teaford, Jon C. *City and Suburb: The Political Fragmentation of Metropolitan America.* Baltimore: Johns Hopkins University Press, 1979.

———. *The Municipal Revolution in America: Origins of Modern Urban Government.* Chicago: University of Chicago Press, 1975.

———. *The Unheralded Triumph: City Government in America, 1870–1900.* Baltimore: Johns Hopkins University Press, 1984.

Tinker, Edward Larocque. *Creole City: Its Past and Its People.* New York: Longmann, Green, 1953.

Tocqueville, Alexis de. *Democracy in America.* Ed. Richard D. Heffner. New York: Mentor, 1956.

Tomlins, Christopher L. *Law, Labor, and Ideology in the Early American Republic.* Cambridge: Harvard University Press, 1993.

Tregle, Joseph G., Jr. "Early New Orleans Society: A Reappraisal." *Journal of Southern History* 18 (1952): 20–36.

Trexler, Richard. *Public Life in Renaissance Florence.* New York: Academic Press, 1980.

Tunnell, Ted. *Crucible of Reconstruction: War, Radicalism, and Race in Louisiana, 1862–1877.* Baton Rouge: Louisiana State University Press, 1984.

———. "Free Negroes and the Freedmen: Black Politics in New Orleans during the Civil War." *Southern Studies* 19 (1980): 5–28.

Turner, Victor. *Celebrations*. Washington, D.C.: Smithsonian Institution Press, 1982.

Upton, Dell. "Another City: The Urban Cultural Landscape in the Early Republic." In *Everyday Life in the Early Republic*, ed. Catherine E. Hutchins. Winterthur, Del.: H. F. du Pont Winterthur Museum, 1994.

———. "The Master Street of the World: The Levee." In *Streets: Critical Perspectives on Public Space*, ed. Zeynep Celik, Diane Favro, and Richard Ingersoll. Berkeley: University of California Press, 1994.

Upton, Dell, ed. *America's Structural Roots: Ethnic Groups That Built America*. Washington, D.C.: Preservation Press, 1986.

Vance, James E. *Geography and Urban Evolution in the San Francisco Bay Area*. Berkeley: Institute for Governmental Studies, University of California, Berkeley, 1964.

Vandal, Giles. *The New Orleans Race Riot of 1866: Anatomy of a Tragedy*. Lafayette: University of Southwestern Louisiana Press, 1983.

Vincent, Charles. *Black Legislators in Louisiana during Reconstruction*. Baton Rouge: Louisiana State University Press, 1976.

———. "Black Louisianians during the Civil War and Reconstruction." In *Louisiana's Black Heritage*, ed. Robert Macdonald, John R. Kemp, and Edward F. Haas. New Orleans: Louisiana State Museum, 1979.

Wade, Richard. *Slavery in the Cities: The South, 1820–1860*. New York: Oxford University Press, 1964.

Walker, James Blaine. *Fifty Years of Rapid Transit, 1864–1917*. New York: Law Print. Co., 1918.

Walker, Richard. "Landscape and City Life: Four Ecologies of Residence in the San Francisco Bay Area." *Ecumene* 2 (1995): 33–64.

Warner, Michael. *The Letters of the Republic: Publication and the Public Sphere in Eighteenth-Century America*. Cambridge: Harvard University Press, 1990.

Warner, Sam Bass. *The Private City: Philadelphia in Three Periods of Its Growth*. Philadelphia: University of Pennsylvania Press, 1987.

Weibe, Robert H. *Self-Rule: A Cultural History of American Democracy*. Chicago: University of Chicago Press, 1995.

Weinbaum, Paul O. *Mobs and Demagogues: The New York Response to Collective Violence in the Early Nineteenth Century*. Ann Arbor: UMI Research Press, 1979.

———. "Temperance, Politics, and the New York City Riots of 1857." *New York Historical Society Quarterly* 59 (1975): 246–70.

Werner, M. R. *Tammany Hall*. New York: Doubleday, 1920.

Westbrook, Robert B. *John Dewey and American Democracy*. Ithaca: Cornell University Press, 1991.

White, Shane. "'It Was a Proud Day': African-American Festivals, and Parades in the North, 1741–1834." *Journal of American History* 81 (1994): 13–50.

Whyte, William. *City: Rediscovering the Center*. New York: Doubleday, 1988.

Wilentz, Sean. *Chants Democratic: New York City and the Rise of the American Working Class, 1788–1850*. New York: Oxford University Press, 1985.

——. "Crime, Poverty, and the Streets of New York City: The Diary of William H. Bell, 1850–1851." *History Workshop Journal* 7, no. 6 (Spring 1979): 126–31.

——. "The Rise of the American Working Class, 1776–1877." In *Survey in Perspectives on American Labor History: The Problem of Synthesis,* ed. J. Carroll Moody and Alice Kessler-Harris. De Kalb: Northern Illinois University Press, 1989.

Williams, Mary Floyd. *History of the San Francisco Committee of Vigilance of 1851.* 1921. Reprint, New York: Da Capo Press, 1962.

Yellin, Jean Fagan, and John C. Van Horne, eds. *The Abolitionist Sisterhood: Women's Political Culture in Antebellum America.* Ithaca: Cornell University Press, 1994.

Young, Alfred. *The Democratic Republicans of New York.* Chapel Hill: University of North Carolina Press, 1967.

Young, Iris. *Justice and the Politics of Difference.* Princeton: Princeton University Press, 1990.

Young, John P. *San Francisco: A History of the Pacific Coast Metropolis.* San Francisco: Clarke, 1912.

INDEX

Adams, John, 9
African Americans: ceremonies, participation in, 46, 90, 227, 254–55; citizenship for, 65, 121–22, 253–54, 257, 260–64, 266, 297–99, 302; clashes with whites, 83, 138; draft riot violence against, 169, 175, 177; elite, 178; free vs. enslaved, 90–91; identity based on color, 262; as majority in New Orleans, 65, 89, 189; organizations of, 88–89; participation in war, 65, 88, 254; racist verbal attacks on, 121, 173, 268, 295; sought as voters, 269; suffrage for, 121–24, 172, 177–78, 263–64, 270–71, 309; as workers, 255
Alger, Horatio, Jr., 200
All Saints' Day, 68, 238, 245
almshouses, 104, 156
Alta Californian (San Francisco), 79, 93, 98, 113, 125, 139; as partisan, 140, 141, 145
Alvarado, Governor Juan Bautista, 29
American Exchange (New Orleans), 36
American identity, 174
American Indians. *See* Native Americans
American Museum (New York City), 37–38
American Party, 148–50, 158
American Theater (New Orleans), 37
American Ward (New York City), 191
Ancient Order of Hibernians (New York City), 79, 224, 234
Anderson, Benedict, 81

Anglo-Saxon elites. *See* Seventh New York Regiment
Anthony, Susan B., 179–80, 251, 297
antiabolitionists, 121
anti-coolie clubs, 286
Anti-Sabbatarian riot (1821), 131
apartment buildings, 195, 196
Appleton's Journal (New York City), 214, 222
Arc de Triomphe (New Orleans), 62–63, 63 (fig.)
Arendt, Hannah, 5, 8
army, U.S., 218
Arnesen, Eric, 283
Aryan race, 251–52
Asian Americans, 189. *See also* Chinese-Americans
assembly, right of, 110, 131, 230–31
associations. *See* organizations
Astor, Mrs. John Jacob, 250
Astor and Company, John Jacob (New York City), 196–97
Astor Place Theater (New York City), 37; riot of 1849, 136, 137 (fig.), 138
Atlantic cable celebration (New York City), 228
auction business, 42
Aunt Fanny, 49
austerity, 160, 163–64, 204
autonomy of cities, 158, 159, 164–65
Ay Tcy, 49

Designer: Nola Burger
Compositor: Impressions Book and
          Journal Services, Inc.
Text: 10/13 Galliard
Display: Stymie
Printer: Edwards Bros.
Binder: Edwards Bros.